Faultlines

OF CONFLICT

in Central Asia and the South Caucasus

Implications for the U.S. Army

D1153511

RAND*MR1598-b*

The South Caucasus

Central Asia

This report is the final product of a project entitled "Sources of Conflict in the South Caucasus and Central Asia." The project was intended to help Army intelligence analysts improve their understanding of the potential for armed conflict in the region of Central Asia and South Caucasus and how such outbreaks might escalate to a level that could involve U.S. forces.

This report identifies and evaluates the key conflict-producing faultlines in Central Asia and South Caucasus. The faultlines include the role of state political and economic weakness; the impact of crime and the drug trade; the effects of ethnic tensions and foreign interests and influence; and the impact of competition for natural resources. The analysis then examines the ways in which the emergence of conflict could draw the United States into the strife. The report also examines the operational challenges the region poses for possible Army deployments in the 10- to 15-year time frame.

This research was completed largely prior to the September 11 attacks on the United States. The report has been updated to take into account the changed security environment and the U.S. military presence on the ground in the Central Asian and South Caucasus region. The operations in Afghanistan have not altered the faultlines. They are long-term and structural in nature. The current U.S. presence on the ground means that they need to be taken into account even more than previously.

The research was sponsored by the Office of the Deputy Chief of Staff for Intelligence, U.S. Army, and conducted in the Strategy, Doctrine, and Resources Program of RAND Arroyo Center. The Arroyo Center is a federally funded research and development center sponsored by the United States Army.

Comments or requests for further information are welcome; please contact the report editors, Olga Oliker *(oliker@rand.org)* and Thomas Szayna *(szayna@rand.org)*.

For more information on RAND Arroyo Center, contact the Director of Operations (telephone 310-393-0411, extension 6500; FAX 310-451-6952; e-mail donnab@rand.org), or visit the Arroyo Center's Web site at http://www.rand.org/ard/.

CONTENTS

FIGURES

TABLES

Violent conflict is likely to be a continuing problem in Central Asia and South Caucasus over the next 10 to 15 years. Violent clashes within and between states in this region have already occurred, and they are likely to occur again. Depending on how the region develops, the form and degree of conflict may or may not grow to involve other states, including the United States and its interests. This analysis considers some of the most important factors underlying the likelihood of conflict in the region, assessing their implications for regional stability and for U.S. interests and potential involvement over the next 10 to 15 years. It also provides some preliminary thoughts on the implications of the ongoing U.S. presence in and near the region.

None of the sources of conflict described in this report operate in a vacuum. Economic, political, ethnic, and religious factors all combine with the impact of foreign interests to make conflict more or less likely. This analysis suggests, however, that the key factor for the likelihood of regional conflict is the regimes themselves; their weaknesses and volatilities leave them increasingly unable to withstand challenges posed by other faultlines. When regimes collapse, these politically and economically weakened countries may experience armed strife.

The specifics of how this happens can vary. Unintegrated and/or alienated minorities who link their economic deprivation and political oppression to ethnicity or religion can be expected to organize. But if there are no political institutions to channel their participation, their efforts to do so will put them in conflict with the state and possibly with each other. The absence of effective political institutions makes it more likely that public discontent will take extralegal forms. Moreover, civil strife and potential state failure resulting from a succession crisis is possible in the next 15 years in almost all of these states, except perhaps Armenia. It is most likely in the near term in Azerbaijan and Georgia. Azerbaijan's president is aging and ailing. He has indicated that he hopes his son will succeed him. Georgia's president Eduard Shevardnadze, also over 70 years of age, has said that he will not run again when his term expires in 2005.

Ethnic heterogeneity, a necessary but not sufficient condition for ethnic conflict, is present in almost all the states of the region (Armenia and, to a lesser extent, Azerbaijan are the exceptions). In this part of the world, however, ethnic diversity exists side by side with wide economic disparities and state policies of "ethnic redress" that privilege the titular nationality over others—including those who once enjoyed more advantages. Weak institutions and limited central control make it more likely that dissatisfied groups will have the capacity to mobilize and acquire weaponry. If this happens, the state itself is likely to respond with violence.

At the interstate level, these internal dynamics may well make conflict with other states more likely, as leaders seek to unite a people of an increasingly contested state behind them, or seek to strike first before another state can undermine their power, or simply behave in an aggressive manner. Pretexts for interstate conflict in this region abound, as borders drawn up in Soviet times fail to follow ethnic lines (or, in most cases, economic "common sense" lines), giving many states a claim on the territory of others. It is expected that territorial disputes may well lead to some forcible readjustment of borders. Such disputes may also serve as a proximate cause of cross-border adventurism by some states. In addition to insurgency attacks, territorial claims and efforts to "defend" co-ethnics by one or another state could escalate conflict to an interstate level. In Central Asia, border conflicts are most likely in the Ferghana Valley. In the South Caucasus, the risk remains that Nagorno-Karabakh will flare up once again.

The states' economic condition reflects the political situation. Both poverty and economic dependence are prevalent in all eight states under consideration. The people of Central Asia and South Caucasus are by and large in worse shape economically than they were under Soviet rule, with at least half living at or below the poverty line according to their own national statistics. What wealth there is, is highly concentrated in the hands of a very small minority, and social services are minimal. Moreover, while trade has begun to shift somewhat toward partners in Europe, the states of Central Asia and South Caucasus remain significantly dependent on Russia. Russian efforts to increase regional economic integration could, if successful, keep these states from many of the potential benefits of involvement in the globalized economy. Finally, while the energy producers may place most of their hope in expected revenues from energy exports (although they then run the risk of both resources and foreign investment becoming diverted entirely to the energy sector, with little gain for the rest of the economy), all the states of the region will require fundamental—and probably painful—reforms before their economies can truly begin to develop.

In an economically backward and depressed situation such as this, it is not uncommon to see the rise of criminal activity and corruption. The drug trade and other criminal activities give people a means of economic activity, alleviating poverty and providing employment. Corruption and bribery make it possible to get things done. Thus, crime in such a situation has both positive and negative effects. Estimates suggest that in much of the Central Asian and South Caucasus region, the shadow, or illegal, economy is approaching the size of the legal economy. If it could be quantified and included, it would double the GDP. This means both that studies of the legal economy alone understate the economic deprivation, and that the prospects for growth are probably lower than the studies indicate, because the long-term effects of a criminalized economy are overwhelmingly negative. Bad business drives out good, preventing investment and growth. Corruption weakens the state's ability to govern, decreasing trust in it and making it tremendously inefficient, as nothing gets done without bribes. Moreover, in Central Asia and South Caucasus, the significant component of the criminal economy that is linked to the drug trade has its own repercussions. The region has already become an important route for drugs flowing from Afghanistan. Increasingly, production is moving into states like Tajikistan, as well. Drug use is on the rise, straining already limited public health resources and increasing the danger of AIDS, and proceeds from drug trafficking are reportedly sometimes used (although the extent is unknown) to fuel the insurgencies that threaten local governments.

Resource development, too, has its positive and negative aspects. The Caspian oil-producing states, Azerbaijan and Kazakhstan, have the greatest prospects for finding hard currency markets abroad. Turkmenistan and Uzbekistan, which produce gas but have very little export potential for their limited oil production, are unlikely to find a market outside the regional one, as monetization of natural gas resources is a far more difficult endeavor. As for the rest of the states of the region, Georgia has hopes of becoming a transit state for Caspian oil and reaping some economic benefits in this way, but Armenia, Tajikistan, and Kyrgyzstan have few prospects in this regard. Moreover, recent droughts have exacerbated the fact that the have/have-not situation with energy is largely reversed when it comes to water. The fossil fuel–poor upstream countries, Kyrgyzstan and Tajikistan, lie at the headwaters of the Syr Darya and Amu Darya rivers, which provide the means for hydroelectric power generation. The fossil fuel–rich downstream countries, Kazakhstan, Uzbekistan, and Turkmenistan, rely on this water for the irrigation of extensive cotton and grain fields. Arguments over when to release this water have led to repeated energy shut-offs and international disputes, while among the Caspian littoral states, disagreement over the division of the seabed has led to the increasing militarization of that body of water, as each state seeks to protect its claims.

Resource competition and crime and the drug trade are overall less likely to serve as proximate causes of conflict than as aggravating factors, making conflict more likely, more intense, and more likely to spread. However, disputes over territory in the resource-rich Caspian Sea itself can also heighten tension. Foreign involvement to contain a developing crisis may also exacerbate the situation, for example, prolonging conflict and involving more states, while criminal support of insurgency groups, perhaps with drug money, can keep the conflict going longer than it otherwise might.

Foreign interests, whether or not they themselves spur conflict, will have an impact on how it develops, and outside actors are likely to get involved if it does. Russia, China, Turkey, Iran, and the United States may seek to defend their interests in the region, whether those derive from shared ethnic characteristics, hopes for pipelines to carry

Caspian energy resources to and through their states, fears of conflict spreading beyond the region, or a desire to demonstrate strength and influence. Foreign state and nonstate actors have also supported insurrectionist and secessionist movements within Central Asia and South Caucasus, seeking to advance strategic and/or ideological (and religious) goals. And as the U.S. response to terrorist attacks on its soil in September 2001 evolves, the region acquires a new set of concerns, including the implications of continued war in Afghanistan, the possibility of unrest in Pakistan, and the short- and long-term impact of U.S. force presence in the region.

The situation in Afghanistan and Pakistan, as well as the troop presence of U.S., Russian, and other forces in the region may serve to catalyze state failure in a number of ways, perhaps making significant conflict more proximate than it might otherwise have been. Refugee flows into the region could strain the treasuries and stretch the capacities of states to deal with the influx. They can also potentially be a mechanism for countergovernment forces to acquire new recruits and assistance. This is of particular concern given the history of Al Qaeda and Taliban support to insurgent groups in Central Asia, as well as the ethnic links and overlaps between Afghanistan and the Central Asian states. To date, the rise of insurgencies linked to radical Islam has either caused or provided an excuse for the leadership in several states to become increasingly authoritarian, in many ways aggravating rather than alleviating the risk of social unrest, and it is entirely plausible that this trend will continue. Moreover, if the U.S.-Russian relationship improves, Russian officials may take advantage of the opportunity, combined with U.S. preoccupation with its counterterror campaign, to take actions in Georgia and Azerbaijan that these states will perceive as aggressive. Meanwhile, U.S. forces in the region may be viewed as targets by combatants in the Afghanistan war and by insurgent efforts against the Central Asian governments.

The situation in Afghanistan will almost certainly have an impact on the faultlines in Central Asia and possibly those in the South Caucasus. While it remains too early to predict just what that impact might be, regardless of the situation in Afghanistan, there remains excellent reason to believe that over the next 15 years separatists will continue to strive to attain independence (as in Georgia) and insurgency forces to take power (as in Uzbekistan, Kyrgyzstan, and Tajikistan).

This could spread from the countries where we see it currently to possibly affect Kazakhstan, Turkmenistan, and Azerbaijan. It could also result in responses by states that see a neighboring insurgency as a threat, and by others that pursue insurgents beyond their own borders. Insofar as U.S. forces stay involved in the region, it could draw the United States into these Central Asian and South Caucasus conflicts.

Even before September 11, 2001, the United States was involved in Central Asia and South Caucasus. Diplomatic ties, economic assistance, economic interests, and military engagement through NATO's Partnership for Peace and bilateral cooperation varied in intensity from state to state, but were significant with several. Caucasus states Georgia and Azerbaijan hoped that U.S. engagement, as well as close ties with neighbor Turkey, might translate into NATO support against Russian political, economic, and military pressure (or, at least, a perception by Russia that NATO support was possible). Central Asian states such as Uzbekistan and Kyrgyzstan received assistance that they hoped would help them with challenges posed by Al Qaeda- and Taliban-supported insurgency groups that sought to destabilize their governments. These states also saw U.S. assistance as a possible alternative to dependence on Russia, and, in the case of Uzbekistan, a means of further strengthening its own regional role. Thus, while in the near term it seems likely that the United States presence will be geared to the counterterror campaign in and around Afghanistan, U.S. interests in the region extend beyond the present campaign. Depending on how ties with the Central Asian states develop, and on the future path of the counterterrorist effort, future activities may involve more counterterrorist efforts into Afghanistan (and perhaps Pakistan), supporting the Central Asian states in their counterinsurgency efforts, peacemaking or peacekeeping after conflict emerges in the region, or responding to terrorist groups on the territories of Central Asian states themselves. Moreover, even if the United States is less involved, a crisis in Central Asia or in the South Caucasus could lead to the deployment of international peacekeepers or peacemakers, to include U.S. forces, protection of energy and pipeline infrastructure throughout the region, and protection and evacuation of U.S. and other foreign nationals.

The same factors that make conflict more likely—ethnic cleavages, economic hardship, high crime rates, rampant corruption, etc.—also complicate any and all efforts, military, economic, or otherwise, in the region. Whatever the extent and form of the longer-term U.S. presence in the region, it will therefore be challenging—and challenged. Even without these problems, the terrain is difficult and distances are substantial, while infrastructure throughout the region leaves much to be desired. With U.S. troops already in place to varying extents in Central Asian and South Caucasus states, it becomes particularly important to understand the faultlines, geography, and other challenges this part of the world presents. U.S. forces will face them in one way or another regardless of the depth of their commitment to the region. The current situation, however, suggests that they may face them somewhat sooner than might once have been expected.

ACKNOWLEDGMENTS

The authors would like to thank LTG Robert W. Noonan, Jr., for sponsoring this research. We also thank Mr. William Speer, Mr. Eric Kraemer, LTC John D. Cecil, and MAJ Donald L. Gabel, currently or previously with the Office of the Deputy Chief of Staff for Intelligence, U.S. Army, under whose auspices this work was undertaken. We would like to acknowledge the useful insights provided in discussions following intermediate briefings of this project at DCSINT by DCSINT staff as well as by Mr. Lester Grau of FMSO, Mr. Alan R. Goldman, Mr. David Merchant, and LTC David O. Grimmet of NGIC, Dr. Joel Shapiro of DIA, and Mr. Shaughnessy of HQ TRADOC.

At RAND, David Kassing provided many valuable suggestions and comments throughout the research and writing process, and Roy Gates assisted in gathering and interpreting information on regional airfields and other facilities. Valuable insights were gleaned from meetings and discussions with LTC Peter A. DeLuca (then at U.S. European Command); LTC Keith D. Solveson (then at the Center for Army Analysis); LTC Prine-Rincon, Mr. Creque, Mr. Fowler, LTC Glover, LTC Cozzie, LTC Hayman, LTC Bonnadonna, MAJ Kron, and LTC Hill at U.S. Central Command; Commander Thom W. Burke of the Joint Staff; and Ms. Lorna Jons, MAJ Walter Grissom, and LTC Richard C. Choppa at the Office of the Secretary of Defense. The suggestions and comments of Dr. Nora Bensahel and Dr. Adam Stulberg greatly enhanced the report's quality, and we are grateful to them for their time and effort. Pamela Thompson and Joanna Alberdeston at RAND were crucial in the preparation of the report, and Nikki Shacklett served as editor.

Chapter One

INTRODUCTION
Thomas S. Szayna and Olga Oliker

THE CONTEXT

The breakup of the Soviet Union led to the emergence of eight new states in the strategically important crossroads located north of the Middle East and the Persian Gulf region, west of China, and south of Russia. Three of them (Georgia, Armenia, and Azerbaijan) are situated in the European periphery—the mountainous area between the Greater Caucasus mountain range (defined by geographers as the boundary of Europe) and Turkey and Iran. In the Soviet lexicon, based on a Russo-centric viewpoint, this area was referred to as the Trans-Caucasus. A name for this subregion that is more neutral in connotation—and one that is preferable in the post-Soviet era—is South Caucasus. The other five states (Kazakhstan, Kyrgyzstan, Tajikistan, Turkmenistan, and Uzbekistan) are situated in the vast steppes and deserts stretching eastward from the Caspian Sea to the Altai and Pamir mountain ranges of Central Asia. For a variety of reasons, Soviet officials differentiated between Kazakhstan and what were then the other four Soviet republics, referring only to the latter as Central Asia. However, in the post-Soviet era the term has come to denote all five states. The term is geographically accurate, since the area encompasses a good portion of central-western Asia. Although the two areas, South Caucasus and Central Asia, are quite distinct from each other in many ways, their common Soviet legacy and similar problems have led the two subregions to be lumped together in a geostrategic sense.

The issue that placed the Central Asia and South Caucasus region on the geostrategic map was the presence of energy reserves (oil and gas) of a size that is significant at the global level. Until September 11, 2001, strategic and fossil fuel–driven competition was the central motivation behind any foreign involvement and interest in the area. In fact, competition over how to exploit the resources sharpened in the late 1990s, with disagreements between the United States, the European Union, Russia, and Iran. There were few other reasons for the extensive foreign interest in the area, since the investment climate in the region was not attractive, all of the new states in this region went through a massive decline in the standard of living during the 1990s, and all of them made only a partial (at best) transition to market economies and democratic political systems.

The attacks on the United States on September 11 changed the geostrategic context in the region and elevated its importance to the United States. Because of access problems the U.S. military has faced in carrying out combat operations in Afghanistan, the importance of the Central Asian states (especially Uzbekistan) to the United States has grown to a level unimaginable prior to September 11. Based on their own problems with political Islam and the Taliban regime in Afghanistan, some of the Central Asian regimes have been among the staunchest supporters of U.S. combat operations in Afghanistan. If those operations continue, the importance of the region to the United States, as well as U.S. involvement with the states of Central Asia, is bound to grow further. This makes it all the more important to note that all of the states of Central Asia and South Caucasus face a multitude of internal problems that potentially could complicate U.S. relations with them—and U.S. operations on or near their territories.

Most of the research effort that led to this report was conducted prior to the September 11 attacks and had the aim of discerning the potential faultlines and catalysts of conflict in South Caucasus and Central Asia internally and in the context of international competition over the manner of exploitation of the area's energy resources. The launching of U.S. combat operations in Afghanistan and the deployment of U.S. troops to several Central Asian and South Caucasus countries as part of the global war on terrorism have changed the context for U.S. views of the region. They have elevated greatly the strategic importance of Central Asia and South Caucasus to the United States, and security cooperation with some of the countries in the region has increased tremendously. However, all of the faultlines and catalysts of conflict in the region still remain. The information cutoff date for this report is mid-2002.

The Army had an interest in tracking the faultlines in the region because of the emerging rivalry and competition over the area, its remoteness, the relative lack of expertise in the Army regarding the region, and the potential for eventual U.S. military involvement in the area in the long-term perspective. That interest has taken on a new meaning in the post–September 11 security environment. With Army troops on the ground in Central Asia, the need to develop a better awareness of local sensitivities and understand the constraints that U.S. military forces operating in the region might face (including force protection issues) have assumed major importance.

OBJECTIVES, APPROACH, AND ORGANIZATION

This study began with the goal of seeking to assist the U.S. Army in understanding the operational environment that it may face should it deploy forces to Central Asia and South Caucasus. The September 11 attacks have given the effort greater urgency and importance. The effort had the following key objectives:

- Identify and define sources of conflict in the South Caucasus (Armenia, Azerbaijan, and Georgia) and in post-Soviet Central Asia (Kazakhstan, Kyrgyzstan, Tajikistan, Turkmenistan, and Uzbekistan) in the next 10–15 years.

- In the 10–15 year time frame, assess the likelihood and ways in which potential conflicts in this region might escalate to a level that could involve U.S. forces, and define the operational environment those forces would face.

- Develop intelligence indicators and signposts to forecast crises that could affect Army contingency planning.

To address these questions, we proceeded with a multifaceted assessment of the major types of faultlines that may lead to conflict, with each chapter organized around a major potential source of conflict. This report presents the results of that research.

Chapter Two focuses on the domestic political realm and traces the political evolution of the region since it gained independence. The problem areas in this category include regime types, extent of participation in the political process, and major political cleavages, which combine with limited economic development to make conflict more likely. The chapter makes use of the political science literature, especially as it pertains to state capacity, democratization, and extralegal forms of participation. The chapter outlines the theoretical background, applies it to the states in question, and then discusses some of the most likely sources of conflict in the near and medium term in greater detail.

Chapter Three deals with the economic contributors to conflict and instability in the region. The problem areas in this category include the partial (at best) economic reform, the wide-ranging poverty, external economic dependence, and the specific difficulties stemming from a reliance on the development of one type of extractive industry. The chapter makes use of the literature on development economics and economic liberalization and draws on the author's decades-long experience with the Soviet economy and more recent studies of this region and its economic development and relationships.

Chapter Four tackles the issue of the pervasive presence of organized crime and the drug trade in Central Asia and South Caucasus and its consequences for the political and economic evolution of the region. The chapter addresses the ways in which the criminalization of political and economic life can have positive effects in the short term, especially in societies riddled with the political and economic problems that are present in these countries. In the long term, of course, the effects are pernicious, and greatly increase the risks of economic and political state failure. The indicators and issues are examined both on a state-by-state basis and for the region as a whole. The chapter makes use of the political science literature, especially as it pertains to regime types, and draws on the author's comparative knowledge of criminalization and international organized crime.

Chapter Five deals solely with the issue of exploitation of natural resources in the region. It provides an assessment of the region's energy and other natural resources and discusses the difficulties inherent in exploiting and transporting these resources, as well as the areas of disagreement between states on these issues. It presents the stark contrasts between the likely "winners" and "losers" in the future exploitation of these resources and discusses how the development of technology will affect this balance. It discusses possible areas of conflict and also the potential for energy and other resource-related infrastructure to become a target for combatants in the event of conflict. The chapter draws on the development economics literature, recent estimates of regional energy resources, and previous work on infrastructure vulnerabilities.

Chapter Six focuses on the potential for ethnically based conflict to erupt in the region. Such strife has taken place in the states of Central Asia and South Caucasus during the 1990s, and it is among the most likely types of violence to erupt in the future. The preconditions for violence along ethnic group lines stem from ethnic heterogeneity that is present in most of the countries of the region, combined with an understanding of ethnicity in an ascriptive fashion, politics of ethnic favoritism, regimes inefficient in conflict resolution, high poverty levels and widespread unemployment, and fundamental socioeconomic disruptions that lead to a climate of fear and insecurity. The chapter makes use of the social science literature on ethnicity and politics and, in its predictive portion, refers to a RAND-developed model of ethnic conflict.

Chapter Seven addresses the issue of foreign interest and competition over the region. It considers the interests in and influence on Central Asia and South Caucasus of a variety of third-party states, including Russia, China, Iran, Turkey, the United States, and Afghanistan, as well as the perspectives of regional states on relations with neighbors and other interested parties. The chapter draws on the political science literature on international relations and international conflict as well as on the work of regional specialists.

Chapter Eight deals with the likely operational environment that any Army troops deploying to the region are likely to face. It considers, on a country-by-country and regionwide basis, the issues that terrain, political environment, economic environment, and ecological environment present for operations, the capacities of local states to support force deployments, and the capacities of local military forces to support or oppose U.S. military presence. The particular challenges of moving forces to and through this part of the world are considered in depth. While this is primarily considered in the 10- to 15-

year time frame, the chapter also discusses some key issues for the near term.

Chapter Nine presents the overall conclusions for the prospects and type of armed conflict in the region, links them to likelihood of U.S. military involvement, and sets out some indicators for intelligence analysts to use in their assessments. It then discusses some of the mitigating factors that work to minimize risk of conflict in the region, although its final assessment is that conflict is likely, and U.S. involvement is increasingly probable.

To reiterate, the analysis here takes a long-term perspective, though most of the faultlines described are already in evidence. It is still too early to assess definitively the long-term impact of the U.S. combat operations in Afghanistan on the conflict faultlines described in this report. What is certain is that the faultlines are of a long-term structural nature and will not go away. Thus, the more the United States is involved militarily in this part of the world, the more these factors will challenge and affect its efforts. Furthermore, there is a dynamic interface between U.S. involvement and military presence in Central Asia and South Caucasus and regional developments. Army analysts and planners need to keep the faultlines in mind as they consider options for further involvement in the region.

Chapter Two

THE POLITICAL EVOLUTION OF CENTRAL ASIA AND SOUTH CAUCASUS: IMPLICATIONS FOR REGIONAL SECURITY

Tanya Charlick-Paley with Phil Williams and Olga Oliker

INTRODUCTION

Ten years after independence, transitions from Soviet authoritarianism and planned economies to democracy and market economies have not been successfully completed in any of the states of Central Asia and South Caucasus (henceforth CASC). Although there are variations among them, each of the eight states in question faces serious challenges to peace and growth. The lack of real economic reform or sustainable development, the persistent centralized controls built on the foundation of Soviet bureaucracy, and the growing problems of corruption and public cynicism all constrain efforts to build effective and popular governance. The capacity of state structures and police and military forces to effectively de-escalate or deter conflict remains highly questionable.

Conflict could result from any of a wide range of factors present in this part of the world. Potentially explosive ethnic tensions and irredentist border challenges, severe poverty, drug trafficking, and, for Central Asia, the threat of Islamic insurgency and conflict across the border in Afghanistan could all separately or together lead to fighting within and between states. Political, social, religious, ethnic, and economic structures are such that the risk of conflict spreading from one state to another is significant. Moreover, there are few mechanisms for effective regional cooperation that could mitigate these problems.

But warning signs for serious conflict do not necessarily translate into conflict itself. Considering the ten years of predictions to the contrary, CASC has seen surprisingly little conflict since independence. The exceptions include Georgia, which has been plagued by small-scale rebellions and kidnappings in its western portions, border skirmishes near Chechnya (and an influx of refugees from that territory—probably including at least some militants), repeated attempts to assassinate or overthrow the president, separatist movements in Abkhazia and South Ossetia, and general lack of central control; Azerbaijan and Armenia's war over Nagorno-Karabakh; and civil war in Tajikistan. Overall, however, conflict has remained at fairly low levels, and although it has sometimes crossed state borders, it has yet to threaten outright interstate war. Armenia, for example, has maintained a relatively stable domestic situation despite economic stagnation, debilitating emigration, and the murders of a prime minister and a speaker of parliament. It has been able to do so in large part because the cease-fire in its conflict with Azerbaijan over the Nagorno-Karabakh conflict, although oft-challenged, remains in place. In Central Asia, the Tajik conflict has cooled to a simmer, although incursions by Islamic militants into Uzbekistan and Kyrgyzstan in 1999–2000 worried leaders in the region and beyond.

This situation, however, could be exacerbated if active conflict continues or worsens in Afghanistan, creating an influx of refugees (and very likely militants) into the Central Asian states. This could potentially reignite the civil war in Tajikistan and would strain Uzbekistan's and Kyrgyzstan's capacity to maintain state control—even assuming U.S. and other foreign assistance. Even stability in this region is a decidedly relative concept, as the best of times have been marked by assassination attempts on government officials and the occasional bombing. But if there is little doubt that this sort of low-level conflict will continue in this part of the world for the foreseeable future, the real question is to what extent, and under what circumstances, these situations might be expected to escalate into full-fledged war.

This chapter will consider some of the political-institutional factors that have been linked to political instability and conflict and apply them to the CASC region. It will then consider both aggravating and constraining factors for conflict, and provide a tentative assessment of the likelihood of an outbreak of civil and/or multistate war in the region.

POLITICAL INSTITUTIONALIZATION, DEPRIVATION, AND STATE AND SOCIETAL CAPACITY: A FRAMEWORK FOR RISK ANALYSIS

In the last decade, global sectarian violence has been accompanied by a renewed academic interest in the ways in which changes in institutional structures and elite strategies for regime legitimacy can either exacerbate or dampen the risk of civil conflicts. While spreading democracy and increasing civil and economic liberties in newly independent countries may be an important policy goal of certain western democracies, it is not without risk, particularly in the near term. Most of the states or territories with bloody ethnic conflicts in the 1990s shared a common trait, a move toward a more open election or greater civil liberties in the year or so before conflict erupted. These included Burundi, Yugoslavia, Armenia and Azerbaijan, and Russia (Chechnya).[1] Thus, one strategy for regime legitimacy, that of increasing democratic liberties, provides a means for groups to organize but has the danger of increasing social mobilization without adequate institutional capacity to fully enable effective political participation. This can increase the risk of conflict. Moreover, some have argued that the actual liberalizations that attend political openness can help increase the danger of violence by making it easier for leaders to mobilize on the basis of societal divisions, exacerbating sectarian hatred.[2] Groups and individuals competing for power may appeal to ethnic or nationalist symbols and allegiances, fostering conflict with those of other ethnicities or those who disagree with the nationalist concept advocated.[3]

In addition, decades of research on the relationship between economic growth and sustainable state-building argue that when there is a downturn in economic growth, particularly when it is accompanied by a gap in the expectations that the citizens have of their eco-

---

[1] Jack L. Snyder, "Nationalism Among the Ruins," in Jack L. Snyder, *From Voting to Violence: Democratization and Nationalist Conflict,* New York: W.W. Norton, 2000, p. 18.

[2] See Snyder and Karen Ballentine, "Nationalism and the Marketplace of Ideas," *International Security,* Vol. 21, No. 2 (Fall 1996), pp. 5–40.

[3] See Snyder, *From Voting to Violence.* See also his previous work with Edward D. Mansfield, "Democratization and the Danger of War," *International Security,* Vol. 20, No. 1 (Summer 1995), pp. 5–38.

nomic future, conflict is a possible outcome. Scholars have also identified a host of risks that accompany increased social mobilization in situations when economic and political change increase popular grievances.[4] Samuel Huntington argued in the 1960s that propensity to conflict is increased by social and economic modernization, particularly when such modernization is rapid. His argument was based on the notion that when social mobilization moves at a faster rate than does economic development, social frustration results at both the individual and group levels. When there is limited capacity for individuals and groups to take action to improve their economic situation (per Huntington, "mobility opportunities," such as a move from a rural to an urban area), those socially mobilized individuals and groups will seek to change the situation through political participation, that is, demands on the government for change. But if political institutionalization in a country is insufficient for the socially frustrated to express those demands through existing legitimate channels, they may seek other illegitimate channels, increasing instability and the risk of violence. Huntington writes, "Political instability in modernizing countries is thus in large part a function of the gap between aspirations and expectations produced by the escalation of aspirations which particularly occurs in the early phases of modernization."[5]

Economic and political inequality and instability are also a part of this equation, as social mobilization makes people more aware of the inequalities that exist in society, and demands for change are often demands for redistribution of wealth and privilege. While in the long run development will lead to a more equitable distribution of wealth,

---

[4]The argument that economic reversals combined with expectations gaps can lead to conflict was formulated as the J curve of social insurrection in Crane Brinton, *Anatomy of Revolution*, New York: Vintage Books, 1957, and has been further developed in James C. Davis, "The Revolutionary State of Mind: Toward a Theory of Revolution" in James Chowning Davies (ed.), *When Men Revolt*, New Brunswick: Transaction Publishers, 1997, pp. 133–148. See also Barrington Moore, *Social Origins of Dictatorship and Democracy*, Boston: Beacon Press, 1966, on the importance of the middle class to democratization, and D. Rueschmeyer, E.H. Stephens et al., *Capitalist Development and Democracy*, Chicago: University of Chicago Press, 1992, on the importance of the working class.

[5]Samuel P. Huntington, *Political Order in Changing Societies*, New Haven: Yale University Press, 1968, pp. 39–56.

in the short term it more often exacerbates existing inequalities, increases corruption, and further heightens frustration.[6]

The key to this argument is the combination of rising expectations that are not met, the lack of existing political institutions to channel popular demands for change, and a perception of inequality. Weak states, that is, those whose institutions are not considered legitimate by the population,[7] are at particular risk. If institutions are not sufficiently developed, then participation is likely to be in forms that threaten social order and state capacity.[8] Moreover, when perceived (and real) inequality can be clearly linked to divisions between specific social groups (ethnic, economic, etc.), this leads to tension within society, as well as against the state. This further exacerbates the danger of conflict, and to some extent helps determine its form.

When weak institutionalization and political mobilization combine to create instability, the result can be termed the "contested state." Such a state is characterized by the following:

- **Low levels of legitimacy and authority of the government.** This can be the result of a lack of consensus about the basic principles on which society should be governed. For states in transition from communism to capitalism, a lack of consensus can be an extremely serious problem, with continuing divisions between those who cling to the old principles and those who want to move toward democracy and the free market. Alternatively, low legitimacy and authority result where government is monopolized or dominated by one ethnic group in societies that are ethnically diverse.

- **Low state capacity for governance.** This is often reflected in a variety of domains, including poor economic management, ineffective foreign and domestic policy implementation, and a

---

[6]Huntington, pp. 56–59.

[7]Karl Deutsch, "Social Mobilization and Political Development," *American Political Science Review*, 55 (September): pp. 493–514, 1961.

[8]On state failure, see Steven R. David, "Saving America from the Coming Civil Wars," *Foreign Affairs*, Vol. 78, No. 1 (Winter 1999), pp. 103–116; Gerald Helman and Steven R. Ratner, "Saving Failed States," *Foreign Policy*, No. 89 (Winter 1992–1993), pp. 3–20; and David Hoffman, "Yelstin's Absentee Rule Raises the Specter of a 'Failed State,'" *Washington Post*, February 26, 1999, p. A1.

criminal justice system where there are serious gaps in both the legal framework and enforcement capabilities. Such characteristics facilitate criminalization.

- **Nonstate affiliations and loyalties.** Where primary loyalties are not to the state, but to the family or clan, the ethnic group, or the region, the state is not seen as the arbiter of disputes and disagreements, but as the prize of politics. Once the state has been captured, the benefits can then be distributed to members of the clan, those of the same ethnic identity, or those from the favored region. The concomitant, of course, is that nonmembers are discriminated against. Indeed, politics based on clan, ethnicity, or region can also be understood as the politics of exclusion.

- **Violent politics.** Political competition may take forms that are not well structured or carefully regulated. In the more extreme cases, of course, political competition degenerates into violence. The failure to convince all too easily leads to a willingness to coerce or, as Jack Snyder put it, "from voting to violence."[9] This can take the form of riots, assassination attempts, ethnic strife, insurgency, or contract killings. The essential point is that violence in the society is an accepted and legitimate continuation of politics by other means.

- **The existence of many areas of society to which the writ of the state does not extend.** These can be informal economic activities beyond the purview and regulation of the state or geographic regions that are essentially beyond the control of the government, and in some cases constitute no-go areas for government representatives, including law enforcement.

The contested state is the last stop on the road to complete state failure. However, a strategy of liberalization is not *solely* tied to increased civil conflict. Contested states are not the inevitable outcome of political and economic liberalization. Some argue that as states relax the limits on political expression and reform their economies to become more open economic systems, conflict can be managed through growing institutions. In addition, greater stability can be attained when economic gains reach beyond the ruling class

---

[9]Snyder, *From Voting to Violence*.

to benefit middle- and working-class members of society. In other words, an increased risk of conflict may well be only a temporary risk in the short term if elites manage the transition well.

In addition, even high levels of discontent, if the discontented lack the resources, capability, or leadership to mobilize, will not present much threat to a regime.

Much depends, then, on the strategies that elites choose to legitimize their regimes, the institutions they build to further these strategies, and the regime's capacity to effectively utilize these governance structures and strategies. Liberalization is only one option for regime legitimacy. The capacity of society to develop and utilize resources and capabilities, and to follow opposition leaders, can be effectively constrained by a state that is willing and sufficiently strong to use such authoritarian means as an effective internal security force to stifle overt dissent. This is, of course, the model the Soviet Union followed for three-quarters of a century.

A second option is to postpone the dangers of conflict arising from democratization (albeit by halting the democratization itself). Useful for understanding this second elite strategy is the concept of "sultanistic regimes."[10] This notion has its origin in the work of Max Weber and was initially developed in relation to Latin American countries.[11] Such a regime is characterized by personal rule and a system of fears, rewards, and extensive corruption. The staff of the government is often chosen directly by the ruler to include his family, friends, and business associates. In sultanistic regimes, the most important politics is what might be termed "palace politics," where the leader distributes both rewards and penalties with little or no external constraint. Greed and fear are used as inducements for loyalty and support. Position becomes a privilege that is granted by the leader and is valued because it provides access to rent-seeking opportunities. Because there are no countervailing factors, decisionmaking is generally arbitrary, and guided by expediency and calculations of self-interest and self-aggrandizement.

---

[10]See H.E. Chelabi and Juan Linz (eds.), *Sultanistic Regimes*, Baltimore: Johns Hopkins University Press, 1998, and the review thereof by Anatol Lieven, posted November 8, 2000, on *www.eurasianet.org*.

[11]Ibid.

The sultanistic regime makes up for its weak institutions with strong and repressive leadership.[12] Sultanism effectively halts or never initiates the progress of a transition to democracy and thereby mitigates the problems such a transition engenders, for as long as the ruler can maintain control of the state through repression. Thus, although the level of political institutionalization is very low in this type of regime, while it is in place, the potential for domestic conflict is also very low. However, these regimes are inherently unstable in the longer term because their lack of institutionalization makes them prone to succession crises when and if something happens to the leader. Finally, in a repressive state led by a single strongman, the leader's need to maintain power and privilege can easily degenerate into political paranoia that brooks no dissent or opposition. Although successful as a short-term palliative, when regimes of personalistic rule fail, the factors that make conflict more likely—those that the repressive leadership was able to keep under control—re-emerge with a vengeance (literally), and create a strong likelihood that the formerly sultanistic regime will become a contested one. However, it is never clear when this implosion will occur. Sultanistic regimes can sometimes be maintained for the very long term, with successive authoritarian rulers following one another.

Clearly, transitions involve both factors that mitigate and those that increase the danger of conflict. A risk analysis for domestic conflict in CASC should therefore examine the constraining and facilitating factors for conflict in several key domestic areas that are at the core of these arguments: economic growth, political institutionalization, elite strategies for regime legitimacy and stability, and the strength of civil society in states across the region.[13] Such an analysis will yield a nuanced view of the short- and longer-term risks of civil conflict within CASC states. It is such an analysis to which we now turn.

---

[12]Ibid.

[13]Juha Auvinen, "Political Conflict in Less Developed Countries 1981–1989," *Journal of Peace Research*, Vol. 34, No. 2 (1997), pp. 177–188.

INSTITUTIONALIZATION IN CENTRAL ASIA AND SOUTH CAUCASUS: RATING THE RISK OF INTERNAL CONFLICT

The states of CASC do not score well on the indicators identified by scholars who link institutionalization and conflict. Unexpectedly independent in 1991, many of the states in the CASC region lacked the infrastructure of governance, the bureaucratic tools, and the political and administrative experience needed to effectively run a state.[14] Although a decade of independence has differentiated some countries from others, institutional weakness in the region continues to be the norm. The strategies and risks for conflict differ across the region and between the two subregions of CASC. The elites in Central Asian states as a whole have not gone as far in liberalizing their political and economic systems as the countries of the South Caucasus have. Georgia, Armenia, and Azerbaijan have most closely approximated a transition to a more liberal political and economic system. This choice, however, at least in the near term, has left them with large gaps between high levels of mass political participation and underdeveloped political institutions as well as problems with the distribution of economic resources to middle-class and working-class sectors of the economy. Thus, these countries face the risks discussed in the section above on liberalization and conflict in contested states.[15]

In Central Asia there are even fewer mechanisms for resolving the economic, ethnic, or political grievances and ambitions, many of which were unleashed and/or aggravated by the processes of independence. None of the CASC states has come all that far in creating coalition and power-sharing arrangements between key groups of elites, much less opposition parties. Instead, in many of them a "strong leader" has emerged to balance the "weak institutions." The effectiveness of the Soviet system at eliminating alternative elites left the Communist republic elites the most credible leaders of the states that emerged from the Soviet dust. Of the eight republics in CASC,

---

[14]Ronald Grigor Suny, "Southern Tears: Dangerous Opportunities in the Caucasus and Central Asia," in Rajan Menon, Yuri Federov, and Ghia Nodia (eds.), *Russia, the Caucasus and Central Asia: The 21st Century Security Environment*, Armonk, NY: M.E. Sharpe, 1999, pp. 147–176.

[15]Snyder, *From Voting to Violence*, Chapter 6, "Nationalism Amid the Ruins of Communism."

five are ruled by former Communist first secretaries. (Tajikistan, Armenia, and Kyrgyzstan are the exceptions.) The development of both these leaders and Kyrgyzstan's Askar Akaev into nascent "sultans" is evidenced by the fact that for the most part, the same men are still in power. Although there were elections in almost all Central Asian countries in 2000, the result was largely the maintenance of the status quo.[16] Incumbents retained their hold on power and showed they were willing to use any means to continue to do so. New elections are not expected in the region until 2003, although in the past sitting presidents have called elections early to show their popular support.[17]

Of the regional states moving toward sultanism, the clearest examples are Turkmenistan and Uzbekistan. In a very real sense, Turkmenistan and Uzbekistan have not undergone political transitions but have preserved the old system, thus largely avoiding the overt threats to the regime that more open political systems in the region have faced. The political elites' choice in both of these countries to govern through personalistic rule is directly tied to their ability to create effective and loyal internal security forces, capable of stifling any overt challenges to their legitimacy.

In Turkmenistan, President Saparmurat Niyazov has led a repressive regime likened by some to Stalin's cult of personality. Not only have political parties been banned and all media controlled by the government, but meetings of any kind are forbidden and torture and execution are common "law enforcement" measures.[18] Although President Niyazov has been named president for life, he has recently announced that he will step down in 2010—when an election will be held to select his successor. There are many who fear, however, that this election will not occur and that Niyazov will instead proclaim himself king and pass power to his son. If Niyazov chooses to be

---

[16]Uzbekistan held presidential elections, Tajiks voted on a new parliament, and Kyrgyz voters held both presidential and parliamentary elections.

[17]Valery Tsepakalo, "The Remaking of Eurasia," *Foreign Affairs*, Vol. 77, No. 2 (March/April 1998), pp. 107–126, and Zbigniew Brezinski, "The Eurasian Balkans," in *The Grand Chessboard*, New York: Basic Books, 1997, pp. 123–150.

[18]Ahmed Rashid, "The New Struggle in Central Asia: A Primer for the Baffled," *World Policy Journal*, Vol. 17, No. 4 (Winter 2000/2001), pp. 33–45.

crowned, as some rumors suggest he might, opposition leaders (in exile) are promising a coup.[19]

In Uzbekistan, President Islam Karimov has banned opposition parties, set heavy restrictions on the press, and imposed state control over mosques. Arguing that the only way to avoid the fate of Tajikistan was to quash dissent, the regime crushed the internal democratic opposition in a series of crackdowns in 1993–1997, and it has forced regime opponents, particularly Islamic militants (largely based in Ferghana), underground. The government's control of the press is sufficient to limit coverage of the U.S. presence in Uzbekistan, and of the war in Afghanistan itself (although Uzbek residents can often pick up Russian television stations).[20] Moreover, closer ties with the United States do not appear to have driven Karimov to greater democratization. On January 27, 2002, Karimov was able to extend his presidential term from five to seven years by means of a referendum in which 91 percent of voters apparently supported the extension.[21]

There are signs that other elites in the region may chose to follow Uzbekistan's and Turkmenistan's lead. To a lesser extent, most leaders in the region share elements of the sultanistic model, most commonly corruption (which is pervasive throughout the region) and personal leadership.

In Kazakhstan, power has increasingly become concentrated in the hands of President Nursultan Nazarbayev and his clan, alienating the majority of the urban population as well as the resource-rich western part of the country.[22] Corruption at every level of government has become routine, as oil companies are offering bonuses simply for the privilege of submitting contract bids. In June 2000 through a parlia-

---

[19]"Turkmen Leader Prepares to Step Down," *BBC News Sunday,* February 18, 2001.

[20]Tamara Makarenko and Daphne Biliouri, "Central Asian States Set to Pay Price of US Strikes," *Jane's Intelligence Review* (2001).

[21]George Gedda, "U.S. May Remain in Central Asia," *Johnson's Russia List (AP),* February 6, 2002.

[22]Nurbulat E. Masanov, "The Clan Factor in Contemporary Political Life in Kazakhstan," translated by Mark Eckert, *Johnson's Russia List,* February 20, 1998.

mentary bill, Nazarbayev and his family were granted lifetime immunity from any charges of corruption.[23]

Kyrgyzstan, once cited as a model of Central Asian democracy, is also exhibiting dangerous signs of authoritarianism. The parliamentary and presidential elections of 2000 were widely criticized by international monitors. President Akaev, who came to power upon the Soviet Union's collapse, shows no signs of loosening his hold on its reins. Moreover, Akaev has been under significant pressure from his neighbors (including China) to clamp down on Islamic fundamentalism through arrests, press restrictions, and electoral rigging, and he appears to be increasingly in agreement that those are the right mechanisms to deal with the rise of opposition in his country. Akaev's government has placed opposition members under arrest on a number of probably fictional charges and has assisted neighboring Uzbekistan in its efforts to pursue its own opposition with the arrest and extradition of individuals.[24] In all of these states, elites have made the choice to buy current stability at the price of political and economic liberty, fostering significant grievances in the population that may ultimately threaten the regime.[25]

In the remaining states the commitment to liberalization is not always clear. Azerbaijan, for example, shares aspects of both a democracy and an authoritarian state, and it is difficult to predict where its future lies. While Azerbaijan does have an active and diverse opposition, opposition leaders who are perceived to pose a real threat to the Aliev government are in prison, in exile, or under constant surveillance. Elections are manipulated, and while there is some freedom of the press, there is also serious censorship.[26] The

---

[23]Rashid, *The New Struggle in Central Asia,* p. 39.

[24]*The IMU and the Hizb-Ut-Tahrir: Implications of the Afghanistan Campaign,* Osh/Brussels: International Crisis Group, 2002. Also available *at www.crisisweb.org/ projects/showreport.cfm?reportid=538.*

[25]There may be interesting comparisons here to certain states in the Middle East, who have found that various combinations of political repression and democratization have proven sustainable over some years. See Nora Bensahel, *Political Reform in the Middle East,* unpublished manuscript.

[26]Svante E. Cornell, "Democratization Falters in Azerbaijan," *Journal of Democracy,* Vol. 12, No. 2 (2001) pp. 118–131; "Heidar Aliev, Maestro of the Caucasus," *The Economist,* Vol. 356 (September 2, 2000), p. 48; Ronald Grigor Suny, "Provisional Stabilities," *International Security,* Vol. 24, No. 3 (1999).

ailing Heidar Aliev's moves to appoint his son his successor, and the grumblings this has engendered, illustrate the danger of a succession crisis in Azerbaijan.

This leaves Georgia, Armenia, and Tajikistan. Georgia and Tajikistan have made moves toward political liberalization, but their tremendous fragmentation and limited central control threaten their success (even assuming real commitment and political will on the part of their governments). Tajikistan is still recovering from its bitter civil war of 1992–1997, which pitted government loyalists against a coalition of Islamic, democratic, regional, and ethnic opposition factions.[27] The current power-sharing regime represents a step forward for state stability and regime legitimacy; but tension continues as regional armed authorities retain significant control, while the central government can claim to control little territory outside the capital (although it has been cracking down with raids and attacks). Tension between groups and regions remains a volatile factor, and many regional leaders, despite ostensible incorporation into the government, are not trusted by the Rakhmonov regime—often with good reason. Local groups, in turn, assert that the government does not distribute funds and resources to former opposition strongholds. Tajikistan remains tremendously poor, with poverty rates over 50 percent and unemployment over 80 percent in some regions. In parts of the country the economy is entirely dependent on the efforts of aid organizations such as the Aga Khan foundation. The drug trade has become one of the few sources of income for local residents, and insurgent groups such as the Islamic Movement of Uzbekistan (IMU) have repeatedly taken advantage of good relations with local leaders in parts of the country outside of central government control to establish and maintain bases. Finally, Tajikistan also exhibits some of the authoritarian aspects identified in connection with its neighbors. In addition to crackdowns on opposition members, it should be noted that in 1999 President Emomali Rakhmonov

---

[27]See "Tajikistan: An Uncertain Peace," (Osh/Brussels: International Crisis Group, 2001). Matthew Evangelista, "Historical Legacies and the Politics of Intervention in the Former Soviet Union," in Brown, *International Dimensions*, p. 123.

won the presidential election with a reported 97 percent majority—
and a difficult-to-credit 98 percent turnout.[28, 29]

Georgia has chosen to legitimize its regime (at least to the outside
world) through a public commitment to political and economic liberalization, but corruption is particularly acute in Georgia, even
compared to the rest of the CASC region, and the central government
has largely failed to consolidate its borders and ensure stability in
such areas as Abkhazia, South Ossetia, and the Pankisi Gorge, where
large numbers of refugees from Chechnya (including some number
of rebels and their leaders) have fled. As in Tajikistan, little that
could be described as central control extends beyond the city limits
of the capital. While primarily a contested state, Georgia exhibits at
least one indicator of sultanism in the very personal rule of Eduard
Shevardnadze. Shevardnadze's capacity to command respect abroad
has helped him maintain the foreign support that he, in turn, has
used to retain power at home. However, opposition to Shevardnadze's continued rule is growing, in large part due to his failure to
take real steps to combat corruption, and the president himself, at
73, is aging and appears visibly tired at public appearances. He has
said that he will not participate in the presidential elections of 2005.
While it is possible that after Shevardnadze leaves power, by whatever means, Georgia will begin to truly develop as a democratic state,
it is also quite plausible that a succession crisis will completely
undermine the few government structures and institutions that do
exist.

Armenia is something of an outlier in this part of the world.
Although it faces severe economic decline largely tied to its continued hold on the enclave of Nagorno-Karabakh within Azerbaijan
(discussed in greater detail below), Armenia is neither a sultanistic
nor a contested state. While corruption is astronomical here, popular discontent with the government is openly manifested in protests
and demonstrations. While there has been some significant discord
and even violence in the parliament, Armenia appears to be in less

---

[28]"Tajikistan: An Uncertain Peace."

[29]Vladimir Davlatov and Turat Akimov, "Dushanbe Alarmed Over IMU Activity";
"Central Asia: Drugs and Conflict," (Osh/Brussels: International Crisis Group, 2001);
"Tajikistan: An Uncertain Peace."

danger of a succession crisis than of a contentious election between bitter political party divisions. In addition, its ethnically homogenous population exhibits few ethnic cleavages that might otherwise be exploited in ways that foment conflict. Thus, the likelihood of internal conflict stemming from Armenia's political transition is comparatively low, although the risks of renewed interstate conflict with Azerbaijan remain.

THE ROLE OF ISLAM

A discussion of the political landscape of CASC would be incomplete without consideration of the additional wrinkle of the rise of political Islam, alluded to previously. The Central Asian regimes are faced with a strange dilemma in that the one factor that could be thought to unite their multiethnic and tribal countries is a shared Islamic religion, which, in Central Asia, also takes on aspects of identity somewhat divorced from religion itself.[30] At the same time, these increasingly sultanistic regimes feel that political Islam directly threatens their hold on power, as groups such as the IMU and Hizb ut-Tahrir openly seek to overthrow existing secular governments and to replace them with ones founded on the Shari'a, or Islamic law. Rather than addressing the particular brand of Islam that these groups represent and embracing a more moderate Islamic identity, however, secular governments in Central Asia (particularly Uzbekistan) have deemed Islam the enemy and sought to suppress Islamic political movements more broadly. Every Central Asian republic except Tajikistan currently prohibits Islamic political groups, regardless of agenda, and most are fairly broad in defining "political."[31] Moreover, Tajikistan's neighbors see its incorporation of the Islamic Renaissance Party (IRP) into the government, and thus the legit-

---

[30]Georgia and Armenia are predominantly Christian, and Azerbaijan does not face the challenges of a multiethnic society, see Chapter Five. Suny, "Provisional Stabilities," compares Islamic identity in Central Asia to the emerging European identity, to differentiate it from an identity that implies affinity with Muslims outside of the region. He argues that post-Soviet Muslims see themselves as a community, separate from both non-Muslims generally and Muslims elsewhere.

[31]Ebon Lee, "Central Asia's Balancing Act: Between Terrorism and Interventionism," *Harvard International Review,* July 2001, pp. 30–33.

imization of political Islam, as a dangerous precedent.[32] But by
suppressing Islam, the region's elites may have eliminated their best
available mechanism for cultivating a unifying multiethnic nationalism that could compete with fundamentalist Islamic movements for
the loyalty of their citizens. Moreover, by treating all political Islam
as a singular antagonistic force, they have left their countries and the
region that much more vulnerable to ever-more extremist strains of
Islam. This problem is exacerbated by the support such groups
received from the Taliban while it controlled Central Asia's southern
neighbor Afghanistan (support may also continue to flow from nongovernment actors in Pakistan and the Middle East).[33]

Islam in CASC under Russian imperial and later Soviet rule was in
many ways isolated from Islamic development in the rest of the
world. This factor is important to understanding some of the pecu-
liarities of religious and ethnic identity in the post-Soviet space as a
whole. Official policies on Islam changed over time, from efforts to
undermine it (at times with violence and deportations) to a more
accommodating stance, with officially approved clerics, after World
War II. The closing years of the Soviet Union saw a renewal of state-
sponsored anti-Islamic propaganda. The result of Soviet policies was
secularization to a significant extent, but coupled with a popular
identification with Islam as somewhat more of an ethnic/identity determinant than an indicator of religious belief or practice. Moreover,
in South Caucasus particularly but in rural areas of Central Asia as
well, a "parallel" Islam developed, an Islam with unofficial (i.e., unsanctioned by government) religious leaders and mystical brother-
hoods. Observant Muslims in the region, denied opportunities to
make pilgrimage to Mecca, often visited saints' graves and various
shrines as another aspect of their religious faith.[34]

---

[32]"Central Asia: Fault Lines in the New Security Map," (Osh/Brussels: International
Crisis Group, 2001).

[33]See *The IMU and the Hizb-Ut-Tahrir: Implications of the Afghanistan Campaign.*

[34]On Islam under Tsarist and Soviet rule, see Ira M. Lapidus, *A History of Islamic
Societies,* Cambridge: Cambridge University Press, 1988, especially Chapter 29: "Inner
Asia under Russian and Chinese Rule," pp. 784–822; Michael Rywkin, *Moscow's
Muslim Challenge, Soviet Central Asia,* Armonk, NY: M.E. Sharpe Inc., 1982; Alexandre
Benningsen and S. Enders Wimbush, *Mystics and Commissars, Sufism in the Soviet
Union,* Berkeley: University of California Press, 1985. See also Shireen T. Hunter,
Central Asia Since Independence, Westport, CT: Praeger, 1996, pp. 14–16, 35–36;
Martha Brill Olcott, *Central Asia's New States,* Washington, D.C.: United States

Today, levels of observance of the Islamic faith vary widely through-out the post-Soviet Muslim world. As elsewhere in the former Soviet Union, however, political independence brought with it a resurgence of religious feeling, and Islam was no exception. There is a wide range of movements, including those modeled on the Wahabist traditions of fundamentalist Islam.[35] To some extent this can be attributed to the broad range of religious material (books, schools and teachers, and religious leaders, as well as funding) that arrived in the region at the time of the Soviet collapse and independence from Islamic states worldwide (including Turkey, Iran, Pakistan, Saudi Arabia, and others). The isolation of Central Asian Islam from global Islamic movements for so many years in some ways dampened some of the aversion that might have been expected by largely Sunni Cen-tral Asia to Shi'ite efforts to influence Islamic development in the region, even as, as Suny notes, primary identification remained with fellow Central Asian Muslims. With a newfound interest in religion combined with distrust of the Soviet Union's approved clerics, many new messages found ready ears.[36]

There can be little doubt that there has been a flourishing of new mosques, religious schools, and institutes (numbering in the thou-sands), all founded and built over the last ten years. Moreover, many new Islamic organizations go unregistered, in part to avoid un-wanted government attention. This makes the actual extent of Islamic resurgence difficult to measure.[37]

Like ethnicity, Islam can be a rallying cry for the frustrated, and thus a mechanism for political participation. In a region where Soviet rule made Islam far more a question of identity than religion, this is par-

---

Institute of Peace Press, 1996, pp. 31–33; Suny, "Provisional Stabilities"; and Ronald Grigor Suny, *The Revenge of the Past: Nationalism, Revolution, and the Collapse of the Soviet Union*, Stanford, CA: Stanford University Press, 1993.

[35]Although Wahabism is often used by post-Soviet and other political leaders to refer to Islamic political movements generally, its roots are the fundamentalist form of Islam practiced in Saudi Arabia. Wahabism is a puritanical movement that rejects the Sufi tradition that was common in Central Asia and the Caucasus. See Lapidus, pp. 673–675; M. Ehsan Ahrari, *Jihadi Groups, Nuclear Pakistan, and the New Great Game*, Carlisle, PA: Strategic Studies Institute, 2001, pp. 20–21.

[36]See Poonam Mann, "Fighting Terrorism: India and Central Asia," *Strategic Analysis*, Vol. 24, No. 11 (February 2001); Olcott, p. 33.

[37]Ahrari, pp. 21–22. See also Hunter, pp. 36–37.

ticularly important since as a religion Islam also provides a useful mobilizing mechanism in that it is an acceptable reason for people to gather, and mosques are an acceptable place for them to do so—even if religious political parties are banned. As Nora Bensahel points out, when Islamic groups and parties are incorporated into the political process they appear (admittedly on rather little data) to behave more moderately,[38] but Islam as an underground opposition force may focus on more divisive and radical agendas. In Central Asia, where Islamic political parties are banned everywhere except in Tajikistan, Islamist fundamentalist movements tend specifically to focus their appeal on the economically and politically disadvantaged. Insofar as these appeals are successful, continued government repression of political Islam then becomes another in a series of grievances that can unite the disadvantaged against the government; in the absence of legal institutions for channeling political participation, the religion serves as an extralegal channel of participation to voice grievances both about economic disadvantage and repression. To date, the extremes of illegal actions have been limited to isolated acts of terrorism or minor border incursions. However, the broadening (although still very small) base of support enjoyed by groups such as the Hizb ut-Tahrir, which does not explicitly advocate the violent overthrow of the state but does urge the creation of an Islamic government (and which is discussed in more detail below), suggests that the danger to the states of Central Asia may still be developing.

The IMU, created in Uzbekistan in the late 1980s, aims to establish an Islamic state first in the Ferghana Valley, and then in Uzbekistan. Its political leader, Tahir Yuldashev, reportedly fought in Tajikistan's civil war on the side of the United Tajik Opposition (UTO) and spent part of the mid-1990s in Afghanistan. IMU military commander Juma Namangani (also known as Djumbai Hodzhaev and Tadzhibai) fought in Afghanistan during the Soviet Union's war there as a member of a Soviet paratrooper unit. He developed an interest in Islam and Islamic political activism after he returned home to Uzbekistan. His involvement in Islamic political and religious groups brought him to fight with UTO forces in Tajikistan and to train in Afghanistani Mujahideen training camps. Namangani, who is now

---

[38]Bensahel.

believed to have been killed in Afghanistan fighting in late 2001, controlled a multinational militia whose size is estimated by various sources as between 2,000 and 7,000 men.[39] Russian sources linked him to Pakistani security forces, who reportedly guided aspects of his training, and to Saudi intelligence, as well as to a wide range of nongovernmental Islamic groups throughout the world.[40] His probable successor, Tohir Yuldash, had held responsibility for external fundraising under Namangani, and thus reportedly has his own contacts in the Middle East and South Asia.[41] The IMU as a whole appears to have received significant assistance from the Taliban, Osama bin Laden's Al Qaeda group, Pakistani radical Islamic movements Sepakhe Sakhaba and Kharakat-ul'-Mujeheddin, and other groups in Pakistan and elsewhere.[42] As will be discussed in Chapter Four, they also reportedly receive some financial assistance from the drug smuggling business in Central Asia.[43] Russian sources indicate that training takes/took place at IMU camps in Tajikistan, as well as in Afghanistan, Pakistan, and Chechnya at camps run by Al Qaeda, Kharakat ul-Ansar, Hizbi-Islami, Kharakat ul-Mujeheddin, Djamaat at-Tablig vad-Daua, the Taliban, and, in Chechnya, by the warlord Khattab.[44] Other Islamic groups in the region, including the IRP (now officially incorporated into government in Tajikistan, although Tajik President Rakhmanov clearly continues to see the group and its offshoots as threatening) also reportedly receive(d) foreign support from Afghanistan and Pakistani movements.[45]

---

[39]Ahrari, pp. 17–19; Dmitri Nikolayev, "They Want to Turn Central Asia into a Tinderbox" (in Russian), *Nezavisimoye Voyennoye Obozreniye*, August 31, 2001, Internet edition, *nvo.ng.ru/wars/2001-08-31/2_asia.html.*

[40]Nikolayev. Groups reported to have taken an interest in his career and provided support for his activities include the Islamic Renaissance Party of Tajikistan and Djamaat-e-Islami.

[41]*The IMU and the Hizb-Ut-Tahrir: Implications of the Afghanistan Campaign.*

[42]Ahrari, Mann, Nikolayev. Other groups include, according to Nikolayev, Islamic Relief Worldwide, Djamaat-e-Islami, Qatar (transliterated from Russian), the Saudi International Islamic Rescue Organization (translated from Russian), Ihvan al-Muslimun (transliterated from Russian), and the Global Assembly of Islamic Youth.

[43]Ahrari, p. 17; Nikolayev; "Central Asia: Drugs and Conflict"; *The IMU and the Hizb-Ut-Tahrir: Implications of the Afghanistan Campaign.*

[44]Nikolayev. Organization names transliterated from Russian.

[45]Mann.

It is, of course, the IMU that was behind incursions into Uzbekistan and Kyrgyzstan in the late 1990s and early 2000s. From bases in Afghanistan and Tajikistan, the IMU has also played an important role in destabilizing southern Tajikistan, which in turn made it difficult for the opposition Northern Alliance in Afghanistan to receive supplies and assistance.[46] The IMU was also involved in continuing fighting in Afghanistan.[47] At present, the targeting by allied forces of IMU bases and camps in Afghanistan, as well as the death of military commander Namangani and countless others, appears to have dealt the IMU a heavy blow. While it may be able to regroup to some extent at bases in poorly controlled parts of Tajikistan, the International Crisis Group estimates that further incursions of the sort the IMU carried out in recent years are probably unlikely. Smaller-scale operations, however, like bombings and possibly attacks on U.S. or allied bases and facilities in the region, may become the new *modus operandi* for the group.[48]

The Hizb ut-Tahrir also advocates Islamic rule, in fact, its ultimate goal, like that of many revolutionary Islamic political groups, including Al Qaeda, is the restoration of a Caliphate and the spreading of the Islamic message to the world. While it does not explicitly advocate taking up arms in this cause, its literature directs that when an Islamic emir calls on the people to take up arms as Muslims, they should do so, and more recent statements in the wake of U.S. and allied attacks on Afghanistan have moved closer to advocating violent action. Its stated goal is "to carry the Islamic call in a political way, so as to change the current corrupt society and transform it to an Islamic society."[49]

Hizb ut-Tahrir propaganda on the subject of Uzbekistan argues that Uzbek president Karimov is of Jewish ancestry and "not one of our own." It calls on Muslim Uzbeks to work for his removal and the in-

---

[46]Ibid.

[47]Nikolayev.

[48]*The IMU and the Hizb-Ut-Tahrir: Implications of the Afghanistan Campaign.*

[49]See the group's web site at *www.hizb-ut-tahrir.org.* Accessed September 16, 2001; October 24, 2001. See also *www.khilafah.com,* another site operated by the Hizb ut-Tahrir.

stitution of Islamic rule.[50] The Hizb claims a global membership and tends to focus recruitment on the young, unemployed, uneducated, and/or rural, and minority groups often prove most responsive. Its cell structure makes accurate assessments of the group's size and makeup difficult, but there is good reason to believe that the group has grown significantly in recent years, although most estimates for even those areas where it is believed to be most active remain below 10 percent of the population. Certainly its distribution of leaflets and propaganda in the region, particularly in the Ferghana Valley but spreading to such states as Kazakhstan, is growing, and is a concern to regional leaders.[51] Even Tajikistan, which accepts a measure of Islamic participation in government, has cracked down on the group with mass arrests of presumed members as well as those possessing Hizb ut-Tahrir leaflets.[52]

Changes in patterns of support for the Hizb ut-Tahrir and similar groups may prove to be an important factor. It is notable that the Islamic Renaissance Party has seen a growing membership in previously predominantly secular parts of Tajikistan, and that the Hizb ut-Tahrir appears to be gaining membership at the expense of the IRP, suggesting an increasing radicalization and perhaps a dissatisfaction with the IRP's involvement in secular government structures. The Hizb's support base in Tajikistan has also enlarged from a primarily ethnic Uzbek population to include more Tajiks and others.[53] The Hizb is also moving beyond its Uzbek base of support in Uzbekistan and Kyrgyzstan, and there are reports that it and similar groups are spreading beyond rural villages and into urban areas throughout Central Asia.[54]

---

[50]Bismillah ir-Rahman ir-Raheem, "Is Uzbekistan Really Independent?" *www.hizb-ut-tahrir.org*, Wilaya Publications link, issued August 28, 2001, downloaded September 16, 2001.

[51]*The IMU and the Hizb-Ut-Tahrir: Implications of the Afghanistan Campaign.* Ahrari, p. 19.

[52]"Tajikistan: An Uncertain Peace."

[53]Ibid.

[54]Ivan Aleksandrov, "Is the Islamic Threat to Uzbekistan Real," *Nezavisimaya Gazeta—Religii*, October 10, 2001; *The IMU and the Hizb-Ut-Tahrir: Implications of the Afghanistan Campaign.*

Increasing popularity of the Hizb ut-Tahrir, which disseminates literature telling Central Asian Muslims that they are oppressed by their current secular leadership and duty-bound to overthrow it, may prove more dangerous in the long term than the threat posed by the IMU. The IMU attracts those already committed to the cause of violent action, whereas Hizb ut-Tahrir and similar groups appeal to those rediscovering their faith and then encourage them to see that faith as commanding their opposition to secular state power. Moreover, continued crackdowns on this group by Central Asian governments will probably only enhance its popular support—and possibly further radicalize its membership. The International Crisis Group notes that in Tajikistan, at least, individuals arrested for fairly minor offenses can be imprisoned for up to five years. In prison, they come in contact with a more radical group of individuals and can emerge with more fundamentalist views—as well as ties to criminal and militant groups.[55]

POLITICAL LANDSCAPE: CONCLUSIONS

In conclusion, a survey of the political landscape illustrates the limited progress in transitioning to democracy and market economies in CASC. The levels of institutionalization and the capacity of states to institutionally manage conflict vary, but even the comparatively democratic regimes exhibit striking institutional weaknesses. The impact of these institutional weaknesses is mitigated in some states by sultanistic and repressive rule, and in others by the fragmentation of opposition movements. In the former, however, it seems likely that by stifling any overt dissent, the governments in question have reduced conflict in the near term but, by sending dissent (and with it religion) underground, perhaps provided more societal support to the most extreme of their opponents in the longer term.

The one clear near-term indicator of a significantly increased risk of internal strife in this region is expected succession crises in several states over the next 10–15 years. While only Aliev in Azerbaijan and Shevardnadze in Georgia are currently over 70, Uzbekistan's Karimov, Turkmenistan's Niyazov, and Kazakhstan's Nazarbaev will be

---

[55] *The IMU and the Hizb-Ut-Tahrir: Implications of the Afghanistan Campaign.*

senior citizens within a decade.[56] Moreover, the sudden death of any of these "strongmen" from illness, accident, or assassination would throw their countries into turmoil no less, and probably even more, than death from old age. These regimes will not have institutions of succession to rely on when the current leaders die or retire. Successions will almost certainly be a catalyst for unrest and civil strife. While it is possible that this will be merely a brief period of instability while elites challenge each other for power, to be followed by yet another individually powerful leader, in the longer term, these regimes based upon personalistic rule are not sustainable, and they carry with them a significant risk of longer-term conflict and strife.[57]

PROXIMATE CAUSES OF CONFLICT IN CENTRAL ASIA AND SOUTH CAUCASUS

As the previous analysis has demonstrated, CASC states remain institutionally weak. This increases not only the risk of civil strife, the mechanisms for which were discussed above, but also the danger of interstate conflict. States that see themselves as weakening may seek to wage pre-emptive war, hoping to fight while they retain sufficient strength to win—and thus perhaps retain control of assets and power. Increasing domestic political disorder and chaos within a state may bring its leaders to wage war as a means of overcoming internal strife and dissent by building popular unity against a common enemy.[58] And even if the weak or declining state is not itself interested in war, its weakness may invite attack from those who see in it a window of opportunity to increase their own power through victory and/or conquest.[59] Geoffrey Blainey points out that states fight wars in large part because they believe they can win them. Another state's weakness can lead to such a belief on the part of others, while the weak state itself, particularly if it is in transition, may not realize the extent of its weakness, and therefore join in battle rather

---

[56]Kyrgyzstan's Akaev is in his mid-50s.

[57]Chelabi and Linz.

[58]See discussion in Geoffrey Blainey, *The Causes of War*, New York: The Free Press, 1988 edition, pp. 72–86.

[59]For an argument on how and why conquest continues to be advantageous to the conqueror, see Peter Liberman, "The Spoils of Conquest," *International Security*, Vol. 18, No. 2 (Fall 1993), pp. 125–153.

than surrender.[60] Moreover, many processes of internal transition, such as revolution, make a state appear weak and vulnerable to outsiders.[61] As we have discussed, the factors of state weakness in the CASC region are far from ambiguous.

In addition to the potential for weak adversaries, the pretexts for internal and interstate war in the region are plentiful. Concentrated resources such as soil, water, and agriculture,[62] competing historical claims to large swaths of land, and national borders disconnected from ethnic and cultural borders,[63] all provide potential proximate causes for war and reasons to believe that it might be profitable. Moreover, the lack of cooperation between regional elites means that—to paraphrase from U.S. history—they are increasingly prone to hanging separately, having failed to hang together. Finally, insofar as Islamic revolution can be thought to be on the rise as a mobilizing revolutionary ideology throughout much of the region, particularly in Central Asia, the likelihood that conflict spurred by its adherents could remain confined within one state's borders appears slim.

All that said, there are other factors that make interstate war somewhat less likely. The economic incentives, particularly for the development of Caspian energy resources, appear to balance out the possible spoils that war might bring. While cooperation among regional leaders remains limited, there is a growing recognition that it is necessary, and it is possible that increased foreign involvement may spur more cooperation.[64] Moreover, the presence of regional, Russian, and now Western security forces in the region has played a stabilizing role in the past, particularly in Tajikistan, and may do so again in the future.

---

[60]See Blainey, pp. 72–86, 123.

[61]Stephen M. Walt, *Revolution and War,* Ithaca and London: Cornell University Press, 1996, p. 32.

[62]See Chapter Five of this report.

[63]See Chapter Six of this report.

[64]However, the opposite effect is also a possibility. If neighbors believe that Uzbekistan is using the opportunities presented by the foreign presence and assistance to consolidate power, for instance, they will feel threatened and may respond by seeking allies against the threat.

The balance of this chapter will examine some of the most likely proximate causes for conflict in CASC, specifically the situation in the Ferghana Valley and the rise of militant Islamic political movements in the region, the Nagorno-Karabakh dispute, and secessionism in Georgia. It will then conclude with some tentative insights for the prospects for large-scale conflict in CASC.

THE FERGHANA VALLEY AND CROSS-BORDER INCURSIONS

Central Asia offers numerous possibilities for interstate border conflict. Existing borders separate ethnic Tajiks from their principal cities. Tajikistan can, in theory, lay claim to all of historic Bukhara, which largely lies in Uzbekistan. While Tajikistan as a state is much weaker than Uzbekistan, the Uzbek leadership remains concerned that small but determined Tajik terrorist cells might wreak significant havoc on Uzbek territory. Turkmenistan also has claims on Khiva in Uzbekistan. Kazaks can make a claim to Tashkent, Uzbekistan's capital. Uzbekistan, for its part, has claims on all three of these countries as well as on Kyrgyzstan's Osh oblast (which has received de facto limited extraterritorial rights to Uzbekistan). The large Uzbek diaspora in various states of the region fuels fears of an Uzbek intervention on behalf of its nationals—or that such an intervention will serve as a pretext for Uzbek imperialism.

The implications for conflict of ethnic divides in Central Asia as a whole are discussed in detail in Chapter Six. This chapter will highlight only the most likely setting for large-scale conflict in the Central Asian subregion: the Ferghana Valley. The valley has already hosted both localized border incursions by the IMU and other groups and counterterrorist operations conducted by a coalition of regional forces with the significant support of Russia and others. Regional cooperation for keeping the peace in Ferghana is crucial, as jurisdiction over its territory is complex to say the least. The valley includes portions of eastern Uzbekistan, southern Kyrgyzstan, and northern Tajikistan, with borders that look like nothing so much as a difficult puzzle (see Figure 2.1, as well as the frontispiece). One hundred fifteen miles long and sixty-five miles wide at its widest point, with a population of 10 million, the Ferghana Valley is one of the most densely populated and agriculturally rich areas of Central Asia. It

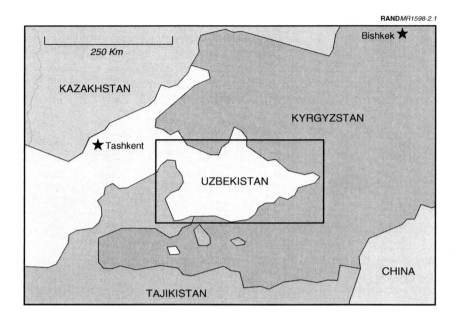

Figure 2.1—The Ferghana Valley

includes 5 percent of the territory but 20 percent of the population of the five states of Central Asia, and almost the entire Uzbek population of Kyrgyzstan lives within it.[65]

The Ferghana Valley's heritage as the political and cultural center of Islam in Central Asia was what led Stalin to divide it among the three states with its present convoluted borders, ensuring control from Moscow by a divide-and-conquer mechanism. The valley is the major source of food and water for the subregion. In recent years, it has been a primary target of IMU recruitment and activities.

The true extent of the threat from Islamic militant revolutionary groups such as the IMU remains subject to extensive debate. As the discussion above indicates, state policies of suppression may in

---

[65]Senator Sam Nunn, Barnett Rubin, and Nancy Lubin, "Calming the Fergana Valley," *Report of the Fergana Valley Working Group for Preventative Action,* New York Century Foundation Press, 1999; Tsepakalo, "The Remaking of Eurasia."

some ways drive more people to a more radical form of Islam, which is dangerous in the longer term for overall state stability. Evidence suggests that at present, however, these movements remain relatively small.

In addition to widespread arrests and crackdowns on a range of Islamic groups, Central Asian leaders have repeatedly sought to increase cooperation in their efforts to strengthen border enforcement. They have also established a rapid-reaction force, at least on paper, with Russia's leadership and logistical support, to counteract the perceived threat.

Actual cooperation among the current leaders has, however, been hindered by distrust and personal animosities between them—and the fact that border incursions are often thought to be supported by one or another regional state. The presidents of Uzbekistan and Kazakhstan, Karimov and Nazarbayev, still regard each other as regional rivals for pre-eminent power. Uzbekistan has complained that former members of the Tajik opposition—now in the coalition government—have aided the IMU, providing basing areas and other support. There is truth to these reports. For example, Tajikistan's Minister of Emergency Situations Mirza Ziyayev, who fought with Namangani in the UTO, helped him maintain bases in the Tavildara region at least into 2000.[66] Tajikistan, in turn, recounts the believed Uzbek support to former Rakhmonov associate Khudojberdiev, who took refuge in Uzbekistan and in 1998 staged an attack into Tajik territory, briefly taking control of Sughd Province.[67] Uzbekistan has mined its borders with Kyrgyzstan and Tajikistan, in some cases in contested areas, and the result has been numerous civilian casualties. Tajikistan and Kyrgyzstan also suffered from unsanctioned Uzbek air force attacks into their territories after the 2000 IMU incursions. Kyrgyzstan, too, has mined its borders with Tajikistan and used explosives to make some mountain passes between the two countries impassable, actions that have not found favor with Tajikistan.[68]

---

[66]Aleksandrov, "Is the Islamic Threat to Uzbekistan Real"; "Central Asia: Fault Lines in the New Security Map."

[67]"Tajikistan: An Uncertain Peace."

[68]"Central Asia: Fault Lines in the New Security Map."

In addition, the convoluted and porous borders in the Ferghana Valley make it extremely difficult to patrol effectively. This difficulty has led to a concern that the region's leaders are not capable of containing a rebellion and will be unable to prevent its escalation into a regional conflict over power and territory. If the situation continues to deteriorate, there is a chance that Uzbekistan may unilaterally move to consolidate the Ferghana Valley under its jurisdiction, redrawing borders to consolidate its defenses.[69] Instability as a result of the actions of the IMU or similar groups may thus provide an opportunity and an excuse for Uzbekistan to achieve territorial expansion. As the mining and air force strikes show, Uzbekistan's evolving security policy seems to include the right to intervene in neighboring states if it perceives its own interests to be threatened.

The impact of the U.S. force presence in the region is likely to be primarily positive, as long as the forces remain in place. That said, the potential for continued low-level conflict in and near the Ferghana Valley puts U.S. forces in danger of becoming targets of attacks by radical revolutionary groups. Moreover, U.S. military presence increases the likelihood that U.S. forces will get involved if conflict breaks out for other reasons. Finally, if U.S. troops do play a significant stabilizing role while in place, there is a risk that their eventual withdrawal will spur deterioration of the situation, particularly if local and regional conflicts remain unresolved.

NAGORNO-KARABAKH

The South Caucasus subregion is also not immune to the danger of border conflict. Azerbaijan and Armenia have yet to settle their territorial dispute over Nagorno-Karabakh, an area that is populated by Armenians but was located inside the territorial borders of Azerbaijan. The Nagorno-Karabakh war that ended in a cease-fire in 1994 left 20 percent of Azerbaijani territory under Armenian control. Since the May 1994 cease-fire, which left Nagorno-Karabakh *de facto* independent but linked to Armenia, the conflict over the status of the Armenian enclave has been in a deadlock.

---

[69]This was suggested by John Schoeberlein, Director of the International Crisis Group's Central Asia Project, at an Open Forum on April 27, 2001, sponsored by the Central Eurasia Project of the Open Society Institute.

Recently, intensified peace talks have increased hope that a settlement can be reached.[70] Several factors have contributed to this shift. First, the leaders of both Azerbaijan and Armenia, Heidar Aliev and Robert Kocharian, no longer consider the status quo to be viable. Armenia's economy has been seriously damaged by the war and both Armenia and Azerbaijan recognize the need for broader relations with Turkey and the West. Secondly, both the United States and Russia have been more committed to reaching a settlement. Russia has been playing a more constructive role in the process and has sought to cultivate a closer relationship with Azerbaijan. While Russia's motives for this are far from selfless, Russian-Azerbaijani rapprochement has the potential to increase the likelihood of a settlement.

If peace talks fail, opposition movements in both Azerbaijan and Armenia are likely to be strengthened, and a new phase of military escalation between the states is probable. There are already warning signs that this escalation, at least in rhetoric, is already under way. Both sides are currently increasing military spending. Armenia is in the process of preparing a new military doctrine that envisions a larger army. In Azerbaijan, parallels have been drawn to Croatia's 1995 cleansing of Krajina as a precedent for regaining territory.[71]

Conversely, a peaceful settlement of the Nagorno-Karabakh conflict would have a significant stabilizing effect on South Caucasus. It would enable the reconstruction of war-damaged areas, and the more peaceful transportation of goods across the region. It would also strengthen Azerbaijan and Armenia and limit their vulnerability to Russian direct interference.

But reaching settlement has been difficult because it requires painful compromise for both sides. Moreover, public opinion in both states is a long way from being committed to peace. Armenian politics have been largely dominated by those determined to hold onto the territory and to annex it to Armenia. In addition, the withdrawal of

---

[70]Stephen Blank, "Armenia at the Crossroads of War and Peace," and Blanka Hancilova, "Prospects and Perils of an Armenian-Azerbaijani Settlement," Bi-Weekly Briefing, *The Analyst*, Wednesday, May 23, 2001.

[71]Seymour Selimov, "Peace Over Nagorno-Karabakh Remains Elusive As Populaces Drift Further Apart," *Transitions Online*, August 24, 2001.

Armenian units from Azerbaijani territory, which is a necessary element of any deal, will certainly be followed by the return of hundreds of thousands of internally displaced persons in Azerbaijan back to their homes in those areas. Estimates are that there are between 700,000 and 1,000,000 internally displaced people in Azerbaijan, or about 10 percent of the population.[72] Such a major population movement would be a strain on the economy of Azerbaijan, as well as a potential political problem.

GEORGIAN SEPARATISTS AND RUSSIA

In Georgia, President Eduard A. Shevardnadze has sought to balance a desire for a more Western orientation for his country, one that ends 200 years of Russian dominance, with the historical and economic relations that tie Georgia to the rest of the post-Soviet world. This challenge has been exacerbated by political and military challenges to Georgia's integrity since independence. In 1992, independent Georgia's first president, Zviad Gamsakhurdia, was ousted from power, the first step in an underground conflict that continues to simmer in the form of military sabotage operations. Secessionist movements in Abkhazia and South Ossetia pose additional complications, as does the situation in the Pankisi Gorge, where a large number of Chechen refugees are believed to include Chechen and other potentially Al Qaeda–linked extremist leaders and insurgents.

Abkhazia, in northern Georgia, enjoyed a measure of political independence under the Soviets. Soon after Georgia declared independence, Abkhazia demanded autonomy from Georgia and asked for Russian help. At the time (and since), some in Georgia accused the Russians of stirring up the unrest in the first place. As the conflict intensified, Russia was accused of supporting the rebels (in part via forces stationed there), and there is no question that the Abkhaz separatists wanted Russian support. By 1993, reports suggested that they had it, as well as assistance from Chechens and other North Caucasus peoples. Fighting continued until the Abkhazians (with the assistance of Russian forces and aid) forced the Georgians out of the region in fall 1993. Two hundred thousand Georgian refugees fled

---

[72]Nancy Lubin, "An Old Story With a New Twist," in Menon et al., p. 222.

into the rest of Georgia. At that time, Russian peacekeepers were deployed to the region. Commonwealth of Independent States (CIS) peacekeepers, which are predominantly if not entirely made up of Russian forces, remain there to this day, and Russia provides energy and economic support to keep the de facto independent region functioning.[73]

The situation in South Ossetia has significant parallels with that in Abkhazia. South Ossetia enjoyed less formal autonomy than did Abkhazia under Soviet rule, and it is a more ethnically homogenous region (fewer than 20 percent of Abkhazia residents are ethnic Abkhaz, while over 60 percent of those in South Ossetia are Ossetian). Moreover, North Ossetia, which shares the same ethnie, is just across the border in Russia. Even before Georgian independence, South Ossetian leaders expressed a desire to secede and join Russia (and North Ossetia). This led to violence in 1990, in which Russia supported Georgian efforts to prevent secession. But in the winter of 1990–1991, an effort to impose direct rule from Tbilisi over the region resulted in outright civil war, and Russian forces intervened. Russian and Georgian peacekeepers continue to separate the factions in this conflict, creating a stable, if not peaceful, situation. Ossetian separatists continue to voice their aims.

Although it is now drawing down its presence, Russia continues to maintain military bases within Georgia, including ground and air forces. It is widely believed that Georgia's initial acquiescence to Russian military presence was based on a Russian promise to help Georgia regain Abkhazia. As this has clearly not occurred, the Georgian parliament has refused to ratify the 1995 treaty on the bases with Russia and is seeking a full Russian withdrawal. At an Organization for Security Cooperation in Europe (OSCE) summit in Istanbul in November 1999, Russia agreed to close down two military bases in Georgia, at Vaziani (near Tbilisi) and Gadauta (in Abkhazia), and it has largely done so. It also agreed to negotiate on the fate of the remaining two Russian bases in Georgia (Akhalkalaki and Batumi) and to complete those negotiations by the end of 2001. Even now that Russian forces have withdrawn from two bases, Russia will con-

---

[73]Rajan Menon, "The Security Environment in the South Caucasus and Central Asia," in Menon et al., pp. 3–27; Emil Pain, "Contagious Ethnic Conflicts and Border Disputes Along Russia's Southern Flank," in Menon et al., pp. 177–202.

tinue to maintain high troop levels inside Georgia.[74] Moreover, in light of the continuing Chechen conflict, Russia has clear strategic reasons to maintain forces in Georgia.

The situation in Pankisi, and the recent revelations that the United States will be assisting Georgia with its efforts to take control of the region, create a number of additional complications. Russia has been arguing for several years that Chechen rebels are hiding in Pankisi, with Georgia generally denying that this was the case and refusing Russia's repeated offers of assistance. In early 2002, rumors that Al Qaeda militants might also be taking shelter in the area led initially to Georgian denials that it would be launching joint operations with either the United States or Russia, and then, of course, to the admission that the United States would be providing assistance in the form of training and equipment.[75]

While the United States has been careful to assert that its presence in Georgia would be minimal and would not include combat operations, the result is that at this point in time, both U.S. and Russian forces are engaged on the territory of this ravaged country. Insofar as Georgia's leadership hopes to hasten the end of Russian military presence in their country, they may see the U.S. involvement as a mechanism to achieve this goal. Certainly, an end to Russia's military presence in Georgia would mitigate at least some aspects of Russia's leverage over Georgia, something Russia is loath to give up, while a greater U.S. involvement would potentially involve the United States in the difficult (and perhaps hopeless) effort of consolidating central control over Georgia and preventing further conflict within its borders. This, of course, has implications for the interests of the United States and Russia, as well as Georgia, interests that are discussed in Chapter Seven of this report.

---

[74]Brian Whitmore, "Bear Hug Pulls South Closer," *Moscow Times*, January 29, 2000, electronic edition.

[75]"Georgian Officials Exclude Bin Laden's Presence in Pankisi," *RFE/RL Newsline*, Vol. 6, No. 32, Part I, February 19, 2002; Vernon Loeb and Peter Slevin, "U.S. Begins Anti-Terror Assistance in Georgia," *Washington Post*, February 27, 2002, p. A1.

CONCLUSIONS

While the above discussion has focused on some specific regions where conflict has emerged in the past and is likely to flare up again in the future, as the balance of this report indicates, there are many other potential areas of conflict in CASC. The fragile political and economic structures of these states will have difficulty containing conflict if and when it emerges. Domestic authoritarianism can stem the tide in the short term but is unlikely to be sustainable, particularly given the economic and political weakness of these states. Foreign presence can play a mitigating role to some extent, but it can also exacerbate the level of conflict once it begins, in part by involving outside states and their interests (see Chapter Seven). Although sources of conflict are varied, it is possible to identify key developments to watch for. Political change, that is to say, movement toward either greater authoritarianism or democratization, has the potential to create conditions favorable to armed strife in all of these states. Political developments ought therefore be watched closely, particularly with regard to the mechanisms and approaches to popular mobilization that develop in coming years.

Successions will almost certainly take place in Azerbaijan and Georgia within the next decade, and are also possible in other states in the 10- to 15-year time frame. While much could change over that period, absent significantly increased political institutionalization, the retirement or death of a leader may well bring one or more states into crisis and domestic unrest. Ongoing efforts within states to define succession ahead of time bear careful monitoring. If these efforts are successful, they will determine the next leader. If they are not, they will at least provide insight into whom the players in the contest for power will be.

The situations in the Ferghana Valley, in Georgia, and around Nagorno-Karabakh are also crucial to the future of CASC. The growth and shape of Islamic movements throughout the region will have an important impact on the future political development of these countries. Such groups' links to organizations abroad and their political and religious agendas are key components of both their goals and their capacities. Tajikistan also cannot be ignored. Central control remains lacking in most of the country, and Dushanbe has been deemed so unsafe that the U.S. Ambassador and his staff commute from Kazakhstan. Tajikistan, and to a lesser but still significant extent Uzbekistan, Turkmenistan, and Kyrgyzstan, are also vulnerable to developments in neighboring Afghanistan. Refugees, drug traffickers, and militants have been crossing these borders with relative ease for years. Continued or resumed unrest and conflict in Afghanistan could, as noted above, reignite the Tajik civil war and strain the state capacity of other neighbors.

At the time of this writing, U.S. troops have arrived at Central Asian airfields and bases (in Uzbekistan, Kyrgyzstan, and also, according to some reports, Tajikistan) in conjunction with the U.S. military response to the September 11, 2001, terrorist attacks on the World Trade Center and the Pentagon. How this situation will evolve depends tremendously on the actions and reactions of a wide variety of actors, but there can be no question that it will both affect and be affected by the situation in Central Asia. Force protection for U.S. forces will involve worries about cross-border incursions and IMU activity. Presence in the region will also require significant coordination with Russian forces, as Central Asian states, particularly Tajikistan, are already heavily dependent on Russia for assistance with border security.[76]

---

[76]Moshe Gammer, "Post-Soviet Central Asia and Post-Colonial Francophone Africa: Some Associations," *Middle Eastern Studies*, Vol. 36, No. 2 (April 2000), pp. 124–149.

Chapter Three

SOME ECONOMIC DIMENSIONS OF SECURITY IN CENTRAL ASIA AND SOUTH CAUCASUS
Abraham S. Becker

INTRODUCTION

What are the economic dimensions of destabilization of a society? Under what economic conditions is the political and social order likely to be subjected to radical change, widespread internal disorder or major external violence? Regrettably, neither the general question nor its application to Central Asia and South Caucasus can be answered with confidence. The links between the economic and the political-social orders are too complex—both the direction of causation and the forms of the functional relations are often ambiguous—for prediction without extensive qualification.[1] This seems particularly true in what may be the early stages in the development of a long-term U.S. and allied presence in Central Asia.

This analysis begins with a general discussion of the principal economic connections to societal destabilization. The main, second section elaborates the application to CASC of two of the most important links. A final section examines the regional prospects, especially in the new, post-September 11 context.

There is a first-order distinction between exogenous and endogenous sources of destabilization, but the two may interact in various ways, in which the political-strategic and the economic intertwine. For example, the penetration of armed forces from outside the coun-

---

[1]It might appear that the effect of political instability on economic growth is intuitively clear and negative, but Nauro Campos and Jeffrey Nugent ("Who's Afraid of Political Instability?" William Davidson Institute Working Paper, No. 326, July 2000) show otherwise.

41

try represents the most obvious exogenous source of security disruption. In turn, the armed encroachment may trigger internal upheavals resulting from pre-existing faultlines in the society, or the latter may be the pretext for or magnet drawing the external incursion (e.g., Islamic militant activities in Central Asia in recent years).[2] The ability of the affected governments to cope with such intrusions will depend heavily on the size, character, and skill levels of their armed forces, which are shaped in part by the magnitude and distribution of military budgets. In the long run, budgets depend on the size of the economy, but in the short run they also hinge on noneconomic factors, including politics and social structure.[3]

International trade and finance are the economic links between the external and domestic arenas. Trade can and most often does bring economic benefits in lower prices, higher quality, and greater variety of goods and services, as well as gains in income and employment. But trade may also hinder broad economic progress—and hence may threaten social and political stability—in several different ways.[4]

1. High levels of participation in trade (measured by trade values as a proportion of GDP) can also mean high exposure to price fluctuations in regional and world markets. To the extent that primary commodity markets experience greater price volatility than those for industrial goods and services, primary product exporters, who are also likely to be importers of industrial goods, can suffer from instability of their export revenues and rigidity of their import costs. This double handicap will lead to instability in foreign exchange reserves and government revenues, not to speak of downward pressures on domestic production, income, and employment.

---

[2] External factors may support particular factions in internal conflicts or one state in conflict with another, without actual invasions by armed forces. The alleged involvement of Russia in the Georgian civil war in the early 1990s and in the assassination attempts against Georgia's President Shevardnadze in later years form prime examples of the first case. A prominent example of the second is Russia's arms supply to Armenia, which Azerbaijan has continually protested.

[3] Discussed in greater detail in Chapters Two and Four of this report.

[4] The first four numbered paragraphs below adapt, with thanks, material suggested by Tanya Charlick-Paley and Sergej Mahnovski.

2. When resource extraction conducted largely by multinationals is the main source of primary product exports, large-scale repatriation of profits may deprive the economy of much-needed investment and thus help perpetuate low-income status. The oil and gas producers in the Caspian region are aware of that danger, and their exploration and development contracts with the multinationals have been drawn to siphon off a good share of the expected financial returns. It is another matter altogether whether that share ends up in productive and efficient investment or in the maintenance of a repressive, corrupt regime. All too often, natural resource producers act largely as "rentier" states, sustaining the nondemocratic status quo by placating the population with low taxes and enhanced public spending but stifling dissent.[5]

3. Energy development through multinational export attracts foreign direct investment, but it is often not a suitable vehicle for diversification of the industrial structure. Most developing countries look to manufacturing to provide a more complex division of labor and higher standards of living, and there are few forward and backward linkages from primary exports to manufacturing. Azerbaijan and Kazakhstan are now setting up so-called oil funds to accumulate proceeds from energy development and direct them to other sectors of the economy.

4. Natural resource export booms have been linked to output declines in traditional export sectors like agriculture and nonextractive industry via the mechanism of the "Dutch disease." This is a coinage of the 1970s that refers to the deleterious effects on the Dutch economy of significant gas discoveries in the North Sea. The surge of oil or gas revenues threatens appreciation of the country's real exchange rate, as inflows of foreign currency reduce its price, and domestic price inflation through growth of the money supply. Both effects tend to raise the supply prices of nonresource exports and lower domestic prices of competing imports. This can lead to reduced competitiveness of nonresource exports and therefore to decline in the economic for-

---

[5]Hazem Beblawi and Giacomo Luciani, *The Rentier State*, London: Croon Helm, 1987, and Terry Lynn Karl, *The Paradox of Plenty*, Berkeley, CA: University of California Press, 1997.

tunes of agriculture and nonextractive industry.[6] One purpose of the oil funds mentioned earlier is to prevent infection from "Dutch disease" by segregating export proceeds and infusing them into the economy gradually over time.

5.   Finally, excessive dependence in external economic relations—the concentration of trade in few commodities or with few partners, or investment and credit relations with particular sources—may create vulnerabilities to external influence and pressure that could pave the way to destabilization.[7] All the CASC states have high trade participation rates. Their trade is characterized by strong concentration in two or three commodity categories and, for several of the states, major reliance on a small number of trade partners.

In the category of mainly endogenous sources of destabilization, two sets of conditions, poverty and economic disorder, merit attention. Poverty does not necessarily generate instability, nor does relative affluence guarantee internal peace. Poverty and general economic dissatisfaction under authoritarian regimes may be indefinitely stable, as long as the regime is not confronted by powerful external threats, retains its cohesion, self-confidence, and a monopoly of force, and exercises tight controls on political participation (see Chapter Two). As Tocqueville taught us, authoritarian regimes tend to get into trouble when they liberalize.

In the turbulent corner of Central Asia where Kyrgyzstan, Tajikistan, and Uzbekistan intersect, the threat to the three governments develops from the combination of high unemployment, income levels at or below subsistence, and the challenge of insurgents with political Islamic ideologies. An especially heady ingredient of the radical message appeals to the generally perceived sense of the moral deterioration of society, with governments viewed as the prime source of the corruption. Even Turkmenistan's unchallenged president has

---

[6]See also Karl, *The Paradox of Plenty*.

[7]A special case of trade dependence is the availability of only one or two transport routes for landlocked countries. Armenia, for example, depends heavily on transport through Georgia to the latter's Black Sea ports; the only alternative is overland through Iran. Georgia apparently charged Armenia higher freight tariffs than it did Azerbaijan. *RFE/RL Newsline*, V:125, July 2, 2001.

been sufficiently concerned about possibilities of internal unrest to provide the population with free gas, water, energy, and salt, "subject to generous limits on usage and a highly subsidized price thereafter." The price of bread is regulated, and families with per-capita incomes below the official average wage receive a free allowance of flour.[8]

Poverty becomes especially difficult to endure when people become aware of great inequality in the distribution of income and wealth. This perception of deprivation, relative to other social groups within the society or to counterparts in other countries, can be destabilizing. Economic measurement of inequality may point to the potential for trouble, but it is not the magnitude of the deprivation alone that will determine the likelihood and scale of the possible instability. Again, political-social factors are important determinants (see Chapter Two).

Poverty and external debt dependence can be interrelated. The need for higher outlays on poverty-reduction programs may bump up against a weak fiscal revenue base, possibly leading to the financing of budget deficits by external borrowing. Over time, the growing burden of debt service on the budget can reduce the scope for spending on domestic programs. This was the case in both Georgia and Kyrgyzstan.[9]

Economic disorder may be viewed as having two components. *Macroeconomic disturbances* encompass high rates of inflation, severe market imbalances (goods shortages and shopping queues), high levels of wage arrears, or waves of labor strife. What has come to be called *misgovernance* of economic institutions is popularly identified with large-scale corruption and economic crime (see Chapter Four), but it also includes inadequately defined property rights and protections for investors, unregulated financial markets, etc.

---

[8]IMF, *Turkmenistan: Recent Economic Developments*, Staff Country Report 99/140, December 1999, pp. 12 and 30.

[9]IMF and World Bank, *Armenia, Georgia, Kyrgyz Republic, Moldova, and Tajikistan: External and Fiscal Sustainability—Background Paper*, February 6, 2001. Hereafter in the notes, this source is designated "IMF/World Bank, February 6, 2001," to distinguish it from the companion piece with the same title except for the words "Background Paper" and dated February 7, 2001. This latter piece is designated "IMF/World Bank, February 7, 2001."

Each of the states under review experienced high rates of price inflation—in some cases, hyperinflation—in the early to middle 1990s. All of them managed to bring inflation under some degree of control with strict monetary and fiscal policies. High inflation persists in Tajikistan and Uzbekistan,[10] and problems of wage arrears and labor discontent are evident in several states of the region, but macroeconomic disturbance is not otherwise a significant feature of the current economic landscape. This does not, of course, mean that such problems will not reappear in the near future.

Misgovernance, in contrast, is a conspicuous and painful condition of the economic life of all the countries of the region. Each has a large "second economy," high levels of public and private corruption, and, a factor closely connected to the previous two, varying but still far from complete transitions to market institutions. Popular perception of widespread corruption undermines the legitimacy of the regime, and corruption, if unchecked, can metastasize to the point of throttling the "first" economy. Paradoxically, attempts to stamp out corruption can be destabilizing too. Because informal economic activities are only quasi-legal or even outright illegal, they almost inevitably depend for their functioning on corruption of local and national authorities. The corruption is likely to be the rule rather than the exception where policing forces are badly underpaid. If the authorities then attempt to siphon off ill-gotten gains of the shadow economy and excise the corruption, the reactions may be violent, particularly if there are well-rooted protection networks in place (see also Chapter Four).

The assertion of misgovernance is clearly warranted, but the scale of the threat to the political-social order is difficult to assess. Several commercial firms and nongovernment institutions have developed and published quantitative indicators of governance,[11] but they may provide misleading comparative evidence on the vulnerability of the states of the region. Ultimately, the stability of misgovernance

---

[10]*Monitor* (Jamestown Foundation), VII:53, March 16, 2001, and VII:172, September 20, 2001.

[11]Daniel Kaufmann, Aart Kraay, and Pablo Zoido-Lobaton, "Aggregating Governance Indicators," Policy Research Working Paper, No. 2195, World Bank, October 1999; "Toward More Operationally Relevant Indicators of Governance," PREM Notes, No. 49, World Bank, December 2000.

depends far less on its absolute size, however defined, than on the national political-social structures. The next, main section of this chapter is therefore limited to discussion of two principal issues, poverty and external economic dependence.

REGIONAL OVERVIEW

Two preliminary remarks seem necessary. First, the weaknesses of national statistical systems in CASC suggest strong caution in interpreting the data presented here. In all cases they should be viewed as indicative only, not as precise measures of the magnitudes they describe.

Second, treatment of the eight CASC states as a single region does some violence to the reality. Tables 3.1 and 3.2 display considerable variation among the eight in important demographic and economic parameters of development. To offer only a few examples: Kazakhstan is 90 times the size of Armenia in area and 15 times as large as the three South Caucasus states combined. Uzbekistan's population is six times that of Armenia and 1.5 times that of the South Caucasus states combined. On the other hand, Armenia's degree of urbanization is almost twice as high as Uzbekistan's. In some demographic respects, the South Caucasus three are more like each other than they are like the Central Asian five. Urbanization is higher, fertility lower, infant mortality lower, and life expectancy higher in the former than in the latter group. The economic differences between the two groups of states are, however, less clear.

Poverty

Evidently, these are all poor states. A decade ago, their education, health, and welfare standards exceeded those of their non-Soviet neighbors, but the Central Asian states especially fell below the average income and welfare levels of the Soviet Union. All the CASC states depended heavily on subsidies from the union budget, artificially low prices for energy and raw materials, and planned direction of trade within the Soviet Union. The dissolution of the Soviet Union disrupted trade links, sharply reducing interrepublic trade flows. Exposure to world market prices revealed the hollowness of valuations at administered prices and therefore the noncompetitiveness of

Table 3.1

Central Asia and South Caucasus: Demographic Indicators, 1999

	Armenia	Azerbaijan	Georgia
Total population, millions	3.8	8	5.5
Urban population, % of total	70	57	60
Fertility rates, births per woman	1	2	1
Infant mortality/1,000 live births			
At birth	14	17	15
Age 5 and below	18	32	20
Maternal mortality/100,000 live births	33	43	N/A
Life expectancy at birth, years	74	71	73

	Kazakh-stan	Kyrgyz-stan	Tajiki-stan	Turkmeni-stan	Uzbeki-stan
Total population, millions	14.9	4.9	6.2	4.8	24.4
Urban population, % of total	56	34	28	45	37
Fertility rates, births per woman	2	3	3	3	3
Infant mortality/ 1,000 live births					
At birth	22	26	20	33	19
Age 5 and below	28	38	34	45	29
Maternal mortality/ 100,000 live births	N/A	6[a]	N/A	N/A	35[b]
Life expectancy at birth, years	65	67	69	66	70

[a]1997.

[b]2000.

N/A = information not available.

SOURCES: World Bank, World Development Indicators database, except: Armenia, maternal mortality, from Republic of Armenia, *Interim Poverty Reduction Strategy Paper,* March 2001, p. 20; Azerbaijan, infant and maternal mortality, from *Azerbaijan Economic Trends,* January–March 2001, p. 140; Uzbekistan, infant and maternal mortality, from *Uzbekistan Economic Trends,* January–March 2001, p. 92.

Table 3.2

Central Asia and South Caucasus: Economic Welfare Indicators, 1999

	Armenia	Azerbaijan	Georgia
1. Government social outlays			
A. Per head, $			
Education	19	24	11
Health	7	6	5
B. Percent of GDP			
Education	4	4	1
Health	1	1	**
2. Physicians per 10,000 pop.	34[a]	36	N/A
3. Hospital beds per 10,000 pop.	67[a]	90	48[b]
4. GNI per head, $	490	460[c]	620
5. Average monthly wages, $	38	45	33
6. Poverty rate, % of population	44/55[d]	60[d]	60[d]
7. Income inequality, Gini coeff.	0.59	N/A	0.53
8. Human development index, rank among 174 countries†	93	90	85

	Kazakh-stan	Kyrgyz-stan	Tajik-istan	Turkmen-istan	Uzbek-istan
1. Government social outlays					
A. Per head, $					
Education	44	10	3	14	14–56
Health	25	6	2	22	4–18
B. Percent of GDP					
Education	4	2	2	5	9
Health	2	4	1	3	3
2. Physicians per 10,000 pop.	34	N/A	21		
3. Hospital beds per 10,000 pop.	73	N/A	68	N/A	N/A
4. GNI per head, $	1250	300	290	670	720
5. Average monthly wages, $	94	25	10	62	66
6. Poverty rate, % of population	N/A	64	83		
7. Income inequality, Gini coeff.	N/A	0.43/0.37	N/A	62[e]	N/A
8. Human development index, rank among 174 countries†	N/A	98	115	100	106

†Based on per-capita income, school enrollment, and life expectancy.

N/A = information not available.

** = less than half the unit indicated.

[a]1998.

[b]1996.

[c]$565 for GDP.

[d]Poverty levels defined as: Armenia (44 percent) $2.15/day and (55 percent) $1/day; Azerbaijan, $4/day; Georgia, $2/day.

[e]Percent of households earning below official average wage.

SOURCES TO TABLE 3.2

Rows 1A and 1B. Azerbaijan: *Azerbaijan Economic Trends,* January–March 2001: percent of GDP (Annex 4.8, p. 153); dollars per capita calculated from budget expenditure in manat (Annex 4.8, p. 152), revalued in dollars at the exchange rate (Annex 2.2, p. 138), and divided by population (Table 3.1 above). Kazakhstan: *Kazakhstan Economic Trends,* January–March 2001: percent of GDP (Annex 4.3, p. 108); dollars per capita calculated from tenge outlays (Annex 4.4, p. 108), revalued in dollars at the exchange rate (p. 8), and divided by population (Table 3.1 above). Turkmenistan: IMF, *Turkmenistan: Recent Economic Developments,* Staff Country Report 99/140, December 1999: percent of GDP (Table 16, p. 106); dollars per capita calculated from budget expenditure in manat (Table 15, p. 105), revalued in dollars at the parallel exchange rate, first half of 1999 (Table 23, p. 113) and divided by population (Table 3.1 above). Uzbekistan: Percent of GDP from IMF, *Republic of Uzbekistan: Recent Economic Developments,* Staff Country Report 00/36, March 2000 (Table 32, p. 69); dollars per capita calculated from budget expenditure in sums, from Ibid. (Table 31, p. 68), revalued in dollars at, alternatively, the official and market exchange rate, from *Uzbek Economic Trends,* January–March 2001 (Table 2.2, p. 35). Other countries: Percent of GDP (except Georgia) from IMF and World Bank, *Armenia, Georgia, Kyrgyz Republic, Moldova and Tajikistan: External and Fiscal Sustainability—Background Paper,* February 6, 2001, Tables 6 (p. 44), 13 (p. 51), 20 (p. 58), and 33 (p. 71); dollars per capita from IMF and World Bank, *Armenia, Georgia, Kyrgyz Republic, Moldova and Tajikistan: External Debt and Fiscal Sustainability,* February 7, 2001, Table 9, p. 28. Percent of GDP for Georgia from *Georgia Economic Trends,* Quarters 3–4, 2000, Table 3.4, p. 19.

Rows 2, 3. Armenia: World Bank and IMF, *Armenia, Georgia . . . Background Paper,* February 6, 2001, Table 7, p. 45. Azerbaijan: *Azerbaijan Economic Trends,* January–March 2001, Table 3.1, p. 39. Georgia: IMF, *Recent Economic Developments and Selected Issues,* Staff Country Paper 00/68, May 2000, p. 4. Kazakhstan: *Kazakhstan Economic Trends,* January–March 2001, Table 3.1, p. 33. Tajikistan: IMF, *Republic of Tajikistan: Statistical Appendix,* Country Report 01/69, May 2001, p. 3.

Row 4. Azerbaijan: *Azerbaijan Economic Trends,* October–December 2000. All other countries: World Bank, World Development Indicators database.

Row 5. Armenia: *Armenia Economic Trends,* October–December 2000, Table 3.3, p. 73. Azerbaijan: *Azerbaijan Economic Trends,* January–March 2001, Graph 3.6, p. 45. Kazakhstan: *Kazakhstan Economic Trends,* January–March 2001, p. 8. Other countries: IMF, *Kyrgyz Republic: Selected Issues and Statistical Appendix,* Staff Country Report 00/131, October 2000, Box 3, p. 29. The figure reported for Turkmenistan in this source is most likely valued at the official exchange rate. It would be much lower at the "curb" rate of exchange. According to IMF, *Turkmenistan: Recent Economic Developments,* p. 11, the average wage in December 1998 was $58 at the official exchange rate and $25 at the "curb" rate.

Row 6. Armenia: The low figure is from IMF and World Bank, *Armenia, Georgia . . . Background Paper,* February 6, 2001, Table 7, p. 45. The higher figure is for 1998, from Republic of Armenia, *Interim Poverty Reduction Strategy Paper,* March 2001, Table 2, p. 20. In 1996 the poverty line was set at a value of the minimum consumption basket of 11,735 drams per month. The average exchange rate then was 413.42 drams/$, which indicates a poverty level of about $0.95 per day. An additional 14 percent of the population was marginally above the poverty line (Ibid., p. 3). Azerbaijan: *Azerbaijan Economic Trends,* January–March 2001, p. 99. Georgia: *Poverty Reduction and Eco-*

nomic Growth Program of Georgia. Intermediary Document, Tbilisi, November 2000, p. 5 (at $2/day). Kyrgyzstan: IMF, *Kyrgyz Republic: Selected Issues and Statistical Appendix,* Table 11, p. 47. According to World Bank and IMF, *Armenia, Georgia . . . Background Paper,* Table 20, p. 58, the poverty ratios were 49 percent at $2.15/day and 84 percent at $4.30/day. Tajikistan: Government of the Republic of Tajikistan, *Interim Poverty Reduction Strategy Paper,* Dushanbe, 2000, p. 2. Turkmenistan: IMF, *Turkmenistan: Recent Economic Developments,* p. 12 (percent of households earning below the official average wage).

Row 7. Armenia: Republic of Armenia, *Interim Poverty Reduction Strategy Paper,* Figure 1, p. 4. Georgia: *Poverty Reduction and Economic Growth Program of Georgia,* p. 5. Kyrgyzstan: The income coefficient is from Kyrgyz Republic National Statistical Committee *(http://stat-gvc.bishkek.su/Eng/Annual/Social.html),* the consumption coefficient from Kyrgyz Republic, *Interim National Strategy for Poverty Reduction,* 2001–2003, June 13, 2001, Table 2, p. 5.

Row 8. Georgia: *Poverty Reduction and Economic Growth Program of Georgia,* p. 6. Tajikistan: Government of the Republic of Tajikistan, *Interim Poverty Reduction Strategy Paper,* p. 2 (figure for 1997). Other countries: *Azerbaijan Economic Trends,* January–March 2001, p. 98.

much if not most of the industrial structure. Productivity in agriculture was low, and most of the post-Soviet regimes were reluctant to institute radical land reform. The difficulties of casting off the yoke of central planning, inept fiscal-monetary policy that helped bring on high inflation, and inherited health and environmental disasters (e.g., the drying up of the Aral Sea) contributed to the deterioration of economic prospects. Political factors specific to particular countries—such as civil war in Georgia and Tajikistan, or war between Armenia and Azerbaijan and the subsequent blockade of Armenia by Turkey and Azerbaijan—also played an important role. All eight states, in consequence, suffered declines in total output in the early 1990s, with accompanying reductions in living standards. The recessions were sharp and prolonged, except in Uzbekistan.

Official statistics[12] state that only Uzbekistan among the eight has now regained the GDP level of 1991, the last year of the Soviet Union's existence. Comparison of current national income statistics with those of Soviet times is certainly imprecise and potentially misleading, but it is probably indicative that in 2000, six of the eight had GDP levels estimated to be but half (Georgia) to less than four-fifths

---

[12]Interstate Statistical Committee of the CIS, *Main Macroeconomic Indicators on CIS Countries (www.cisstat.com/mac1_an.htm).*

(Armenia and Kazakhstan) of the 1991 level. (Turkmenistan did not report in this format.) With the exception of Uzbekistan again, the ratios of reattainment of 1991 levels were even lower for agricultural output.

At present only Kazakhstan has reached a gross national per-capita income exceeding $1,000 (Table 3.2). Tajikistan and Kyrgyzstan, the poorest of the eight by this measure, had per-capita incomes about one-quarter as large as Kazakhstan's, but the Armenian and Azerbaijan proportions were not much larger. The middle group of Georgia, Turkmenistan, and Uzbekistan averaged (unweighted) a little over half of the Kazakhstan figure. Kyrgyzstan and Tajikistan were at about the income level of Laos and Uganda; Armenia was comparable to Nicaragua and Georgia to Cameroon.[13]

It is no surprise, after viewing these numbers, to observe that reported average monthly wages range from $10 in Tajikistan to $94 in Kazakhstan. CASC national authorities consider that at least half, and in most cases much more, of the population lives near or below the poverty line, defined in stringent terms. Even in Kazakhstan, 30 percent of the population is found below that line.[14] The burden of poverty is exacerbated by the minimal level of public sector outlays on social services, which are constrained by the small size of the economies and government budgets under continual stress. For that reason, too, the levels of health provision to the population are considerably worse than is indicated by the normalized number of physicians and hospital beds, owing to poor training and shortages of medicines and other supplies.

Poverty also comes tied to considerable inequality of income distribution in the region. The Gini coefficient, where zero measures perfect inequality and one perfect equality, is about 0.25 for the Czech Republic, 0.3 for Poland, and 0.35 for Hungary, whereas it is about 0.4 in Kyrgyzstan, 0.5 in Georgia, and almost 0.6 in Armenia.[15] The prevalence of "informal" or "second economy" features in the region

---

[13]"IMF/World Bank, February 7, 2001." Table 8, p. 27.

[14]*RFE/RL Central Asia Report*, 1:23, December 27, 2001.

[15]Republic of Armenia, *Interim Poverty Reduction Strategy Paper*, March 2001, Figure 1, p. 4.

means that in several cases the inequality of consumption is lower than that of income distribution.

High or growing levels of inequality of distribution—or, as noted in the introduction to this chapter, of poverty in general—are neither necessary nor sufficient conditions for political instability. Witness the sharp rise in the Russian Gini coefficient from a 1985 level of about the current Czech figure to 0.48 by 1997, putting Russia in the class of Ecuador, Venezuela, or Nigeria, but without significant threat to the social-political order.[16] A decade of independence has not brought the gains in mass consumption and distributional equity that the CASC leaders promised upon taking power. This failure was surely not lost on the region's inhabitants, and it may well have been a factor in the ethnic-religious tensions that have marked recent years, but it did not visibly shake the political foundations of the national regimes.

Dependence

In 1990 the Soviet republics traded mainly within the Soviet Union; foreign trade involvement as a share of national output was far smaller than a decade later (Table 3.3). In 1999, the CASC states were, except for Uzbekistan, heavily dependent on imports; five of the eight states had import ratios of 50 percent or higher. Export participation in 1999 was generally lower, except in the cases of Kazakhstan, Tajikistan, and Uzbekistan. As developing economies, the eight states generally tend to run substantial trade and current account deficits.

Their trade is highly concentrated in terms of commodity structure (Table 3.4, part 1). Three categories of goods constitute 60 percent or more of exports and imports in seven of the eight countries. It takes only two categories to make up 55 percent or more of total exports by six of the eight states. Azerbaijan presents the extreme degree of concentration among them: petroleum alone accounts for 83 per-

---

[16]Cited in William H. Buiter, "From Predation to Accumulation? The Second Transition Decade in Russia," SITE Working Paper No. 156, Stockholm School of Economics, July 2000, p. 7.

cent of exports.[17] All the fuel producers—Kazakhstan, Turkmenistan and Azerbaijan—show heavy concentration, with more than half of total exports derived from fuel. Energy in the form of electric power is also a principal export of Kyrgyzstan and Tajikistan. Each depends heavily in addition on the sale of a single commodity—gold and aluminum, respectively. Uzbekistan appears to have the most balanced structure of the eight.

The degree of concentration is only somewhat less on the import side. As might be expected of developing countries, machinery and equipment is the principal import by six of the eight countries and the third most important by Armenia. Food appears in the lists for five of the eight. Tajikistan's aluminum exports depend heavily on alumina imports.

Table 3.3

Central Asia and South Caucasus: Trade Dependence Ratios, 1990 and 1999
(Exports, Imports and Current Account as Percent of National Output*)

	Exports		Imports		Current Account Balance
	1990	1999	1990	1999	1999
Armenia	16	21	13	50	−17
Azerbaijan	3	34	13	51	−28
Georgia	N/A	27	N/A	46	−8
Kazakhstan	2	43	8	42	−1
Kyrgyzstan	2	43	15	57	−15
Tajikistan	5	68	13	63	6
Turkmenistan	4	42	9	62	−17
Uzbekistan	5	19	10	19	0

*Net material product in 1990 and GDP in 1999; 1990 trade is with non-USSR.
N/A = not available.
SOURCE: 1990 trade from Informatsionno-izdatel'skii tsentr po statistike, *Vneshniaia torgovlia suverennykh respublik i pribaltiiskikh gosudarstv v 1990 godu*, Moscow 1992; net material product from Statisticheskii komitet SNG, *Strany-chleny SNG. Statistich-eskii ezhegodnik*, Moscow, 1992. 1999 data: WTO, International Trade Statistics, 2000; World Bank, and Country Briefs (*www.worldbank.org*).

---

[17]In the first nine months of 2001, fuel and energy accounted for over 90 percent of Azerbaijan's exports. *Monitor*, VII:228, December 12, 2001.

Table 3.4

Foreign Trade Concentration in Central Asia and South Caucasus, 2000
Part 1: Commodity Structure

Goods Forming 60 Percent of Exports or Imports (percent of total exports or imports)			
Exports		**Imports**	
Armenia			
Precious stones, metals, and articles	41	Food, animals	25
Base metals	15	Mineral products	21
Machinery, equipment	12	Machinery, equipment	17
Azerbaijan			
Petroleum products	84	Machinery, equipment	40
		Food, animals	19
		Metals and articles	11
Georgia			
Food, vegetable products	29	Machinery, equipment	26
Base metals	24	Food, vegetable products	20
Mineral products	19	Mineral products	19
Kazakhstan			
Fuel, oil products	53	Machinery, equipment	38
Ferrous metals	13	Fuel, oil products	11
		Ferrous metals, products	9
Kyrgyzstan			
Nonferrous metals	47	Machinery	27
Electric power	16	Oil and gas	22
		Food	8
		Light industry products	7
Tajikistan			
Aluminum	50	Electric power	24
Electric power	23	Alumina	21
		Oil and products, natural gas	15
Turkmenistan (1998)			
Oil products, natural gas	55	Machinery, equipment	45
Cotton fiber	22	Industrial materials, excluding chemical and building materials	27
Uzbekistan			
Cotton fiber	31	Machinery, equipment	39
Energy products	12	Chemicals, plastics	15
Metals	8	Food	13

Table 3.4
Foreign Trade Concentration in Central Asia and South Caucasus, 2000
Part 2: Geographic Structure

Exports

	Armenia	Azerbaijan	Georgia	Kazakhstan	Kyrgyzstan[a]	Tajikistan[a]	Turkmenistan[a]	Uzbekistan
CIS	24	14	41	26	40	46	56	36
Russia	15	6	21	20	16	17	7	17
Caucasus	5	4	10	0	N/A	N/A	4	N/A
Central Asia	2[b]	1[b]	N/A	3	23	28	4	3
Others	2	3	10	3	2	1	42	16
Non-CIS	76	86	59	74	60	55	44	35
EU	40	60	21	23	38	36	23	18
Iran	9	**	N/A	N/A	2	2	12	2
Turkey	N/A	6	22	1	1	**	1	3
Others	31	20	16	50	19	17	7	12
U.S.	13	1	2	2	2	**	1	N/A

Imports

	Armenia	Azerbaijan	Georgia	Kazakhstan	Kyrgyzstan[a]	Tajikistan[a]	Turkmenistan[a]	Uzbekistan
CIS	19	32	32	55	43	78	52	35
Russia	15	21	13	49	18	14	7	16
Caucasus	2	1	9	N/A	N/A	N/A	3	N/A
Central Asia	N/A	6[b]	N/A	3	22	55	29	7
Others	2	4	10	3	2	9	13	2
Non-CIS	81	68	68	45	57	22	48	65
EU	34	19	24	20	18	13	26	21
Iran	9	7	N/A	N/A	2	2	4	N/A
Turkey	N/A	10	16	3	4	**	**	9
Others	38	32	28	22	33	7	18	35
U.S.	12	7	10	6	9	**	2	9

[a] 1999.

[b] Armenia: exports to Turkmenistan. Azerbaijan: exports to Turkmenistan and imports from Kazakhstan and Turkmenistan.

N/A = information not available.

** = less than half the unit indicated.

SOURCES TO TABLE 3.4

Armenia: *Armenia Economic Trends*, October–December 2000, Table LA3, p. 134 (commodity structure) and January–March 2001, Annexes 6.6 and 6.7, pp. 155–156 (geographic structure).

Azerbaijan: *Azerbaijan Economic Trends*, January–March 2001, Annexes 7.6 and 7.8, pp. 180–181 (commodity) and Annexes 7.10 and 7.12, pp. 183 and 185 (geographic).

Georgia: *Georgian Economic Trends*, Quarters 3–4, 2000, Tables 5.3 and 5.4, pp. 29–30 (commodity) and Tables 5.1 and 5.2, p. 28 (geographic).

Kazakhstan: *Kazakhstan Economic Trends*, January–March 2001, Annexes 7.3 and 7.5, pp. 139, 141 (commodity) and Annexes 7.7 and 7.9, pp. 143, 145 (geographic).

Kyrgyzstan: Kyrgyzstan National Statistics Committee *(http://nsc.bishkek.su/Eng/Database/Index.html)* (commodity); IMF, *Kyrgyz Republic: Selected Issues and Statistical Appendix*, Staff Country Report 00/131, October 2000, Table 44, p. 110, and National Statistical Committee of the Kyrgyz Republic, Direction of Trade Statistics *(http://nsc.bishkek.su/Eng/Annual/Xc.html and Mc.html)* (geographic).

Tajikistan: IMF, *Republic of Tajikistan: Statistical Appendix*, Country Report 01/69, May 2001, Tables 40 and 41, pp. 44–45 (commodity) and IMF, *Direction of Trade Statistics Yearbook 2000* (geographic).

Turkmenistan: IMF, *Turkmenistan: Recent Economic Developments*, Staff Country Report 99/140, December 1999, Tables 28, 30, pp. 118, 120 (commodity) and IMF, *Direction of Trade Statistics Yearbook 2000* (geographic).

Uzbekistan: *Uzbek Economic Trends*, January–March 2001, Annexes 7.1 and 7.2, pp. 101–102 (commodity: the distributions are calculated net of services, unidentified in this source but labeled as such in previous editions); and Annexes 7.3 and 7.4, pp. 102–103 (geographic).

Armenia is a heavy importer of oil and gas (under "mineral products"); so are Tajikistan and Kazakhstan (because of the latter's huge size and unique energy geography). Indicated Kyrgyz oil imports may be understated: 85 percent of its oil consumption originates abroad but half of all fuel is smuggled into the country.[18] Fuel is not a major import by value for Azerbaijan, but when Russian gas supplies were cut off in October 2000 the deprivation was painful; thousands of Azeris took to the streets in protest.[19]

Part 2 of Table 3.4 shows the relative importance of regional neighbors as well as the outside world in the geographic direction of trade. When the CASC states emerged out of the Soviet Union, they were still largely tied to the Soviet trade network. Over the next decade, however, the direction of trade shifted substantially. Only Turkmenistan now sends more than half its exports to the CIS region, and that is because of gas sales to Ukraine. Nevertheless, Russia is the market for 15–20 percent of the exports by six of the eight countries. The South Caucasus countries do not loom very large as either the export destinations or import sources for both Central Asia and the South Caucasus itself, with a minor exception for Georgia. In two cases, in contrast, Central Asian states are important customers of their immediate neighbors: in order of size of trade share, Kazakhstan and Tajikistan for Kyrgyzstan's exports and Uzbekistan for Tajikistan's.

Extra-CIS states are the destination of 55 percent or more of the exports by six of the eight states of the region. The European Union is now a major customer of the region's exports, its share ranging from 18 percent (Uzbekistan) to 60 percent (Azerbaijan). There are substantial unidentified residuals in the extra-CIS group, but partial breakdowns suggest that most cases involve multiple destinations. Kazakhstan's 50 percent residual consists largely of crude oil sales to offshore locations, particularly Bermuda and the Virgin Islands.[20]

---

[18] *Monitor,* VII:151, June 7, 2001.

[19] Ariel Cohen, "The New Tools of Russian Power: Oil and Gas Pipelines," *UPI,* December 29, 2000.

[20] *Kazakhstan Economic Trends,* April–June 2000, Table 9.3, p. 184.

The CIS remains the major source of supply for three of the eight CASC states. Russia provides roughly half of Kazakhstan's imports and 80 percent of the country's purchases from the CIS states. Otherwise, Russia's share ranges from a low of 7 percent in Turkmenistan to a high of 21 percent in Azerbaijan, in a pattern roughly similar to Russia's role in CASC exports. On the import side, three Central Asian countries rely substantially on their Central Asian neighbors: again, in order of size of share, Uzbekistan and Kazakhstan for Tajikistan imports; Uzbekistan for Turkmenistan's; and Kazakhstan and Uzbekistan for Kyrgyzstan's. The South Caucasus states draw most of their imports from extra-CIS sources. Considering how ardently Turkey has sought closer relations with most of the region, its trade is significant only with Georgia. Iran's role is also generally small, again with a single exception—its purchases of Turkmenistan's exports. China is included in the miscellaneous category because of inadequate data.

Russia's supplier role is weightier than indicated in Table 3.4, Part 2, because much of its export to the region consists of fuels, which are vital to the importing economies. This is particularly true for Georgia, which is totally dependent on Russia for natural gas, but Russia is also the main supplier of gas to Armenia. All three South Caucasus states as well as Kyrgyzstan and Tajikistan have experienced temporary cutoffs of oil or gas from Russia or regional partners (Turkmenistan or Uzbekistan). The suppliers usually blamed the consumer states' large arrears of energy debts, but the latter suspected political motives as well.[21]

External economic dependence may occur not only with trade but also with credit. Table 3.5 supplies some indicators of the relative size and burden of external public debt in the region. Kyrgyzstan and Tajikistan carry the largest debt burdens, measured as a percent of GDP, followed by Georgia, Uzbekistan, and Armenia. Calculation of

---

[21]See, for example, *Financial Times*, January 4, 2001 (Georgia); *RFE/RL Newsline*, V:18, January 26, 2001 (Kyrgyzstan); *FSU Oil and Gas Monitor*, June 19, 2001, p. 11 (Tajikistan). Kyrgyzstan and Tajikistan in turn have exploited their position as water resource suppliers to exert pressure on Uzbekistan and Kazakhstan. Sadji, "Natural Resources Are Being Used as Political Trump Cards," *Prism* (Jamestown Foundation), VII:5, May 2001, Part 5.

Table 3.5

Central Asia and South Caucasus: Public Sector
Debt and Debt Service, 1999

	Debt as percent of			Debt service as % of	
	GDP[a]	Exports	Fiscal revenue	Exports	Fiscal revenue
Armenia	45/30	154[b]	168[b]	16[c]	19[c]
Azerbaijan	21/NA	73	NA	2	3
Georgia	60/56	213[b]	688[b]	13[c]	45[c]
Kazakhstan	24/NA	73	NA	27	NA
Kyrgyzstan	140/94	188[b]	386[b]	24[c]	24[c]
Tajikistan	110/86	128[b]	504[b]	5[c]	20[c]
Turkmenistan	NA	NA	NA	NA	NA
Uzbekistan	23/NA	120	NA	16	NA

NA = not available.

[a]First figure, debt at nominal value; second figure, debt at net present value.

[b]Debt in net present value; includes public enterprise and private nonguaranteed debt for debt/exports but only government and government-guaranteed debt for debt/revenue.

[c]Debt service includes payments on public enterprises and private nonguaranteed debt for export ratios but only government and government-guaranteed debt for revenue ratios.

SOURCES: Azerbaijan: *Azerbaijan Economic Trends*, January–March 2001, Graph 7.13, p. 95. Kazakhstan: *Kazakhstan Economic Trends*, January–March 2001, pp. 70, 72, 137. Uzbekistan: *Uzbek Economic Trends*, October–December 2000, p. 89. The Uzbek debt/GDP ratio is evidently valued at the official exchange rate; the figure would be considerably higher at a weighted average rate, based on Chart 2, p. 102. Other entries from IMF and World Bank, *Armenia, Georgia, Kyrgyz Republic, Moldova, and Tajikistan: External Debt and Fiscal Sustainability*, February 7, 2001, pp. 4, 5, 7, 19.

net present values reduces the ratios because of conditionality features of the loans—particularly, in relative terms, for Armenia and Kyrgyzstan. The debt burden on Georgia, Kyrgyzstan, and Tajikistan appears especially heavy in terms of ratios of exports or budget revenues. Georgia's debt problems may be worse than indicated because exports may be overstated and debt underestimated.[22]

A level of debt service exceeding 25 percent of the value of exports is usually regarded as a threat to financial stability. In extreme cases, as

---

[22]"IMF/World Bank, February 6, 2001," pp. 5 and 15.

Argentina has demonstrated recently, financial instability can lead to popular disorder. The only country exceeding the 25 percent figure in 1999 was Kazakhstan, but its oil and gas export prospects are so promising, assuming that oil prices remain steady, that the debt/export ratio is likely to decline sharply in the next few years. The same cannot be said for Kyrgyzstan and Georgia; in the latter's case, debt service obligations absorb almost half the government's budget revenues. The Kyrgyzstan situation may have deteriorated further: the republic's finance minister indicated at the end of June 2001 that debt service obligations on the national budget left almost nothing over for socioeconomic purposes.[23]

Table 3.6 looks at the structure of external debt in the four weakest states. Georgia and Tajikistan not only have large public-sector external debts, in absolute value and relative to GDP, but also half or more of the external debt falls to bilateral debt. The CIS region accounts for 36 and 50 percent, respectively, of these two states' totals and, therefore, the lion's share of their bilateral components.

Table 3.6

Public-Sector External Debt of Four CASC States, End 1999

	Armenia	Georgia	Kyrgyzstan	Tajikistan
Total government and gov't-guaranteed debt, million $	854	1,678	1,383	887
Structure in percent of total				
Multilateral	75	50	68	36
Bilateral	21	50	32	60
Russia	13	11	12	32
Other FSU	14	25	1	18
Commercial and guaranteed	4	0	0	5

SOURCE: IMF and World Bank, *Armenia, Georgia, Kyrgyz Republic, Moldova, and Tajikistan: External Debt and Fiscal Sustainability,* February 7, 2001, Table 1, p. 6.

---

[23]*RFE/RL Newsline,* V:125, July 2, 2001. The minister reported that the government's foreign debt on January 1, 2000, was $1.76 billion, notably higher than the figure shown in Table 3.6, and reached $2 billion as of the date of his report, one-third greater than GDP. *FSU Oil and Gas Monitor,* April 10, 2001, p. 7; *RFE/RL Newsline,* V:137, July 23, 2001; *RFE/RL Newsline,* V:239, December 19, 2001.

Russia is a particularly large creditor of Tajikistan, but it is also the source of 11–13 percent of the total government and government-guaranteed debt in the other three states.

Concentration of trade joined to debt dependence makes a potentially dangerous combination. Armenia, for example, has struggled to cope with its debts for Russian natural gas and nuclear fuel. In a debt-equity swap, the Russian gas suppliers Gazprom and Itera together acquired 55 percent of the Armenian gas distribution monopoly Amrosgazprom. In the second half of 2001, Moscow was negotiating for a stake in various Armenian state-owned enterprises, in return for writing off Yerevan's remaining $88 million debt.[24] It has been reported that Moscow offered deep discounts on future gas supplies if Armenia joined the Eurasian Economic Community (consisting of Russia, Belarus, Kazakhstan, Kyrgyzstan, and Tajikistan).[25]

Armenia is not the sole case in point. The agenda of the September 2001 session of the Kyrgyzstan-Russia Intergovernment Committee on Trade and Cooperation included the transfer to Russia of shares in 27 domestic industrial enterprises in partial repayment of Kyrgyzstan's $150 million debt to Moscow.[26] The leadership expressed strong interest in having Russian companies buy into Kyrgyz businesses, evidently due to the apparent failure of Kyrgyzstan's privatization effort in enlisting Western participation.[27] In any case, the political-economic implications of a substantial Russian stake in Kyrgyzstan's economy remain the same. Economic subordination to a regional hegemon, if that is what results from such negotiations, is of course not equivalent to political destabilization. The implicit conflict with national goals and interests, however, can intensify internal political discontents.

---

[24]*FSU Oil and Gas Monitor*, April 10, 2001, p. 7; *RFE/RL Newsline*, V:137, July 23, 2001; *RFE/RL Newsline*, V:239, December 19, 2001.

[25]*Russia's Week* (Jamestown Foundation), VI:935, September 26, 2001.

[26]*RFE/RL Newsline*, V:173, September 12, 2001.

[27]*Interfax Daily News Bulletin*, November 11, 2001. See also *RFE/RL Central Asia Report*, 1:17, November 15, 2001.

PROSPECTS

The solutions to the economic problems posed by CASC poverty and external dependence ultimately reside in structural reform and economic growth. Reform is likely to be a necessary condition for sustained growth and a co-determinant of success in reducing poverty significantly. Stepping up the rate of growth, in turn, would contribute to poverty reduction directly, by increases in employment and incomes, as well as indirectly, by augmenting the resources available for poverty reduction. Growth could help ease the burden of debt by increasing government revenues and perhaps also by boosting exports, but enlarging the government's revenue base is also the task of fiscal reform. The content of the required reforms, in addition to fiscal changes, is well known. It includes (in no particular order) reducing public-sector corruption; further privatization, but to profit-seeking entrepreneurs rather than would-be asset strippers; strengthening the rule of law in all spheres of the society; instituting or extending nondiscriminatory regulatory regimes; creating a modern banking system; repairing the social safety net by restructuring the social services; land reform; eliminating disguised unemployment, which distorts labor resource allocation; and so on. The seriousness with which the CASC states prosecute reform programs, however, remains to be seen; the record of the 1990s was disappointing in most cases.

All eight states recorded economic growth in 2000 and 2001, but this period of progress is too brief, against the background of sustained misadventure in the 1900s, to warrant unconstrained optimism. The eight states appear to fall into two groups in terms of their current growth prospects, the three major energy producers and exporters in one category and the other five states in a second. Azerbaijan, Kazakhstan, and Turkmenistan have large oil and gas deposits, which have attracted the interest of the major international conglomerates. (Uzbekistan has large gas reserves but has not yet become a significant energy exporter.) Because of the region's isolation from world markets, distribution—essentially, via pipelines—has been more of a problem than production. It is likely, however, that the pipeline problems will be resolved in one fashion or another, if oil and gas prices remain in roughly the current range.[28]   In that case, energy exports should become an increasingly important driver of the three states' economic growth. By the same token, their debt management burdens, which are already relatively low, should be further reduced. On the other hand, the introduction to this chapter pointed to a number of potential downsides of energy concentration, apart from market price fluctuation: failure to channel oil and gas proceeds into productive investment, tenuous links between primary product extraction and development of manufacturing and services, "Dutch disease," and vulnerability to external pressure. As already noted, the energy producers are aware of these difficulties and hope to be able to sidestep them.

The growth prospects of the other five states will be conditioned in part by the character of the external environment. Russia's relative weight in the CASC's trade and debt is not what it was in the early and middle 1990s, but the Russian financial crisis of August 1998 hurt several of the region's economies badly, if temporarily. Another sharp reduction in Russian demand, especially if accompanied again by steep devaluation, would naturally be damaging. It seems less likely at this time because of the improvement in Russia's growth prospects and macroeconomic management. In general, however, the high trade participation ratios shown in Table 3.3 indicate that external trade shocks, whether coming from Russia, the European Union, or other significant partners, could set back growth substantially in the second group of CASC states. Finally, reluctance of lenders to reschedule debt on favorable terms or insistence on hardening of credit terms for new debt would also constitute a form of external shock.

Domestic policy and action are, however, fundamental for the group of five. Four of them—Uzbekistan is the exception—have specific poverty-reduction programs, worked out in the context of IMF/World Bank lending programs, with targets for increasing income levels of the poor, decreasing infant and child mortality, raising education and health standards and service, and the like. Whether these programs will succeed to any extent will depend in part on success in

---

[28]For more detail and a somewhat different point of view, see Chapter Five of this report.

fiscal-monetary policy—increasing budget revenues, decreasing deficits, and controlling the money supply. More important perhaps is increasing investment in the economy, particularly by attracting foreign investment, which in turn depends on transforming the domestic business climate through the structural reforms noted earlier. The IMF and World Bank believe that Georgia, Kyrgyzstan, and Tajikistan face difficult situations of balance of payments and debt over the current decade, even under a relatively benign scenario of internal macroeconomic adjustment and reform coupled with a shockless external environment. An alternative scenario with less favorable internal and external conditions yields near-crisis conditions. Armenia's debt sustainability problem seems manageable.[29] Uzbekistan's situation is obscured by doubts about the reliability of government statistics.[30] Persistent government refusal to liberalize its foreign exchange and trade regimes, which has only recently begun to yield to international pressure, raises additional questions about Uzbekistan's near- and mid-term prospects.

All forecasting for the CASC economies, however, will now have to be examined in the light of a potentially cardinal transformation of the regional environment: the U.S. government's war against terrorism triggered by the events of September 11, 2001. Heightened U.S./allied presence in the wake of military action that was supported to varying degree by all eight states—but especially by Kyrgyzstan, Tajikistan, and Uzbekistan—will surely have an impact on the region. The potential economic effects of sustained foreign presence may be of various kinds:

- When the U.S. military campaign began, it was feared that perhaps hundreds of thousands of Afghan refugees would flee to the neighboring Central Asian states and disrupt their economies. That concern has abated with the defeat of the Taliban–Al Qaeda regime, but tribal-ethnic conflict may yet erupt in dimensions that could resurrect the specter of large-scale refugee movements.

---

[29]"IMF/World Bank, February 6, 2001," and "IMF/World Bank, February 7, 2001," along with an additional companion paper.

[30]IMF, *Republic of Uzbekistan: Recent Economic Developments*, Staff Country Report 00/36, March 2000, p. 7.

- In recent years, Central Asia in particular has experienced a major influx of drugs, mainly enroute from south Asia to Russia and Europe but also increasingly distributed to the Central Asian populations. The danger of widespread drug addiction was exacerbated by an incipient AIDS epidemic, a combination that threatened to play havoc with the regional economies and seriously disrupt their political-social order. Coalition military action may have disrupted Taliban drug flows, but they may be replaced by production in Afghanistan, still far from centralized control by the new Kabul government, or in parts of Central Asia. Presumably, replacement of drug flows would be accompanied by a reorganization of distribution networks. As the drug trade is intertwined with local criminal networks and depends on the corruption of government officials, such reorganization could upset political balances and lead to a refashioned struggle for power.

- Depending on the scale, character, and duration of the U.S./ allied presence, significant foreign exchange injections into the national economies could stimulate economic growth and employment. It could also, however, accelerate local currency price inflation, increase the inequality of income distribution, and perhaps even intensify economic crime and corruption. War tends to stimulate capital flight and inhibit the inflow of foreign investment, but extensive military action in Afghanistan has been brief. Restoration of military security in the region, even without substantial political reform, joined with augmented foreign exchange resources for the national governments, could stimulate external credits and the inflow of foreign investment.

- Military conflict does not ordinarily promote trade. Kyrgyzstan and Tajikistan depend heavily on trade with other Central Asian states and could be hard hit if significant hostilities resumed. Realization of the promise of security stabilization in the region, in contrast, would probably stimulate intra- and extraregional trade.

- Caspian basin energy development may also be affected. With military action confined to Afghanistan and its neighborhood, oil and gas pipeline construction in the Caspian–Black Sea area should be able to proceed unhindered, particularly if energy prices stabilize. The dream of piping gas from Kazakhstan and

Turkmenistan through Afghanistan to Pakistan, India, and, via the Arabian Sea, to East Asia may be revived. But if disturbances spread westward, possibly even to the Persian Gulf, the shock to energy development could be severe.

- An interesting question concerns the political economics of CASC interstate relations. For example, Uzbekistan's currently central role in supporting the coalition might strengthen its economic as well as political leverage over its weaker neighbors. The principal issue, however, is the future role of Russia in the region. Before September 11, three of the five Central Asian states (Kazakhstan, Kyrgyzstan, and Tajikistan) had joined Russia and Belarus in a customs union, which was raised in status to the Eurasian Economic Community. The economic and political integration of the CIS is a Russian government goal that antedated the accession of Vladimir Putin, but he energized what appeared to be a moribund policy. In the past, CIS integration was retarded and distorted by the clash of interests of the participants, especially by the opposition of the smaller states to what they perceived as Russia's hegemonic ambitions. Such a conflict characterizes much of the history of Caspian oil and gas development over the last seven or eight years.[31]

- Resistance by the smaller CIS states to Moscow's integrationist ambitions was made possible by Russian economic and military weakness. Recent strengthening of the Russian economy has raised the possibility of a reversal of the power balance. Uzbekistan's President Karimov noted that "present-day Russia is not the Russia of the 1990s." He warned that "if the ruble and Russian economy strengthen, none of us will be able to escape its influence."[32]

- If the members of the Eurasian Economic Community are serious about implementing their unity promises, they will be opting for one form of economic integration against an alternative, with

[31]On Russian policy regarding integration of the CIS, see Abraham S. Becker, "Russia and Economic Integration in the CIS," *Survival*, XXXVIII:4, Winter 1996–97, pp. 117–136. On the Caspian oil and gas conflict, see Becker, "Russia and Caspian Oil: Moscow Loses Control," *Post-Soviet Affairs*, XVI:2, 2000, pp. 91–132.

[32]Cited by Igor Torbakov, "Economic Clout Gives Russia Growing Power in CIS," *Eurasia Insight*, December 6, 2001 *(www.eurasianet.org)*.

the increasingly globalized world market and especially with Europe. It is difficult to believe that such a choice would not have major consequences for the economic growth and welfare of these economies. The most important Central Asian member of the community, Kazakhstan, evidently seeks a Janus-like position. On a visit to President Bush in Washington, Kazakh President Nazarbayev and his host proclaimed a "long-term strategic partnership and cooperation" between the two states and stressed the need to integrate a prosperous, democratic Kazakhstan into the global economy.[33] At the same time, Nazarbayev is CASC's most consistent and enthusiastic supporter of CIS economic integration and the Eurasian Economic Community in particular. Riding two horses heading in different directions seems, however, inherently unsustainable.

- Russia exhibits signs of uneasiness about the prospect of long-term American presence in Central Asia. This is partly evoked by such statements as U.S. Secretary of State Colin Powell's declaration that the American "interest in the region should be permanent and these relations will continue after the [Afghan] crisis," or President Bush's promise to seek "long-term partnership" with Uzbekistan.[34] One visible Russian reaction is to bolster its military position in the region. The CIS summit meeting in Moscow on November 30, 2001, called for closer cooperation between CIS security organs to strengthen the new CIS counterterrorist center. The center was viewed as a step toward the creation of "a global system to counteract terrorism in close coordination with all interested nations and organizations, and with the United Nations (UN) and Security Council playing the leading role."[35] Russia is now seeking permanent military facilities for its forces deployed in Tajikistan.[36]

- In sum, Russian political-military pressure on Central Asia—perhaps on the South Caucasus too—to prevent the solidification of

---

[33] *RFE/RL Central Asia Report,* 1:23, December 27, 2001.

[34] *RFE/RL Central Asia Report,* 1:21, December 13, 2001.

[35] *RFE/RL Central Asia Report,* 1:20, December 6, 2001.

[36] *RFE/RL Newsline,* V:232, December 10, 2001; *RFE/RL Central Asia Report,* 1:21, December 13, 2001.

a long-term U.S. presence, along with a possible clash of political-economic interests over integration in the CIS and the Eurasian Economic Community, are also potential threats to regional stability.

These considerations of the possible implications of the Afghanistan war and its aftermath point in different directions, toward economic progress and political stabilization or toward conflict and destabilization. It was noted at the beginning of this chapter that generalizations about the connection between economic factors and political stability are problematic and controversial. The difficulties loom larger in a period of rapid change in the external environment, as is now the case in the CASC. Whether we will indeed see a substantial, long-term U.S./allied presence in the region and, if so, what character it will take are very much open questions at present. So too therefore are the possible consequences for the CASC countries. They may become clearer over the next year or two as the direction of U.S. policy and the reactions of regional actors unfold.

Chapter Four

CRIMINALIZATION AND STABILITY IN CENTRAL ASIA AND SOUTH CAUCASUS
Phil Williams

INTRODUCTION

In assessing the prospects for stability in Central Asia and South Caucasus, it is essential to consider the impact of crime and corruption. Since the collapse of the Soviet Union there has been a process of criminalization in both subregions that make up CASC, involving drug trafficking, organized crime, shadow economies, and corruption and rent seeking. Once on the margins—or more accurately in the shadows—of the Communist systems, in the post-Soviet world these phenomena have moved to the center of political and economic life. They play a critical role in the success or failure of transitional measures toward democracy and free markets. It is generally assumed that their impact is negative, not only complicating and inhibiting the transition process but contributing significantly to instability and creating new insecurities in society. Yet their effects do not point unequivocally in this direction: the criminalization of societies has many negative consequences but also provides some benefits. The precise balance between positive and negative varies from country to country and changes over time. Indeed, in the short term, organized crime, drug trafficking, and the operation of shadow economies and informal markets give to many citizens means of economic advancement that are not available in the legal economy. Consequently, they act as both a safety valve and a safety net. But this is not to ignore either their negative short-term consequences or their even more serious long-term effects. In the long term, the criminalization process is likely to add significantly to the prospects for instability. The choice of illegal over legal economic activity is a rational short-term choice, but it chokes off legitimate activity and reduces the flow of resources to the state by avoiding taxation.

These negative consequences are particularly marked in relation to the fourth component of this criminalization syndrome: corruption and rent seeking by political elites. Long-term political corruption combined with inadequate state capacity in other areas can ultimately lead to widespread disaffection. In such circumstances protest movements, whatever their origin or impulse, will very likely garner widespread support, not necessarily because of their intrinsic appeal to populations but as a means of channeling broader political and economic dissatisfactions. Indeed, Central Asia has already witnessed the emergence of an Islamic insurgent movement fueled not only by support from elsewhere in the Islamic world but also by the alienation of populations that are politically oppressed and economically depressed.[1]

If one component of the criminalization process is likely to catalyze support for insurgencies, such movements can also benefit from the direct or indirect involvement of their own in illegal activities. Crime can be lucrative, and drug trafficking in particular can provide opportunities for insurgent groups to fund their activities—either through direct participation or through the imposition of taxes on traffickers or growers. This pattern has been evident elsewhere in the world, particularly Colombia and the Balkans, and it is unlikely that Central Asia deviates markedly from it. Thinking 10 to 15 years into the future, therefore, it seems likely that any short-term stabilizing effects of the criminalization syndrome will be more than outweighed by the long-term destabilizing consequences.

Before elucidating and developing these themes, however, it is necessary to identify characteristics of CASC that determine the extent and impact of the criminalization syndrome. That is followed by an analysis of the major components of the criminalization syndrome, with reference both to the region as a whole and to individual states. Succeeding sections explore the relationship between criminalization and the dominant regimes, then consider several plausible sce-

---

[1] The Islamic Movement of Uzbekistan is generally referred to as a terrorist movement but is better understood as an insurgent movement.

narios for the period 2010 to 2015. The final section offers some brief concluding observations.

CHARACTERISTICS OF CENTRAL ASIA AND SOUTH CAUCASUS

Central Asia is sometimes seen as a unified region in which the member states share many characteristics. There are good reasons for this. The five "stans" occupy a large swath of land marked by aridity and the need for irrigation agriculture. They also share a history of integration within the Soviet empire and subordination of their own economic needs to those of the bloc as a whole, a subordination that left them with massive environmental problems, highly skewed trade patterns, and distorted production bases. Since independence, they have all suffered to one degree or another from hyperinflation, the growth of unemployment, the loss of traditional markets and trade outlets, and limited investment capital. The transition process has proved both painful and protracted—and progress in all five countries toward democracy and a market economy has been limited. Much the same is true of the South Caucasus. In this subregion, animosities between Azerbaijan and Armenia provide an added complication, while Georgia has exhibited severe growing pains.

Looking at CASC from a regional perspective, one of the most significant factors is the high level of poverty. The collapse of the Soviet Union and the subsequent transition process were enormously disruptive, involving large-scale economic dislocation, serious social and economic deterioration, and major hardship (See Chapter Three). It is estimated that the economies of former Soviet republics are, on average, 40 percent lower than in 1989.[2] In Armenia, for example, an estimated 80 percent of the population lives in poverty on less than $25 a month, and although the official unemployment rate is 17 percent, there are claims that the real figure is 50 percent.[3]

---

[2]Gustavo Capdevila, "Former Soviet Republics Still 40% Worse Off," CIS, *Inter Press Service*, May 14, 2001, *www.atimes.com/c-asia/CD11Ag02.html*.

[3]"Despite Foreign Aid, 80% Live in Poverty," Armenia, May 2, 2001, *www.times.kg*.

The problems confronting the two subregions are reflected in the Human Development Index (HDI) used by the UN to assess overall quality of life around the globe. The HDI is a composite index that encompasses a variety of factors such as GDP per capita, availability of water, and accessibility of health and welfare services.[4]   The countries of CASC generally fall into the level of "medium" development as ranked by the HDI.[5]   In 2000, they were ranked as follows: Kazakhstan 76 (down from 64 in 1995), Georgia 85, Armenia 87, Uzbekistan 92, Turkmenistan 96 (down from 86 in 1995), Kyrgyzstan 97 (down from 86 in 1995), Azerbaijan 103, and Tajikistan 108 (down from 103 in 1995).[6] Within this broad category, clearly there are considerable variations.   Kazakhstan, for example, because of its oil potential, has attracted considerable foreign investment, while Tajikistan, the lowest-ranked state, has little or no appeal for outside investors.   Uzbekistan, for its part, witnessed the withdrawal of some foreign investment in 2001, partly in response to overregulation and corruption.

In terms of economic growth, in 2000 and 2001 many of these economies started to improve, with some instances of double-digit growth.   The overall outlook remains gloomy, however.   Even where there has been foreign investment in the oil industry, this has generated sectoral dynamism but has contributed to a two-tier economy rather than comprehensive across-the-board growth.   In short, these are countries in which many of the needs of citizens are not met by government or by business, and where there is considerable capacity for alienation and subsequently violence in an attempt to improve conditions.

Common problems, however, should obscure neither the political diversity of the countries in CASC nor the differences between the two subregions.   In many respects, for example, the five states of Central Asia—Kazakhstan, Kyrgyzstan, Turkmenistan, Tajikistan, and Uzbekistan—differ markedly from one another.   This is not surpris-

---

[4]For an overview and explanation of the HDI, see *www.undp.org/hdro/anatools.htm.*

[5]The "high" development category encompassed countries ranked from 1 to 46 in 2000; "medium" countries were ranked 47–139 and "low" 140–174. Sierra Leone was ranked last, Canada first.

[6]The Human Development Annual Reports can be found at *www.undp.org/hdro/ highlights/past.htm.*

ing: although Soviet rule and central planning deformed the politics and economics of the Central Asian states, each state was affected differently.[7] The same is true in the South Caucasus. Each country has unique problems that, in some cases, greatly complicate the general regionwide problems. Among these regional problems is an ethnic kaleidoscope that results in cross-national loyalties and a potential for intercommunal violence that could in turn seriously increase tensions among governments. Ironically, this is accompanied by incomplete nation building. Even within ethnic groups, national identities constantly have to compete with tribal and clan affiliations.[8] This has been a huge problem in Tajikistan and Georgia, but it also has the potential to be troublesome in other countries.

Both Central Asia and the South Caucasus are vulnerable to external forces that could all too easily combine with internal weaknesses to create far-reaching instability. These forces differ, of course, between the two subregions. In the South Caucasus, Georgia in particular faces the danger of spillover from the Chechnya conflict. For its part, Central Asia needs to be viewed as a border region with Afghanistan and Iran, with close proximity to Pakistan. In other words, it has the misfortune to be located next to the largest heroin-producing region in the world. Moreover, states bordering Afghanistan have suffered to one degree or another from the spillover effects of the drug trafficking and internecine warfare in that country. The rise of religious fundamentalism has also created new dangers and tensions for Central Asia. And because borders in both subregions are so porous, weapons are easily transshipped into and through the countries of the region, offering easy opportunity for those intent—for whatever reason—on challenging the regimes, revising the political status quo, or pursuing ethnic agendas.[9] The ready availability of arms is a potent vulnerability for countries in which governments have limited legitimacy and state capacity is low. In sum, the permeability of the region to external forces adds to the

---

[7]S. Frederick Starr, "Making Eurasia Stable," *Foreign Affairs*, January/February 1996, p. 81.

[8]S. Akiner, "Post-Soviet Central Asia: Past Is Prologue," in P. Ferdinand (ed.), *The New Central Asia and Its Neighbors*, London: RIIA/Pinter, 1994, pp. 10–11.

[9]See Bobi Pirseyedi, *The Small Arms Problems in Central Asia: Features and Implications*, Geneva: UNIDIR, 2000.

demands placed on governments, while also offering more serious opportunities for interethnic violence, terrorism, or insurgencies.

The removal of the Taliban regime in Afghanistan as part of the U.S. war against terrorism is likely to have both positive and negative consequences. On the one side, it has removed from the region a destabilizing regime. On the other, it could contribute significantly to the radicalization of Islamic forces in Central Asia and possibly even in the South Caucasus. Part of the reason for this latter danger is the other long-term characteristic of most of the countries of CASC: the alienation of populations. Rooted in both political oppression and the stark contrast between mass poverty and elite wealth, the alienation process has been accentuated by the collapse of basic social provisions such as health services that were widely and readily available during the Soviet era. The lack of progress toward democratic accountability combines with continued elite dominance and exclusivity to limit opportunity for legitimate expressions of political opposition. The corollary is that political opposition is increasingly likely to take violent forms.

With the blocking of both economic advancement in the legitimate economy and the effective articulation of legitimate grievances in the political arena, alternative strategies for both economic and political advancement are increasingly attractive. Drug trafficking or involvement in organized crime and black market activity become a means of making money for those with few or no legitimate alternatives, while political frustration can all too easily result in violent strategies to articulate grievances. The addition of Islamic fundamentalism renders the mix even more volatile. In some respects, turning to religion is an understandable response to material deprivation: salvation in the next world is possible even if there are acute problems in this world. Yet the attraction of Islam is not confined to spiritual comfort: Islam also offers an attractive form of political activism (see Chapter Two). Although Islam is, in some quarters at least, a messianic religion, recruitment in Central Asia is propelled as much by domestic factors as by the crusading activities of external forces. The irony of the U.S. military attack on Afghanistan and its cooperation with Pakistan is that this has eliminated the prospect of Taliban-inspired militancy while strengthening the domestic forces in Central Asia contributing to the rise of Islamic militancy—including the desire of Uzbekistan's government to clamp down on all political dissent.

The implications of alienation for the rise of organized crime, insurgency, and Islam are profound. Disenfranchised, poor, and alienated populations provide an excellent recruiting pool for criminal organizations, insurgent groups, or fundamentalists intent on replacing the dominant secularism with a religious state. Criminal groups offer economic advancement and higher status; insurgencies offer opportunities for political expression; and religious groups offer salvation and an alternative vision of political life. In looking at the rise of fundamentalism in Central Asia, therefore, its broad appeal is obvious. Repressive societies, in which benefits are concentrated within the elite, encourage citizens to turn to any movements that offer some promise of alleviation. In this sense, growing support for militant Islamic movements is in large part a protest against economic and social conditions. In sum, the quality of governance in CASC states is such that citizens will turn to crime, political violence, or religious fundamentalism as a means of coping with political oppression and economic deprivation. It is against this background that the criminalization syndrome must now be elucidated.

THE CRIMINALIZATION SYNDROME

One of the most important components of the new reality in CASC is what is termed here the "criminalization syndrome." This term is particularly useful because it encompasses several distinct but reinforcing components:

- The involvement of many of the countries (in both subregions but particularly in Central Asia) in the drug trafficking industry that has centered around Afghanistan and its huge opium production.

- The emergence of organized crime as an intrusive force in political, economic, and social life in both Central Asia and the South Caucasus.

- The emergence of large shadow economies that encompass illegal economic activities and informal activities that are beyond the reach of the state (and outside both tax and regulatory systems) and provide an important means of subsistence for many people.

- The prevalence of corruption and rent seeking on the part of government officials and even law enforcement personnel.

Each of these components of the criminalization syndrome must be examined in turn, with particular emphasis on its scope and characteristics in CASC.

Organized Crime

The concept of "organized crime" has long been controversial, with many competing definitions. While most observers agree that organized crime is about the provision of illicit goods and services, there are intense arguments about the structure of criminal organizations. Those who focus on traditional "mafiya" families emphasize the need for a structured hierarchy and centralized leadership and control. Others contend that organized crime often manifests itself through loose, fluid, network-based organizations. Even recognizing that the "organization" of organized crime differs in different places and circumstances, the latter argument is generally more compelling: networks are highly functional and sophisticated organizational forms and offer criminals an efficient and effective way to conduct their activities while minimizing and countering the risks they face from law enforcement.

The UN grappled with the issue of definition for several years as it moved toward the creation of a convention against transnational organized crime, finally unveiled in Palermo in December 2000. The convention defined an organized criminal group as "a structured group of three or more persons existing for a period of time and acting in concert with the aim of committing one or more serious crimes or offenses established pursuant to this Convention, in order to obtain, directly, or indirectly, a financial or other material benefit."[10] Although there can be argument about the number of people required, the part of the definition that captures the core of organized crime is the idea of profit through crime. Indeed, rather than

---

[10]For the text of the convention, see *www.odccp.org/palermo/convmain.html.*

becoming preoccupied with definitional issues, it is preferable to focus on essences. In this context, in a parallel to Clausewitzian thought, one can argue that organized crime can best be understood as the continuation of business by criminal means.[11] This obscures some aspects of organized crime—especially the fact that organized crime is often rooted in family and kinship and in patron-client relations—but it leads to a clear understanding of the pragmatism of organized crime and the desire to exploit any situation to maximize opportunities for profit so long as the risks are tolerable.

Organized crime is highly acquisitive and highly rational—and this has important implications for developments in CASC. Indeed, the most salient feature of organized crime in the transitional states of the former Soviet Union is the extent to which it pervades economic life: it has infiltrated most sectors of the economy to one degree or another and has influence or control over large chunks of economic activity—not simply the provision of illegal goods and services. Although it provides alternative employment opportunities and some income generation, organized crime is one of the most pernicious forces in contemporary political, economic, and social life in CASC: it undermines the rule of law, challenges the state monopoly on the use of violence, has a corrosive effect on state institutions, drives out legitimate economic activity, and frightens off foreign investment.

These consequences are pervasive throughout both subregions. Yet the manifestations of organized crime differ from country to country. In Kazakhstan, organized crime succeeded in establishing a strong foothold in the early 1990s. Racketeering and organized prostitution were merely two components of a much broader portfolio, which included infiltration of the banking system and the use of corrupt bank officials and forged letters of credit to conduct large-scale financial fraud.[12] Moreover, although there is little public discussion of this development, it is very likely that criminal organizations, operating through various front companies, are heavily involved in the oil sector in Kazakhstan, a development that could pose prob-

---

[11]The Clausewitzian concept of organized crime has been enunciated by the author.

[12]Sergey Skorokhodov, "Kazakhstan—Morals Will Be Policed" (in Russian), *Moscow Rossiyskaya Gazeta*, March 22, 1994, p. 6.

lems for Western oil companies.[13] In Kyrgyzstan, extortion activities in the Osh market received a lot of attention, but these were part of a much wider phenomenon that encompassed car theft, trafficking in women, illegal trafficking in wildlife (particularly falcons smuggled to the Middle East), drug trafficking, money laundering, and a wide variety of financial crimes. Theft of livestock was also a problem— with many of the perpetrators never being identified.

In Uzbekistan, by the middle 1990s, there were close links between leaders of the major criminal organizations and the political elite.[14] It was thus not entirely surprising when in 2000, Australia refused to allow two Uzbek officials with the Olympic team to enter the country on the grounds that they were implicated in organized crime. If the political-criminal nexus was well developed in Uzbekistan, however, it did not preclude the successful operations of groups from outside the country.[15] Korean criminal organizations, for example, developed a strong base in the Fergana Valley and a handle on trade with the Far East, as well as important influence in the restaurant business.

In Georgia too, it is difficult to overestimate the political importance of criminal organizations. With deep roots in Georgian and Soviet history, they have been particularly important from the inception of Georgia's independence. When Eduard Shevardnadze took over the reins of power, he had to make expedient alliances with warlords and mafia figures such as Iosseliani and his paramilitary followers, the Mkhedrioni or "horsemen." Although Shevardnadze subsequently arrested his erstwhile ally and banned the Mkhedrioni, problems remain. Warlords are less important than they were in the early 1990s, but organized crime is still a powerful factor in Georgian political and economic life.

---

[13]For a fuller analysis, see Tamara Makarenko, "Patterns of Crime in the Caspian Basin," *Jane's Intelligence Review,* April 1, 2001.

[14]This observation is based on a personal interview by the author with a U.S. official in Tashkent in March 1996.

[15]For a full articulation of the notion of the political-criminal nexus, see "Special Issue: Confronting the Political-Criminal Nexus," *Trends in Organized Crime,* Vol. 4, No. 3 (Spring 1999).

Indeed, the Georgian criminal world shares many characteristics with the Russian. There is pervasive penetration of the economy. Organized crime controls not only motor vehicle construction plants but also "manganese mining and ferrous-alloy producing enterprises in western Georgia."[16] As in Russia, the looting of major enterprises is continuing, with rare metals being smuggled out of the country.[17] There are also close links between leading criminal figures and Georgian politicians and members of the government. As one report noted, criminal leaders "take a ride in the cars belonging to senior officials in the Georgian authorities, give business advice to businessmen, and if arrested, enjoy support from bureaucrats."[18] Members of parliament even intercede with law enforcement on behalf of leading criminals who have been arrested.

Among the most influential criminal leaders are Shakro Kalashov, alias Molodoy, Dato Tashkenteli, Tariel Oniani, Gia Kvaratskhelia, and Babua Khasan. Kalashov, a young Russian, reportedly controls a number of banks and casinos in Russia, including the popular Kristall in Moscow, from his base in Georgia. Another criminal authority, Melia [Fox] in Kutaisi, controls banks and is believed to be involved in money laundering.[19] Most of the criminal authorities live in Tbilisi, with 120 in Kutaisi, 12 in Rustavi, and 21 in Khoni.[20] Even more of the authorities are based in Russia, particularly Moscow, although there are some reports that their influence there is declining. In January 2001, Mindadze, a key figure in a "West Georgian organized crime affiliate specializing in extortion, fraud, carjacking, drug pushing, and abductions" was arrested in Moscow.[21] In Georgia itself, however, they remain well entrenched. Indeed, in

---

[16]"Georgian president bans armed vigilante units in troubled eastern Georgian area" (in Georgian), Georgian Radio, Tbilisi, July 23, 2001, BBC Worldwide Monitoring.

[17]Ibid.

[18]Giorgi Kapanadze, "Members of Parliament Take Crime Bosses Under Their Wing" (in Georgian), *Tbilisi Rezonansi,* August 22, 2000, p. 1.

[19]A criminal authority is a criminal leader with high status in the criminal world. Although it is tempting to translate this as "godfather," there are important differences that preclude a facile equivalence.

[20]Ibid.

[21]Andrey Mukhin, "A 'Proper Criminal' Nabbed on Narcotics: the Georgian Criminal Community Is Sustaining Losses" (in Russian), *Moscow Segodnya,* January 13, 2001, p. 7.

some quarters the number of leaders is regarded as an indicator of criminal influence, with some commentators suggesting that Georgia is becoming a criminalized state.[22] At the very least, there are parts of the country where the presence of the Georgian state is weak, if it even exists at all. This was evident in the crisis that erupted in the Pankisi Gorge in July 2001. Populated by ethnic Chechen citizens of Georgia and Chechen refugees, the gorge had become a "safe haven for criminals involved in drug trafficking and hostage-taking."[23] An armed criminal group of about 70 people operates from the gorge, engaging in drug trafficking, kidnapping, and extortion. In the gorge itself, the writ of the state is meaningless, law enforcement is absent, and anarchy is tempered only by a criminal order based on relative power. This was evident in the offer of one of the criminal leaders, Vepkhia Margoshvili—who is wanted by Georgian law enforcement for drug trafficking and kidnapping—to guarantee order in the gorge in return for an amnesty. Although the tensions were gradually diffused, the episode revealed that while Georgia has come a long way from the violence of the early 1990s, stability remains fragile. Indeed, there have been several developments in recent years that indicate a possible intensification of competition among the elites. The Mkhedrioni have become an overtly political force, while the localized mutiny of an army detachment in spring 2001 highlighted the fragile nature of critical institutions.

The complexity of crime and politics in Georgia is surpassed only by that in Tajikistan. The civil war of 1992 to 1997 was a complex struggle between the old Communist leadership on the one side and a combination of democratic reformers and Islamic fundamentalists on the other. This was overlaid by old clan feuds (between the ruling "kuliab" clan—whose members, from the city of Kuliab, provided the Communist leadership in Tajikistan—and the rebellious clan groups "Lali Badahkshan" and "Rastochez"). The conflict also involved ethnic rivalries that reflected longstanding tensions between Tajiks and Uzbeks. It was exacerbated by a struggle among rival warlords, criminal groups, and drug traffickers for control of drug routes and

---

[22]Giorgi Kapanadze, "Shevardnadze and godfathers of the thieving fraternity" (in Georgian), *Tbilisi Rezonansi*, September 1, 2000, p. 1.

[23]See "Georgian president bans armed vigilante units."

markets.[24] Moreover, in a country in which the major economic activity centered on drugs and arms, drug traffickers and rival warlords were able to consolidate their position and power into the resulting peace. Although Tajikistan managed to restore a semblance of stability in the late 1990s, organized crime continues to have significant influence. This was particularly evident in the apparent contract murder of Tajikistan's deputy interior minister, Khabib Sanginov, in Dushanbe in April 2001. Significantly, Sanginov had been leading a government effort to combat organized crime. The assassination was reportedly carried out by eight gunmen, and Sanginov's driver and two bodyguards were also killed. The Islamic Renaissance Party said the killings posed a threat to stability in the country.[25]

In sum, although organized crime differs in some of its incidentals, in its essentials it is a major player in the economic and political life of CASC. In several countries it clearly overlaps with drug trafficking.

Drug Trafficking

Although organized crime has taken on a variety of forms in CASC, in Central Asia much of it revolves around the drug trade. While some organized crime groups traffic in drugs as simply one among several illegal commodities, there are many groups that specialize in drug trafficking, developing expertise in moving the commodity, in circumventing or corrupting border guards, and in developing transnational linkages. A certain amount of cultivation also takes place in Central Asia, and several countries in the region produce acetic anhydride, an important precursor for heroin. The real problem for the countries of Central Asia, however, is that they are natural transshipment points for opium and heroin from Afghanistan on its way to the markets in Russia and Western Europe. In the late 1990s, Afghanistan emerged as the world's largest opium producer, surpassing Burma in the process. Producing 2,693 metric tons of raw opium in 1998, Afghanistan—in part as a result of the stability imposed by

---

[24]See Richard Pomfret, *The Economies of Central Asia,* Princeton N.J.: Princeton University Press, 1995, pp. 98 and 193.

[25]Gregory Gleason, "Tajikistan Minister's Murder Points to Drug-Route Conflict," *The Times of Central Asia, www.times.kg/times.cgi?D=article&aid=1017175.*

the Taliban—produced 4,581 tons in 1999.[26] Although the Taliban had condemned drug cultivation, the exigencies of power encouraged both toleration and taxation of the activity, at least in the short term. In 2000, partly because of weather conditions, production fell to 3,275 tons.[27] There is some evidence that in 2001 the Taliban was implementing its promised ban on cultivation.[28] Prior to September 11, however, this had not led to a real reduction in trafficking, partly because of extensive stockpiles and partly because the opposition Northern Alliance was heavily involved in the business. Indeed, there appeared to be a clear relocation of heroin laboratories to northeastern Afghanistan near the border with Tajikistan. On July 15, 2001, Russian border guards on the Afghanistan-Tajikistan border seized over two tons of raw opium to complement the 1,000 kilograms of heroin and 1,500 kilos of other drugs they had already seized in 2001. As one commentary noted,

> Three aspects of this incident are striking. First, it is officially described as the largest drug consignment ever seized "on any CIS border." Second, the raw opium came from the northern Afghan area opposite Tajikistan, controlled by Russian-backed, anti-Taliban forces, where poppy cultivation has increased after the Talibs suppressed it in their territory. And, third, the massive smuggling of raw opium across that border, as recently reported, indirectly confirms the information about heroin-making laboratories thriving in Tajikistan.[29]

There have been reports for some years that the processing of opium into heroin is taking place in Tajikistan, especially in the Pamir mountains, and this seizure certainly gives credence to such contentions.

Nor is this the only way Tajikistan is becoming more centrally involved in the drug business. Widespread poverty has lent a certain attraction to participation, if only as couriers, in drug trafficking—

---

[26]These figures are taken from S. Redo, "Uzbekistan and the United Nations in the Fight Against Transnational Organized Crime," in Tadeusz Bodio (ed.), *Uzbekistan: History, Society, Policy*, Warsaw: Elipsa, 2001.

[27]Ibid.

[28]Ibid.

[29]*Jamestown Foundation Monitor*, July 18, 2001.

with the result that Tajiks have been increasingly obvious among those arrested for drug trafficking in Moscow and elsewhere in Russia. Yet there is also some evidence that Tajiks are being forcibly recruited by Afghan drug traffickers to act as couriers. Reports from the southern Shuroabad district suggest that

> Shuroabad's key location has made its residents an easy target of Afghan dealers looking for Tajiks to carry the drugs on to the next point of transit—the capital Dushanbe, or even a location outside the country. The involuntary couriers are given a strict selling price for the drugs they are conveying. If the money they bring home is insufficient, the Afghan dealers may seize property or even a family member until the balance is paid. Some dealers have reportedly kidnapped relatives to ensure that the family will take their instructions seriously.[30]

As well as engendering violence and intimidation, the drug business also brings with it rampant corruption. With customs and police officers receiving extremely meager salaries, bribes from drug traffickers simply to look the other way are an attractive means of income augmentation. There have even been claims that the safest way to move heroin is to hire Russian border guards. In December 1997, twelve servicemen from Russia's 201st mechanized infantry division stationed in Tajikistan were arrested in a Moscow aerodrome while trying to carry in more than 8 kilos of drugs, including 3 kilos of heroin.[31] Perhaps most disturbing of all, however, is the high-level bureaucratic involvement. One official Tajik report acknowledged that "many drug merchants and couriers are members of Tajik state agencies, including law enforcement bodies and security services."[32] The report criticized state authorities for "failing to implement presidential decrees, governmental programs, and Security Council decisions against the narcotics trade" and suggested that one cause of failure was "law enforcement officers themselves being involved in the drug trade and making it possible for the

---

[30]Vasilina Brazhko, "Afghanistan Remains Main Supplier of Illegal Drugs to Central Asia and the CIS," *The Times of Central Asia*, July 19, 2001.

[31]Ibid.

[32]"Drug Trade Engulfs Tajikistan, Spills into Russia," *Jamestown Foundation Monitor*, January 31, 2001.

dealers to evade the law."[33] Not surprisingly, the report concluded that the drug business "poses a direct threat to national security."[34] Yet there are also allegations that personnel in the state security ministry are "complicit in the interrelated trades with drugs and arms. The president's Kulob clan is over-represented in that ministry, and the Kulob area near the Afghan border is known as a major transit point for Afghan-made drugs."[35] It is also where the Tajik state security ministry and Russian military intelligence operate the Parkhar airfield, by means of which they supply anti-Taliban forces in northeast Afghanistan—and, according to some allegations, bring drugs back to Tajikistan for onward shipment to Russia.[36]

Although one estimate suggests that the interdiction rate in Central Asia is about 0.4 percent, there are increasingly large seizures.[37] Russian authorities seized 30 kilos of heroin on July 2, 2000, in Astrakhan on a train arriving from Dushanbe, 100 kilos arriving by truck in Samara on July 7, and 120 kilos in Astrakhan on July 10.[38] The size of the loads suggests that the traffickers operate with a high confidence level. They are also diversifying routes and markets. Russian authorities, for example, have identified a trafficking channel that goes from Tajikistan through Kyrgyzstan and Kazakhstan to Novosibirsk in Siberia. In December 2000, Kyrgyzstan authorities seized 1,828 pounds of opium and 5.5 pounds of heroin that was en route to Russia, where unofficial estimates suggest that the number of addicts exceeds 3 million.[39]

Turkmenistan has also become a transshipment country. As the International Narcotics Control Strategy Report published in March 2001 noted,

---

[33]Ibid.

[34]Ibid.

[35]Ibid.

[36]Ibid.

[37]Redo, op. cit.

[38]*Jamestown Foundation Monitor,* July 13, 2001.

[39]Scott Peterson, "Fabled Silk Road Now Paved With Narcotics," *Christian Science Monitor,* January 8, 2001.

Turkmenistan is not a major producer or source country for illegal drugs or precursor chemicals, but it remains a transit country for the smuggling of narcotics and precursor chemicals. The flow of Afghan opiates destined for markets in Turkey, Russia and Europe, including drugs such as heroin, opium and other opiates enters Turkmenistan directly from Afghanistan, and also indirectly from Iran, Pakistan, Tajikistan and Uzbekistan.[40]

Turkmenistan is also a transshipment country for the precursor chemical, acetic anhydride, significant quantities of which are produced in India.

When countries are involved in transshipment, however, they also develop local consumer markets that result in a growing addict population—a development that can be particularly harmful where medical and health services are overstretched and underfunded. According to official U.S. estimates, there are "200,000 drug abusers among Uzbekistan's 24 million inhabitants," while in Kazakhstan, although "the official number of drug abusers is approximately 37,408," authorities estimate the real number to be 7 to 8 times higher.[41] Increasing numbers of children (1,946) and women (3,488) were arrested in 2000 for drug abuse.[42] Marijuana and heroin are the drugs most often abused. For its part, the Turkmen ministry of health estimates that approximately 6 to 7 percent of the population use illegal drugs, though, according to the 2001 INCSR, unofficial estimates put the user population at 10 to 11 percent, up from 8 to 9 percent in 2000.[43] In Kyrgyzstan, there is enormous concern that drug addiction and the use of needles will also contribute enormously to the spread of HIV—a further burden on inadequate health services.

---

[40] *International Narcotics Strategy Control Report 2001*, Washington, D.C.: Department of State, March 2002.

[41] *International Narcotics Strategy Control Report 2000*, Washington, D.C.: Department of State, March 2001. For the electronic text, see *www.state.gov/g/inl/rls/nrcrpt/2000/index.cfm?docid=891*.

[42] Ibid.

[43] The lower figure is from the 2000 INSCR report. The higher figure is from the 2001 report.

With this litany of consequences, it is easy to categorize drug trafficking as an unmitigated negative and to ignore the possibility that there are positive consequences—particularly in countries where opportunities in the legal economy are limited and legitimate routes to capital accumulation are few. The drug business provides employment, the importance of which is underlined by the fact that peasants often engage in what can be termed spontaneous crop substitution, moving from other crops into opium cultivation. During the mid-1990s in both Kyrgyzstan and Tajikistan, opium became the one currency that was accepted in countries wracked by widespread poverty. Acknowledging this, however, is not to ignore the reality that drug trafficking provides a potentially important source of revenue for insurgent organizations. Moreover, the drug business can also be a prize of military competition—and under some circumstances the desire for this prize can provoke conflict. Any short-term positives, therefore, are outweighed by the negatives, particularly in the medium and long terms.

The Shadow Economy

The term "shadow economy" is comprehensive. It encapsulates not only illegal or black markets but also the informal economy that helps to provide subsistence and sustenance to ordinary citizens. Barter trade, undeclared second jobs, and economic activity that is not controlled by governments and is not reflected in official government statistics about the economy are the kinds of activity included here. These informal activities are sometimes captured in the notion of the gray—as opposed to the black—market. In most Western countries the shadow economy is a relatively small part of the totality of economic activity. In major advanced economies such as those of Western Europe and the United States, for example, the shadow economy is rarely more than 10 to 15 percent of economic activity. In many developing countries and states in transition, in contrast, the shadow economy is much more important, accounting for a more significant portion of total economic activity. Precisely how important, however, is often difficult to assess, as there are many problems in calculating the size of the shadow economy. Such activity is difficult to assess precisely because it is not open, easily observed, or carefully regulated. Nevertheless, economists and scholars of the transitions in the former Soviet Union have developed various methodologies to use in calculating the size of the shadow economy. The figures here are drawn from a study undertaken by Yair Eilat and Clifford Zinnes, two scholars at Harvard who developed a composite index using a combination of several different methodologies of measurement.[44] The figures in Table 4.1 reflect assessments of the countries of CASC in 1997 and show the size of the shadow economies in relation to the official GDPs. Russia and Ukraine are included as comparisons. Although this assessment is somewhat dated, and it is unlikely that the numbers in Table 4.1 are still valid today, they can be taken as an indication of the situation at that time, the aftereffects of which continue to be felt. Three observations can be made about these figures:

- In Tajikistan and Kyrgyzstan, unofficial economic activity was approximately as large as the formal economy. While not quite as high, in Georgia, Armenia, and Azerbaijan it was close to this level. The figure for Uzbekistan, in contrast, was surprisingly low, but this is consistent with continued government control of economic activity and the slow pace of economic reform at that time.

- Although they conform to international norms regarding GDP assessments, the official figures—by ignoring the shadow economy—no doubt continue to greatly underestimate the extent of economic activity in most of the countries of CASC. In some cases, the inclusion of the shadow economy might effectively double the size of GDP, providing a de facto (as opposed to de jure) assessment. The implication of this, of course, is that the shadow economy—depending on its character and structure— goes at least some way toward alleviating poverty and providing opportunities for the unemployed. It mitigates, even if it does not offset, the economic dislocation that occurred through the 1990s. In other words, there are elements of both safety valve and safety net inherent in these figures.

- The positive consequences cannot be understood without also considering the negatives. The shadow economy is outside the

---

[44]See Yair Eilat and Clifford Zinnes, "The Shadow Economy in Transition Countries: Consequences for Economic Growth and Donor Assistance," on the Internet at *www.hiid.harvard.edu/caer2/htm/content/papers/paper83/paper83.htm.*

taxation system and therefore deprives the state of much-needed revenues that could contribute to the building of state capacity. Moreover, for individuals participating in the informal economy and the gray market, it is a slippery slope to the illegal economy and the black market. Certainly, they are a potential target for criminals seeking new recruits.

Table 4.1

Shadow Economy Size Relative to Official GDP

Country	Shadow Economy Size Relative to Official GDP (percent)
Armenia	78
Georgia	85
Azerbaijan	90
Uzbekistan	13
Kazakhstan	39
Turkmenistan	60
Kyrgyzstan	100
Tajikistan	100
Russia	53
Ukraine	80

Corruption and Rent Seeking

Economists use the term "rent seeking" to cover nonproductive activities that are designed to generate personal wealth. Political corruption comes under this heading. Generally accepted as the use of public office for private gain, corruption is pervasive in the states in CASC. In large part, it is related to forms of government that still place a premium on government control over economic activity, that maintain exclusive and strict control over political and economic life, and that have few checks in place against the use of public office for private gain. As Robert Klitgaard has noted, corruption generally occurs when there is both monopoly and discretion and an absence of accountability.[45]   The states in CASC generally exhibit these conditions.

This is reflected in the rankings contained in the annual Corruption Perception Index issued by Transparency International, an NGO based in Berlin.[46] These rankings generally encompass between 90 and 100 states and go from least to most corrupt. Based on reports by transnational corporations and businessmen subject to requests or demands for bribes, the rankings do not always include all the countries in CASC. When they are included, however, these countries appear near the bottom of the list (among the most corrupt countries). Azerbaijan, for example, appears to have a particularly acute corruption problem. Although its position improved slightly between 1999 and 2001, it comes close to the bottom of the rankings: in 1999 it was ranked 96 of 99 countries; in 2000 it was ranked 87 of 90, on a par with Ukraine and only a little above Nigeria, the lowest country; and in 2001, it was ranked 84. Uzbekistan was ranked 94 in 1999 but improved to 71 in 2001, the same position as Kazakhstan. Armenia generally does a little better than most other countries in CASC, while Kazakhstan has improved its ranking. In 1999 Kazakhstan was ranked 84, along with Georgia, and Kyrgyzstan 87. In spite of the annual variations, the rankings make it consistently clear that the countries of CASC suffer from pervasive and systemic corruption that has debilitating and ultimately destabilizing consequences.

Although corruption in these countries exists at all levels of society, one of its pernicious manifestations is elite corruption and rent seeking. In Kyrgyzstan, for example, parliamentary deputy Zainitdin Kurmanov complained that "only the bureaucrats live well—giving no material benefit to the country but keeping tight controls over all state mechanisms."[47] In Georgia, television correspondent Akaki Gogichaishvili stated that "owing to corruption, the state budget is losing an annual one billion laris from customs. This sum is equal to

---

[45]See, for example, Robert Klitgaard, "International Cooperation Against Corruption," *Finance and Development*, Vol. 35, No. 1 (March 1998), pp. 3–7.

[46]The figures are drawn from the annual TI reports found on *www.transparency.org*.

[47]Igor Grebenshchikov, "Central Asian Leaders Think Alike," *www.iwpr.net/index.pl?archive/rca/rca_200103_45_4_eng.txt*.

the official state budget, which means that Georgia has two budgets—the official one, which is applied to five million citizens, and an unofficial budget, which is exploited by fewer than a hundred high-ranking officials."[48] Rent-seeking behavior is particularly pernicious in that it enriches leaders but not governments. In effect, it places private interests above the collective interest.[49] It can also perpetuate the power of corrupt elites and help them maintain their ruling position with all the attending privileges and perquisites. A good example of this occurred with the Milosevic regime in Serbia. Members of the governing elite maintained monopolies on such basics as oil and food supplies and were able to enrich themselves personally while also consolidating—in the short term—their grip on power. The situation in CASC has not been quite as blatant, but the potential for more ostentatious displays of corruption is clearly present.

The negative consequences of corruption and rent seeking include a reduction in state building capacity, increased gaps between elites and publics, a loss of faith in government and the free market economy, the radicalization of political opposition, and the alienation of youth groups and political activists. In the short term, rent seeking helps to maintain authoritarian regimes in power; in the longer term it can contribute to their collapse. This is not surprising: corruption and rent seeking can have a profoundly alienating impact on the populace—especially when the corruption benefits are concentrated rather than diffused more broadly to ensure a higher degree of support. Another adverse consequence of corruption and rent seeking is an inhibition on foreign investment—something that is crucial to the success of transitional economies because of the deficits in indigenous capacity to finance new ventures. In view of all these negative effects, the overall, long-term impact of corruption and rent seeking is the creation of profound domestic instabilities that can all too easily feed into regime collapse, revolution, or civil war.

---

[48]Quoted in Michael Specter, "Letter from Tbilisi: Rainy Days in Georgia," *New Yorker*, December 18, 2000.

[49]The importance of this point is elucidated very effectively in a different context by William Reno. See his *Warlord Politics and African States,* Boulder: Lynne Rienner, 1999.

Costs and Benefits of Criminalization

Criminalization can be understood in part as coping mechanisms for people in societies and economies that are not working effectively. From this perspective, drug consumption is a means of escape from difficult social and economic conditions; drug cultivation is a means of subsistence; and drug trafficking is an opportunity to become part of a transnational business that provides one of the few forms of regional economic integration in Central Asia. Similarly, organized crime is a form of entrepreneurship, providing economic opportunities, a basis for capital accumulation, and multiplier benefits that would otherwise be absent in economies characterized by slow economic growth or even decline. On occasion, criminal organizations can even be paternalistic, sharing the spoils of their activities, an approach that often results in increased information and support from citizens. Even corruption can be understood as a way of circumventing regulations and allowing things to happen that would otherwise be severely hampered. Low-level corruption by police and other public servants is a form of income augmentation that is essential given the low wages they typically receive. Finally, the informal or shadow economy is a means of subsistence. Shadow economies flourish when, for whatever reason, legal economies are not working effectively in providing jobs and incomes. Indeed, organized crime, drug trafficking, corruption, and shadow economic activity can be understood as symptoms of underlying problems in both political governance and economic management. The presence of these phenomena, particularly on a large scale, is a critical indicator that other things are going wrong. The difficulty, of course, is that they exacerbate the conditions that give rise to them and render the underlying problems even more resistant to solution. The positive aspects of criminalization cannot be ignored, but they are far outweighed by the negatives.

Criminalization has seriously adverse implications for the effective functioning of the economy, for the integrity and legitimacy of the state and its institutions, for public confidence and faith in the transition process, and for the stability of society. Criminal capitalism inhibits the development of legitimate capitalism: it is difficult for legitimate entrepreneurs to compete with organizations that combine a maximum of liquidity with a minimum of accountability. Consequently, drug trafficking and organized crime can have a dampening effect by hampering economic competition, stifling legitimate entrepreneurship, and discouraging foreign investment. In short, illicit capital either frightens off or pushes out licit capital.

Another consequence of drug trafficking and organized crime is the creation of a class of nouveau riche citizens who combine ostentatious wealth with political power. The danger is that in straitened economic circumstances and amidst widespread unemployment, these newly rich will be objects of emulation, with little consideration given to the manner of money making. The obvious result is an increasing number of recruits for drug trafficking and criminal organizations; the less obvious result is the development of a form of economic Machiavellianism in which the end—the accrual of wealth—justifies any means. Once again, licit entrepreneurship is placed at a major disadvantage.

In the final analysis, drug trafficking and organized crime are sources of illegitimate wealth and power, provide an important means of finance for terrorist and insurgency groups, and can spark conflict among rival clans or factions seeking control of lucrative routes and markets. Similarly, corruption undermines the functioning of government and the operation of civil society. High-level rent seeking by political and administrative elites provides personal enrichment at the expense of the state and its citizens. Moreover, the interplay among these phenomena significantly increases their adverse impact—particularly in CASC, where the vulnerability to instability is accentuated by the very nature of the regimes, the lack of state capacity, and the contrast, in many cases, between strong leaders and weak institutions. Indeed, the nature of the regimes in the CASC countries—and the relationship to criminalization—must now be examined.

GOVERNANCE AND CRIMINALIZATION IN CENTRAL ASIA AND SOUTH CAUCASUS

The dynamics of governance in CASC can be understood in terms of two kinds of conditions: sultanistic regimes and contested states (see Chapter Two). The main characteristics of each of these forms of governance are such that they both encourage and facilitate key manifestations of the criminalization syndrome.

Sultanistic Regimes[50]

The notion of a sultanistic regime has particular relevance to the countries of CASC and the way they have evolved since the collapse of the Soviet Union. This becomes obvious from a brief overview of the characteristics of such regimes.[51] Personal rule, a system of fears, rewards, and corruption, arbitrariness, repression, and the juxtaposition of weak institutions and strong leaders are all in evidence, to varying degrees, in most of these states. This system has perhaps gone furthest in Turkmenistan, where the president is known as Turkmenbashi and has developed a clear cult of personality. Karimov in Uzbekistan has gone in the same direction. Even in Kyrgyzstan, which a few years ago appeared to be moving toward greater freedom, President Akaev has consolidated personal power at the expense of democratic reform and the creation of a truly open society. Of course, the sultanistic regime's vulnerability to a succession crisis is magnified in both Central Asia and the South Caucasus because of the age of many of the leaders.

Not surprisingly, sultanistic regimes—as authoritarian regimes elsewhere—are prone to develop alliances with criminal organizations. In Uzbekistan in the mid-1990s, for example, there were three major criminal organizations, and it was common knowledge that each one had a cabinet-level protector.[52] Moreover, criminals provide services for the sultan and his family, offering an unofficial capacity to coerce or eliminate rivals and opponents of the regime. They also offer further opportunities for elite enrichment. Rent seeking by government elites often finds a perfect match in the use of corruption by criminal and drug trafficking organizations seeking to extend their influence into the higher reaches of government. Criminals use corruption to obtain support, protection, information, and knowledge and, in effect, to neutralize the instruments of social control—at least as these instruments apply to their particular criminal activities. Put in systemic terms, drug trafficking and criminal organizations

---

[50]Much of the following discussion was stimulated by Anatol Lieven's review of H.E. Chelabi and Juan J. Linz (eds.), *Sultanistic Regimes*, Baltimore: Johns Hopkins University Press, 1998, posted November 8, 2000 on *www.eurasianet.org*.

[51]Discussed in greater detail in Chapter Two.

[52]See note 13 above.

flourish where state capacity is weak—and in spite of outward appearances, many sultanistic regimes are rooted in weak states. Moreover, criminals have a vested interest in ensuring that the state remains weak or at the very least willing to acquiesce in their activities. There is, in effect, a convergence of the interests of the sultan and his followers on one side and of criminal organizations on the other—in that neither of them wants a political process characterized by widespread legitimacy and accountability and that places collective interests above their private interests.

This is not to suggest that all criminal or drug trafficking organizations have equal importance. Clearly, some of them have far greater access and influence than others. The corollary is that efforts by sultanistic regimes to combat organized crime and drug trafficking will generally be selective, targeted against the criminal organizations not connected with the elite. In effect, the sultan, his family, and the members of his court will seek to combat those criminal activities that they do not control or benefit from through bribery and corruption.

Regimes will also seek to perpetuate the benefits they obtain from their links with organized crime and drug trafficking groups. Moreover, the natural desire of elites to limit the degree of openness in politics and society is likely to be intensified when individual members of the government apparatus who are benefiting from links with criminals wish to ensure that their activities do not become the focus of public and media scrutiny. When organized crime and trafficking is deeply embedded in symbiotic relationships with political elites, the entrenched interests in limiting the emergence of democratic forms of governance are formidable. Indeed, there is a major irony here: the lack of a free press, an effective opposition, and a high degree of transparency greatly weaken the prospects for reducing and containing criminal corruption; yet the regime can use drug trafficking and organized crime as pretexts for authoritarian measures that themselves stifle change. In effect, the political-criminal nexus both benefits from and obstructs the development of transparency in government, one of the key elements of democratic governance.

In the long term, of course, such conditions are highly corrosive—of governance, of institutions, and of the level of public trust. Corruption undermines the effectiveness of law enforcement, the impartiality of the judiciary, and the efficiency and fairness of administration. If a high level of corruption makes it more difficult to establish a civil society based on the rule of law, it also means that eventually, political activism will take other forms. It is at this point that a sultanistic regime can find itself operating what has become a contested state.

Contested States

In contested states, too, organized crime and drug trafficking can become a significant factor in domestic politics. Such states are similar to sultanistic regimes in that the government or regime suffers from a lack of legitimacy, but in a contested polity, control of the state becomes the prize of political competition, in part because of the lucrative rent-seeking opportunities it provides.[53]   The elites are usually divided, and in some cases this coincides or overlaps with ethnic divisions within the country. In these circumstances, tensions among different ethnic groups about the distribution of responsibilities and privileges within politics and society interlink with competition among the elites in ways that are generally destabilizing. Moreover, when there are ethnic agendas that are not being fully satisfied, dissatisfied groups will tend to resort to organized crime activities or drug trafficking to generate the resources necessary to pursue their agendas through campaigns of violence. Within contested states, violence also becomes a continuation of domestic politics by other means, as competing elites seek alliances with the more powerful criminal organizations in an effort to promote their own agendas. There is also an amplifying effect because of competition in the criminal world itself over control of legal markets such as oil and gas as well as illegal markets such as drugs. The dynamics of these cross-cutting alliances exacerbate tensions in both the legitimate and illegitimate worlds and intensify violence and instability in the society. In almost all societies in which they appear, drug traffickers and organized crime challenge the state's possession of an effective monopoly on the use of force within the society. When an ethnically diverse population leads to a fragile sense of nationhood, the chal-

---

[53]Characteristics of contested states are discussed in greater detail in Chapter Two of this report.

lenge is even greater. Local wars, separatist ambitions and movements, and the drug trade are deeply interconnected in pernicious and damaging ways in the countries of CASC. This has been especially true in Tajikistan and Kyrgyzstan, where the drug trade is closely bound up with competing structures of power in society.

Drug trafficking can also be a source of funding for disaffected groups within a society and one that allows them to arm themselves for the struggle against the existing government. In CASC, where several states do not yet command overriding loyalty and support from the population and where drug trafficking and organized crime are pervasive, groups that have separatist ambitions or are otherwise disaffected have a readily available source of funding. Control of drug trafficking routes and markets can be a source of considerable profit and can be seen therefore as a prize that particular ethnic groups or clans are willing to fight for. Areas bedeviled by civil war or ethnic strife sometimes experience increasingly intense fighting as groups vie for control over growing areas, trafficking routes, processing laboratories, or local drug markets. Although the civil war in Tajikistan had complex and multifaceted causes, one of them was control over drug routes.

A corollary is that drug traffickers can take advantage of ethnic strife or civil war to pursue their activities, secure in the knowledge that although they have to transit some difficult areas, they do not have to worry about the threat from government. Perhaps the ideal situation is one in which there is a fragile cease-fire but in which the government has not yet been able to re-establish its power and authority and is unable to implement effective law enforcement activities. Tajikistan has been in this position for a few years, and it is hardly surprising that much of the drug trafficking activity in Central Asia has focused on Tajikistan.

In sum, the dynamics of criminalization feed naturally into both sultanistic regimes and contested states in CASC. Both sets of conditions provide environments in which organized crime and drug trafficking flourish. This is not entirely surprising. Although sultanistic regimes and contested states are in some respects ideal types that, at a superficial glance, appear to be at the opposite ends of a spectrum, in practice they share certain traits. These include the weakness of state structures and institutions, the absence of the rule of law, the lack of accountability (cloaked in secrecy in sultanistic regimes and obscured by chaos in contested states), and the weakness of civil society. One implication of this is that governance in some countries in CASC might involve a hybrid of both types. Another implication is that it is possible for a country to go from one type to the other rather more easily than might be expected. In a contested state, for example, if one clan or faction emerges as the dominant force and is able to subjugate the opposition, it might rapidly develop many of the characteristics of a sultanistic regime. Conversely, sultanistic regimes almost invariably contain the seeds of their own destruction and at some point are likely to be transformed into contested states. In both these eventualities, organized crime and drug trafficking could play a significant role. They could increase domestic instability by creating no-go zones that undermine efforts at governance, by driving out the legal entrepreneurship that is essential to transitional economies, by intensifying divisions among political elites, and by supplying weapons or funding for protest movements and terrorist organizations or insurgencies.

GOVERNANCE, CRIMINALIZATION, AND INSTABILITY IN CENTRAL ASIA AND SOUTH CAUCASUS

In considering the prospects for stability and instability in CASC, regional factors are important in providing a broad assessment. At the same time, variations among states make it necessary to move from the regional to the national level. Accordingly, the analysis now turns to the prospects for instability in several countries, within the framework of sultanistic regimes and contested states outlined above.

The Collapse of Sultanistic Regimes

In considering the prospects for instability in CASC over the next 10 to 15 years, it seems probable that some of the sultanistic regimes in the region will weaken or collapse, resulting in the emergence of more states that are fundamentally contested. It is possible, of course, that sultanistic regimes will prove far more resilient than suggested here—not least because their monopoly on coercive and repressive power compensates for their limited legitimacy. But the inherent long-term weaknesses of sultanistic regimes, juxtaposed with the major trends in the region and particularly the alienation of populations, suggest that there is an inexorable quality about their ultimate collapse—and it is really only a matter of the timing. It also seems clear, as one commentary noted, that when sultanistic regimes die, "they die hard."[54] The collapse is unlikely to be smooth or sudden, and the resulting dislocation will almost certainly be far-reaching as various groups vie for the patronage and privileges that have come with power. As sultanistic regimes begin to collapse, the battle for the spoils that come with leadership will rapidly come to the fore.

Uzbekistan is perhaps the prime candidate for such a contingency. There are several reasons for this:

- Uzbekistan has a corrupt and repressive sultanistic regime that has maintained tight control over significant portions of the country's economy, suppressed political dissent, and responded harshly to any criticism of President Karimov and his government. As one human rights observer has noted, "the escalation of repression has involved the forced displacement of people from their home villages, the indiscriminate use of mines along borders, the organization of 'hate rallies' against 'enemies of the people,' and widespread torture of political prisoners."[55] The regime has almost certainly bought short-term stability through the immediate consolidation of power rather than through transitional processes that offer the prospect of enhanced long-term legitimacy.

- The government has maintained control of rent-seeking opportunities and has also established symbiotic relationships with organized crime. The concentration of corruption has continued, and the regime has done little to establish a wider power base through fuller and more comprehensive distribution of corruption benefits.

---

[54]Anatol Lieven; see note 50.

[55]"Uzbekistan, Kazakhstan . . . : Repression Spreads in Central Asia," *The Times of Central Asia*, February 16, 2000.

- The alienation process that is evident throughout CASC is particularly pronounced in Uzbekistan—and could well take a greater toll there than in some of the other states.

- The use of the threat from Islamic fundamentalism as the main rationale (or rationalization) for government oppression is a short-term expediency—buttressed, of course, by developments since September 11—that could prove highly counterproductive, leading in the longer term to a self-fulfilling prophecy. A militant Islamic movement has a much easier time gaining recruits when the government itself provides reasons for opposition.

- At present there are a few indicators of splits within the elite in Uzbekistan.[56] Although these are limited, they could presage a transition toward a contested state in which rival political factions are allied with rival criminal organizations.

One possibility, of course, is that nascent jealousies and rivalries within the political elite, resulting perhaps from unequal access to the benefits from corruption and rent seeking, will spill over into violence against Karimov and his key supporters. Another kind of split that can occur is between members of the elite and their criminal or drug trafficking allies. Such a development would be evident in contract killings targeted against political figures and criminal bosses. Although this might seem unlikely, it is certainly not out of the question, especially given the brutal nature of competition in the criminal world, the desire of criminal organizations to carve out monopolies, and the tendency to use violence in response to real or imagined slights. Indeed, something like this seems to have occurred in Belgrade prior to the collapse of the Milosevic government—which itself had many of the characteristics of a sultanistic regime. There was a period in which both government figures and organized crime leaders were victims of contract killings. If either kind of split happened in Uzbekistan, the competition could easily take on a dynamic comparable to that in Tajikistan during the early and middle 1990s.

The other possibility in Uzbekistan is of a grassroots opposition movement that gradually obtains sufficient political appeal or mili-

---

[56]Ahmad Rashid, "Central Asia: Trouble Ahead," *Far Eastern Economic Review,* May 9, 2002.

tary power to challenge the regime. The prime candidate here is the Islamic Movement of Uzbekistan (IMU). The IMU represents domestic dissent and concern over the regime's repressive nature, backed by external forces. Prior to the U.S. military campaign in Afghanistan, the IMU appeared to have several characteristics that give it the potential to cause considerable problems for the regime.

Perhaps the IMU's most important asset was Juma Namangani, a charismatic leader who in 1992 was himself the victim of the Karimov regime's repressive policies. In some parts of Uzbekistan as well as Tajikistan, Namangani was a folk hero willing to challenge a government that has been patently unresponsive to both economic needs and basic freedoms of its citizens. The death of Namangani while he fought alongside the Taliban and Al Qaeda in Afghanistan in the fall of 2001 was a huge blow to the IMU.

The introduction of U.S. military forces into Afghanistan and the fall of the Taliban could also erode some of the funding for the IMU. Until the collapse of the Taliban and the flight of Al Qaeda, the IMU appeared to be well placed with respect to resource generation. As a result of developments in late 2001, however, the external funding that the IMU received from the Taliban, Bin Laden, and even the Pakistani intelligence service was obviously disrupted. Although Uzbek Saudis who intensely dislike Karimov and several other Islamic organizations are likely to continue with some funding, resources could be less readily available than they were.[57]

Yet these losses might have a silver lining. The collapse of the Taliban has enabled many Afghan farmers to start cultivating the opium poppy once again without fear of reprisals. Although the United States along with the UN is hoping that the Western presence will provide an opportunity to prevent the resurgence of opium growing, there is a recognition that drug cultivation and trafficking are "so ingrained in the economy of Afghanistan, and the economy is so wrecked, that it's an easy thing for the population to turn back to."[58] Unless eradication efforts are successful, the drug trade could be an

---

[57]Mikhail Falkov, "The Islamic Movement of Uzbekistan" (in Russian), *Moscow Nezavisimaya Gazeta* (Internet Version), August 25, 2000.

[58]U.S. Assistant Secretary of State Rand Beers, quoted in Ed Blanche, "West Turns Attention to Afghan Drugs Trade," *Jane's Intelligence Review*, January 1, 2002.

increasingly important source of funding for the IMU. Indeed, even before the U.S. military involvement, there were frequent reports that the IMU had become a major player in the drug trafficking business, with claims that it was responsible for as much as 70 percent of the heroin and opium moving through Central Asia. One observer even argued that the IMU, although portraying itself as a group fighting for Islam, was "primarily concerned with financial gain" and had "successfully used terrorism to destabilize Central Asia to maintain and secure narcotics transportation routes."[59] These allegations have to be treated with some caution, having come primarily from governments in Kyrgyzstan and Uzbekistan intent on stigmatizing and discrediting any opposition. At the same time, it would not be surprising to learn that the IMU had engaged in drug trafficking directly or imposed taxes on the traffickers. Such behavior would certainly be consistent with insurgencies elsewhere—and is likely to be more significant than before, given that other funding flows have been interrupted or dried up.

The IMU has two additional assets that speak against writing it off. The first is a safe haven in the Pamir mountains.[60] The importance of a sanctuary or safe haven for an insurgency or protest movement is well understood to be critically important. In this case, it continues to provide opportunities for recruitment and replenishment as well as a safe base from which to move into Uzbekistan when weather conditions permit and other circumstances are favorable. The second asset is the underlying alienation of the population: the IMU benefits considerably because it is the most obviously available funnel for the political, social, and economic dissatisfaction existing in Uzbekistan. In spite of the setbacks suffered by the IMU in late 2001 and early 2002, it could ultimately prove resilient enough to become a formidable adversary for the Karimov regime, particularly if the regime continues to use its existence to justify even more repression.[61] One possible scenario is that the IMU will actually

---

[59]Tamara Makarenko, "Crime and Terrorism in Central Asia," *Jane's Intelligence Review,* Vol. 12, No. 7, July 1, 2000.

[60]Ahmen Rashid, "Pamirs Offer IMU Secure Base," *Eurasia Insight,* August 12, 2001.

[61]Gregory Gleason, "Counterinsurgency in Central Asia: Civil Society is the First Casualty," January 8, 2001, *www.eurasianet.org/departments/recaps/articles/eav092200.shtml.*

trigger government measures that are so unpopular they provoke even more opposition. Although the IMU still has to go beyond seasonal military activity and mobilize grassroots support that can challenge the regime and provide a viable political alternative, such a development is certainly not out of the question over the next 10 or 15 years. It is worth bearing in mind the old adage about insurgency movements (and the IMU, in spite of U.S. categorization, is far better understood as an insurgent movement than a terrorist group) that if they can avoid defeat in the short term, they have a reasonable prospect of securing victory in the long term.

At the same time there is no guarantee of such an outcome. Indeed, there is an alternative scenario very different from either of the instability scenarios. Sultanistic regimes, for all their shortcomings and weaknesses, can prove more resilient and enduring than suggested above. It is possible that Karimov has sufficient control over his repressive forces to maintain himself in power with relative ease.

Perhaps the most intriguing and important issue concerns U.S. military involvement in the region (as well as the involvement of the international community more broadly)—and its impact on the plausibility of these very different scenarios.

On the one hand, international involvement might provide opportunities to do something about the drug trade, especially if plans for cultivating alternative crops are implemented with any degree of success. This would probably result in some reduction in criminalization in the region and would certainly make it more difficult for the IMU to maintain its funding. On the other hand, both a military presence and an international aid presence provide new markets and new opportunities to generate criminal proceeds. The commercial sex trade, for example, which is largely controlled by organized crime, generally receives a boost from the insertion of a large foreign presence.

Perhaps the more serious issues, though, concern the relationship between the United States and the sultanistic regimes in the region, especially that of Uzbekistan. As the International Crisis Group has noted,

> Far too often, the region's nondemocratic leadership has made repression its instrument of choice for dealing with religion and

civil society as a whole, thus creating greater public sympathy for groups whose agendas, methods and rhetoric are deeply troubling. There is a danger that the international community, in its understandable eagerness to combat terrorism, will give the regions' governments a free hand to continue and expand repression of all groups that are viewed as political threats—a dynamic that will only boomerang and further destabilize the region over time.[62]

Unqualified support for the Karimov regime that allows it to perpetuate repressive policies would buy short-term stability at a high price. It would involve a loss of legitimacy for the United States that, in turn, could intensify an impending legitimacy crisis for the Karimov regime. The Bush Administration needs to be sensitive to the possibility that—as with Iran in the 1970s—U.S. support for an unpopular regime could be the kiss of death.

It is clear that increased U.S. economic assistance has been the price to pay for Uzbekistan's support for U.S. military actions in Afghanistan. Yet there are also opportunities for U.S. policy. Support for Uzbekistan that is made conditional upon economic liberalization and more serious moves toward democracy and respect for individual rights offers some prospect for engineering reform. The danger here, however, is that this process will weaken the regime's coercive power while doing little to increase its legitimacy and authority.

The Escalation or Resurgence of Violence in Contested States

Tajikistan is at the other end of the spectrum. During the 1990s it was clearly a failed state, wracked by a civil war driven by a complex mixture of religion, ideology, clan rivalry, and greed. At least one component in the war was the struggle for control of drug routes and markets. The cessation of hostilities in 1997 brought into being a fragile peace in what remained an intensely competitive state. The continued enmities and divisions in Tajikistan have been intensified by a collapsing infrastructure and a continued decline in living standards. An important spark to what remains a highly combustible mixture could well be provided (albeit inadvertently) by future de-

---

[62]*The IMU and the Hizb-ut-Tahrir: Implications of the Afghanistan Campaign.*

velopments in Afghanistan. If the international community succeeds in reducing opium production in Afghanistan, then it is likely that a form of geographical displacement will occur, with some of the neighboring countries making up the shortfall. The prime candidate for this—partly because of geography and partly because of the weakness of the government—is Tajikistan. As suggested above, there is already some cultivation and processing in Tajikistan, and Tajiks are playing a major role in drug trafficking to Russia. The implications of deepening Tajik involvement in the drug industry could be far-reaching. Almost certainly there would be intense competition for control of cultivation areas, processing facilities, and trafficking routes. As a result, fierce and violent competition among rival warlords would probably result in yet another outbreak of civil war. Rather than being a period of postwar reconstruction, the present peace could simply be an interlude between two periods of intense fighting.

Another country providing a potential flashpoint is Georgia. Although President Shevardnadze has been an important unifying and calming influence, the country still has numerous problems that could all too easily degenerate into political instability. Criminal control over large sectors of the economy combines with corruption and widespread disillusionment and disaffection among the population to provide a potentially combustible mixture. In spite of continued Western aid, therefore, it would not be surprising if Georgia became a contested state without a viable and effective government—particularly after Shevardnadze ceases being the president. Once again the United States is in danger of supporting a regime with a low level of legitimacy. Although the United States has understandably agreed to help Georgia deal with Chechen rebels in the Pankisi Gorge, there are dangers in a longer-term commitment. In a contested or potentially contested state, U.S. military involvement could all too easily become a rallying cry for those forces opposing the existing government.

None of this is intended to suggest that Georgia, Tajikistan, and Uzbekistan provide the only potential for failed states in CASC. The analysis of the potential for collapse and instability in these states is intended to be illustrative rather than exhaustive. Kyrgyzstan, for example, has been identified by the International Crisis Group as a potential flashpoint.[63]

CONCLUSIONS

The war against the Taliban and U.S. military involvement in the region introduced additional elements of uncertainty into the evolving situation in CASC. Yet many of the underlying long-term realities remain starkly unchanged. One of these is widespread poverty. Although the recent trends toward rapid economic growth in several countries in CASC are promising—and suggest that formal economic activity might eventually become as important and dynamic as the illegal and informal versions—the overall prospects for large segments of the populations remain dismal. Not surprisingly, therefore, organized crime, corruption, and the alienation of people from their governments continue to provide a volatile mixture that could easily explode into violence and instability in particular countries. This was temporarily obscured by September 11, which allowed existing regimes to play the "Islamic card" with the United States sooner and with far more effect than would otherwise have been possible. Requests for financial and military assistance cast in terms of combating the forces of Islamic fundamentalism, and particularly associated terrorism, naturally found a receptive ear in Washington. The underlying reality, however, is that the policies of some of the regimes are doing much to galvanize support for fundamentalism, as well as the continued growth of organized crime and drug trafficking. The exigencies of the war in Afghanistan meant that these problems could, in the short term, be ignored. In the longer term, however, the United States may not have this luxury.

---

[63]See International Crisis Group, *Central Asia: Crisis Conditions in Three States, www.intlcrisisgroup.org/projects/showreport.cfm?reportid=291*, August 2000.

Chapter Five

NATURAL RESOURCES AND POTENTIAL CONFLICT IN THE CASPIAN SEA REGION
Sergej Mahnovski

INTRODUCTION

Since the collapse of the Soviet Union, the petroleum-endowed states of Central Asia and South Caucasus have sought, with varying degrees of success, to attract foreign direct investment in their respective energy sectors, with the hope of securing a steady stream of revenues and bolstering their political legitimacy. Hamstrung by their landlocked geographic position, decaying infrastructure, and non-cash-paying neighbors, the Caspian Sea littoral states have struggled with the issue of how to profit from their remote fossil fuel reserves in a practical and timely manner. As petroleum revenues increase in the next 10–20 years, each of these states will be faced with increasing expectations for improved standards of living from their populations and internal competition over the distribution of this wealth, with potential long-term social dislocations resulting from natural resource-based economic growth. The energy picture is further complicated by divergent claims to the scarce water resources in the region, which are a critical element in both regional energy trade and long-term agricultural plans for many states.

The potential contribution of natural resources to armed conflict in the Caspian Sea region must be placed in the context of existing grievances and aspirations of the former Soviet states, as developed in the other chapters of this report. History has shown that a heavy reliance on extractive industries can lead to severe political and economic pathologies that can be precursors to civil conflict. At the same time, the development of oil and gas resources provides a unique window of opportunity for the Caspian energy producers to modernize their economies and gain political clout. Whether the Caspian leaders have the political will and ability to husband their indigenous resources for the long-term benefit and stability of their societies is unclear.

FOSSIL FUEL PRODUCTION IN THE CASPIAN SEA REGION[1]

Crude Oil

Today, the combined crude oil production in the Caspian Sea region is recovering from a period of stagnation in the early 1990s. At peak output, the Caspian Sea region is forecasted to contribute approximately 3 to 4.5 percent of total world crude oil production, and 6 to 9 percent of non-OPEC crude oil production, as illustrated in Figures 5.1 and 5.2, respectively.[2] These forecasts do not include Russian or Iranian sectors of the Caspian Sea, which are not expected to contribute substantially to total Caspian production.

Six projects—Kashagan, Tengiz, Karachaganak, Azeri-Chirag-Guneshli, Shah-Daniz, and the Severnyi block—contain approximately 68 percent of the region's 39.4 billion barrels of liquid reserves. According to forecasts based on *existing* discoveries, oil production in the region will be dominated by Kazakhstan and Azerbaijan, and it will likely plateau in the 2010–2015 time frame, as illustrated in Figure 5.3. Future exploration successes could push the eventual decline in production beyond 2020. Azerbaijan, once thought to be the linchpin of future Caspian oil exports, is increasingly seen by energy analysts as a natural gas producer, following a

---

[1] For this chapter, Caspian Sea fossil fuel *production* forecasts are based on analysis by the Wood Mackenzie consulting agency: Hilary McCutcheon and Richard Osbon, "Discoveries Alter Caspian Regional Energy Potential," *Oil & Gas Journal*, December 17, 2001. Domestic Caspian fossil fuel *consumption* forecasts are from: Robert Smith, "Politics, Production Levels to Determine Caspian Area Energy Export Options," *Oil & Gas Journal*, May 28, 2001.

[2] World and non-OPEC production forecasts are from Energy Information Administration's *International Energy Outlook 2001*, March 2001, p. 42. Caspian state-level production scenarios are from Robert Smith, "Politics, Production Levels. . . ."

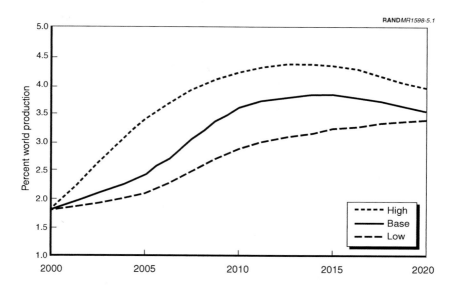

Figure 5.1—Caspian Contribution to World Crude Oil Production

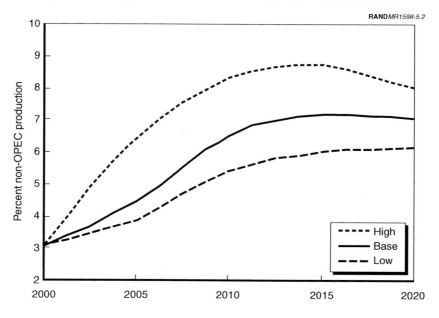

Figure 5.2—Caspian Contribution to Non-OPEC Crude Oil Production

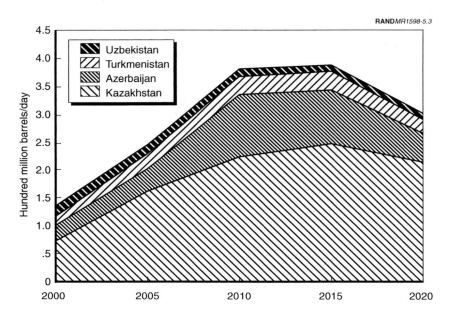

Figure 5.3—Caspian Crude Oil Production Forecasts

string of disappointments in exploratory drilling in 2000 and 2001. In light of successful exploration efforts in the Kashagan field since 2000, Kazakhstan is forecasted to be the dominant regional producer and exporter of crude oil over the next two decades.

Macroeconomic and demographic developments in the region will affect export potential primarily through the growth in domestic consumption. For example, Turkmenistan's share of Caspian (non-Russian and Iranian) export potential, as shown in Figure 5.4, will steadily decrease from 7 percent to approximately 4 percent in 2020. By 2005, Uzbekistan is expected to become a net importer of crude oil, importing almost 150,000 barrels per day (b/d) by 2020.

NATURAL GAS

Caspian gas production, based on existing discoveries, will also reach a peak in the 2010–2015 time frame, driven by projects in Kazakhstan's Karachaganak, Tengiz, and Kashagan projects, as illustrated

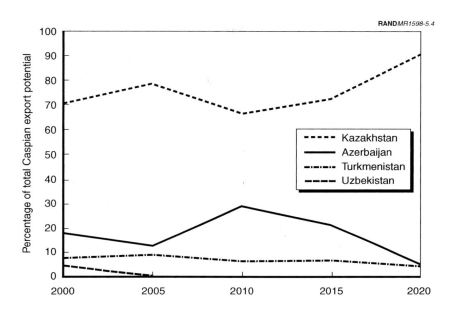

Figure 5.4—Caspian Crude Oil Export Potential Forecasts

in Figure 5.5. In the near term, the lion's share of Caspian natural gas export potential will come from Turkmenistan, with Uzbekistan's production share declining rapidly in the next decade, as shown in Figure 5.6. Although Uzbekistan will still be a major regional producer of natural gas for some time, its export potential will become insignificant by 2005 because of its high levels of domestic consumption, as the most populous state in the region. Azerbaijan's export potential will depend greatly on successes in the Shah Daniz project.

One important caveat in this analysis is that these figures represent production forecasts, which are highly dependent on assumptions about producers' actions in matching supply and demand. This is particularly relevant for both Turkmen and Uzbek estimates, where great uncertainty remains in the viability of export options. For example, Uzbek gas production will probably reflect domestic demand more than theoretical production capability, while Turkmen gas production will depend on securing Turkish and Far Eastern markets.

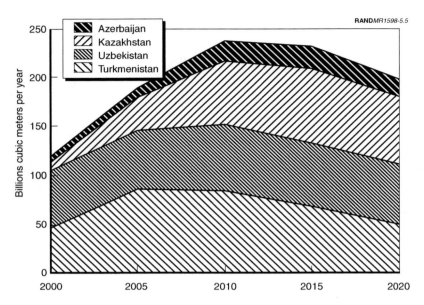

Figure 5.5—Caspian Natural Gas Production Forecasts

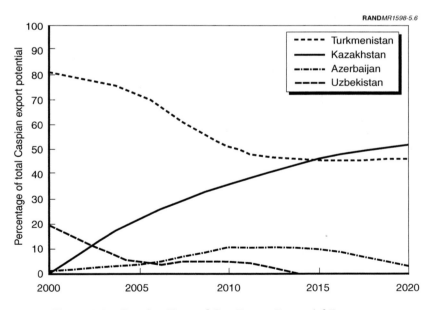

Figure 5.6—Caspian Natural Gas Export Potential Forecasts

FOSSIL FUEL TRANSPORT TO MARKETS

Although they face similar obstacles, such as low domestic demand and high transportation costs to foreign markets, crude oil and natural gas producers must consider fundamentally different transportation options. With the exception of large markets with overland routes, such as China, potential crude oil pipeline expansions would likely terminate at high-capacity ports with access to international waterways in the Black Sea, Persian Gulf, Mediterranean Sea, and possibly the Indian Ocean. In contrast, natural gas pipelines would lead directly to regional hubs near demand centers, since large-scale maritime transport is impossible without capital-intensive liquefaction plants. Existing and proposed oil and gas pipelines are illustrated in Figure 5.7.

CRUDE OIL

Current Transport Options

Today, the existing transport options for Caspian oil are dominated by Russian-European pipelines, seaborne exports from Black Sea terminals, and low-volume swaps with Iran. The Black Sea terminals include the Russian ports of Novorossiysk (with a maximum capacity of 680,000 b/d) and Tuapse (200,000 b/d), the Ukranian port of Odessa (200,000 b/d), and the Georgian ports of Supsa (200,000 b/d) and Batumi (70,000 b/d). To reach the Mediterranean Sea and beyond, tankers must pass through the increasingly congested straits of the Bosphorus, posing a potential environmental threat to Turkey and the Black Sea littoral states. Kazakhstan exports have relied on an existing pipeline to Samara, Russia (200,000 b/d), where Kazakh crude is blended with West Siberian crudes, ultimately arriving at Russian terminals on the Black Sea, or to European markets via the Druzhba pipeline. Kazakhstan has also engaged in low-volume oil swaps with Iran, whereby Kazakhstan transports oil via barge to northern Iranian terminals and refineries, while Iran sells an equivalent[3] amount of oil from its Persian Gulf terminals to world markets. With the recent construction of the Caspian Pipeline Consortium

---

[3]This is modified somewhat by Iranian markups for lower Kazakh crude oil quality.

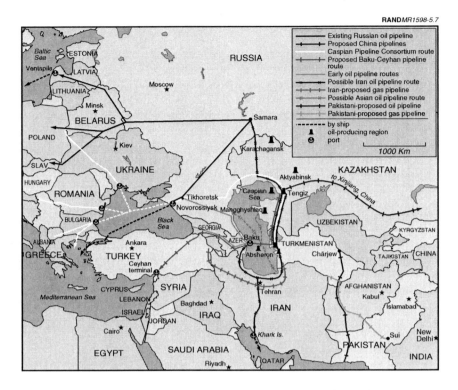

Figure 5.7—Oil and Natural Gas Existing and Proposed Pipelines (EIA)

(CPC) pipeline from Tengiz to Novorossiysk, Kazakhstan will enjoy the most diversified export options among Caspian nations. Azeri oil relies on a "western route" from Baku to Supsa, and a "northern route" from Baku to Novorossisyk, for which a bypass was recently built to avoid the risks associated with transit through Chechnya.

Medium Term (until 2005)

The most pivotal decision regarding Caspian liquids transport over the next several years concerns the construction of a "main export pipeline" to accommodate the bulk of increased production capacity from Kazakhstan and Azerbaijan over the next two decades. Azerbaijan, Georgia, Turkey, and the United States have supported the construction of the Baku-Tbisli-Ceyhan (BTC) pipeline, a transportation option that would bypass Russian and Iranian territory altogether. As originally envisioned, it would begin in Baku, Azerbaijan, pass through Georgia and eastern Turkey, and terminate at the Mediterranean port of Ceyhan, Turkey. This route would offer Azerbaijan more export flexibility, generate transit revenues for Turkey and Georgia, stem tanker traffic through the Bosphorus and Dardanelles, and prevent Russia and Iran from exerting added influence in the Caspian crude oil market. Russia, Iran, Armenia, and some energy analysts in the United States and elsewhere have criticized the BTC plan for being a politically inspired and economically unviable route.

Recent disappointments with dry wells in the Azerbaijani sector have made Kazakhstan's participation potentially critical to the future success of the project. Kazakh crude, transported by tanker or pipeline from Tengiz to Baku to supplement Azeri crude, would help ensure the economic viability of the project by reducing the risks from potential Azeri production shortfalls.[4] It is expected that the BP-led Azerbaijan International Operating Company (AIOC)[5] will make a decision after it reviews the results of a twelve-month detailed engineering study to be completed by June 2002, determines the extent of Kazakhstan's commitment in crude oil shipments to Baku, and secures assistance from U.S. government lending agencies such as the Export-Import Bank and the Overseas Private Investment Corp. Recent comments by U.S. Deputy Secretary of State Richard Armitage[6] and President Bush's waiver of economic sanctions[7] against Azerbaijan certainly bode well for the project.

---

[4]The BTC project will hereafter be referred to as the TBTC project.

[5]AIOC is a consortium of 10 major oil companies and the State Oil Company of Azerbaijan (SOCAR).

[6]Although he has not explicitly stated that the United States would play any financial role in the development of the BTC pipeline, Armitage said at a U.S.-Azerbaijan Chamber of Commerce meeting on March 7, 2002, that he expects the pipeline to be completed by 2005 and on budget. Maureen Lorenzetti, "Iran Should Not Interfere with Caspian Interests, Top U.S. Official Says," *Oil & Gas Journal Online*, March 8, 2002.

[7]On January 25, 2002, President Bush signed a waiver of Section 907 of the Freedom Support Act to end restrictions on U.S. economic assistance to Azerbaijan, which was approved by Congress in October 1992 during the Nagorno-Karabakh conflict with Armenia. Although the waiver was initiated most directly to enlist Azeri support for U.S. efforts to fight international terrorism, energy analysts view it as a prelude to U.S.

Technical analyses performed by AIOC and its contractors concerning the TBTC pipeline are not available in the public domain. However, several consulting agencies, under the auspices of the European Union's Tacis INOGATE program,[8] have published a comparison of nine different export options for Caspian oil to the European market.[9] The clear winner, in terms of lowest total transportation costs (20.2 euro/ton), would involve transporting Tengiz crude via a trans-Caspian pipeline to Baku, where Azeri crude would be added, followed by a pipeline route to Supsa on the Georgian Black Sea coast, parallel to the existing early-oil pipeline. Transport from Supsa to Trieste would be via tanker, crossing the Turkish straits. This option is vehemently opposed by Turkey, on the grounds that more tanker traffic would increase the probability of an oil spill or other accident within the overcrowded Turkish straits. The second-best (23.6 euro/ton) and third-best (24.1 euro/ton) options involve tanker transport from Supsa to the western shores of the Black Sea, followed by various pipeline routes on the European continent. The TBTC pipeline is the fourth-best option (24.8 euro/ton), but it has the advantage of being the only option under consideration that involves absolutely no transport through the Turkish straits or within the Black Sea itself. This option is clearly favored by the Turkish government.

In the meantime, before a main export pipeline is built, the CPC pipeline from Tengiz to Novorossiysk will accommodate additional Kazakh oil streams. Kazakhstan and Turkmenistan will increase their oil swaps with Iran. The well-developed gathering, refining, and distribution infrastructure in northern Iran will be able to handle increases in Kazakh and Turkmen crude for refining into products for domestic use, up to a point. Iran is unwilling to accept more than approximately 500,000 b/d of Kazakh and Turkmen crude, since further imports would involve major investments in refinery infrastruc-

---

support of the TBTC pipeline. "US Waives Economic Sanctions Against Azerbaijan," *Alexander's Gas and Oil Connections*, Vol. 7, Issue 4, February 21, 2002.

[8]Tacis = Technical Assistance to the Commonwealth of Independent States; INOGATE = Interstate Oil and Gas Transports to Europe.

[9]Orhan Degermenci, "EU Study of Caspian Area Oil, Gas Pipelines Compares Routes, Costs," *Oil & Gas Journal*, Vol. 99.45, November 5, 2001.

ture, which is tailored for domestic crude oil quality.[10] Furthermore, the capacity of the oil pipeline between Iran's Caspian terminal at Neka and a refinery complex in Tehran is limited to about 370,000 b/d.

Russian exports through the Black Sea are not expected to increase substantially, unless intensive exploration and production efforts in the nascent Russian sector of the Caspian shelf prove successful. However, Russia will have access to a deepwater terminal in the Mediterranean by 2003, making exports to the United States and Asian Pacific Rim much more economical than shipments from Novorossiysk, which are limited to 150,000 deadweight ton (dwt) vessels (Suezmax size and smaller) because of restrictions through Turkey's Bosphorus Straits.[11] By 2003, the Druzhba-Adria pipeline system will have an initial capacity of approximately 100,000 b/d.

Longer Term (2005–2010)

Growing demand in Russia, Ukraine, and Belarus may divert some Russian oil away from Black Sea routes, unless substantial discoveries are made in the Russian sector of the Caspian shelf. Furthermore, the Druzhba-Adria pipeline system, reaching a capacity of 300,000 b/d by 2013, will be able to transport some Caspian crude via the Odessa-Brody pipeline system.[12] Ukraine, Romania, and Bulgaria have substantial slack in refining capacity, and are actively looking to secure feedstock from the Caspian via Bosphorus bypass routes such as Burgas-Alexandroupolis, Burgas-Vlore, or Romania-Trieste. The upgrading of the Baku-Supsa pipeline would help support these bypass routes, while the construction of TBTC might obviate the need for them, since it would direct Caspian oil straight to the

---

[10]Robert Smith, "Politics, Production Levels . . . ."

[11]As a result of Ukrainian ratification of a tariff agreement, Russian Urals blend will flow through 1,987 miles of pipeline from Samara (Russia), via Belarus, Ukraine, Slovakia, Hungary, and Croatia, terminating at the Adriatic port of Omisalj. However, the existing pipeline from Omisalj to Sisak must be reversed, for approximately $120 million. The port of Omisalj will be able to handle 500,000 dwt (ultra large crude carriers—ULCCs) tankers. Source: "Tariff Accord Clears Way for Russian Oil Exports Through Med," *Oil & Gas Journal*, Vol. 100.9, March 4, 2002, p. 64.

[12]"Tariff Accord Clears Way for Russian Oil Exports Through Med," *Oil & Gas Journal*, Vol. 100.9, March 4, 2002, p. 64.

Mediterranean. Pipelines through Iran or Afghanistan will depend on highly uncertain political developments, while routes to China are thought to be economically unfeasible under current circumstances.

NATURAL GAS

The most salient difference between oil and gas markets today is that gas markets are almost entirely regional, due to prohibitively high transportation costs.[13] In fact, many energy analysts believe that approximately one-half of the natural gas reserves in the world are currently "stranded"—economically or technically unfeasible to transport to existing markets with today's technologies. Abundant gas reserves in many parts of the world are either flared or reinjected into oil wells to boost reservoir pressure, rather than transported to markets, due to the high capital costs associated with natural gas pipeline construction and operation.

Because of limited domestic demand and chronic payment problems, Caspian states with abundant gas reserves are concentrating on transporting their gas to lucrative foreign markets. However, natural gas pipeline transport involves a careful matching of forecasted supply and demand.[14] Whereas crude oil and other liquid products can be transported by some combination of rail, truck, or ship without major processing, natural gas must be compressed, liquefied, or chemically transformed to take advantage of nonpipeline transport. Although there are other options for "monetizing" stranded gas, as illustrated in Table 5.1, the most realistic options for utilizing most of the Caspian gas in the near to medium term involve pipeline transport.

---

[13]It is thought that the evolution of a more robust liquefied natural gas (LNG) trade will tend to link regional markets more closely in the long term. In particular, improvements in LNG technologies and increased capacity in maritime transport and infrastructure will allow for shorter-term contracts that more closely reflect piped natural gas costs.

[14]Since the energy density of natural gas is low relative to crude oil, the opportunities for storage are more limited. Natural gas can also be stored within the pipeline itself by increasing pipeline pressure up to a limit, but this strategy is only feasible for transient mismatching of supply and demand.

Table 5.1

Options for Monetizing Stranded Natural Gas

Method	Advantage	Disadvantage
Dedicated pipeline	• Lucrative foreign markets • Control over exports	• High capital cost • Transit fees eat up profit
Liquefied natural gas (LNG)	• Can reach distant, overseas markets • Europe has established LNG regasification capability/infrastructure • Usually involves long-term contracts, offering possible hedge against daily price fluctuations	• High capital cost • Best if near open-water coast with established maritime infrastructure • Safety and Bosphorus problem
Electricity generation	• Transport over existing wires • Utilize slack in system: many natural gas plants in FSU switched from natural gas to fuel oil, but could switch back, with some modifications	• Significant investment in plants and transmission to implement on a large scale • Local markets saturated quickly • Neighboring states are typically noncash customers
Synthetic fuels (i.e., Fischer-Tropsch Diesel)	• Can use an existing crude oil pipeline, or a variety of standard liquid transport options (i.e., rail, ship, truck) • Hedge against low gas prices (which translates to cheap feedstock)	• High capital cost • Low demand for high-quality synthetic fuels in region (greater potential in Europe)
Chemicals (i.e., methanol, ammonia, dimethyl ether, hydrogen)	• Potentially higher-value products • Hedge against low gas prices	• High capital cost • Limited domestic demand, still needs to be transported • Price fluctuations and tough competition

The primary export markets for Caspian gas will be Russia, Ukraine, and Turkey, followed by southeast Europe, and then more remote possibilities in Pakistan, India, and China. It is highly unlikely that any Caspian gas would ever reach the United States, since liquefaction is probably not a realistic option for Caspian gas.

Western Markets

The Turkish gas market has been coveted by all Caspian natural gas producers, not only because of burgeoning Turkish demand, but also because it could serve as a non-Russian gateway to European markets.[15]   However, many independent energy analysts believe that Turkish forecasts of natural gas demand have been overstated, since they depend on optimistic scenarios for the construction of a large number of natural gas–fired electrical generation plants. As a result, it is believed that the Turkish market will not be able to accommodate all of the interested regional suppliers. Despite Turkish economic problems, the remaining underwater portion of the Blue Stream gas pipeline from Russia will probably be constructed,[16] with Russia exporting natural gas directly to Turkey sometime in 2002–2003.[17] Supplies from Azerbaijan and Iran will probably saturate the Turkish market, rendering the proposed Trans-Caspian pipeline from Turkmenistan unrealistic.[18]

In the short to medium term, Turkmenistan will continue to rely on Russian and Iranian infrastructure to transport its natural gas to foreign markets. Since Russia itself is a major natural gas exporter, this strategy might not be sustainable for Turkmenistan if Russia decides

---

[15]Currently, the main transmission line between Europe and the western Anatolian peninsula originates in Russia, passes through Ukraine and Moldova, runs along the western coast of the Black Sea in Romania and Bulgaria to Istanbul, and terminates in Ankara. The direction of flow is from Russia to Turkey. Its length is 1,257 kilometers, with a total capacity of 8.6–8.7 billion cubic meters per year (bcm/year), with expansion plans up to 20 bcm/year under way. *Black Sea Energy Survey*, IEA, 2000.

[16]See Chapter Seven of this report.

[17]Robert M. Cutler, "The Blue Stream Gas Project: Not a Pipe Dream Anymore," *Alexander's Gas & Oil Connections*, Vol. 6, Issue 16, August 28, 2001.

[18]Bhamy Shenoy and William James, "Caspian Energy Exports: Turkmenistan Fumbling Opportunities Afforded by Trans-Caspian Pipeline," *Oil & Gas Journal*, May 28, 2001.

to charge prohibitively high transit fees or simply refuses to transport Turkmen gas. Furthermore, Ukraine, a significant market for Turkmen gas, is indebted to Turkmenistan and pays for its gas partly in barter trade instead of hard currency. Turkmenistan's failure to secure a trans-Caspian route and consequent dependence on Russian and Iranian infrastructure has led it to explore riskier options on the eastern market.

Caspian gas will have a difficult time penetrating the European market. Recent movement toward gas deregulation in Europe, LNG cost reductions by North African competitors, and the potential emergence of competitors from the Middle East will tend to depress gas prices. Furthermore, even substantial improvements in the infrastructure to accommodate this gas will not free the Caspian states from their dependence on Turkey and Russia as gateways to the European market. Still, Europe's desire to diversify its supply in the wake of declining North Sea production, the decommissioning of nuclear power plants in Germany in favor of gas-fired plants, and tougher EU regulations on double-hulled LNG tankers could benefit Caspian gas.

Eastern Markets

Although China remains a potential long-term market for Kazakh gas reserves, the volumes of reserves are too low and the transit distance to the western provinces too great for the foreseeable future. In the near to medium term, Russian supplies from western and eastern Siberia and Sakhalin Island are the most promising candidates for the Far Eastern market.

One potential solution to Turkmenistan's stranded gas problem is the large market in India. However, the necessary pipeline routes would have to traverse either Iran or Afghanistan, and then Pakistan, in order to reach India.[19] As a result, India is hesitant to depend on

---

[19]A gas pipeline terminating in Pakistan is probably not an option, since Pakistan has enough gas reserves to satisfy its domestic consumption needs for approximately 18 years. Rather, Pakistan would benefit from transit fee revenues amounting to approximately $600 million/year, and an option to purchase the piped gas, if one was built with India as the final destination. Source: Hassaan Vahidy and Fereidun

Turkmen gas because Pakistan would be able to control the through-put. Iran and India have discussed the possibility of transporting LNG from Iran's South Pars gas field by tanker, or of constructing a deepwater offshore gas pipeline to bypass Pakistan.[20] However, U.S. sanctions against Iran would preclude American participation and potentially constrain international involvement in the exploration of Iranian fields and the construction of appropriate infrastructure.

From October 1997 to December 4, 1998,[21] Unocal had served as the development manager of the seven-member Central Asian Gas (CentGas) pipeline consortium, whose purpose was to evaluate and potentially participate in the construction of a gas pipeline from Turkmenistan to India via Afghanistan and Pakistan. Civil war, low oil prices, and public pressure over the Taliban's human rights record led to Unocal's withdrawal from the consortium. After Unocal's decision and the victory of the Taliban, the Afghanistan pipeline option had been considered untenable by major energy companies.

In the wake of the September 11 attacks on the United States, it is too early to tell how developments in the region will unfold, and whether the United States will fundamentally review its sanctions and energy policies in the region. Some analysts have argued that a rebuilding of Afghanistan's infrastructure, with a Turkmenistan-Afghanistan-Pakistan-India natural gas pipeline at its heart, could be a powerful incentive for peace in the region.[22] However, it is not clear whether the construction of such a pipeline would actually increase the pos-sibilities of sabotage and extortion from local power centers within Afghanistan. President Niyazov of Turkmenistan and Afghanistan's interim leader Hamid Karzai have expressed interest in reviving

---

Fesharaki, "Pakistan's Gas Discoveries Eliminate Import Need," *Oil & Gas Journal*, Volume 100.4, June 28, 2002, pp. 24–34.

[20]Fiona Hill and Regine Spector, *The Caspian Basin and Asian Energy Markets*, Conference Report No. 8, Washington, D.C.: The Brookings Institution, September 2001.

[21]The official Unocal statement concerning its withdrawal from the consortium is available on its web site: *www.unocal.com/uclnews/98news/centgas.htm*.

[22]David Young, "Mideast Political Changes Seen Creating Oil Opportunities," *Oil & Gas Journal*, October 1, 2001, p. 30.

these plans, albeit with a different group of investors.[23] In addition to pipelines, Afghanistan and Turkmenistan have discussed investments in highways and electricity infrastructure between the two nations.[24] Whether major energy companies and financial institutions would be willing to gamble in such a politically and militarily unstable setting is highly uncertain at this time.

Other Options for Natural Gas?

In time, improvements in regional economic performance and domestic payment, elimination of distribution losses, and the growth of natural gas as an electric-generation fuel will create more robust natural markets within the Caspian region itself. Although lucrative export markets in major industrialized countries would provide the most promising revenue sources, there are other options for nations, such as Turkmenistan, that have heretofore failed to secure sufficient transport capacity and diversity in light of their sizable resources. Apart from pipeline transport to foreign markets, stranded natural gas can be "monetized" by physical or chemical transformation, followed by more flexible modes of transportation.

Physical transformation involves compression or liquefaction in order to facilitate transport via truck, rail, or ship. Liquefied natural gas is an important source of energy in parts of East Asia, but it entails significant capital investments in ports and liquefaction facilities by the supplier, and regasification facilities by the recipients. This option is typically pursued by coastal nations without feasible overland demand centers and so is not a serious option for land-locked Caspian nations.

Natural gas can also be chemically transformed, which would entail supplying something other than natural gas. One method is to generate electricity in a natural gas–fired power plant and then transport the energy by transmission line. There is some slack in the current electricity generation system in the region, which is composed of

---

[23]Gulshen Ashirova, "Trans-Afghan Pipeline Project a Reality?" *The Times of Central Asia Online*, February 27, 2002.

[24]"Afghan, Turkmen Officials Discuss Electricity and Gas Cooperation," Associated Press, February 12, 2002.

Soviet-built power plants that burn fuel oil, after having substituted away from natural gas during the supply disruptions of the 1990s.[25] Some of these facilities, with modifications, could switch back to natural gas, increasing domestic demand for this resource. However, these opportunities would be limited and any major effort to build additional natural gas–fired power plants would have to be met with a concomitant upgrading of the transmission infrastructure.

Another option for utilizing natural gas reserves is producing chemicals or ultraclean liquid fuels, such as Fischer-Tropsch (FT) diesel. Both benefit from the flexibility of transportation options associated with liquid products. Increasingly stringent diesel sulfur regulations in the United States and Europe have improved the prospects for FT diesel worldwide. However, the capital cost of a gas-to-liquids (GTL) facility could be prohibitive, since these high-quality fuels would probably have limited demand in Central Asia and South Caucasus in the near future. Chemicals produced from natural gas, such as methanol, ammonia, hydrogen, and dimethyl ether (DME) also suffer from high capital costs and insufficient domestic demand. However, the technologies to produce chemicals and synthetic fuels are not yet mature and could potentially benefit from significant cost reductions in the next several decades.

For example, India's demand for DME could become important in the next decade. India's natural gas supply is not expected to meet its growth in electricity generation–driven gas demand in the next decade. Since import options from deep offshore Iranian pipelines or LNG would be very expensive, and overland options from Turkmenistan fraught with uncertainty, several Indian energy companies have partnered with BP Amoco[26] to develop an alternative fuel to natural gas. As a result, India is striving to develop DME[27] as a fuel in electricity generation and residential appliances, and as a diesel

---

[25]*Black Sea Energy Survey,* IEA, 2000.

[26]See the India DME Project web site: *www.dmeforpower.net/pg_theproject.html.*

[27]DME is an extremely clean-burning synthetic fuel with a high cetane number that handles like liquefied petroleum gas. Initial tests have shown that it can be used as a diesel substitute that produces negligible soot, smoke, and SO_2, and significantly lower NO_x. It has also shown promise as a replacement for natural gas in some gas turbine applications and LPG in residential appliances.

alternative in compressed ignition (CI) vehicles. DME is manufac-
tured from natural gas, but its advantage lies in its ease of handling,
since it can be offloaded and stored using conventional unloading
and storage equipment for liquid fuels. It is likely that the natural gas
producers in the Persian Gulf, rather than the Caspian region, would
be the first to reach the Indian market by converting natural gas to
DME and then shipping it in conventional LPG tankers to the Indian
coast. However, it is not clear at this point whether these developments will have any significant impact on the dynamics of gas trade
in the region.

Natural gas producers will decide among these various options for
profiting off their stranded gas, based on technological advance-
ments, volumes of production, distance to markets, existing infrastructure, specific characteristics of their natural gas reserves, foreign
investment behavior, and regulatory idiosyncrasies in the region.
Although many of these alternative options are probably not economically feasible at this time, it is important to understand that
pipeline transport is not the sole method for utilizing natural gas
resources.

ENERGY RELATIONSHIPS IN THE CASPIAN SEA REGION

Interstate Dynamics

At its heart, the rivalry over the development of Caspian resources
and infrastructure can be represented as a series of bilateral negotiations among rent-seeking stakeholders wielding different types of
market power, whose objectives are illustrated in Table 5.2. The
main actors are (1) states endowed with natural resources but lacking export routes; (2) states endowed with favorable transit geography but negligible natural resources; and (3) a multitude of private
industries, dominated by a smaller subset of major multinational
energy companies. This situation is further complicated by (4) outside political actors whose objectives are not necessarily financial,
but who can steer the course of infrastructure developments through
economic, diplomatic, and even military means.

However, the political component must be placed in the context of
Caspian resources not being particularly competitive in foreign mar-

Table 5.2

Stakeholders in Caspian Energy Developments

Stakeholder	Objectives	Actions
Private industry	• Maximum long-term profits • Manage risk	• Develop economically viable infrastructure • Promote government subsidies • Hedge by waiting
Energy-rich, but infrastructure-poor states (i.e., Azerbaijan, Kazakhstan, Turkmenistan)	• Maximum revenue stream • Energy independence and political clout • Maintain power	• Attract foreign direct investment • Secure lucrative foreign markets
Energy and infrastructure-rich states (i.e., Russia, Iran)	• Maintain status quo and market power over transport	• Undermine competing projects • Upgrade existing infrastructure, lower tariffs
Pure transit states (i.e., Georgia)	• Steady revenues • Reliable and affordable supply	• Maximum transit fees without alienating project on its territory˙
Energy-poor neighbors (i.e., Turkey)	• Cheap, secure supply with as many routes as possible	• Support several options • Overestimate demand • Guarantee cost overruns
United States	• Promote former Soviet Union independence • Bolster non-OPEC supply • Support U.S., companies	• Support multiple pipelines through pro-U.S. countries

kets after transportation markups are added to the already high well-head prices, since these resources are both expensive to produce and distant from major industrial demand centers and transshipment routes. Therefore, economics will always be an important driver, since enormous amounts of financing would be needed to promote economically unsound routes for the sake of purely political objectives.

Furthermore, certain combinations of pipeline routes are mutually exclusive, because suppliers do not have inexhaustible resources and because demand hubs can become saturated. This puts "first movers" at a distinct advantage. With the enormous levels of financing needed to bring drilling rigs and other specialized equipment into this remote area and the ensuing slow capital stock turnover, infrastructure investment decisions will be largely irreversible in the short to medium term, locking stakeholders into particular relationships for some period of time. For the next several decades at least, oil—and to an even greater extent, gas—will not be supplanted by other energy sources that involve fundamentally different infrastructure options in the region.[28]

Decisions on oil and gas transportation routes will have significant implications for the revenue streams and energy security of the Caspian states. For example, Chevron has estimated that the CPC oil pipeline will add approximately $84 billion to Russia's GDP and $23 billion in tax revenue (Kazakhstan will receive approximately $8 billion in tax revenue) over its 35- to 40-year lifetime. Furthermore, the lack of a dedicated pipeline has already been shown to be risky to some players. For example, Azerbaijan's northern oil pipeline route to Novorossiysk proved unreliable, with up to 25 percent downtime due to transit fee disagreements, technical problems, and sabotage.[29]

The construction of the Tengiz-Baku-Tbilisi-Ceyhan pipeline would create a secure export route for Azerbaijan and transit revenues for Georgia and Turkey, and it would alleviate significant amounts of oil tanker traffic through the Bosphorus, if it is shown to be economically feasible. Kazakhstan, which already benefits from export flexibility with the CPC pipeline, the traditional Samara pipeline, and Iranian oil swaps, will also have the option to invest in the TBTC pipeline.

As currently envisioned, the TBTC pipeline would not transit Armenia. Advocates of an Armenian portion of the main export pipeline point out that transit through Armenia, instead of Georgia, would decrease the length of the pipeline and thereby reduce transit

---

[28]Energy grids, which currently comprise natural gas and electricity infrastructures, will be more thoroughly integrated, with the natural gas pipelines potentially carrying hydrogen in the long-term future (past 2050), according to Ger Klaassen et al., "The Future of Gas Infrastructures in Eurasia," *Energy Policy*, Vol. 29 (2001), pp. 399–413.

[29]*Black Sea Energy Survey*, IEA, 2000.

costs. H. Con. Res. 162,[30] introduced on June 14, 2001, discourages the use of U.S. government funds and other kinds of support for oil and gas projects in the South Caucasus that explicitly exclude Armenia. However, there are indications that the United States is increasingly calling upon Azerbaijan to help in the fight against international terrorism since September 11, 2001. President Bush's waiver, on January 25, 2002, of Section 907 of the Freedom Support Act to end restrictions on U.S. economic assistance to Azerbaijan could be a sign of closer cooperation between the two countries. Furthermore, Armenia's traditional ally in the region, Russia, has begun to share similar views with Azerbaijan with respect to Caspian seabed demarcation, cross-border regulation and trade, and use of the Gabala radar station.[31] Under these circumstances, the inclusion of Armenia in the main export pipeline is not likely. In an effort to diversify its energy resources, Armenia plans to import natural gas from Iran and eventually decommission its Metsamor nuclear power plant.[32] So far, plans for a $140-million, 35-bcf pipeline that would carry gas from northern Iran to Armenia have passed the initial feasibility study.

Intrastate Dynamics

There are also important implications for relationships among the power centers within each state. It can be argued that the pace of petroleum development has been hindered more by multinational corporations' hesitation to operate in states with ad hoc regulations, insecure contractual agreements, and impermanent regulatory regimes than by the fear of interstate armed conflict. Transparent legal and regulatory institutions, including internationally recog-

---

[30]Thomas web site:
   http://thomas.loc.gov/cgi-bin/query/D?c107:1:./temp/~c107fSDwwu::.

[31]Douglas Blum, "Political Implications of the U.S. Military Intervention for the Transcaspian," *PONARS Policy Memo,* No. 211, January 25, 2002.

[32]Armenia shut down its Metsamor Nuclear Power Plant at Yerevan in 1989 because of safety fears after the 1988 earthquake. As a result of an economic blockade from Turkey and Azerbaijan and ensuing energy shortages, Armenia resumed operation of Unit 2 of Metsamor in 1995, supplying about 45 percent of its electricity. The Armenian government is planning on decommissioning the power plant by 2004 if it secures sufficient alternative energy sources, because of safety concerns. EIA web site: *www.eia.doe.gov/emeu/cabs/armenia.html.*

nized territorial rights, are essential in the quest to entice foreign companies to invest in exploration and drilling, secure financing in international capital markets, and arrange economically feasible transit fee contracts with downstream parties. Necessary internal reforms within petroleum-rich nations have historically been met with institutional inertia and rent-seeking individuals protecting their favored positions. One potential remedy for insulating substantial petroleum revenues from political machinations is the establishment of an independently managed, transparent "oil fund."[33] The course of these developments will be crucial to the stability and health of these regimes.

THE ROLE OF WATER AND ELECTRICITY IN CENTRAL ASIA

The hydrological and fossil fuel infrastructures of the Caspian Sea region, and Central Asia in particular, are inextricably linked. States near the headwaters of major river systems, such as Georgia, Tajikistan, and Kyrgyzstan, have benefited from high per-capita hydroelectric generation capacity and still untapped potential, as illustrated in Figure 5.8. However, the rest of the region, excluding Armenia, benefits from a rich endowment of fossil fuels. Armenia has a nuclear power plant whose future is uncertain.

The early 1990s were marked by disruptions in natural gas supply throughout the Caspian region, leading to the substitution away from natural gas toward fuel oil in thermal power plants.[34] Another post-Soviet trend has been the politicization and inefficient use of the former Soviet Trans-Caucasus Interconnected System, resulting in significant declines in interstate electricity trade. Furthermore, electricity trade has been hampered by disrepair resulting from the lack of investment in the transmission sector. Within Central Asia, the transmission grid is chronically overloaded, leading to frequent blackouts.

According to the International Energy Agency, the Caspian region could benefit from a more efficient allocation of electric power

---

[33]See the "Some Potential Mitigating Factors to Conflict" section in this chapter.

[34]*Black Sea Energy Survey*, International Energy Agency, Paris, 2000.

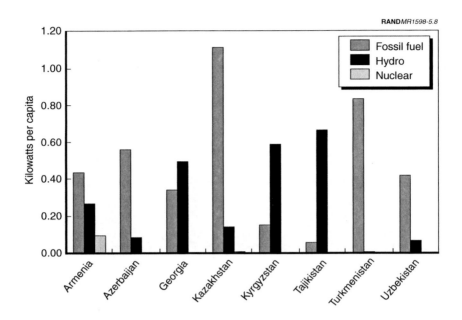

Figure 5.8—Per-Capita Electricity Generating Capacity by Plant Type
(Energy Information Administration, 1998)

within the region. Turkey will offer a potentially significant market for electric power generation from South Caucasus.

Table 5.3 illustrates a clear difference between states that are dependent on hydroelectric power generation and those dependent on fossil fuel–powered generation. The fact that those states lacking hydroelectric power are relatively rich in fossil fuels but in great need of water for irrigation, while the hydro-rich states have less need for water but own negligible oil and gas reserves, has led to a fundamental dichotomy between "upstream" and "downstream" states in Central Asia.

The upstream countries, Kyrgyzstan and Tajikistan, lie at the headwaters of the Syr Darya and Amu Darya rivers, which provide the means for hydroelectric power generation. However, natural gas and oil must be purchased from downstream neighbors. The down-

Table 5.3

Water Relationships in Central Asia

Stakeholders	Fossil Fuel Endowment	Water Endowment and Control of Hydrological Infrastructure	Actions
Upstream (Kyrgyzstan, Tajikistan)	Poor	Rich	• Prefer to release water from reservoirs to generate hydroelectric power during peak winter demand • Must import fossil fuels from downstream neighbors
Downstream (Uzbekistan, Kazakhstan, Turkmenistan)	Rich	Poor	• Prefer water to be released from reservoirs in summer for irrigation

stream countries, Kazakhstan, Uzbekistan, and Turkmenistan, rely on this water for the irrigation of extensive, water-thirsty cotton and grain fields. Furthermore, these states differ in demand for water according to season. Upstream countries prefer to release water from their reservoirs to create power during peak electricity demand in the winter. Downstream countries, on the other hand, prefer that water levels be maintained in these reservoirs until the spring and summer, when water demands are at their peak in the arid lowlands.

Recent droughts have exacerbated these historic grievances between upstream and downstream states. Uzbekistan maintains that excessive volumes of water are released from the Toktogul reservoir in Kyrgyzstan to generate electricity during winter months, resulting in chronic water shortages during the summer. As a result, Uzbekistan cut off natural gas supplies to Kyrgyzstan for lack of timely payment during the winter of 2001, leaving residents in the northern regions of Kyrgyzstan without natural gas for part of the winter. The management of water demand among stakeholders in the region will have a large impact on this relationship in the long term.[35]   Thus far, attempts at regional water management have been largely theoretical, overshadowed by bilateral and sometimes trilateral barter arrangements.[36]

CAN NATURAL RESOURCES CONTRIBUTE TO ARMED CONFLICT?

Resources as Target of Conflict: Infrastructure Sabotage

In recent years, the vulnerability of oil and gas infrastructures has been highlighted by incidents of pipeline sabotage in Chechnya and Daghestan in Russia, Colombia, Nigeria, and elsewhere. Rebels and disenfranchised groups have disrupted pipeline operations in an attempt to deprive governments of petroleum revenues and, in some cases, to steal petroleum products. Although such incidents have generally failed to win major concessions from these regimes, they have increased the cost of petroleum operations and drawn international attention to these regions.

Both oil and gas infrastructures are elaborate systems that include production, gathering, processing, transmission, storage, and distribution elements. Long-distance pipelines provide the most attractive and unprotected targets for saboteurs, but they also have the least impact on both the infrastructure itself and the surrounding community, depending on the location, timing, and magnitude of such an attack. For example, over the past decade, more than 750 attacks on oil pipelines have occurred in Colombia, mostly from the Caño Limón oil field complex in the Llanos basin to Coveñas.[37] Rebels in Colombia bombed the overground Caño Limón-Coveñas oil pipeline 77 times in 1998, and more than 60 times in 1999, as a protest against the alleged involvement of foreign oil companies with

---

[35]See the "Some Potential Mitigating Factors to Conflict" section in this chapter.

[36]Martha Brill Olcott, "Regional Cooperation in Central Asia and the South Caucasus," in Robert Ebel and Rajan Menon (eds.), *Energy and Conflict in Central Asia and the Caucasus,* Lanham: Rowman & Littlefield, 2000, p. 137.

[37]"Nigeria, Colombia Pipeline Deaths Mounting," *Oil & Gas Journal Online*, October 26, 1998.

right-wing paramilitary forces in Colombia.[38] Although there have been several tragic fires that have devastated local villages, most of the bombings have had major impact on neither the surrounding communities nor the operation of the pipeline itself. On the other hand, natural gas or LPG pipelines, which operate at higher pressures than crude oil or refined liquid products pipelines, are generally more dangerous and costly to repair. These dangers are mitigated, to some degree, by the amount of pipeline that is built underground.

The destruction of a critical component of a pumping or compressor station, which cannot be purchased "off the shelf," could significantly affect operations. On the other hand, such stations are typically located in small, fenced-in areas that can be protected more easily than the entire length of pipeline itself. For example, the proposed 42-inch diameter, 1-million b/d TBTC oil pipeline would be 1,743 kilometers long, with seven pumping stations.[39] Clearly, seven distinct pumping stations could be guarded more securely than the entire length of the pipeline.

Cascading failures from one infrastructure to another could multiply the impact of a damaged system. For example, oil or gas pumping stations could be affected by electric power failures. This contingency has been considered by the Caspian Pipeline Consortium, which has recently outfitted the 1,500-kilometer Kazakhstan-Russia Caspian Pipeline with backup power systems, which will help lower the probability of a cascading failure from the electrical infrastructure to the pipeline system.[40]

It is highly unlikely that infrastructure sabotage could lead to catastrophic disruption of oil and gas operations in the region. For an act of infrastructure sabotage to have anything but a local and transient effect, it would involve extensive planning, resources, knowledge,

---

[38]John Wade, "Violence, Crime Continue to Cast Shadow over Future Oil Investment in Colombia," *Oil & Gas Journal Online*, January 17, 2000.

[39]"Construction of the $2.8 Billion Baku-Tbilisi-Ceyhan Oil Export Trunkline Could Begin in the Second Quarter of 2002," *Oil & Gas Journal*, June 18, 2001, p. 9.

[40]One of the battery backups is dedicated to SCADA and telecommunications loads and can last 48 hours in the event of an electrical grid disruption. "Caspian Crude Oil Pipeline Gets Power Systems," *Oil & Gas Journal*, June 18, 2001.

and luck, and would certainly need to be state-sponsored or at least involve a dedicated group with significant financial means and trained personnel.

Resources as Cause of Conflict: Competition over Distribution of Wealth

While few scholars have proposed that the development of natural resources[41] contributes directly to civil strife,[42] most studies of the "natural resource curse" suggest that a high degree of dependence on primary exports tends to have detrimental effects on a state's institutions and long-term economic development, particularly when the development of these resources coincides with modern state-building.

Anecdotal evidence of the "natural resource curse" has been known for many years, from the fate of Spain's economy in the 15th and 16th centuries in the wake of its mercantilist policies in the New World, to the aftermath of the Australian gold rush of the 1850s.[43] More recently, the peculiar economic decline of oil-producing nations in the wake of the oil booms of the 1970s has spurred a wealth of scholarly research on the macroeconomic and political consequences of natural resource development. For example, one study showed that economies with a high ratio of natural resource exports to GDP tended to have low growth rates, even after controlling for other variables known to influence economic growth, such as initial per capita income, trade policy, government efficiency, and

---

[41]A distinction must also be made between nonrenewable natural resources, such as oil and gas, and renewable resources, such as water and cropland. The discussion in this section concerns nonrenewable resources.

[42]For example, Collier and Hoeffler find that an important risk factor for civil war is dependence on primary commodity exports. Paul Collier and Anke Hoeffler, "Greed and Grievance in Civil War," October 21, 2001. Available on World Bank web site: *www.worldbank.org/research/conflict/papers/greedandgrievance.htm.*

[43]According to Graham A. Davis, economist John Elliot Cairns described the negative effect of the Australian gold rush as early as 1859. Graham A. Davis, "Learning to Love the Dutch Disease: Evidence from the Mineral Economies," *World Development,* Vol. 23, No. 10, 1995.

investment rates, among others.[44] In fact, only two natural resource–dependent developing countries had sustained per-capita growth rates of greater than 2 percent per annum for the period from 1970 to 1992.[45]

First coined in the late 1970s, as a result of the stagnation of the Dutch economy following significant gas discoveries in the North Sea, the term "Dutch disease" has been used widely to describe the dilemma facing countries that have enjoyed a windfall in oil revenues. Although the term has become a catch-all phrase for a host of macroeconomic pathologies, it refers more specifically to the appreciation of a state's real exchange rate caused by a dramatic rise in primary exports, followed by the flight of capital and labor away from the manufacturing and agricultural sectors. While energy development attracts foreign direct investment, it is not necessarily a vehicle for diversification of the industrial structure, a goal of most energy producers. Some have argued that the draining of factors away from the agricultural sector has more serious implications for developing countries than the contraction of their often uncompetitive manufacturing industries, especially for societies whose cultures are fundamentally challenged by the uprooting of the agricultural employment and lifestyle.

More recently, scholars have supplemented this purely economic view with a synthesis of political, institutional, and economic explanations of the pathologies of natural resource development. The relevant issue is that regimes fail to take well-established corrective actions, instead placating their populations with low taxes and enhanced public spending, or stifling emerging public grievances by excessive spending on a loyal security apparatus. Using time series

---

[44]The sample included 97 developing countries. Resource-based exports include agricultural products, minerals, and fuels. A "developing country" here is defined as having less than $5,000 per-capita income on a PPP (purchasing power parity) basis in 1971. "Natural resource dependent" is defined as being in the top quartile of resource-dependence (defined as the ratio of primary product exports to GDP in 1970) of countries in the sample. Source: Jeffrey D. Sachs and Andrew M. Warner, "Natural Resource Abundance and Economic Growth," *Development Discussion Paper*, No. 517a, Harvard Institute for International Development, October 1995.

[45]These countries were Malaysia and Mauritius, known for their efforts to stimulate labor-intensive manufacturing exports through the use of Export Processing Zones and other manufacturing promotion policies.

cross-national data from 121 states between 1971 and 1997, one researcher found that oil has a consistently antidemocratic effect on states.[46] The effect is stronger for states that are highly dependent on oil than those that are moderately dependent on oil. In fact, what may seem as inefficient decision-making can be an integral part of the calculus of rulers hoping to maintain their power. Under these circumstances, competing factions would tend to fight over the distribution of these rents, inefficiently exhausting the public good.

Although the Caspian states have made significant strides in macroeconomic reform over the past several years, there are indications that the OPEC experience of rent seeking and corruption will be an important aspect of the political landscape in this region.[47] The paths of recovery that Norway and the Netherlands took in the 1990s will probably not provide a simple blueprint for those countries with authoritarian political regimes, weak state institutions, and embryonic private sectors. However, the fact that the Dutch Disease appears curable is encouraging. Experience has shown that the transparent handling of oil revenues, privatization of state enterprises, and fiscal discipline are necessary, but not sufficient steps in handling the natural resource "curse." Whether the leaders of the Caspian states have the political will and ability to genuinely implement these remedies is unclear.

SOME POTENTIAL MITIGATING FACTORS TO CONFLICT

Caspian Sea Territorial Disputes

Despite lingering disputes over the legal status of the Caspian Sea and the division of its fossil fuel–rich seabed since the fall of the Soviet Union, there has been little direct military confrontation among the littoral states until recently. On July 23, 2001, Iranian gunboats threatened to use force against a BP research vessel operat-

---

[46]For a review of the literature on the natural resource curse, see Michael L. Ross, "The Political Economy of the Resource Curse," *World Politics*, Vol. 51, January 1999, pp. 297–332.

[47]Terry Lynn Karl, "Crude Calculations: OPEC Lessons for the Caspian Region," in Robert Ebel and Rajan Menon (eds.), *Energy and Conflict in Central Asia and the Caucasus*, Lanham: Rowman & Littlefield, 2000, pp. 29–54.

ing in what Azerbaijan considers its territorial waters. This was followed immediately by a declaration from Turkmenistan that Azerbaijan was illegally claiming oil fields in the Caspian Sea, since no demarcation line had yet been agreed to between the two nations. Although Turkmenistan has claimed portions of the Azeri and Chirag fields to which the Azerbaijan International Operating Company (AIOC) holds rights, it has concentrated its dispute chiefly over the oil field that Baku calls Kyapaz and Ashgabat calls Serdar, with estimated reserves of 500 million barrels.

These events can be seen as an attempt, on the part of the "losers" of the Caspian Sea investment race, to exert pressure on the "winners" to agree to a multilateral framework on the status of the Caspian Sea that is more favorable than the status quo to the resource-poor states. These actions have helped accelerate the militarization of the Caspian Sea. A successful resolution would involve a multilateral agreement with possible international mediation.

A long-delayed summit of Caspian states is expected to take place in Ashgabat, Turkmenistan by the end of 2002, in order to resolve the legal status of the Caspian Sea. Over the last several years, Russia has advocated a solution whereby the seabed and subsoil of the Caspian would be divided into national sectors along international boundary lines, according to a variant of the median-line principle, while the waters would be held in common.[48] This approach has won the support of Kazakhstan and Azerbaijan, which have signed bilateral treaties with Russia. Iran has advocated dividing the Caspian seabed and waters so that each littoral state receives 20 percent of the total oil and gas resources. Turkmenistan has been ambivalent in its stance until recently, advocating a condominium principle whereby each littoral state would have a national coastal zone extending 10–20 miles into the sea. However, Turkmenistan insists that no development should take place on subsoil gas and oil deposits on disputed territories until a final multilateral agreement is reached.

---

[48]"More Discussions on Caspian Legal Status Issue," *Alexander's Oil & Gas Connections*, Vol. 7, Issue 3, February 6, 2002.

Petroleum Funds

The most direct approach to insulating oil rents from political gaming is to establish a legally sanctioned "oil fund," which is a method of transforming a nonrenewable into a renewable resource by investing oil rents in financial assets. Typically, these funds are composed of a mixture of domestic and foreign financial assets, and are conservatively managed. Current examples of such funds vary in their purpose and the degree of government involvement, such as the Alaskan and Norwegian petroleum funds.[49]

The Alaskan Permanent Fund is unique in its legal independence from both the legislative and executive branches of government. It is unlikely that leaders (or legislatures, when appropriate) in developing countries would be willing to tie their hands by voluntarily proposing such stringent measures. However, different degrees of independence are possible. A Norwegian version, whereby the transparency of a government's budget is ensured, at least with respect to its use of oil rents, could be a very useful tool for many oil-producing governments in promoting fiscal discipline and trans-

---

[49]For a review of these oil funds, see Rognvaldur Hannesson, *Petroleum Economics: Issues and Strategies of Oil and Natural Gas Production*, Westport, CT: Quorum Books, 1998, pp. 123–140.

According to Hannesson, the most independent petroleum fund in the world is the Alaska Permanent Fund, whose investment and withdrawal rules are enshrined in the Alaskan Constitution. At least 25 percent of oil revenue must be deposited into the fund, after which only the real return on the fund can be disbursed every year. All Alaskan residents, including children, typically receive a $1,000 annual check in the mail from the fund. The fund is independent of the state legislature, and the statutes that govern its management can be changed only by popular vote. The fund is known for its conservative investment strategy and a small and effective administration, whose operating expenses are roughly 1.5 percent of its total revenue. The income from the fund in 2010 is expected to reach the value of state oil revenues at their peak in 1981.

Hannesson points out that the Norwegian Petroleum Fund, established by law in 1990, contrasts sharply with the Alaskan Permanent Fund. The Norwegian Petroleum Fund is simply an account in the Bank of Norway, with no independent administration. Whereas the Alaskan fund emphasizes not only the independent, but "permanent" nature of its operations, the Norwegian fund was established to make the government's use of oil revenue more explicit and transparent. For example, government budgets that are passed with deficits are automatically covered by the fund's assets, so that the fund had no positive balance until 1996. Although the Norwegian fund seems to have been handled properly over the past decade, its future success will depend on the discipline of future legislators much more than will the Alaskan Fund.

parency. Furthermore, the addition of an egalitarian dividend policy could place enormous pressure on a government to use such public funds wisely.

One of the IMF's conditions for extending to Azerbaijan a recent installment of loans has been the creation of a transparent national oil fund. Although the fund has already been established, the IMF and President Aliyev are at odds over whether the management should reside within the purview of the legislative or executive branches of government, with Aliyev favoring more direct control over this institution. Samir Sharifov, the executive director of the Azerbaijan State Oil Fund, expects Azerbaijan to channel more than $52 billion during 2008–2014 into the fund.[50] Recognizing the need for the fund's independence, Sharifov does not favor using the fund to finance deficits in the national budget.

As of May 2001, Kazakhstan had already transferred $862 million into its own national oil fund, known as the National Strategic Fund for Future Generations, with the purpose of funding social welfare projects for future generations, according to President Nazarbayev.[51] The fund is managed by Kazakhstan's National Bank and is supported by revenues and royalties from oil development projects and certain privatization sales. It remains to be seen how viable and transparent these institutions will become.[52]

Water Management Strategies

Since ambitious, Soviet-style plans to increase water supply by manipulation of the natural environment, such as the diversion of Siberian rivers to Central Asia,[53] are no longer possible, it is

---

[50]"Azerbaijan Grappling with Prospects of Oil Wealth Dilemma," *Oil & Gas Journal*, June 18, 2001, pp. 30–32.

[51]"Kazakhstan Reports on Money Deposit into National Oil Fund," *Alexander's Gas & Oil Connections*, Vol. 6, Issue 12, July 2, 2001.

[52]For a detailed review of Caspian oil funds and their political context, please refer to Yelena Kalyuzhnova, "The Economics of the Caspian Region and Development of the Oil Funds," presented at the Second CEAS-ROSES Workshop on Enterprise Reform, March 14, 2002.

[53]*Translations on Major USSR River Diversion Projects*, Foreign Broadcast Information Service, JPRS L/9951, Vol. I–III, September 1, 1981.

imperative that the states of the region find ways to manage water demand. Although the potential for a short-term crisis is high, particularly in periods of high demand and drought, there are several long-term mitigating trends that may avert potential water-energy blackmail scenarios in the future. First, a stable, multilateral agreement on water use in both major river systems is crucial. Second, the trend toward the privatization of water, gas, and electric utilities in the region will eventually eliminate the barter relationship among states. As government distortions of the water and energy markets decrease with the elimination of subsidies, there will be a more rational allocation of these resources based on their commodity price. Finally, investments in reservoirs, hydro capacity, irrigation canals, and a more robust, regional electricity grid will provide a hedge against uncertainties in weather.

However, these mitigating strategies represent a long-term approach to the regional water allocation problem. Whether continued drought conditions in the short term will lead to regional conflict remains to be seen. The water-energy dispute in the winter of 2001 did not result in substantial repercussions for the summer of 2001. This nonevent is hardly surprising; although water disputes have triggered low-level military actions throughout history, there is only one recorded incident of war over water, occurring approximately 4,500 years ago between the Mesopotamian city-states of Lagash and Umma.[54] However, it is unclear how appropriate these historical analogies are for the case of downstream states of Central Asia, whose residential water demand is only a small fraction of agricultural demand, as a result of unsustainable agricultural practices from the Soviet era. In the future, much will depend on downstream states' irrigation plans, where large segments of the population are employed, formally or informally, in the agricultural sector. Potential large-scale dislocations among this workforce resulting from severe water shortages or misallocation could provide a powerful destabilizing factor in the region.

---

[54]Sandra L. Postel and Aaron T. Wold, "Dehydrating Conflict," *Foreign Policy*, September/October 2001, pp. 61–67. The authors point out that about one-fourth of water-related interactions have been hostile during the last half-century, with 37 of them leading to some military action.

CONCLUSIONS

At its peak oil and gas production, in approximately 15–20 years, the Caspian Sea region will provide a modest contribution to world oil supply, and it will be an important regional supplier of natural gas. Over the next decade, the region will likely see intense exploration and production activity, along with the gradual creation of a more robust oil, gas, and electricity infrastructure. However, it is too early to tell which direction the Caspian Sea region is going with respect to the management of its natural resource rents, and the ensuing relationships both within and among the littoral states.

The lack of an internationally recognized territorial division of the Caspian Sea has retarded foreign investment in disputed zones, while allowing real and perceived grievances by littoral states to be used as a pretext for the militarization of the region. However, even in the absence of such a multilateral agreement, it is difficult to imagine any of the Caspian states successfully shifting territorial boundaries by force without the implicit approval or explicit backing of Russia, which has a vastly superior military apparatus in the region. The more likely scenario of conflict stemming from the development of these natural resources would be over the internal distribution of revenues, the consequences of social dislocations associated with long-term petroleum-based growth, and the potential for physical sabotage to the infrastructure itself.

The petroleum-endowed states of the Caspian region will find that their government revenues will depend on fluctuating oil and gas prices, successes in exploration, and stability in infrastructure agreements, eventually declining as lower-cost reserves are exhausted in the coming decades. Clearly, fiscal discipline and the implementation of transparent oil funds by Kazakhstan and Azerbaijan are steps in the right direction. However, other legacies of the Soviet-era management of the natural resource infrastructure might prove more difficult to address, particularly in Central Asia, which will face fundamental questions about its potentially unsustainable agricultural policies if severe droughts and disputes among upstream and downstream neighbors continue in the region.

Since the attacks of September 11, there are signs of U.S. support for the TBTC pipeline. At the least, the deployment of U.S. special forces in Georgia, the waiving of sanctions against Azerbaijan, rapprochement between Russia and Azerbaijan, increased Russian cooperation in the development of Caspian resources, and preliminary Kazakh interest will facilitate the project, barring any major problems found in the detailed engineering study. However, the impact of the rapidly changing events in Afghanistan on the energy situation in the Central Asian states, other than Kazakhstan, is highly uncertain. While Kazakhstan has secured the most flexible export options of any of the Caspian states, Turkmenistan is eager to find feasible markets for its natural gas. The building of a natural gas pipeline from Turkmenistan to India, transiting Afghanistan and Pakistan, is unlikely in the near term. However, it may prove to be a valuable lever for the United States and the international community in dealing with the political and military crises in the region.

Chapter Six

POTENTIAL FOR ETHNIC CONFLICT IN THE CASPIAN REGION
Thomas S. Szayna

INTRODUCTION

A number of incidents of communal violence have taken place in the Central Asia and South Caucasus region in the late Soviet period (late 1980s) and the initial decade of independence (1990s). In Central Asia, the incidents include riots in Kazakhstan and periodic flare-ups of violence in the Ferghana Valley (Uzbekistan). In South Caucasus, the incidents include flare-ups of violence (Azerbaijan, Georgia), and outright secessionist wars with outside intervention (Azerbaijan, Georgia). The incidents of strife differ greatly in terms of intensity, length, and immediate causes, but the warring parties in all the incidents have been differentiated largely along ethnic lines, thus justifying the use of the term "ethnic conflict" in their description.[1]

While the catalytic events that led to the previous incidents of ethnic conflict are case-specific, the preconditions for the violence and tensions along ethnic group lines stem from the combination of the presence of many ethnic groups in a given polity and the presence of

---

[1]We use the following definition of ethnicity: Ethnicity is a constructed social phenomenon. The concept refers to the idea of shared group affinity and a sense of belonging that is based on a myth of collective ancestry and a notion of distinctiveness. The constructed bonds of ethnicity may stem from any number of distinguishing cultural characteristics, such as common language, religion, or regional differentiation. Within a polity, the "markers" are widely known, internalized, and allow for easy categorization of individuals. Thomas S. Szayna and Ashley J. Tellis, "Introduction," in Thomas S. Szayna (ed.), *Identifying Potential Ethnic Conflict: Application of a Process Model,* Santa Monica, CA: RAND, MR-1188-A, 2000, pp. 13–14. The above definition, with slight variations, is widely used by scholars of ethnic conflict.

most of the following factors: authoritarian political regimes that are by nature inefficient in conflict resolution, low income levels and widespread unemployment, official nationalist ideologies that favor some ethnic groups over others, perception of ethnicity in an ascriptive fashion, and fundamental socioeconomic disruptions that lead to a climate of fear and insecurity (see Chapter Two for more on the political problems in the region). Since the conditions that led to the previous incidents of violence still persist, and at least some of the contributing factors to violence have no quick remedies and thus will remain a feature of the region for the foreseeable future, further ethnic violence in CASC during the next 10–15 years is probable and, indeed, likely. This does not mean that ethnic conflict is likely to sweep the CASC region or that it will result in state failures in any of the states. The range of ethnic violence that might take place in the region varies greatly in terms of severity and its likely location. Moreover, even frequent ethnic riots do not necessarily pose a threat to a regime or to interstate peace in the region. But communal conflict with an ethnic dimension is among the most likely types of mass violence that may take place in the CASC region in the next 10–15 years and, depending on its specifics, has the potential to affect the security environment in the region as a whole.

From the perspective of impact on U.S. policy, the primary analytical issue is to anticipate the cases under which the potential for ethnic conflict might lead to state failure or a regional war. As a general conclusion, some potential for such dangerous pathways exists in most countries of CASC, though the largest countries (in terms of population) pose the biggest problems.

This chapter addresses the potential for conflict in the CASC region along the lines of communal—primarily ethnic—conflict. First, the chapter examines the current ethnic makeup and the extent to which the preconditions for ethnic conflict are present in the CASC states. Then, the chapter explores the potential for ethnic violence in the CASC region and points out the probable pathways for the eight countries from the perspective of interethnic relations and ethnic conflict.

THE ETHNIC FACTOR IN THE CASC STATES

Estimates of current population in each country in the CASC region vary, sometimes substantially, depending on the source of data. Table 6.1 lists the most reliable external estimates of current population levels in each country, as well as the estimates of what the population is likely to be in 2015. The CASC states exhibit different rates of population growth. According to UN estimates, Georgia and Kazakhstan will decline in population in the period 2000–2015, Armenia will remain essentially unchanged, Azerbaijan will show moderate growth, and Kyrgyzstan, Tajikistan, Turkmenistan, and Uzbekistan will continue to see high population growth. Since population growth varies greatly by ethnic group, both the absolute and relative share of the total by each group is going to change the most in Central Asia. Generally, the ethnic groups eponymous with the Central Asian states will experience a high rate of natural increase. The low natural increase rates (or even declines) in South Caucasus (Georgia, Armenia) stem from a combination of high out-migration and low fertility rates.

Figures concerning the share of the total population by the major ethnic or religious groups in each country need to be taken with some skepticism. Part of the problem is that ethnicity, as a form of

Table 6.1

Overall Population Estimates, CIA and UN, CASC Region

	2001[a]	2000[b]	Estimated in 2015[b]	Percent Growth 2000–2015[b]
Armenia	3,336	3,787	3,808	0.6
Azerbaijan	7,771	8,041	8,725	8.5
Georgia	4,989	5,262	4,775	−9.3
Kazakhstan	16,731	16,172	15,957	−1.3
Kyrgyzstan	4,753	4,921	5,836	18.6
Tajikistan	6,579	6,087	7,097	16.6
Turkmenistan	4,603	4,737	6,059	27.9
Uzbekistan	25,155	24,881	30,554	22.8

[a]From CIA, *The World Factbook*, July 2001 estimates; *www.odci.gov/cia/publications/factbook/index.html*.

[b]From UN, Department of Economic and Social Affairs, Population Division, *www.un.org/popin/*.

constructed identity, is not static. It is malleable, and shifts in state policy affect the ethnic identification of individuals. Moreover, ethnic attachments vary in strength, and population figures alone do not reflect the intensity of the attachments nor do they indicate other aspects of identity (supraethnic or subethnic) that may affect how an individual perceives those belonging to another ethnic group. Censuses have not taken place in many of the CASC countries since their independence, and the accuracy of what censuses have been done is debatable. Consequently, many of the population figures generated both externally and internally concerning the individual CASC countries rely on adjustments and estimates of either the post-independence censuses or even the 1989 Soviet census (the last and probably the most reliable Soviet census). But the estimates also have a substantial error margin because of massive migration flows throughout the region in the last decade (not captured sufficiently in official records) and nontrivial changes in natural increase rates. Last but not least, state policies in each of the CASC states favor certain ethnic groups over others, open discussion of ethnic tensions and even a genuine portrayal of ethnic heterogeneity in each of the CASC countries is politically sensitive, and there exist national-level pressures to inflate the number of individuals belonging to the ethnic groups eponymous with the state.

With the above caveats in mind, all the states in the CASC region have some portion of the population that is not of the eponymous ethnicity, ranging from the mostly monoethnic Armenia to a highly ethnically heterogeneous Kazakhstan. In general, the level of ethnic heterogeneity in states of the South Caucasus is lower than that in the Central Asian states. Tables 6.2 through 6.9 present data on the main ethnic groups in each of the CASC states, keeping in mind that the figures given amount to no more than composite estimates on the basis of poor data and that the categories themselves are, to some extent, always in flux.

Table 6.2

Main Ethnic Groups, Armenia

Group	Populationª	Percent and Trendsᵇ	Linguistic Group	Religionᶜ	Main Area of Settlement
Armenian	3,242,000	97.2 (~)	Armenian	Armenian Orthodox	
Kurd	61,000	1.8 (+)	Iranian	Muslim	Northwest, mainly western Aragatsotn province
Russian	8,000	0.2 (–)	Slavic	Russian Orthodox	Major urban areas, mainly Yerevan
Otherᵈ	25,000	0.8 (~)			
Total	3,336,000	100.0			

ªFigure for Armenians is derived from CIA estimates for 2001; the figure is in agreement with official Armenian sources, based on estimates as of January 2000 and excluding "persons temporarily absent," the term used to denote out-migration (this is also the reason for the large difference between the CIA and UN figures for the population figures for Armenia reported in Table 6.1: UN uses official Armenian figures, which do not take into account the massive out-migration). Figure for Russians is a 1999 estimate by the Russian State Bureau of Statistics (Goskomstat), published in *Nezavisimaya Gazeta,* September 17, 2001. Figures for other groups are estimates based on 1989 census figures, rates of natural increase, and overall migration trends. Total population figure is an estimate (as of July 2001) by the CIA, *The World Factbook, www.odci.gov/cia/publications/factbook/index.html.* No census has taken place in Armenia since 1989. There has been large out-migration in the 1990s. The figures above are likely to have a moderate margin of error.

ᵇFuture trends regarding population share are based on state policies of favoritism, patterns of natural increase, and expected migration flows. + = relative increase, – = relative decrease, ~ = little change.

ᶜReligion associated with the ethnic group; not necessarily an indication of strength of religious attachments.

ᵈThe largest groups are Greeks and Assyrians.

Table 6.3

Main Ethnic Groups, Azerbaijan

Group	Population[a]	Percent and Trends[b]	Linguistic Group	Religion[c]	Main Area of Settlement
Azeri	6,998,000	90.1 (+)	Turkic	Muslim	
Lezgin[d,e]	197,000	2.5 (+)	Caucasic	Muslim	Northeast, along Dagestan border
Armenian[f]	190,000	2.4 (~)	Armenian	Armenian Orthodox	Southwest, Nagorno-Karabakh and nearby
Russian	142,000	1.8 (–)	Slavic	Russian Orthodox	Urban centers, mainly Baku and vicinity
Avar[d]	51,000	0.7 (+)	Caucasic	Muslim	North, Balaken and nearby areas
Talysh[g]	30,000	0.4 (+)	Iranian	Muslim	Southeast, along the Caspian Sea
Tatar	27,000	0.4 (–)	Turkic	Muslim	Urban centers, mainly Baku and vicinity
Tat (Muslim)	24,000	0.3 (~)	Iranian	Muslim	Northeast, eastern range of Greater Caucasus
Kurds	22,000	0.3 (~)	Iranian	Muslim	Southwest, Nakhichevan
Turk	19,000	0.2 (~)	Turkic	Muslim	Southwest, Nakhichevan
Tsakhur[d]	18,000	0.2 (+)	Caucasic	Muslim	North, Zaqatala area
Other[h]	53,000	0.7 (~)			
Total	7,771,000	100.0			

[a]Figures for all groups except for the Russians and Armenians are derived from the 1989 census results, modified by rates of natural increase and out-migration. Figure for Armenians is derived from population figures in the 1989 census for Nagorno-Karabakh and surrounding areas (controlled by the secessionist Armenians). Figure for Russians is a 1999 estimate by the Russian State Bureau of Statistics (Goskomstat), published in *Nezavisimaya Gazeta,* September 17, 2001. Total population figure is an estimate (as of July 2001) by the CIA, *The World Factbook, www.odci.gov/cia/ publications/factbook/index.html.* A census took place in Azerbaijan in 1999 but its results have been widely disputed. There has been moderate out-migration in the 1990s. A large refugee population (575,000 by UN estimates) remains in Azerbaijan in the aftermath of the war over Nagorno-Karabakh. The figures above are likely to have a moderate to large margin of error.

[b]Future trends regarding population share are based on state policies of favoritism, patterns of natural increase, and expected migration flows. + = relative increase, – = relative decrease, ~ = little change.

[c]Religion associated with the ethnic group; not necessarily an indication of strength of religious attachments.

[d]One of the ethnic groups inhabiting Dagestan.

[e]Includes several linguistic subgroups: Khinalugh, Kryts, Budukh, Udi (together amounting to about 16,000 people).

[f]Almost all Armenians inhabit Nagorno-Karabakh and nearby areas that are currently not under control of the Azerbaijani government.

[g]The Talysh category is new. Previously (1989 census) Talysh had been considered Azeris. Estimates of the Talysh population vary tremendously, with some linguistically-based estimates putting the figure at close to 1 million in Azerbaijan. The number of people in Azerbaijan considering themselves as Talysh (rather than considering themselves Azeri and using Talysh) is probably far smaller.

[h]The largest groups are Ukrainians and Georgians.

Table 6.4

Main Ethnic Groups, Georgia

Group	Population[a]	Percent and Trends[b]	Linguistic Group	Religion[c]	Main Area of Settlement
Georgian	3,615,000	72.4 (+)	Georgian	Georgian Orthodox, some Muslim	
Armenian	430,000	8.6 (~)	Armenian	Armenian Orthodox	South, bordering Armenia
Azeri	358,000	7.2 (+)	Turkic	Muslim	South and west of Tbilisi
Ossetian[d]	165,000	3.3 (~)	Iranian	Orthodox Christian, some Muslim	Central, South Ossetia
Russian	140,000	2.8 (–)	Slavic	Russian Orthodox	Urban centers, Abkhazia, coast
Abkhaz[e]	100,000	2.0 (~)	Caucasic	Christian, some Muslim	Northwest (Abkhazia)
Greek	75,000	1.5 (–)	Greek	Greek Orthodox	South-central, coast
Kurd	33,000	0.7 (+)	Iranian	Muslim	Southwest
Ukrainian	23,000	0.5 (–)	Slavic	Orthodox Christian	Urban centers, Abkhazia, coast
Other[f]	50,000	1.0 (~)			
Total	4,989,000	100.0			

[a]Figures for all groups except for the Russians are derived from the 1989 census results, modified by rates of natural increase and out-migration. Figure for Russians is a 1999 estimate by the Russian State Bureau of Statistics (Goskomstat), published in *Nezavisimaya Gazeta*, September 17, 2001. Total population figure is an estimate (as of July 2001) by the CIA, *The World Factbook, www.odci.gov/cia/publications/factbook/index.html.* No census has taken place in Georgia since 1989. There has been large out-migration in the 1990s. The figures above are likely to have a large margin of error.
[b]Future trends regarding population share are based on state policies of favoritism, patterns of natural increase, and expected migration flows. + = relative increase, – = relative decrease, ~ = little change.
[c]Religion associated with the ethnic group; not necessarily an indication of strength of religious attachments.
[d]Majority of Ossetians inhabit South Ossetia, currently not under control of the Georgian government.
[e]Almost all Abkhaz inhabit the Abkhazi Autonomous Republic, currently not under control of the Georgian government.
[f]The largest groups are Lezgins, Turks, Tatars, and Assyrians.

Table 6.5

Main Ethnic Groups, Kazakhstan

Group	Population[a]	Percent and Trends[b]	Linguistic Group	Religion[c]	Main Area of Settlement
Kazakh	7,985,000	53.4 (+)	Turkic	Muslim	
Russian	4,480,000	30.0 (–)	Slavic	Russian Orthodox	North, northeast, and urban centers
Ukrainian	547,000	3.7 (–)	Slavic	Orthodox Christian	North, northeast, and urban centers
Uzbek	371,000	2.5 (+)	Turkic	Muslim	South, Ongtusik Qazaqstan province
German	353,000	2.4 (–)	Germanic	Protestant and Catholic	North, northeast
Tatar	249,000	1.7 (~)	Turkic	Muslim	North, northeast, and urban centers
Uighur	210,000	1.4 (+)	Turkic	Muslim	Southeast, Almaty province
Belarusan	112,000	0.7 (–)	Slavic	Orthodox Christian	North, northeast, and urban centers
Korean	100,000	0.7 (~)	Korean	Buddhist	East, southeast
Azeri	78,000	0.5 (~)	Turkic	Muslim	East, southeast
Polish	59,000	0.3 (–)	West Slavic	Catholic	North
Dungan	37,000	0.2 (+)	Sino-Tibetan	Muslim	Southeast, Zhambyl province
Kurd	33,000	0.2 (~)	Iranian	Muslim	East, southeast
Chechen	32,000	0.2 (~)	Caucasic	Muslim	East, southeast
Tajik	26,000	0.2 (+)	Iranian	Muslim	South, Ongtusik Qazaqstan province
Bashkir	23,000	0.2 (~)	Turkic	Muslim	North, northeast
Other[d]	258,000	1.7 (~)			
Total	14,953,000	100.0			

[a]Figures for all groups are based on the 1999 census in Kazakhstan (census results generally interpreted as reliable). The total population figure from the census differs from the CIA figure of (as of July 2001) 16,731,000. *The World Factbook, www.odci.gov cia/publications/factbook/index.html.* There has been large out-migration from Kazakhstan in the 1990s, coupled with in-migration in the late 1990s. The figures above are likely to have a moderate margin of error.

[b]Future trends regarding population share are based on state policies of favoritism, patterns of natural increase, and expected migration flows. + = relative increase, – = relative decrease, ~ = little change.

[c]Religion associated with the ethnic group; not necessarily an indication of strength of religious attachments.

[d]The largest groups are Moldavians, Ingush, Mordvinians, Armenians, Greeks, Chuvash, Erzya, and Udmurts.

Table 6.6

Main Ethnic Groups, Kyrgyzstan

Group	Population[a]	Percent and Trends[b]	Linguistic Group	Religion[c]	Main Area of Settlement
Kyrgyz	3,130,000	64.9 (+)	Turkic	Muslim	
Uzbek	666,000	13.8 (+)	Turkic	Muslim	Southwest, Osh and Jalal-Abad provinces
Russian	603,000	12.5 (–)	Slavic	Russian Orthodox	North and urban centers
Ukrainian	71,000	1.5 (–)	Slavic	Orthodox Christian	North and urban centers
Tatar	53,000	1.1 (–)	Turkic	Muslim	North and urban centers
Tajik	47,000	1.0 (+)	Iranian	Muslim	Southwest, Osh province
Uighur	45,000	0.9 (+)	Turkic	Muslim	East, Ysyk-Kol and Naryn provinces
Kazakh	44,000	0.9 (+)	Turkic	Muslim	North, Chuy and Talas provinces
German	40,000	0.8 (–)	Germanic	Protestant	North, Chuy province
Dungan	38,000	0.8 (+)	Sino-Tibetan	Muslim	Northeast, Chuy and Ysyk-Kol provinces
Other[d]	86,000	1.8 (~)			
Total	4,823,000	100.0			

[a]Figures for the major groups are based on the 1999 census in Kyrgyzstan (census results subject to some debate). Figures for other groups are based on the 1999 census, and the 1989 census adjusted for natural increase and migration rates. The total population figure from the census differs from the CIA figure of (as of July 2001) 4,753,000. *The World Factbook, www.odci.gov/cia/publications/factbook/index.html.* There has been large out-migration from Kyrgyzstan in the late 1990s. The figures above are likely to have a moderate to large margin of error.

[b]Future trends regarding population share are based on state policies of favoritism, patterns of natural increase, and expected migration flows. + = relative increase, – = relative decrease, ~ = little change.

[c]Religion associated with the ethnic group; not necessarily an indication of strength of religious attachments.

[d]The largest groups are Koreans, Azeris, and Kurds.

Table 6.7

Main Ethnic Groups, Tajikistan

Group	Population[a]	Percent and Trends[b]	Linguistic Group	Religion[c]	Main Area of Settlement
Tajik	4,598,000	69.9 (+)	Iranian	Muslim	
Uzbek	1,691,000	25.7 (+)	Turkic	Muslim	Ferghana valley and southwest
Russian	68,000	1.0 (–)	Slavic	Russian Orthodox	Urban centers, mainly Dushanbe
Kyrgyz	85,000	1.3 (+)	Turkic	Muslim	East
Persian	25,000	0.4 (~)	Iranian	Muslim	Southwest
Turkmen	29,000	0.4 (~)	Turkic	Muslim	Southwest
Other[d]	83,000	1.3 (–)			
Total	6,579,000	100.0			

[a]Figures for the major groups are based on the 2000 census in Tajikistan (census results prone to major discrepancies), CIA estimates, and the 1989 census adjusted for natural increase and migration rates. The total population figure from the census differs from the CIA figure of (as of January 2000) 6,128,000. *The World Factbook, www.odci.gov/cia/publications/factbook/index.html*. There have been large refugee inflows into and out of Tajikistan, as well as substantial out-migration from Tajikistan in the 1990s. The figures above are likely to have a large margin of error.

[b]Future trends regarding population share are based on state policies of favoritism, patterns of natural increase, and expected migration flows. + = relative increase, – = relative decrease, ~ = little change.

[c]Religion associated with the ethnic group; not necessarily an indication of strength of religious attachments.

[d]The largest groups are Kazakhs, Tatars, and Ukrainians.

Table 6.8

Main Ethnic Groups, Turkmenistan

Group	Population[a]	Percent and Trends[b]	Linguistic Group	Religion[c]	Main Area of Settlement
Turkmen	3,613,000	78.5 (+)	Turkic	Muslim	
Uzbek	453,000	9.8 (+)	Turkic	Muslim	North and east, Dashowuz and Lebap provinces
Russian	240,000	5.2 (–)	Slavic	Russian Orthodox	Urban centers and west (Balkan province)
Kazakh	98,000	2.1 (~)	Turkic	Muslim	Northwest
Azeri	37,000	0.8 (~)	Turkic	Muslim	West, Balkan province
Tatar	33,000	0.7 (–)	Turkic	Muslim	Urban centers
Baloch	30,000	0.7 (~)	Iranian	Muslim	Southeast, Mary province
Ukrainian	26,000	0.6 (–)	Slavic	Orthodox Christian	Urban centers
Other[d]	73,000	1.6 (~)			
Total	4,603,000	100.0			

[a]Figures for the major groups are based on the 1995 census in Turkmenistan (census results subject to some debate), CIA estimates, and the 1989 census adjusted for natural increase and migration rates. CIA estimate in *The World Factbook, www.odci.gov/cia/publications/factbook/index.html.* The figures above are likely to have a large margin of error.

[b]Future trends regarding population share are based on state policies of favoritism, patterns of natural increase, and expected migration flows. + = relative increase, – = relative decrease, ~ = little change.

[c]Religion associated with the ethnic group; not necessarily an indication of strength of religious attachments.

[d]The largest groups are Armenians, Lezgins, and Persians.

Table 6.9

Main Ethnic Groups, Uzbekistan

Group	Population[a]	Percent and Trends[b]	Linguistic Group	Religion[c]	Main Area of Settlement
Uzbek	19,233,000	76.5 (+)	Turkic	Muslim	
Tajik	1,395,000	5.5 (+)	Iranian	Muslim	Central, southern, and eastern provinces
Russian	1,150,000	4.6 (−)	Slavic	Russian Orthodox	Toshkent and other urban centers
Kazakh	1,050,000	4.2 (+)	Turkic	Muslim	West, central, and eastern provinces
Karakalpak	577,000	2.3 (+)	Turkic	Muslim	Karakalpakstan
Tatar	398,000	1.6 (−)	Turkic	Muslim	Toshkent and other urban centers
Kyrgyz	219,000	0.9 (+)	Turkic	Muslim	Farghona, Namangan, Andijan provinces
Korean	217,000	0.9 (~)	Korean	Buddhist	Toshkent and northeast
Turkmen	162,000	0.6 (+)	Turkic	Muslim	Karakalpakstan and Khorezm province
Turk	160,000	0.6 (~)	Turkic	Muslim	Toshkent and northeast
Crimean Tatar	155,000	0.6 (−)	Turkic	Muslim	Samarqand and Nawoiy provinces
Ukrainian	107,000	0.4 (−)	Slavic	Orthodox Christian	Toshkent and other urban centers
Uighur	45,000	0.2 (+)	Turkic	Muslim	Northeast
Other[d]	287,000	1.1 (~)			
Total	25,155,000	100.0			

[a]Figures for all groups except for the Russians are derived from the 1989 census results, modified by rates of natural increase and out-migration. Figure for Russians is a 1999 estimate by the Russian State Bureau of Statistics (Goskomstat), published in *Nezavisimaya Gazeta*, September 17, 2001. Total population figure is an estimate (as of July 2001) by CIA, *The World Factbook, www.odci.gov/cia/publications/factbook/index.html*. No census has taken place in Uzbekistan since 1989. There has been large out-migration in the 1990s. The figures above are likely to have a large margin of error.

[b]Future trends regarding population share are based on state policies of favoritism, patterns of natural increase, and expected migration flows. + = relative increase, − = relative decrease, ~ = little change.

[c]Religion associated with the ethnic group; not necessarily an indication of strength of religious attachments.

[d]The largest groups are Persians, Azeris, Armenians, Bashkirs, and Belarusans.

Figure 6.1 portrays the extent of ethnic heterogeneity in the CASC states, as measured by the percentage of the population that belongs to the ethnic group eponymous with the state and the extent of change in the heterogeneity that has taken place in the ten years that followed the independence of the CASC states. Other than Armenia and Azerbaijan, which are largely monoethnic (with the eponymous ethnic group accounting for over 90 percent of the population), all of the other CASC states contain substantial ethnic minorities. The second-largest state in the CASC region, Kazakhstan, is the most ethnically heterogeneous of all the states in this region.

Of course, for purposes of conflict propensity, heterogeneity needs to be supplemented by a more detailed look at the interethnic situation in a given state. A situation of two roughly evenly-sized groups may be potentially more dangerous from a conflict-propensity perspective than a situation in which the dominant eponymous group has to take into account two or more much smaller groups, because the

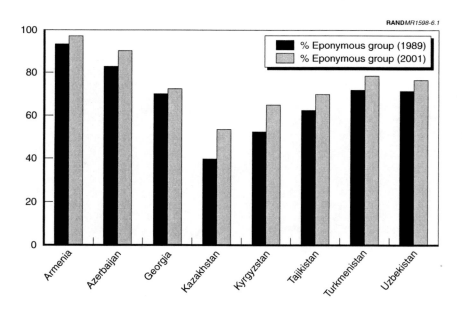

Figure 6.1—Ethnic Heterogeneity in the CASC States

adversaries may be closely matched and an environment of insecurity may pervade relations between them (due to fear of "first strike" by the other). Similarly, groups with a long history of settlement in the territory in question present a different problem than groups composed primarily of recent "settlers." The former are likely to have a higher attachment to the territory and may not see out-migration as an option in the face of discriminatory measures along ethnic lines, whereas the latter may have a weak attachment to the territory and may emigrate rather than resist such measures. A geographically concentrated group presents different problems than a group that is dispersed. In the former case, even a small but concentrated and locally dominant minority group may be stronger than its relatively small population share indicates. Proximity to states composed of co-ethnics and ease (or even the possibility) of assimilation further modify simple heterogeneity calculations.[2]

Keeping in mind the caveats mentioned earlier, there are additional reasons to be cautious when interpreting population figures in the CASC region. For one, the strength of the main ethnic identities in the region is open to question. The ethnic groups eponymous with the states of the region are recent creations (with the exception of Georgia and Armenia). They are byproducts of Stalinist nationality policies from the 1920s and 1930s and the Soviet attempts to impose "national" distinctions (based on Eurocentric definitions of the nation, with its heavy emphasis on language) onto a variety of premodern peoples inhabiting the area. The relative brevity of Soviet control of the region means that important supraethnic and subethnic identities continue to exist. For example, in Central Asia, supraethnic identities include Muslim cultural heritage (differentiating Muslims from non-Muslims, as in, for example, Uzbeks and Tajiks on the one hand, and Russians and Germans on the other hand), Turkic background (establishing shared linguistic and historical bonds between, for example, Turkmen and Uzbeks and differentiating both from Tajiks), historical cultural affinities based on settlement patterns (linking the nomadic Kazakhs, Kyrgyz, and Turkmen, as opposed to the sedentary Uzbeks), and a Turkestani

---

[2]These characteristics are described in more detail in Barry Posen, "The Security Dilemma and Ethnic Conflict," *Survival*, Vol. 35, No. 1 (1993), pp. 27–47.

regional identity (linking many of the indigenous Central Asian groups).

In terms of subethnic attachments, there is much evidence that lineage-based subethnic identities of the pre-Soviet era remain strong and coexist with national identities. For example, before the incorporation of the steppes between the lower Volga and the Altai Mountains into the Soviet Union, the Turkic nomads who inhabited the area distinguished among each other on the basis of three *zhuz* (tribal confederations): the *Kishi Zhus* of the western steppe, the *Orta Zhus* of the north and northeastern steppe, and the *Uly Zhus* of the south and southeast steppe). Further distinctions were made by the variety of *ru* and *taipa* (clans and tribes). The distinctions continue in contemporary Kazakhstan. The nomads of the Kara Kum desert comprised five tribes: Akhal Teke, Yumut, Salar, Ersari, and Kerki. These distinctions persist in contemporary Turkmenistan. Similar distinctions were present among what are now the Kyrgyz, Uzbeks, and Tajiks. The Soviet regime attempted to erase these identities, but they persisted and remain important in most of the Central Asian states. The degree of their importance is a subject of some controversy.[3] The regime in each of the states has in place nation-building policies (meaning an effort to construct a nationality closely identified with the state), and these policies not surprisingly tend to downgrade the significance of subnational identities. Still, independent scholars see the subnational attachments as important. Nor is the importance of subnational identities limited to the Central Asian states. In the South Caucasus, the Azeris follow the pattern of the Central Asians.[4] Even among the groups that have a long history of existence, such as the Georgians, regional distinctions amount to fundamental substate cleavages that mimic closely interethnic patterns of competition.

---

[3]Saulesh Esenova, "'Tribalism' and Identity in Contemporary Circumstances: the Case of Kazakhstan," *Central Asian Survey*, Vol. 17, No. 3 (1998), pp. 443–462; Edward Schatz, "The Politics of Multiple Identities: Lineage and Ethnicity in Kazakhstan," *Europe-Asia Studies*, Vol. 52, No. 3 (2000), pp. 489–506; Hilda Eitzen, "Refiguring Ethnicity through Kazak Genealogies," *Nationalities Papers*, Vol. 26, No. 3 (1998), pp. 433–451; Shahram Akbarzadeh, "National Identity and Political Legitimacy in Turkmenistan," *Nationalities Papers*, Vol. 27, No. 2 (1999), pp. 271–290.

[4]Fereydoun Safizadeh, "On Dilemmas of Identity in the Post-Soviet Republic of Azerbaijan," *Caucasian Regional Studies*, Vol. 3, No. 1 (1998), *http://poli.vub.ac.be/publi/crs/eng/0301-04.htm*.

In any event, though it is clear that the populations of most of the CASC states tend to be ethnically heterogeneous, the quantitative information on the ethnic composition of the population in the region amounts to rough estimates with a potentially large margin of error and should be treated as such. Moreover, ethnic attachments of the main peoples in the CASC region, and especially in Central Asia, are products of relatively short processes of assimilation, and so they seem to coexist on par with other supra- and subnational identities, whose strength is difficult to judge with any degree of accuracy.

PRECONDITIONS FOR ETHNIC CONFLICT

By itself, ethnic heterogeneity is a necessary precondition but insufficient for ethnic conflict to occur. Even the politicization of ethnicity is an insufficient cause of conflict. Actual catalysts are tied to some form of group-level grievances and a perception of threat and insecurity at the group level. Willingness to compromise and mechanisms for conflict resolution generally are not as well developed in authoritarian regimes as they are in democratic ones. Moreover, authoritarian regimes, by definition, tend to be more arbitrary, less transparent in decisionmaking, less willing to allow popular input than democratic regimes, and more prone to foster a climate of group-level insecurity. For all these reasons, authoritarian regimes are not as efficient and effective in heading off severe ethnic conflict. The lower restraint of authoritarian regimes toward the use of coercion amounts to an alternative mechanism for deterring ethnic conflict, but generally it is not an efficient way to deal with group-level grievances.

There are a multitude of group-level grievances in most of the CASC states, varying in their extent by country. In addition, all the political regimes in the CASC region are authoritarian, with some being highly authoritarian. Data from Freedom House illustrate the extent of their authoritarianism. Freedom House is among the best-known and oldest institutions that gauge the political and civil rights of all countries in the world according to a standard methodology.[5] Freedom House ranks both political rights and civil liberties, each on

---

[5]For full explanation of Freedom House methodology and individual country scores, see *http://www.freedomhouse.org/ratings/*.

a one-to-seven scale, with one representing the highest level of freedom and liberty and seven the lowest. Figure 6.2 traces the scores of
all eight CASC states since independence. The chart uses an average
of the political freedoms and civil liberties to establish one figure that
approximates the extent of democratic governance in a given state.
For comparison, current (2001–2002) scores of some countries outside of the CASC region are: Turkey 4.5, Russia 5.0, China 6.5, Iran
5.5, Afghanistan (under Taliban) 7.0. Other than Turkey and Greece
(which has a current score of 2.0), all NATO countries have current
scores of 1 or 1.5.

As a general rule, the states of South Caucasus are less authoritarian
than the states of Central Asia. Georgia and Armenia are the least
authoritarian of the states in the region, and Turkmenistan and
Uzbekistan are the most authoritarian. The data indicate that some
of the liberalization and democratization that occurred in the CASC

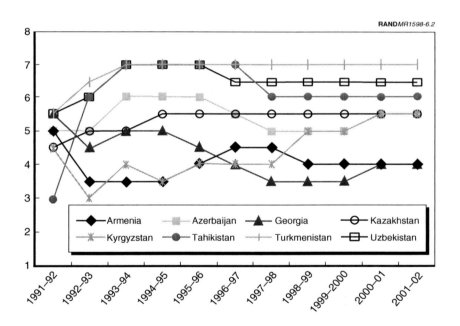

Figure 6.2—Extent of Democratization in the CASC States
(Scale 1–7; 1 = fully democratic, 7 = fully authoritarian)

states after the breakup of the Soviet Union has been reversed. There are also fewer fluctuations in the regime ratings since 1996, seemingly showing that as the regimes have become more authoritarian, they have also become more entrenched. The combination of authoritarian regimes and the presence of large ethnic minorities in most of the states of the CASC region does not mean that ethnically based conflict will necessarily occur, but it does mean that some of the preconditions for such strife are in place because individuals and groups may not have access to conflict resolution mechanisms or ways to channel their grievances in a peaceful fashion (see Chapter Two for more on the political problems in the region).

In terms of ethnically based grievances, the pursuit of nation-building and "ethnic redress" by the regimes in power in all of the CASC states are probably the most important factors because of their symbolism and their implications for the ability of the nonfavored citizens to identify with the country. Regimes in the CASC region have their base of support in ethnic groups eponymous with these states and, since gaining independence, each of them (with varying intensity) has pursued policies that aim to strengthen its group's hold on the structures of power and thereby institutionalize its newly dominant position. In short, the CASC states are "nationalizing" states (to use Rogers Brubaker's term), in that they pursue policies that aim to assimilate, marginalize, or expel the nondominant ethnic groups.[6] Although the pace of nationalizing varies from country to country, the long-term goal of the regimes is clear: to build a large ethnically based pillar of support by shifting the status stratification map to ensure that the eponymous ethnic groups are in an unchallenged position of power. There is nothing unusual about the pattern being followed; a program of nationalist modernization fueled by creating a national identity on the basis of one major ethnic group was a common path to modernity in the 20th century.

Since members of the eponymous groups control the regimes of all the states in the CASC region, they have been able to use the administrative machinery of these states as tools of "ethnic redress." Because the tools are numerous and because they are combined with

---

[6]Rogers Brubaker, *Nationalism Reframed: Nationhood and the National Question Reframed in the New Europe,* Oxford: Cambridge University Press, 1996.

the arbitrariness one would expect from authoritarian regimes, they are effective in an overall sense, even if the administrative capacity of the states is generally weak. The tools range from manipulation of privatization, channeling of foreign direct investment to benefit certain areas or individuals, and selective enforcement of laws so as to benefit some groups, to constitutional clauses that stipulate the primacy of one ethnic group, rewriting and outright fabrication of history to establish symbolic primacy, educational guidelines that elevate the status of the dominant ethnic group, and linguistic policies that privilege the dominant ethnic group.

Implementation of "ethnic redress" has not been so much illegal as extralegal, in that the intent to privilege the dominant group is not outlined specifically in law but is affirmed symbolically and through a number of political cues. In turn, the authoritarian nature of the regimes in power and controls on the media allow for little redress, appeal, or questioning of specific decisions. The general climate of favoritism toward some ethnic groups that emerges is unambiguous, even if there is sometimes substantial leeway in the way that the specific tools are used.

For reasons that vary from state to state, the pace and scope of "ethnic redress" has been relatively constrained so far. Though there has been massive migration, outright state-sponsored violence to drive out members of specific ethnic groups generally has not taken place (other than in Azerbaijan). The reasons include an already strong position by some of the dominant ethnic groups in their states, need for the technical skills that reside primarily among the members of ethnic minorities and the consequent desire not to alienate them further, and potential of stronger steps provoking an international reaction that might then weaken these regimes.

Since "ethnic redress" entails essentially zero-sum competition, in general it causes the ethnic minority populations to be disadvantaged relative to the dominant group. However, the ethnic groups that previously held a position of privilege end up being disadvantaged the most (in terms of status loss relative to the dominant group) or they at least bear the brunt of "redress" actions. In the CASC region, and especially in Central Asia, the most privileged group during the Soviet era had been the Russophones; the current policies of "ethnic redress" penalize these groups the most. The term

Russophones is used here because, in the context of the CASC region, Russians, Ukrainians, and Belarusans formed one supraethnic group that represented the Soviet system in the CASC region (the three ethnic groups were at the apex of the overall Soviet ethnic status stratification map), and Russian was the primary language of members of all three East Slavic groups who lived in the region. On both counts, the Russophones contrasted with the indigenous ethnic groups of the CASC region, who were low on the Soviet stratification map and, especially in Central Asia, often did not have working knowledge of the Russian language.

The above notwithstanding, other (non–East Slavic) ethnic minorities also have been affected by the policies of "ethnic redress." Members of ethnic groups indigenous to Europe, though not necessarily privileged during the Soviet era, have been affected by the policies because of their European physical features and, in the eyes of the new dominant groups, their association with the power structure run by the Russians and East Slavs generally. If they had once held privileged position in the local power structure, even members of noneponymous ethnic groups indigenous to the CASC region have been the targets of some of the "ethnic redress."

Although they are not a sufficient cause of conflict, grievances (either real or imagined) are a necessary component of mobilization of a group for political action along ethnic lines. The mobilization may, in turn, lead to conflict. Mobilization depends on several factors, especially catalytic events that provide a spark and a general sense of danger to the group, a leadership that is willing to take risks, and the extent of organization and resources available to the group that can be harnessed by the leadership.[7] These factors have to be measured against the state's ability to accommodate the demands of the group, to buy it off by extending selective economic benefits, or to simply crack down and repress it. States with political systems that provide representation to aggrieved groups and that have strong conflict-resolution mechanisms can generally accommodate the group's demands. Wealthy states can afford to limit strife by buying off the group. Repressive regimes can rely on their security apparatus to

---

[7]Thomas S. Szayna (ed.), *Identifying Potential Ethnic Conflict: Application of a Process Model*, Santa Monica, CA: RAND, MR-1188-A, 2000.

raise the risk for anyone participating in a group action and thus heighten the costs of collective action to such a level that mobilization is difficult. All of this simply means that mobilization does not automatically follow the presence of grievances. Some groups may remain quiescent for years despite facing repressive conditions.

Even if mobilization takes place, the outcome does not necessarily have to be conflictual. After tough bargaining, the group in question and the regime may reach accommodation. Finally, if conflict follows mobilization, it may be localized and controllable by the regime. Only in select and rare cases does conflict that sometimes follows mobilization lead to state collapse.

KAZAKHSTAN: AN EXAMPLE OF A NATIONALIZING STATE

Kazakhstan provides an example of the policies pursued by the "nationalizing" states of the CASC region. Using the example of Kazakhstan does not mean in any way that the "ethnic redress" policies in Kazakhstan are more severe than in other CASC states, nor does it mean that ethnic conflict is more likely in Kazakhstan than in other states of Central Asia. Kazakhstan simply presents a case of a Central Asian state that is highly ethnically heterogeneous (more so than other Central Asian states), has experienced some ethnically based violence in the 1990s, and is ruled by an authoritarian regime. The case is meant simply to illustrate a pattern that is present, to some extent, in all of the CASC states.

The changing status of the Russian language has both symbolic implications and substantive consequences for the Russophone population of Kazakhstan. Kazakh laws designate Kazakh as the "state language" and Russian as an "official language." Though the meaning of these terms is unclear and left undefined, other laws stipulate the phasing in of exclusive use of Kazakh by state employees.[8] What is especially interesting about the Kazakh language laws is that, even ten years after independence, Russian is still the native language of the majority of the citizens of Kazakhstan (since most of

---

[8]William Fierman, "Language and Identity in Kazakhstan: Formulations in Policy Documents 1987–1997," *Communist and Post-Communist Studies*, Vol. 31, No. 2 (1998), pp. 171–186.

the non-Kazakh ethnic groups as well as at least 25 percent of Kazakhs use Russian as their first language, and proficiency in Kazakh is limited almost entirely to ethnic Kazakhs). Placing Kazakh in a dominant position in such circumstances and erecting formal and informal barriers to certain types of employment based on proficiency in Kazakh represents a case of establishing a preference system that clearly favors ethnic Kazakhs over members of other ethnic groups. Such preferences and biases lead to the staffing of the governmental bureaucracy almost entirely with Kazakhs. But such a pattern of staffing has far-reaching consequences, since there is little experience in Kazakhstan (and in the entire CASC region) with an impartial state bureaucracy. Indeed, there is an expectation of favoritism along ethnic lines by government employees. Thus, laws such as the Kazakh language law have an impact on career choices and prospects for livelihood of nonethnic Kazakhs in Kazakhstan. But they also establish the potential for estrangement of the non-Kazakh population from the administrative machinery of the state. Moreover, the increasing ethnic bias comes on top of the authoritarian nature of the regime in Kazakhstan, making it even more difficult for non-Kazakhs to have their grievances addressed.

Language policy is but one example of the "ethnic redress" measures. Other steps include the favoring of ethnic Kazakhs in promotion policy in the police and security apparatus, and myriad local-level decisions that affect everyday lives. The overall trend is one of making it more difficult for non-Kazakhs to prosper in Kazakhstan in the future. Survey data and focus group discussions confirm the presence of the belief by the Russophones in Kazakhstan that they face an overall antagonistic climate.[9] The following excerpts from focus group discussions with Russophones in Kazakhstan provide an example of the perception of "ethnic redress":

> Female: We are all literate, and if there were courses we would go and learn Kazakh; but that would not remove the problems. They divided the kindergartens, schools, and workplaces. Factories— Russians; banks—Kazakhs. The language is just an excuse.

---

[9]Lowell Barrington, "Russian Speakers in Ukraine and Kazakhstan: 'Nationality,' 'Population,' or Neither?" *Post-Soviet Affairs*, Vol. 17, No. 2 (2001), pp. 129–158.

> Male: Well, say, a situation arises. . . . Let's take specialists. Someone's higher in qualification, someone's lower. Right? If there is a dilemma, whom to leave, you or a Kazakh? Of course, they will leave the Kazakh.[10]

None of the above is to say that the "ethnic redress" policy is driven by ethnically based hatreds. Indeed, any ethnic tensions are the result rather than the cause of these policies. The policy has causes at the level of political competition and is embedded in the nature of the regime and the political patronage networks in place. In the late Soviet period, two such networks ran Kazakhstan, one mainly composed of Russians or Russophones and the other one of Kazakhs. With the collapse of the Soviet Union, the Kazakh network emerged as the victor and has used the machinery of the state to place its staff in positions of power and to pass laws that cement its dominant position.[11] Although the motivation is not one of outright ethnic antagonism, the effect of the policies is one of creating new winners and losers who are identified primarily along ethnic lines.

The policies already have had a far-reaching impact on the demographic makeup of Kazakhstan. The clearest indicator of group-level dissatisfaction among the Russophones is their massive out-migration from Kazakhstan, with estimates showing that in 1989–1999, over 25 percent of the Russians (amounting to over 1.5 million people, or over 10 percent of Kazakhstan's population in 1989) left Kazakhstan permanently. The remaining Russophones show a pattern of consolidating their area of settlement. In other words, the Russophones have largely left the already predominantly Kazakh central, southern, and western areas of the country. In areas of dominant Russophone presence (north and northeast), the margin of Russophone dominance has decreased. All this does not mean that the Russophones have migrated primarily because of the state-sponsored ethnic favoritism. Indeed, probably the most important rationale for the out-migration has been the severe economic contraction and the corresponding decline in the standard of living and

---

[10]Ibid., pp. 137–138.

[11]However, it is worth noting that with the clear victory of the Kazakh patronage network, new cleavages, this time along tribal (*zhuz*) lines, appear to have emerged within it. Timothy Edmunds, "Power and Powerlessness in Kazakstani Society: Ethnic Problems in Perspective," *Central Asian Survey*, Vol. 17, No. 3 (1998), pp. 463–470.

high unemployment, combined with the fact that economic opportunities opened up to them elsewhere. But the policies of "ethnic redress" undoubtedly have contributed to the outflow, for the out-migration has a clear ethnic character. After all, the policies of preferences for ethnic Kazakhs in conditions of much greater scarcity and competition have dimmed the economic prospects of the Russophone population in Kazakhstan and established greater incentives for them to emigrate.[12] Figure 6.3 shows the extent of the population shift in a graph format.

Another indication of group-level dissatisfaction is the emergence of mainly Russian groups and political movements in northern Kazakhstan that have secessionist goals. While these groups have

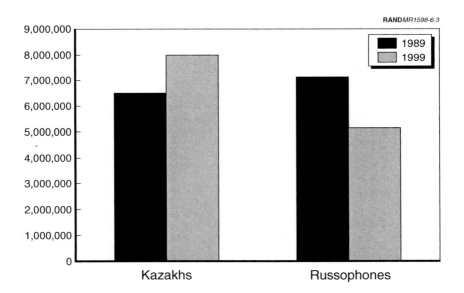

Figure 6.3—Extent of Demographic Shift in Kazakhstan, 1989–1999

---

[12]Richard H. Rowland, "Urban Population Trends in Kazakhstan During the 1990s," *Post-Soviet Geography and Economics*, Vol. 40, No. 7 (1999), pp. 519–552. The same pattern applies to Kyrgyzstan and the other Caspian states: see Rafis Abazov, "Economic Migration in Post-Soviet Central Asia: the Case of Kyrgyzstan," *Post-Communist Economies*, Vol. 11, No. 2 (1999), pp. 237–252.

been minor so far, their small prominence may stem more from the relatively mild "ethnic redress" steps taken by the Kazakhstani regime, media restrictions on information, constraints on their ability to organize, punitive measures by the regime, and lack of support from Russia than from low resonance among the population. In fact, opinion surveys have shown that ethnic Russians in Kazakhstan, especially those in northern Kazakhstan, are more irredentist-oriented than ethnic Russians in other post-Soviet states.[13]

Although the official population statistics need to be considered with a healthy dose of skepticism, the overall trend is clear. Over the course of ten years of Kazakhstan's independence, ethnic Kazakhs have moved from a position of plurality and rough similarity to the number of Russians in Kazakhstan to one of outright majority. Moreover, the shift has come not from any unusual jump in the Kazakh rate of natural increase or any substantial in-migration, but from a large drop in the number of ethnic Russians and Russophones in general. According to the 1999 Kazakhstani census and the 1989 Soviet census, the Russophones dropped from almost 44 percent of the population of Kazakhstan in 1989 to 34 percent in 1999. Out of 21 ethnic groups that numbered over 10,000 in Kazakhstan in 1999, only the groups indigenous to the CASC region, and particularly to Central Asia, showed demographic growth in the period 1989–1999 (Kazakhs, Uzbeks, Uighurs, Dungans, Kurds, and Tajiks). All other groups showed demographic declines, sometimes at drastic levels.[14] Taking their population in 1989 as 100 percent, Russians declined to 74 percent, Ukrainians to 63 percent, and Belarusans to 63 percent. In absolute numbers, Russians decreased by 1,582,401, Ukrainians by 328,639, and Belarusans by 66,012. While future migration patterns will depend on "push" and "pull" factors, it is reasonable to expect that the longstanding Russian settlements in northern and eastern Kazakhstan will remain. If the "ethnic redress" policies continue, the autochtonized Russophones who reside there may

---

[13]Edwin Poppe and Louk Hagendoorn, "Types of Identification Among Russians in the 'Near Abroad,'" *Europe-Asia Studies*, Vol. 53, No. 1 (2001), pp. 57–71.

[14]Even taking into account a moderate margin of error in the Kazakhstani 1999 census, the patterns of growth of some groups and reduction of others are unmistakable.

become increasingly alienated and subject to easy mobilization against the government along ethnic lines.

Dissatisfaction among the Russophones, as demonstrated through their level of out-migration, is real, but the interesting question is why the Kazakh regime has pursued relatively mild policies of "ethnic redress" and eschewed policies aiming at a rapid assimilation or expulsion of non-Kazakhs. The reasons include some that are unique to Kazakhstan[15] as well as others that are generally applicable to the CASC region and Central Asia in particular. The specific reasons include a historical relationship between Kazakhs and Russians that is different from Russian relations with other peoples of Central Asia. They include the long period of Russophone settlement in Kazakhstan, the lengthy period of association with Russia, extensive cultural Russification, and Soviet/Russian origins of Kazakh autonomy and statehood. The more general reasons include a generally cautious policy when it comes to discrimination against the Russophones for fear of provoking a reaction from Russia, combined with the ongoing need to trade with Russia and to employ the mainly Russophone managerial and technical elite to help run Kazakhstan's economy.[16] To a greater or lesser extent, most of these considerations also play a role in the policies of other regimes in the CASC region. Kazakhstan's contiguity with Russia, the Russophone presence in northern Kazakhstan (in areas bordering Russia), and the frequent voicing of irredentist claims toward Kazakhstan on the part of Russian nationalists (including Alexander Solzhenitsyn) make Russian territorial claims on Kazakhstan a distinct possibility and strengthen the likelihood that the regime will act cautiously so as to avoid a potentially catastrophic Russian counterreaction. When a regime has fewer incentives to act carefully toward noneponymous ethnic groups, as in Uzbekistan, the policies of "ethnic redress" have been more pronounced.

---

[15]Michael Rywkin, "Kazakstan and the Rest of Central Asia: Fifteen Shades of Difference," *Nationalities Papers*, Vol. 26, No. 3 (1998), pp. 573–579.

[16]When it comes to the new states' dependency on the technical expertise that resides primarily with the Russophones, the situation in post-Soviet Central Asia resembles that of postcolonial French and Portuguese Africa. Moshe Gammer, "Post-Soviet Central Asia and Post-Colonial Francophone Africa: Some Associations," *Middle Eastern Studies*, Vol. 36, No. 2 (April 2000), pp. 124–149.

Although greater alienation of the Russophones in Kazakhstan is certainly a possibility, there is nothing inevitable about it. The constitution of Kazakhstan adopts a clear territorial (or civil) basis for citizenship rather than an ethnic one. In other words, the constitution refers to the Kazakhstan nation rather than the Kazakh nation (other constitutions in Central Asia are not as clear on this point).[17] As such, the phrasing is more inclusive, and other ethnic groups are not treated in a clearly secondary fashion. The phrasing opens up the possibility that Russophones, despite their non-Kazakh roots, can still develop a Kazakhstani national identity.[18] While no one can fail to recognize that the Kazakhs are "first among equals" in Kazakhstan, the status is better than "first with no others allowed." Interestingly enough, there are indications of the emergence of a Eurasian identity (understood differently from the way the term is used in Moscow) among the Russophones of northern Kazakhstan. In the specific context of northern Kazakhstan, the term refers to a Slavic-Turkic identity that is indigenous to the area. This may be an example of a coping strategy that includes an identity shift and which may be acceptable to the regime in the context of the development of a Kazakhstani national identity and loyalty. However, to paraphrase Gyanendra Pandey, the question of "can a Russian be a Kazakhstani" is unlikely to be answered in the affirmative as long as the Kazakhstani national identity remains built around Kazakh ethnicity and all its attached symbolism.[19]

The case of Kazakhstan illustrates the overall point that grievances alone are not enough to lead to conflict. Similarly, the presence of

---

[17]Of course, the problem is not one of laws but of the regime respecting the laws. On this score, the record of the Central Asian states (and to a lesser extent, the states of South Caucasus) living up to the principles established in their constitutions is poor. The poor record notwithstanding, there is important symbolism in having clear references to a civic rather than ethnic identity underpinning a country. For some examples of the wide difference between theory and practice regarding constitutions and elections in post-Soviet Central Asia, see Rebecca M. Bichel, "Deconstructing Constitutionalism: The Case of Central Asia and Uzbekistan," *Interactive Central Asia Resource Project (ICARP) paper,* 1997, *www.icarp.org/publications/pub-deconstruct.html;* and John Anderson, "Elections and Political Development in Central Asia," *The Journal of Communist Studies and Transition Politics,* Vol. 13, No. 4 (1997).

[18]Edward A. D. Schatz, "Framing Strategies and Non-Conflict in Multi-Ethnic Kazakhstan," *Nationalism and Ethnic Politics,* Vol. 6, No. 2 (2000).

[19]Gyanendra Pandey, "Can a Muslim Be an Indian?" *Comparative Studies in Society and History,* Vol. 41, No. 4 (1999), pp. 608–629.

many ethnic groups in one state, even if some of them have grievances, in no way means that a conflict is either inevitable or even likely. Few countries in the world are more ethnically hetero- geneous than Kazakhstan, but despite an authoritarian regime in place and policies (implemented in an arbitrary fashion) that have created a climate that privileges one ethnic group over others, the country has avoided any violent ethnic incidents since the early 1990s. There is nothing that precludes the current state of affairs from lasting for another decade or longer.

CATALYSTS TO ETHNIC VIOLENCE

Even if all the preconditions for ethnic violence were in place, that still would not mean that such strife is inevitable.[20] For sustained violence to occur, either a group or the state must believe that the opportunity structure allows for a decisive action to eliminate the perceived threat from the other side. Anticipating the occurrence and severity of potential ethnic conflict depends on three main cri- teria: the type of conflict, the issues in contention, and the extent of external involvement. Each type of conflict is explained below, fol- lowed by an examination of the likelihood of each type of conflict in the CASC region.

Concerning the type of ethnic conflict, there are at least three possi- ble patterns. One involves a group or several groups in a coalition against the state. Another involves intergroup conflict, pitting one or more groups against another one or more groups. In this case, the state is involved not as a participant but as a "referee" in the inter- group conflict. Still another involves intergroup conflict but with the state partial to one side. Such a type of conflict is a hybrid of the

---

[20]The analysis here rests on previous RAND work concerning the emergence of ethnic conflict (Szayna, *Identifying Potential Ethnic Conflict*). The three-stage model developed in that work traces the development of ethnic and communitarian strife, beginning with the conditions that may lead to the formation of an ethnic group, then the group's mobilization for political action, and ultimately its competition with the state. The model integrates diverse insights offered by various theories that focus on separate aspects of ethnic and communitarian strife—such as relative deprivation of the populace or the extent of state capacity—into a comprehensive model that speaks to the entire *process* of ethnic mobilization, from the structural roots of conflict all the way to social reconciliation or state breakdown. The model also allows predictions based on the relative strengths and weaknesses of the specific state and group.

group-versus-state and intergroup strife. In any of the above, either the state or the group or groups in question may be the initiators of conflict.

Issues in contention in ethnic conflict can range widely, from redressing a local grievance to desire for national-level legal changes that involve recognition of group rights, all the way to secession. Some regimes have the accommodative capacity to allow secession without resorting to armed conflict. However, such regimes are exceptions to the general rule that the more far-reaching the goals of the group, the greater the potential for severe conflict. When the group that controls the state is the initiator of conflict, it can bring the machinery of the state against a specific group. There can be any number of specific reasons for a regime to turn to violence in such a manner, though generally the group controlling the state does so as a means of increasing its own power by scapegoating another group or because it perceives some kind of a threat (even if distant) from it.

Armed intrastate conflict almost always tends to bring some form of external involvement. But the extent of such involvement ranges widely, from concern over human suffering, to fear of a spillover of conflict onto neighboring territory, all the way to concern over (or desire for) the breakup of the state undergoing strife. The different types of concern motivate divergent types of support for the group(s) or the state. Geographically distant states that are not great powers generally limit their involvement to issuing diplomatic "notes of concern" and sending humanitarian assistance to the affected area. Neighboring states are always involved in some fashion and are forced to take sides to some extent. These steps may stem from internal motives and cost-benefit assessments, such as in the choice of the extent of resources devoted to policing the border to prevent smuggling of supplies to the warring parties and controlling any cross-border refugee movements. But they have implications for the conflict and tend to draw the neighbors into the conflict in one way or another. Neighboring states, great powers, and regional powers also may have goals that motivate outright active support for one of the warring sides. In some cases, such goals may lead to provision of troops and weapons or even an outright armed intervention on behalf of one side.

The potential for severe conflict, meaning a rapid state collapse and/or a civil war with potential intervention, is greater when a combination of certain types of ethnic conflict is matched with certain group characteristics. Of the three types of ethnic conflict, the group (or groups) versus state conflict (regardless of who initiated it) is potentially the most severe if the group in question encompasses a substantial portion of the population. This is so because in cases of ethnic conflict, lines are drawn along group lines, and even though most of the group's members are not combatants or involved in the strife, they are potential sympathizers and supporters and the state treats them as such. But if the state apparatus suspects much of the population of sympathizing with or supporting armed strife against the state, then it is impossible for that state apparatus (and the state itself) to function effectively. When the state is a "referee" among striving groups or even favors one side, there may be disruptions in civic functioning but not a basic state distrust of a large share of the citizenry.

Concerning the continuum of issues in contention, the higher the level of group goals, the greater the likelihood that the conflict will be severe. Any group advocating secession or administrative changes that bring it more power has more potential for sparking severe conflict because a state generally will resist meeting such demands. Finally, if the group in question has substantial resources available to it (relative to the resources available to the state), then the conflict is likely to be more evenly matched and severe. External support is an important factor here, in that it increases the resource base greatly and can make a group that is otherwise dwarfed in terms of resources into a formidable opponent.

The presence of all of the above elements generally foreshadows a particularly severe conflict, one that has the potential to lead quickly to state breakdown. If these elements are not present, however, ethnic conflict taking other forms can still have problematic regional implications. Other types of ethnic conflict can lead to state failure, though they are likely to do so in a more gradual fashion. Especially when the groups in question have a low level of resources relative to the state, the state is likely to keep them under control for some time. But unless the conflict is brought to an end quickly, the dissolution of "normal" functioning of state structures in areas affected by strife is likely to be accompanied by the growth and then the institutionalization of a criminal or "war" economy. In other words, in the absence of state regulating mechanisms, nonstate structures (such as organized crime) are bound to fill the vacuum and adapt to the conflict in order to prosper from it.[21] In the long run, such a development amounts to a dissolution of the state from within.

POTENTIAL FOR ETHNIC VIOLENCE IN THE CASC REGION

The occurrence of ethnic conflict in one or more CASC states during the next 10–15 years does not necessarily mean that such strife will have clear ramifications for the United States. It may take the form of localized clashes that have little further significance, as was the case with ethnically based riots in western Kazakhstan in the early 1990s. But it is also clear that over the next 10–15 years, a number of groups in CASC might be involved in ethnically related strife that fits the description of a severe conflict. If U.S. forces remain engaged in combat or peace operations in central and western Asia, then the likelihood of the United States being at least affected by—or even drawn into—severe ethnic strife in the CASC region is high. Whether the conflict remains potential or becomes actualized depends on the internal evolution within the specific countries as well as among the major neighboring states. The potential for conflict is explored in more detail below, first examining Central Asia and then South Caucasus. Each subsection is organized by origin of the potential for conflict: intraregional, extraregional, and intrastate.

Central Asia

In terms of ethnic conflict that has intraregional origins and implications, Uzbekistan—more specifically, Uzbek aspirations in the Ferghana Valley—is the primary source. The existence of Uzbek extraterritorial enclaves in Kyrgyzstan (administratively part of Uzbekistan's territory but not contiguous to Uzbekistan), heavy intermixing of Uzbek, Kyrgyz, and Tajik populations, tensions over access to resources between Uzbekistan and the other two countries, "ethnic redress" policies in all three countries, Uzbek ambitions of

---

[21]Hugh Griffiths, "A Political Economy of Ethnic Conflict, Ethno-nationalism and Organised Crime," *Civil Wars*, Vol. 2, No. 2 (1999).

regional dominance, and a recent record of ethnic riots and tensions in the Ferghana Valley all suggest the potential for strife. The strife could take the form of Uzbekistani assistance for Uzbeks just beyond Uzbekistan's borders (with a goal, for example, of effecting boundary changes that would attach directly to Uzbekistan the Uzbek enclaves in adjoining countries). Historical Uzbek-Tajik rivalry and, to a lesser extent, Uzbek-Kyrgyz historical distrust (combined with a sense of Uzbek superiority), provides ample room for exploitation by leaders who wish to play the "ethnic card."

In terms of ethnic strife with origins from beyond the region, there are at least three potential sources. Depending on the evolution of domestic Russian politics, the millions of Russians and Russophones in northern Kazakhstan could emerge as a secessionist group supported by Russia. Nationalist figures in Russia, including Alexandr Solzhenitsyn, have called for the incorporation of all or part of Kazakhstan into Russia. If the policies of "ethnic redress" in Kazakhstan lose their current cautious edge, the likelihood of Russian secessionism gaining strength in northern Kazakhstan is strong. Russian leadership in Moscow would be hard pressed not to support their fellow Russians.

Political Islam, supported from abroad, is another potential source of potentially severe communal (not strictly ethnic) conflict in Central Asia.[22] Although political Islam is a homegrown threat to the current regimes, the outside support strengthens it greatly.[23] The potential for strife arising from political Islam is most acute in the southern states of the region (Tajikistan, where it has already contributed to a civil war, as well as Uzbekistan and perhaps Turkmenistan), but geography and Soviet-era boundary lines between the states of Central Asia mean that the strife would be difficult to control.

---

[22]An examination of the relationship between ethnic and religious causes of intrastate strife since the end of the Cold War shows a close correlation between the two. Moreover, Islam is more highly correlated than other religions with ethnic conflict. The study involved the Minorities at Risk data set (the most comprehensive data set of minority populations in the world). Jonathan Fox, "The Ethnic-Religious Nexus: The Impact of Religion on Ethnic Conflict," *Civil Wars*, Vol. 3, No. 3 (2000); Jonathan Fox, "Is Islam More Conflict Prone Than Other Religions? A Cross-Sectional Study of Ethnoreligious Conflict," *Nationalism and Ethnic Politics*, Vol. 6, No. 2 (2000).

[23]Anna Zelkina, "Islam and Security in the New States of Central Asia: How Genuine Is the Islamic Threat?" *Religion, State and Society*, Vol. 27, No. 3–4 (1999), pp. 355–372.

Tajikistan and Kyrgyzstan would also be involved in any strife that centered on the Uzbekistani portion of the Ferghana Valley (as has already happened on one occasion). Complicating matters, the Central Asian regimes have used Islam to further their own nation-building schemes (since Islam is part of the cultural heritage of the indigenous people of the region). But such use of Islam has the potential to backfire, if the officially sanctioned Islam meta-morphoses into political Islam at odds with the secular Soviet-legacy regimes in power across the region.[24] As it currently stands, the most likely path to conflict (based on political Islam) would take the form of the current Soviet-legacy regimes in power (or their similarly inclined successors) in Central Asia attempting to suppress an armed movement aimed at establishing Islamic republics. However, such a movement would probably target the "infidels" (citizens of these countries that are members of ethnic groups not indigenous to the region) as well as the "collaborators" from the groups indigenous to Central Asia. While not strictly ethnic, such strife would have an ethnic dimension. The U.S.-led operations in Afghanistan may have diminished the short-term direct threat of Islamist insurgency to the Central Asian states (by denying bases, support, and expertise to the homegrown militants). But the problems that led to the emergence of the Islamist militants still persist. In the medium term and be-yond, those problems may spawn renewed efforts at insurgency.

A third source of ethnic strife that has origins from beyond the terri-tory of the five Central Asian states is the spillover of conflict from the ongoing low-level insurgency among the Turkic population of China's Xinjiang region (or East Turkestan to the Central Asian groups). The Uighurs, one of the groups involved in the strife in Xinjiang, also inhabit eastern Kazakhstan. Although hardly a mono-lithic group, the Kazakh Uighurs sympathize with their co-ethnics in Xinjiang and support the goal of establishing an independent Uighurstan from a part of Xinjiang.[25] Under certain scenarios, such

---

[24]Shahram Akbarzadeh, "Political Islam in Kyrgyzstan and Turkmenistan," *Central Asian Survey*, Vol. 20, No. 4 (2001), pp. 451–465.

[25]Sean R. Roberts, "The Uighurs of the Kazakhstan Borderlands: Migration and the Nation," *Nationalities Papers*, Vol. 26, No. 3 (1998), pp. 511–530; Witt Raczka, "Xinjiang and Its Central Asian Borderlands," *Central Asian Survey*, Vol. 17, No. 3 (1998), pp. 373–407. For more on Xinjiang, see the special issue (devoted to Xinjiang) of *Inner Asia*, Vol. 2, No. 2 (2000).

as weakening central Chinese control over Xinjiang, the support could become more overt and lead to direct involvement of the Uighurs of eastern Kazakhstan. The reaction of Kazakhstan to such an evolution could range from a crackdown on the Uighurs to covert support for their cause. Either way, if the strife from Xinjiang were to spread to Kazakhstan, it would have extraregional ramifications.

Finally, in terms of ethnic conflict that has internal sources (purely within specific Central Asian countries), the Karakalpaks of western Uzbekistan are the most likely source of potentially severe ethnic conflict. Karakalpakstan has a special administrative status in Uzbekistan, providing it with a large measure of autonomy. Since such a status leads to the development of local elites that have little attachment to the central government, and since autonomous political structures based on ethnicity have already led to secessions in other post-Communist countries, the special status for Karakalpakstan is a potential source of severe conflict. Under the current conditions of the Uzbek government's strong central authority, such an evolution seems unlikely, but under other evolutionary pathways for Uzbekistan (for example a weakened regime, perhaps because of Islamist insurgency), an opportunity structure that might lead to Karakalpak moves toward secession is plausible.[26]

Toward the upper range of the next 10–15 years, if the current regimes in power in Central Asia show signs of unraveling or even sustained weakening, then the subnational identities that now seem secondary may re-emerge. If that were to happen, then additional sources of potential ethnic conflict could also arise.

South Caucasus

The primary source of ethnic conflict in South Caucasus with intraregional origins and implications is the import of strife from the northern Caucasus (predominantly Muslim regions that are a part of Russia). Georgia and Azerbaijan stand to be most affected by such strife. The continuing war in Chechnya is the most obvious case for potential spillover into Georgia, with possible Russian intervention

---

[26]Reuel R. Hanks, "A Separate Space? Karakalpak Nationalism and Devolution in Post-Soviet Uzbekistan," *Europe-Asia Studies,* Vol. 52, No. 5 (2000), pp. 939–953.

and/or actions to detach parts of northern Georgia from central control. Other existing disputes that could evolve to sustained armed strife include the following: the unresolved Ingush-Ossetian conflict (especially as it affects Georgia's South Ossetia), an upsurge in tensions between the Karachai-Balkars and Circassians in the western portion of Russia's north Caucasus (affecting Georgia), the potential for Lezgin nationalism spreading from Dagestan to northern Azerbaijan, and the potential for multifaceted ethnic strife in Dagestan (affecting Azerbaijan).[27] Though all of these conflicts involve Russia, they are in fact intra–Caucausus region conflicts that might be exploited by Russia. The conflict between Azerbaijan and Armenia over Nagorno-Karabakh is not discussed here, since it is essentially an interstate conflict at this stage (though it evolved from an ethnic conflict internal to Azerbaijan) and has to be resolved at the interstate level.

In terms of ethnic strife with origins from beyond the region, further Russian attempts (beyond Abkhazia) aimed at fragmenting Georgia along ethnic lines are the most plausible source of potential severe ethnic conflict in South Caucasus. Given the presence of many ethnic groups and subethnic identities in Georgia, a plausible list of options in the next 10–15 years is long and includes Ossetia, Adjaria, or even support for Armenian designs on the Armenian-inhabited parts of Georgia that are contiguous to Armenia.

Political Islam does not figure as a major potential source of communal strife in South Caucasus in the near term.[28] It pertains only to Azerbaijan and only in the medium or longer time frame (and depends on the political and economic evolution in Azerbaijan over the next decade). Under certain scenarios of the Islamic parties taking power in Turkey, political Islam also would become a more powerful force in Azerbaijan. For political Islam to become a factor in

---

[27]Svante E. Cornell, "Conflicts in the North Caucasus," *Central Asian Survey,* Vol. 17, No. 3 (1998), pp. 409–441; Robert Bruce Ware and Enver Kisriev, "The Islamic Factor in Dagestan," *Central Asian Survey,* Vol. 19, No. 2 (2000), pp. 235–252; Vladimir Bobrovnikov, "Muslim Nationalism in the Post-Soviet Caucasus: The Dagestani Case," *Caucasian Regional Studies,* Vol. 4, No. 1 (1999), *http://poli.vub.ac.be/publi/crs/eng/0401-01.htm.*

[28]It is important to note that religion has played a limited role in the conflicts in the Caucasus (north and south) since 1991. Svante E. Cornell, "Religion as a Factor in Caucasian Conflicts," *Civil Wars,* Vol. 1, No. 3 (1998).

Ajaria (an area inhabited by ethnic Georgians who are Muslims) in the short or medium term is currently beyond the plausible, since ethnic Georgian identity is stronger than any subgroup sectarian attachments and the Ajars tend to secular.

Finally, in terms of ethnic conflict that has internal sources (purely within specific countries of South Caucasus), the multitude of internal fissures in Georgia is the clearest and most immediate potential source of severe conflict. Whether the conflict comes about depends greatly on the institutionalization of rule of the current regime over all of Georgia. Under certain scenarios, especially centering around political succession, the internal fissures may widen. Although Georgia is the weakest of the three states of South Caucasus in terms of internal fissures, should the current regime in Azerbaijan show signs of unraveling, then over the next 10–15 years, subnational identities that now seem secondary in Azerbaijan may re-emerge.

FINAL OBSERVATIONS

Given the multitude of plausible scenarios for further ethnic conflict to arise in the CASC region over the next 10–15 years and the fact that conditions that can lead to these conflicts have been in place for much of the 1990s, the important question is why conflict has been relatively absent in the past decade. The persistence of authoritarian Soviet-legacy regimes in all the countries of the region, and particularly in Central Asia, provides one explanation. All of the regimes have pursued policies of "ethnic redress" but, for reasons of their own, have not followed drastic measures in implementing them. Had they done so, the likelihood of mobilization of the affected groups against these regimes would have been higher. The relative risk aversion and caution toward ethnic minorities shown so far by the regimes of the CASC region are not a given but a specific outcome based on domestic political calculations as well as a cost-benefit assessment of more assertive policies. As Soviet era recedes further into the past and the cumulative effects of a decade of "ethnic redress" become apparent, the calculations are bound to change (either toward even greater acquiescence or toward ethnic assertiveness). In the near term, the regime in Uzbekistan is the most likely to shift to more assertive policies, a move that will have an ethnic dimension and regional implications. In the longer term, potential exists for such a shift in all the states of the CASC region.

Would mobilization of an ethnic group for political action or even ethnically based strife in one country lead to mobilizations or conflict in other countries of the CASC region? The answer varies greatly, depending on the country and the group. At minimum, the potential for spread of ethnic assertiveness or strife between South Caucasus and Central Asia is low. Any such contagion is likely to be within the specific subregion. In Central Asia, strife in the Ferghana Valley is unlikely to be contained to one country because of the way ethnic groups are intermixed and the manner in which the borders were drawn.[29] Political Islam is also unlikely to be limited to just one country. But beyond these easy observations, the situation is too murky and too scenario-dependent to predict the potential for spread of conflict with any degree of confidence.

One thing is clear, however. If an ethnic group were to mobilize for political action in the CASC region under the political and economic conditions approximating the situation today, violence is likely to follow. Using the framework for anticipating ethnic conflict developed by RAND,[30] the types of states prevalent in the CASC region are prone to resort to violence in response to mobilization by an ethnic group for political action. Using the terminology of that work, the CASC states fit three of the eight state types (G, D, or F).[31] These are

---

[29]The republican borders of the Central Asian republics date back to the 1930s and were made to ensure Moscow's control over the region rather than to achieve the most "fair" solution to ethnic-territorial delimitation, one that would include considerations of historical pattern of settlement or economic links. Thus, large numbers of ethnic Tajiks and the historically Tajik cities of Samarkand and Bukhara ended up in Uzbekistan. Conversely, areas historically associated more with Uzbeks, like the Khujand region (overlooking the Ferghana Valley), became part of Tajikistan even though the region remained more linked economically to Uzbekistan than to the rest of Tajikistan. In fact, intracountry surface communication between the Khujand region and the rest of Tajikistan is impossible for half the year because of the Turkestan, Zarafshon, and Hisor mountain ranges, whereas transportation links with Uzbekistan are extensive and operational year-round. Though not as egregious, similar problems exist in other Central Asian states and, to a smaller extent, in South Caucasus.

[30]Szayna, *Identifying Potential Ethnic Conflict: Application of a Process Model.*

[31]The Caspian states are generally type G (strong leadership, weak fiscal position, exclusive regime) or, arguably (and depending on the relative position of the group in

the three most violence-prone of all the state types. The conclusion makes sense intuitively, in that the states of the CASC region do not have the institutions in place to accommodate group demands easily; they are developing states and cannot buy off dissatisfied groups with economic benefits, but they generally have sizable coercive apparati in place. Moreover, the coercive apparati are more suitable for domestic use than for external conflict. The above does not mean that ethnic conflict is a given in the CASC region, since mobilization of an ethnic group for political action may not take place even if the group in question has real and numerous grievances. But it does mean that mobilization of an ethnic group is likely to end up with the state using violence against it.

How the U.S.-led military operations in Afghanistan will affect the potential for ethnic conflict in the CASC region, and especially Central Asia, remains unclear. At a minimum, the ongoing military operations have made forecasts even more difficult, and any predictions beyond the short term are downright foolhardy because of so many unknowns. Suffice it to say that conditions continue to be in place for severe ethnic strife, though there is nothing inevitable about such strife. Any assessment of the potential for ethnically based conflict depends greatly on the situation in Afghanistan (and the extent and length of time of any U.S. military presence in central and southwestern Asia), the extent to which the conflict may spread to other parts of southwestern Asia, the scope of international efforts to assist the CASC states in dealing with the fallout from the conflict, and the overall long-term impact of the conflict on the appeal of fundamentalist Islamist ideas to the Muslim populations of the states of the CASC region. The latter especially deserves to be monitored closely, both in a regional sense as well as in terms of impact on specific ethnic groups (and demographic subgroups within them) within the region.

---

question), types D (strong leadership, strong fiscal position, exclusive regime) or F (weak leadership, weak fiscal position, exclusive regime).

Chapter Seven

CONFLICT IN CENTRAL ASIA AND SOUTH CAUCASUS: IMPLICATIONS OF FOREIGN INTERESTS AND INVOLVEMENT
Olga Oliker

INTRODUCTION

Geography has made the Central Asian and South Caucasus states a historical nexus for trade, competition, and sometimes conflict. Traditionally, foreign powers have seen the region as an economic and strategic gateway to other parts of the world. Somewhat more recently, since the states of the region gained independence from the Soviet Union a decade ago, the region's potential for energy production created new, additional areas of foreign interest. Today, it is increasingly clear that foreign competition over energy is only one component of a complex balance of the economic and strategic short- and long-term goals of a number of interested parties, a balance now complicated further by the crucial importance of Central Asia to the multinational coalition response to terrorist acts against the United States on September 11, 2001. If, in the summer of 2001, the International Crisis Group could safely write (with regard to Central Asia) that "no outside power is sufficiently interested in the region to make major investments in its security," this is clearly no longer the case.[1]

It is therefore highly likely that coming years will see continued competition among outside powers over the region and its resources and allegiances. This does not necessarily mean, however, that great-power conflict will result. In fact, as the exploration of the interests and motivations of various actors undertaken in this chapter will

---

[1]"Central Asia: Fault Lines in the New Security Map," Osh/Brussels: International Crisis Group, 2001.

show, competition is moderated by the many shared interests of the outside powers in question. But strategic and economic interests will also cause foreign states to be increasingly active in the region diplomatically, economically, and militarily. This means that if other factors spur conflict in the region, as analysis elsewhere in this report suggests is likely, there is significant potential for outside powers to get involved—even if their interests are not themselves the reason that conflict emerges.

Because there is room for many states to gain from the region's potential and because regional stability is a shared goal as well, there will be high incentives to cooperate as well as compete. Strategic reasons to maintain good ties among interested third parties will also temper the likelihood of conflict. But because there is also little doubt that some will gain more than others, it is likely that competition will remain a significant factor—and may at times be fierce. Moreover, the existence of incentives for cooperation among outside powers does not imply that third parties cannot be potential sources of regional conflict in other ways, or that one or more of them will not get involved in conflict if it occurs for other reasons.

Even the generally shared interests in the peaceful development of these states may be what leads neighbors and other interested parties to become involved in conflict if it occurs. If the peace that they desire appears threatened, these states may see their interests as threatened as well. Moreover, the weakness of CASC states creates incentives for outsiders to seek to influence the policy directions of local governments and to question the latter's capacity to maintain peace and stability on their own. If these outsiders feel compelled to act to quell conflict, whether real or burgeoning, they will of course themselves become parties to it.

The ways and reasons that third parties could instigate, exacerbate, or otherwise involve themselves in regional fighting are as varied as the countries in question. The most obvious and critical concern today is the situation in Afghanistan. On the one hand, Afghanistan provides a harrowing example of the effects of state failure and factionalism that at least some of the CASC states are at risk of. A new commitment to preventing this sort of disintegration could lead to increased involvement by foreign actors in efforts to stabilize the region. At the same time, the processes of stabilization and state-building in Afghanistan itself have the potential to be long and arduous, involving the reconciling of differences between a large number of conflicting groups—many of which share ethnic, religious, and linguistic ties with neighboring Central Asian states (and China). Moreover, members of the international coalition that is working to help stabilize the situation in Afghanistan are using bases in Central Asian states, which increase their own interests in maintaining stability and peace in this region. Their presence sharply increases the likelihood of their involvement in any unrest or conflict that emerges in this part of the world.

If it proves impossible to quickly quell conflict in Afghanistan, neighboring states may suffer from refugee flows, and possibly even the export of some of the instability. The narcotics trade that fueled what there was of Afghanistan's economy in recent years will also be difficult to eradicate. The production of narcotics remains one of the few trades available to rural Afghans seeking to make a living, and Northern Alliance factions were no less involved in the trafficking than were Taliban groups. Of course, Central Asia has suffered as the primary route for opium and heroin traveling from Afghanistan to Russia and Europe (see Chapter Four).

Russia, whose stakes in the region are historical, political, strategic, and economic, presents a number of complications. One is the fear among CASC states that this large neighbor, recognizing its increasing weakness and fearing a complete loss of influence in the region, will seek to reassert control while it still can, and will attempt to do so by force. Whether or not Russia has the capability to do so successfully is less important than the fact that in trying, it can spark ethnic, religious, and territorial conflict in the region, which would set prospects for reform and development back by decades. Moreover, Russia's deep and fundamental interests in the region all but guarantee that if conflict erupts, for whatever reason, Russia will seek to play a role—and to have a say over the extent to which other outside powers can get involved.

Perhaps even more dangerous is the possibility that Russia, due either to weakness or some other factor, cannot or does not act to stem local conflict, or does so belatedly. While Russia has clear interests in the region, which it has made no secret of, other regional powers, including China, Turkey, and Iran, also have reason to fear conflict and anarchy in this region. To date, these states have to different degrees been deterred from actively pursuing their interests in the region by Russia's clear opposition to their doing so. A regional crisis combined with a seemingly disinterested, incapable, or otherwise insufficiently active Russia, however, could spur one or more of them to attempt to resolve the situation. This could potentially result in a Russian response less to the conflict at the root of the problems than to "interference" in its neighboring states.

The increased U.S. presence in CASC alters this equation in several ways, however. Prior to September 11, most of its interests in CASC could best be described as secondary economic interests (given the relatively low level of energy resource wealth that most estimates for the region assess), derivative of the interests of allies such as Turkey, or based in the pursuit of desired, but far from vital, goals such as democratization. On the other hand, the United States had and continues to have vital interests in responding to transnational threats that, while not specific to CASC, even before September 11, could not be advanced without some attention to this part of the world. These include the prevention of proliferation of weapons of mass destruction, the fight against transnational crime and the drug trade, and of course, the effort to combat and prevent the development and spread of terrorist groups and tactics. Moreover, it is worth noting that even secondary interests can have important second-order effects. Allies and U.S. and multinational energy firms, as well as the transnational threats mentioned above, created imperatives for the United States to be at least somewhat involved in the CASC region. Finally, as recent events have demonstrated beyond a doubt, the region's location between Russia, Afghanistan, China, Iran, and Turkey make it the staging area for a variety of combat scenarios— above and beyond the current one. If anything, the investment that the United States and its allies are now making in developing infrastructure and relationships in CASC states for the Afghanistan operation will make it more likely that these states will be called upon to support future missions and endeavors.

U.S. ties with the states of CASC had been growing and developing for a decade prior to the decision to base forces here for the military effort in Afghanistan. The United States has sought to deepen ties so as to influence regional governments to a wide range of goals (ideological as well as strategic), and U.S. policy, in turn, was also affected by these contacts. Even before September 11, continued and deepening involvement made it likely that even if the United States avoided direct involvement in regional conflict, unrest in CASC would complicate U.S. military and nonmilitary efforts in and near the region. Today, with the likelihood of a significant long-term peacekeeping and humanitarian effort in Afghanistan that includes at least some U.S. involvement, it seems impossible that the United States would not get involved in some way in a Central Asian crisis. This has implications for the United States and the states concerned, but also for Russia and other regional powers. On the one hand, it makes it even less likely that China, for example, will choose to get involved in developing unrest, insofar as it believes that the United States can be relied upon to keep the situation quiet. On the other hand, depending on how the U.S. relationship with Iran evolves, the latter may feel it necessary to protect its interests in the region against the United States by supporting certain groups over others, as it has in Afghanistan. Turkey, as a U.S. ally, may be called upon to play a larger role than it might want. Finally, Russia, depending on the level of cooperation with the United States at the time, could either seek to flummox U.S. efforts or act in partnership, creating complications in either case.

This analysis considers the interests of third parties in the region, seeking to identify the potential for those interests to cause and/or exacerbate conflict. It discusses each potentially interested state in turn to assess its strategic position and threat perception, and how they affect its attitudes toward and relations with CASC states. It assesses the potential for conflict between third parties spurred by their interests and activities in CASC as well as how they might get involved in conflict in the region. It then turns to the states of the region to assess their perspective on these neighbors and other interested parties.

RUSSIA

To understand Russia's attitudes toward Central Asia and South Caucasus, it is imperative to understand the strategic and historical factors that influence Russian decisionmaking. Weakness and perceived vulnerability on the part of a state are generally believed by those adhering to the realist and neorealist schools of political science to result in a view of the world as even more threatening and unfriendly than the anarchic political system already leads it to be.[2] Because stronger states have the capacity to harm, they are seen as dangerous to the weak state and its interests. At the helm of a formerly strong state, now in decline, Russia's leadership seeks to reverse the decline and (insofar as possible) reclaim a position of power and influence. But the state's weakness precludes success in this endeavor. While Russia may in principle be able to stop aspects of its political, economic, and military decline, efforts to re-establish some sort of pre-eminence in the short term by means of influence over other states makes sustainable reform of its own declining state structures even less likely.

Whatever Russia's own situation, however, it has numerous strategic reasons to see CASC as crucial to its security interests. Russia's historical effort to control the region derived from its belief that this control would reap economic and strategic benefits. Russian rule over regions of Turkestan and Transcaspia was cemented by the end of the 19th century, with the inner Asian region divided into spheres of influence by Russia and China.[3] Moscow maintained that control during both the Tsarist and Soviet periods, and CASC states were important sources of resources for the successive empires. Over time, to many in Russia, such imperial possessions became a component of Russia's self-definition, and proof of its importance as a state and as a great power. Thus, the independence of these and other former Soviet states continues to be difficult to accept for many Russians, for whom the Russian empire and the Soviet Union were, to a large extent, Russia itself. As Roman Szporluk writes, "Russia did not *have* an empire, it *was* one."[4] Moreover, many ethnic Russians

---

[2]The classic texts of neorealism are Kenneth Waltz, *Theory of International Politics,* New York: McGraw-Hill, 1979, and Stephen Walt, *The Origins of Alliances,* Ithaca and London: Cornell University Press, 1987. On the impact of state decline, see A.F.K. Organski, *World Politics,* 2nd ed., New York: Knopf, 1968, and Robert Gilpin, *War and Change in World Politics,* Cambridge: Cambridge University Press, 1981. See also Joseph S. Nye, Jr., *Bound to Lead: The Changing Nature of American Power,* New York: Basic Books, 1990.

[3]Ira M. Lapidus, *A History of Islamic Societies,* Cambridge: Cambridge University Press, 1988, Chapter 17: "Islam in Central And Southern Asia," p. 415.

[4]Roman Szporluk, "The Fall of the Tsarist Empire and the USSR: The Russian Question and Imperial Overextension," in Karen Dawisha and Bruce Parrott (eds.), *The End of Empire? The Transformation of the USSR in Comparative Perspective,*

lived in these regions during Soviet times and, despite emigration following the collapse of the Soviet Union, many remain, particularly in Kazakhstan (see Chapter Six).

Strategic/historical interests aside, the economic benefits of continued close ties with CASC states are a strong motivator for Russia to seek to maintain influence over the region. Moscow recognizes that its own economic modernization will be crucial if it is to regain any semblance of the power that it once enjoyed. Caspian energy development provides real opportunities for economic gain, and Russia hopes to play a role. But while both Moscow and the CASC states stand to benefit from Caspian Sea development, Moscow's economic interests are not always aligned with those of its neighbors. Russia, a major energy exporter in its own right (with its own Caspian Sea reserves) has strong incentives, for instance, to charge high transit fees for Caspian oil transported over its territory, to buy up other states' production to keep prices high, and to otherwise prevent or hinder its neighbors from effectively and profitably exporting fossil fuels. The Soviet-designed and built network of pipelines that Caspian energy exporters rely on to get oil and natural gas to customers is one in which all pipelines (and much of the refining and other infrastructure) lead through Russia. This makes other producers dependent on this large neighbor, and because these fossil fuels are among the only export assets these countries possess, this infrastructure perpetuates economic dependence on Russia. It also enables Russia to manipulate Caspian energy exports to its own economic benefit, as well as potentially translating into political leverage over the CASC states. Russia therefore sees it as imperative to maintain these states' dependence on Russian export routes and has tended to oppose new pipelines or other energy export routes that fail to transit its own territory.[5]

Russia also sees a threat in the growth of radical Islamic political movements that seek to overthrow secular governments in Central

---

Armonk, NY: M.E. Sharpe, Inc., 1997, pp. 65–95. Quote is on page 71. See also Ronald Grigor Suny, "Provisional Stabilities," *International Security,* Vol. 24, No. 3 (1999).

[5]That said, Russian energy companies are interested in being involved in Caspian energy development regardless of where the pipelines go, although they do have their preferences. Recent statements by Lukoil, for instance, suggest that the Russian government may drop some of its opposition to various pipeline routes, including Baku-Ceyhan, if Russian companies stand to gain from them.

Asia. With its own large Muslim population (concentrated primarily in the north Caucasus and the Tatar and Bashkir Republics), Russia fears that radical Islamic movements, if successful in Central Asia, will then spread to other states, including Russia itself, perhaps using Chechnya as a foothold, and that this will lead to further unrest and homeland terrorist attacks. Secessionist movements (whether religious in nature or otherwise) in CASC are similarly viewed in Moscow as potential spurs to secessionist activity in Russia's own regions, especially in the north Caucasus. As Grigor Suny writes, Russia, or at least the Russian media, tends to view the area to the south as the source of a variety of threats, including "militant Islam, ethnic mafias, agents of foreign states, and drug traders."[6]

The drug trade and crime are indeed reasons for Russia to be concerned. The narcotics trafficking routes that start in Afghanistan and move through Central Asia then transit Russia, where drug use and abuse is growing, along with the attendant health care problems. Russian and other post-Soviet criminal groups, including those in CASC, maintain close ties.[7] Their growing power and influence threaten government control and the social order throughout the post-Soviet space and have repercussions beyond it, with activities in Europe, Israel, the United States, and elsewhere. At the same time, the Russian leadership also recognizes that for all of these threats, domestic instability keeps CASC states weak, which makes them more reliant on Russian assistance and support and thus more compliant with Russia's political and economic demands.

This has made for fundamental contradictions within Russian policy goals toward the CASC region. The Russians want to prevent unrest and violence, stem the flow of crime and drugs, and ensure that secular governments remain in place and in control, but these interests are at odds with their desire to maintain dominance, which requires that these states remain politically weak and dependent on Russian assistance. Similarly, the Russian desire to profit from Caspian energy development implies significant economic modernization and growth in the region, which of course would make these states

---

[6]Suny, "Provisional Stabilities."

[7]See Chapter Four of this report.

less dependent on Russia (unless, of course, Russia can attain and maintain a monopoly over energy export routes).

Over the last few years, Russia has sought to advance its goals in CASC with a multitracked policy of engaging local states to both build influence and attempt to mitigate the security threats it sees as emanating from the region.[8] Efforts include political, military, and economic ties and assistance. Russia has sought to take advantage of fears of instability and conflict within the region itself by promising security assistance and commitments. (Some even suggest that Russia has supported insurgency movements in Central Asia in order to make the local states less secure.[9]) Military assistance includes the sale of weapons, the stationing of troops to assist with defensive goals, joint counterinsurgency training, and the establishment of a joint regional counterterrorist organization headquartered in Bishkek, as well as an associated joint rapid-reaction unit.

Russian success with military contacts and assistance has been variable. Tajikistan and Armenia have welcomed Russian troops,[10] Kyrgyzstan has accepted some military assistance, and Kazakhstan has been willing to maintain military and political ties (including through the Shanghai Five/Shanghai Cooperation Organization— Russia, China, Kazakhstan, Kyrgyzstan, Tajikistan, and, since June 2000, Uzbekistan). On the other hand, Turkmenistan has remained insistently nonaligned (and increasingly isolationist), Georgia continues to demand that Russian forces leave its soil (and has protested Russian attacks into Georgian territory in pursuit of Chechen

---

[8]Suny, "Provisional Stabilities," argues that Russia is "a relatively benign hegemon in relationship to the Southern Tier rather than a neo-imperialist threat."

[9]Edward Helmore, "US in Replay of 'Great Game,'" *Johnson's Russia List (The Observer)*, January 21 (January 20), 2002.

[10]Russia has about 25,000 men, including border guards and motor rifle troops, under its direct command in Tajikistan, many of them Tajiks. Tajikistan itself only patrols a small fraction, about 70 kilometers, of its 1,300-kilometer border. Russia patrols the rest, and provides training for Tajik forces as well. Agreements between the two countries permit Russia to as much as double its military presence, but the difficulties inherent in attracting personnel to serve in Tajikistan, along with Russia's commitments elsewhere, make it unlikely that Russia will step up its presence to that extent. "Tajikistan: An Uncertain Peace," Osh/Brussels: International Crisis Group, 2001. "Central Asia: Fault Lines in the New Security Map."

rebels[11]), Azerbaijan has been adamant and consistent in its refusal to allow Russian troops to be stationed on its soil and more recently has largely rebuffed Russian efforts to re-establish close ties, and Uzbekistan has repeatedly refused to accept Russian military assistance. Kazakhstan, Kyrgyzstan, Georgia, Uzbekistan, and Azerbaijan have instead sought to build ties with the United States and Turkey, with, until recently, varying degrees of success. Finally, although the efforts at multinational cooperation through CIS and the Shanghai Cooperation Organization look plentiful on paper, implementation has been minimal.[12]

Mixed feelings about Russian overtures are to be expected. Even if Russian behavior today is not neoimperialist, this is a sharp break with the past experience of regional states, and, as Suny points out, it is difficult for them to view Russia as benevolent.[13] And indeed, as already noted, Russia will pursue its own interests, which are at various times more or less congruent with those of its neighbors. If Russia once conquered and held Central Asia by the sword, Russia's real threat to the independence of these states today is one of economic and political pressure, not military incursion. While Russia's military might and capacity is questionable, the pipeline routes through its territory are very real. Not surprisingly, Russia's efforts at coercion have increasingly taken on an economic component. If it previously used tough talk and reminders of its force presence to convince its neighbors that they should be its allies, it has now supplemented words and military posturing with economic action: for instance, a government-supported campaign by Russian firms to invest heavily in the industry of peripheral states, particularly the energy sector. This increasing Russian ownership of industry in the CASC and throughout the former Soviet Union gives Russia more leverage over these states' economies, and provides a hedge in the event that Russia loses its near-monopoly over energy export routes. No matter which way the pipelines go, at least some Russian firms will stand to gain.

---

[11]Vernon Loeb and Peter Slevin, "U.S. Begins Anti-Terror Assistance in Georgia," *Washington Post*, February 27, 2002, p. A1.

[12]"Central Asia: Fault Lines in the New Security Map."

[13]Suny, "Provisional Stabilities."

As with military ties, the record of success is mixed. Caspian oil-producing states Azerbaijan and Kazakhstan, as well as transit state Georgia, hope that by supporting multiple pipeline routes, they can limit Russia's capacity to exert influence through these economic mechanisms. In the meantime, they resist Russian economic pressure in the expectation that these routes will be built. Azerbaijan and Georgia, as well as gas producer Uzbekistan and resource-poor Kyrgyzstan, are also hopeful that political, military, and economic ties with other states will help them withstand Russian pressure. Kyrgyzstan, with less to offer economically or militarily, is more accepting of Russian influence than Uzbekistan. Turkmenistan, on the other hand, whose most important export is natural gas, most of which is transported to customers by pipelines through Russia, has sought to dampen its continuing vulnerability to Russian pressure with a policy of increasing political, economic, and social isolationism. Finally, Armenia and Tajikistan depend on Russia for their security needs and therefore maintain close relations with Moscow.

Russia's mixed record in both the political and the economic spheres can be attributed not only to the history of empire, but also (as Suny notes) to the questionable nature of Russia's ability to deliver on its promises and threats. With Russia unable to establish law and order at home, it seems unlikely that it can assist Central Asia in its efforts to drive out rebellious religious fundamentalists, organized criminals, and drug traffickers. In some ways it is decades of rule from Moscow that has made the region poor, fragmented, conflict-prone, and economically dependent. Today, there is reason to doubt that Russia can do much to fix the situation, even if it wants to, or that it can make it worse without doing itself severe harm in the process.

The fact that others may be able to do something creates additional complications, of course. Because the region has so long been under Russian rule, because it remains one of few where Moscow retains influence, and because Russia, as a weak state, is inclined to perceive all foreign activities near its borders as threatening, Russia throughout the 1990s saw other states' efforts in this part of the world as a form of hostile encroachment. This was particularly true of Moscow's attitudes toward U.S. and Turkish bilateral and multilateral ties with Caucasus and Central Asian states. These activities were viewed as an attempt to woo Russia's natural allies away from its influence. Moreover, U.S. involvement in Central Asia was interpreted by much of the Russian leadership (and the Russian public) as a component of a concerted effort by the United States (along with plans for a national missile defense and NATO enlargement) to lessen Russia's influence and weaken it further. This perception made it all the more important for Russia to maintain influence over this region, not only to assert Russia's power and importance, but also to demonstrate to the world that the United States and its allies have not weakened Russia entirely.

From a neorealist perspective, this can be viewed as a form of "balancing" on Russia's part—a way of increasing its own strength relative to a stronger adversary or potential adversary, in this case the United States and its allies. Continued influence over at least the near abroad makes justifiable Russia's claim to be a great power, even given its political and economic weakness, because it continues to have states in its sphere of influence. Even if the actual military and economic power thus gained is minimal, the ability to attract allies at all augments Russian capacity to demonstrate that it remains a player on the global stage. That a role in the economic and energy development of these states can further benefit Russia makes continued influence over this particular region that much more important.

But the fact remains that Russia is a relatively weak actor on the global stage, even if it remains strong compared to its post-Soviet neighbors. This combination makes Russia a potentially dangerous player in the region over the next 10–15 years. That shifts in state power increase the risk of war is well accepted in the political science literature.[14] In Russia's case, its difficulty in accurately assessing its own capabilities (to say nothing of the difficulties of others assessing them), combined with its desire to maintain influence and control over the CASC region (in part as a way of augmenting Russia's perceived power) could lead to military adventurism by a Russia that overestimates its capacity to attain a military solution. In fact, both Russia's continuing peacekeeping role in Tajikistan and its involvement in Georgia's internal conflicts can be seen as examples of such

---

[14]See Organski, *World Politics,* and Gilpin, *War and Change in World Politics.* On the impact of political transitions to and from democracy and authoritarianism, see also Edward D. Mansfield and Jack Snyder, "Democratization and the Danger of War," *International Security,* Vol. 20, No. 1 (1995), pp. 5–38.

"overstretch" by a declining power. In Tajikistan, the effectiveness of Russia's peacekeeping and border control efforts is debatable, and arguments that the presence is useful depend on assessments of how much worse things would be were the Russians not there. In Georgia, Russian military involvement has exacerbated conflict in ways that significantly weakened the Georgian state, supporting de facto secessionism in North Ossetia and Abkhazia, although it can be argued that Russian military presence more recently helped mitigate violence in Georgia.

Moreover, as discussed elsewhere in this analysis, the region itself is also one of inherently dangerous political transitions. Russia's political and economic interests in the region, combined with its desire to maintain and demonstrate pre-eminence there and the continuing presence of Russian troops in both South Caucasus and Central Asia, all but guarantee that should conflict emerge (for any reason), Russia will play a role in responding to it. Because Russia itself is in the process of profound political and economic changes that are likely to continue for at least the next one or two decades, Russian weakness combines with its interests to create a potentially dangerous situation. If Russia attempts to stem conflict and fails, not only could the fighting spread, but other states might get involved in an effort to complete the job. Unless this is carefully coordinated with Russia, it might be perceived by Moscow as encroachment, leading to hostility and possibly even conflict between Russia and the offending state. Moreover, Russian interests in the region mean that if it does seek a foreign war to demonstrate its capabilities while it still has them, the CASC region is at risk of being a target. Alternatively, Russian weakness, particularly given a significant downturn in the Russian economy, may lead other states to take action in the region to advance their own goals, taking advantage of Russia's incapacity to stop them. Finally, some combination of these scenarios, for instance a foreign power seeking to take advantage of Russian weakness to advance its own regional interests through military force but under the guise of humanitarian intervention or peacekeeping, is another possibility.

Because the potential for much Russia-spurred conflict rests in Russia's perception of stronger (or other) states involved in its neighboring regions as hostile, the potential for conflict can be mitigated if Russia's threat perception can be altered. This is a difficult task, but cooperation with the West in the region, for mutual goals such as economic development and general stability, can play a role. For this to work, however, Russia will have to see both economic and political gains to be had, and many of these run counter to the interests of potential partners.

The military campaign in Afghanistan has caused a re-evaluation of Russian policy on this issue, although to what extent and for how long remain uncertain. President Vladimir Putin of Russia appears to have decided that acceptance of the U.S. presence in his Central Asian and Caucasian backyards, and cooperation in the counterterrorist effort, will serve his country better in the long term than rumblings about encroachment and efforts to battle the United States for influence. That said, every new revelation of U.S. involvement and action sets off murmurs of discontent and complaints of U.S. imperialism among the Russian elite (an example is the late February news that the United States would be assisting Georgia with its efforts to battle insurgents in the Pankisi Gorge, shortly after the Georgian government once again refused Russian assistance), followed by a statement by Putin that this is not a problem. This suggests that Putin's policy is not entirely in keeping with the views of those around him (and often of his own ministers and advisors), and that its political sustainability may be questionable.

Certainly Russia is not willing to entirely give up its interests in CASC. Even those who accept the U.S. presence are loath to suggest that it might extend beyond the present conflict.[15] Moreover, Russian officials have been consistent in their desire to be kept informed, and, if possible, involved in U.S. efforts in the region.[16]

If it can be developed and sustained, cooperation between the United States and Russia to respond to the threat posed by terrorist groups may be an important mechanism for altering Russia's threat perception. Insofar as both the United States and Russia see the danger of asymmetric terrorist threats to their states and their people as the greater danger, Russia's perception of the United States as a

---

[15]Edward Helmore, "US in Replay of 'Great Game,'" *Johnson's Russia List (The Observer)*, January 21 (January 20), 2002; Boris Volkhonsky, "The US Tries Walking in the Shoes of the USSR," *Johnson's Russia List (Kommersant)*, January 23, 2002.

[16]Tamara Makarenko and Daphne Biliouri, "Central Asian States Set to Pay Price of US Strikes," *Jane's Intelligence Review*, 2001.

hostile power will be mitigated. To date, this dynamic has made it possible for the United States to reach agreement with Central Asian states about overflight and the stationing of forces on their territories in conjunction with counterterror efforts without jeopardizing either its own or its Central Asian partners' relations with Russia. But the ambiguities of Russian response reflect a real debate within the Russian Federation about the benefits and costs of cooperation with the United States, and it should not be taken for granted that Russia will continue to see terrorism as the greater evil. In fact, unless the United States matches its rhetoric with actions that signal to Russia that the United States is truly a partner, cooperation is unlikely to prove sustainable.

Moreover, even if the shared interest in fighting global terrorism trumps Russian distrust of the United States, continued and effective cooperation will require compromise on both sides, compromise that will have implications for the CASC states. One way in which the United States could signal Russia that it is not a threat, for example, is to become more reticent in developing its ties with the CASC states, involving Russia in its cooperative efforts. This could have the second-order effect of increasing Russian efforts to pressure those states on a variety of issues, from Chechen refugees in Goergia to oil pipelines. Failure to seek areas of compromise with Russia, however, may also lead to Russian pressure on these states, coupled with increasing hostility toward the United States, which will make it more difficult for the United States to pursue and attain its own goals in the region.

TURKEY

If Russia has a history of imperial control over the states of CASC, Turkey's connection is one of ethnic, religious, and linguistic ties with the Islamic states in the region. Its proximity, interest in Caspian energy development, and desire for a regional leadership role have led it to develop varying degrees of ties with a number of CASC states, including non-Muslim, non-Turkic Georgia. Turkey's efforts are complicated by its important trade relations with Russia and, to a lesser extent, by continuing tension between Turkey and Armenia stemming from mass deaths of Armenians in Turkey in

1915. Armenia views this as a genocidal act by the Turkish government, an interpretation the Turkish government disputes.

As Soviet rule weakened in the late 1980s and finally collapsed in 1990–1991, Turkey took steps to build ties with the post-Soviet Islamic states with which it shared aspects of heritage, ethnic kinship, and language.[17] Turkey hosted the Azerbaijani prime minister shortly before Soviet troops moved in to put a stop to increasing ethnic/political violence in pre-independence Azerbaijan. Turkey was also the first state to recognize Uzbekistan and Kazakhstan when they declared independence in 1991. After the Soviet Union's collapse, Turkey signed a flurry of cultural and economic exchange agreements with these countries and began broadcasting television programs in the region. Toward the end of 1992, it took steps to establish visa-free exchanges of citizens and free up capital flows with Azerbaijan, Kazakhstan, Kyrgyzstan, Turkmenistan, and Uzbekistan. Turkey also provided medical and educational supplies in the early 1990s, and established schools in the region and scholarships for local students to study in Turkey.

Turkey promised the Central Asians and the Azerbaijanis a model of an Islamic secular democracy, which was an appealing concept to the secular post-Soviet governments that were developing at that time. Having been rejected by the European Community, Turkey hoped that by building ties with these new states it could build a sort of Turkic community under its own leadership, a concept put forth by then Turkish President Turgut Ozal. This community would benefit Turkey economically and politically and, by serving as a bridge to the Islamic post-Soviet world, demonstrate Ankara's usefulness to Western states. This approach generally met with widespread support. Both U.S. and international funding organiza-

---

[17]Close ethnic and linguistic ties exist between Turks and the titular ethnies of Azerbaijan, Kazakhstan, Turkmenistan, Kyrgyzstan, and Uzbekistan (as well as some of the minority populations of Central Asia, such as the Uighurs). Although all of these are to varying extents distinct ethnic groups with unique languages, they are all members of the Turkic linguistic family. Tajiks are a Persian ethnie and speak a language closely related to Farsi.

tions, including the World Bank, provided assistance to Central Asian states through Turkey as a means of bolstering its efforts.[18]

The Central Asian states and Azerbaijan initially warmly welcomed Turkish assistance and support. By the end of 1992, however, it was clear that things were not going entirely as hoped. The Central Asians were disappointed that Turkey's help was not sufficient to bring economic health, prosperity, and integration with Western economic institutions. Many in Central Asia expressed frustration with what they saw as Turkey's almost condescending attitude toward the new states and their governments. In Azerbaijan, for instance, the coming to power of President Heidar Aliev resulted in a reversal of predecessor Abulfaz Elchibey. Where Elchibey sought to focus on Azerbaijan's Turkic ethnicity, Aliev in his early days distanced himself from Turkey and reinvigorated relations with Russia, rejoining the CIS (although refusing to allow Moscow to send troops to Azerbaijan).[19]

Meanwhile, Turkey had realized that doing business in the region was more difficult than anticipated, with efforts hampered by high levels of corruption and low levels of business competence. Moreover, its high levels of trade with Russia spurred Turkey to reconsider its initial enthusiasm for a large-scale effort to bring the Central Asian states into a Turkish sphere of influence.[20]

As this history indicates, Turkey's foreign policy, like Russia's, is often one of conflicting interests. While membership in NATO and longstanding friendship with the United States give Turkey a measure of strength in the international arena, this is mitigated by the European Union's continued rebuffs, Turkey's domestic economic crisis, and its domestic political uncertainty. Continuing battles between Islamists and secularists in Turkey's government and society, to say nothing of a disturbingly strong military role in governance, have created problems in the domestic functioning of the Turkish political system that sometimes spill over into its foreign policy.

---

[18]See Martha Brill Olcott, *Central Asia's New States*, Washington, D.C.: United States Institute of Peace Press, 1996, pp. 25–26; Shireen T. Hunter, *Central Asia Since Independence*, Westport, CT: Praeger, 1996, pp. 136–138.

[19]Suny, "Provisional Stabilities."

[20]Olcott, pp. 25–27.

If Turkey backed away from its initial exuberance toward Central Asia in the early 1990s, it has continued to seek ways of building on shared ethnic and linguistic ties with the region (as well as on its sheer proximity). One primary reason is its hopes for Caspian energy, both for its own needs, which it estimates will continue to rise, and for the promise of energy routes through Turkish territory, which bring with them lucrative transit fees and links to consumers in Europe. Turkey currently imports approximately 90 percent of its oil, which supplies half of its energy needs, and almost all of its gas, 70 percent of it from Russia. Although gas today accounts for only about 13 percent of Turkey's energy, Turkey estimates that demands by industry and power plants will increase dramatically, perhaps even sixfold, in coming years.

Turkey's success in wooing the Central Asian states has been limited. While business ties exist, they are a small component of Central Asian economies. Turkish bilateral military assistance to Central Asian states has become substantial only as of late 2000, and even here it focuses primarily on Uzbekistan and Kyrgyzstan, which were willing to accept Turkish equipment and training to help prepare their forces to battle insurgencies. Turkish troops have worked with Uzbek and Kyrgyz special forces units, and in 2001 they gave the Kyrgyz military forces (ground forces and border guards) a variety of nonlethal supplies, including night-vision equipment, all-weather gear, uniforms, and radio stations and transmitters (as well as training in their use and in counterterrorism operations).[21]

The situation in South Caucasus is a different one. If Central Asian states remained hesitant to respond to Turkey's overtures, Caucasian states Georgia and Azerbaijan welcomed Ankara's involvement in the

---

[21]"A Prickly Friend," *The Economist*, June 8, 2000; Energy Information Agency, "Country Analysis Brief: Turkey," August 2000, *www.eia.doe.gov/emeu/cabs/turkey.html*; Laurent Ruseckas, "Turkey and Eurasia: Opportunities and Risks in the Caspian Pipeline Derby," *Journal of International Affairs*, Fall 2000, No. 1, pp. 217–236; "A Turkish Move into Central Asia," *The Economist*, November 25, 2000; "Kyrgyz Border Guards Get Military Aid from Turkey, *BBC Monitoring Service*, from *Vecherniy Bishkek* web site, June 1, 2001; "Central Asia: Fault Lines in the New Security Map"; Marianna Belen'kaya, "Fight for Turkish Gas Market" (in Russian), *Nezavisimaya Gazeta*, August 7, 2001, internet edition, *http://ng.ru/world/2001-08-07/6_market.html*; Liz Fuller, "Turkey Delivers Military-Technical Aid to Kyrgyzstan," *RFE/RL Newsline*, Vol. 5, No. 187, Part I, October 3, 2001; author discussions with U.S. military and government specialists.

middle to late 1990s (Aliev once again shifting his country's foreign policy in a more western direction). Turkey sponsors these countries' participation in NATO-led peacekeeping in the former Yugoslavia (as part of NATO's KFOR stabilization force in Kosovo), where their peacekeepers serve as part of the Turkish contingent, and provides significant military assistance, including training, refurbishment of bases, and so forth. Both Georgia and Azerbaijan cite Turkey as their largest single trade partner.[22]

Energy is a big part of these relationships. Azerbaijan is a primary source of this energy. Georgia and Turkey both stand to benefit from Azerbaijani gas, both as customers and as transit states. Although Turkey lacks any ethnic, linguistic, or religious ties with the majority of the Georgian people, these states' shared interests (and Georgia's desire to identify and build strategic partnerships with NATO member states) have been more than sufficient to form the basis for an excellent relationship. The dark spot in Turkey's relations in South Caucasus, however, is Armenia. Turkey's insistence that the government was not at fault in the deaths of Armenians in Turkey in 1915 has severely constrained any development of bilateral relations between the two countries. Turkish support for Azerbaijan further exacerbates mutual distrust and hostility, as Armenia and Azerbaijan remain at war over the Armenian enclave of Nagorno-Karabakh. While the U.S. Congress prohibited the provision of most forms of U.S. military assistance to either Azerbaijan or Armenia throughout much of the 1990s (a prohibition recently lifted), Turkey faces no such restrictions.

Prior to September 11, the United States and NATO appeared generally willing to let Turkey take the lead for them in CASC, insofar as Turkey was able to do so. But Turkey's mixed success demonstrates the problems with this approach. Alone, Turkey lacks the resources to provide the level of economic and infrastructure assistance needed to make a difference in this underdeveloped region.

---

[22]"A Prickly Friend"; "Turkey gives 2.5m-Dollar Grant to Georgian Defense Ministry," *BBC Monitoring Service*, Georgian News Agency *Prime-News*, June 4, 2001; Speech by Georgian President Eduard Shevardnadze, "Georgia, the United States, and the New Security Paradigm in Eurasia," at the Willard Hotel in Washington, D.C., October 4, 2001; author discussions with U.S. military and government specialists. For more detail on trade relations, see Chapter Three of this report.

Moreover, throughout the region, Turkey's involvement was often seen as a proxy for U.S. involvement, both by local leaders and in Moscow. To Georgia and Azerbaijan, Turkey's assistance was perceived in large part as a means to more direct security assistance from, and alignment with, the United States. On the one hand, this made states more willing to accept Ankara's help. On the other hand, it meant that without U.S. backing, Turkey's independent influence was limited.

As in the early 1990s, Turkey also remained constrained by its economic ties to Russia. While Turkey views Central Asian and Azerbaijani gas as a possible alternative to dependence on Russia, and has been working with these states and Georgia to develop new oil and gas routes, it has also been working with Russia on the Blue Stream natural gas project. Blue Stream is a plan to lay a pipeline underneath the Black Sea in order to improve gas delivery (Russian and Caspian) from Russia to Turkey and beyond. Construction on Blue Stream began in 2001, and the route appears more feasible than do plans for a Trans-Caspian gas route.[23] The latter would require an underwater pipeline to deliver Central Asian gas to Azerbaijan and then parallel the Baku-Ceyhan oil pipeline through Azerbaijan, Georgia, and Turkey.

Turkey's interests over the next decade and a half will be heavily influenced by where the pipelines go. Its cooperation with Russia on the Blue Stream natural gas pipeline demonstrate that it is not averse to closer ties with Moscow, if that is the best way to guarantee delivery of the gas. While Turkey wants to build ties in the region, it is generally likely to steer clear of antagonizing Russia. If pipeline routes avoid Russia, and Turkey is able to diversify away from dependence on Russian gas, that assessment may change, especially with regard to South Caucasus. If they do not, and if Turkey's assessment of its growing gas needs proves accurate, Turkey's interests will dictate closer ties to Russia.

This suggests that Turkey is an unlikely source of conflict in CASC. Its regional interests are primarily economic, and will follow energy flows. To the extent that it is able to diversify energy supplies, Turkey

---

[23]Lyudmila Romanova, "Italian Invasion of Russia" (in Russian), *Nezavisimaya Gazeta*, August 7, 2001, internet edition, *http://ng.ru/world/2001-08-07/1_inroad.html*.

will seek to maintain that diversity, which will lead it to make every effort to maintain stable relations with all suppliers insofar as possible. However, a diversified supply will make Turkey less nervous of offending any one supplier. Thus, if conflict emerges for other reasons, there are several possible ways that Turkey could get involved.

If the oil and/or gas pipeline routes through South Caucasus and Turkey develop in accordance with current plans, Turkey will be linked to the CASC region far more closely than it is now. If it becomes a customer for Caspian gas, and that gas can reach Turkey without first traversing Russian territory, Turkey's dependence on Russia will decrease drastically. Even if only oil pipelines from South Caucasus are laid on Turkish soil, these will become an important component of Turkey's economy. If conflict in South Caucasus or Central Asia then erupts to threaten oil and gas fields, pipelines, or related infrastructure, Turkey would face significant incentives to get involved in an effort to protect its diversified energy sources and control the situation. Moreover, insofar as it is likely that conflict near oil and gas fields and pipeline routes generally presents a threat to the energy trade, Turkey may choose to get involved even before there is a clear danger. While Russia's actions and its perceived capacity to act effectively on its own will have an impact on Turkey's decision calculus, like any other state, Turkey can be expected to act to protect its economic interests.

The other possibility for Turkish involvement in Central Asian or Caucasus conflict is linked to its developing relationships with Georgia and Azerbaijan and, to a lesser, lagging extent, Uzbekistan, Kyrgyzstan, and Kazakhstan. While these ties do not involve formal security commitments on Turkey's part, they do involve military assistance and training, as well as the provision of equipment. This could lead to Turkey's involvement in conflict if Turkish forces are on the ground when conflict occurs and find themselves either in the line of fire or used as hostages by one or another combatant. Furthermore, simple development of close ties makes it likely that should Georgia or Azerbaijan perceive a severe internal or external threat to national security even now (and, if relations develop as Turkey hopes, some Central Asian states may eventually be as close to Ankara as Tbilisi and Baku are today), they may well ask for Turkey's assistance, and Turkey, although faced with conflicting political and economic interests in such a situation, may, having weighed its political, economic, and strategic interests against one another, agree to provide it.

Finally, Turkey's involvement in the multinational counterterror effort now under way could lead it to commit forces to Central Asia. Increasing ties between the United States and CASC states mitigate Turkey's importance to those countries, insofar as Turkey was seen as a means to the true prize: cooperation with the United States. However, Turkey is likely to be involved in any multinational presence in the region. The development of U.S.-Russian relations could also affect this dynamic. If Russia and the United States are cooperating in their approaches to the region, Turkey will have strong incentives to join in that cooperation. This could further improve Turkey's relations with Russia. If U.S.-Russian cooperation proves unsustainable, however, Russia is likely to look even more askance at Turkey's involvement in its backyard, heightening tension between the two countries and potentially complicating their economic relations.

THE EUROPEAN UNION AND ITS MEMBER STATES

With a few exceptions (namely the Baltic states and, to a lesser extent, Ukraine), the European Union states have kept the non-Russian states that emerged from the wreckage of the Soviet Union at arm's length, particularly those in the southern tier. With the United States and Turkey having taken a more active interest, most of the European Union members saw little reason to do more than take a wait-and-see approach to the development of the CASC region. They provided economic assistance and humanitarian aid after natural disasters, but limited their foreign policy involvement. As energy resources began to appear more lucrative, numerous European companies have gotten involved in CASC. While their governments continue to be cautious, these firms' involvement does change Europe's interests in the region. Moreover, European states are likely consumers of Caspian oil, and possibly even natural gas (although its cost makes it less appealing), as its development continues (see Chapter Five of this report). That said, European firms are involved in the entire range of Caspian oil projects, working with Russia (for instance on the Blue Stream pipeline through Turkey) as well as the CASC states. Thus, their interests, and to a large extent, it seems, those of their governments, have been focused on economic rather than strategic goals vis-à-vis CASC states.

The EU (and the EC before it) and its member states have provided significant technical and financial assistance to states in the region, including food aid, market and legal reform efforts, and so forth. EU Partnership and Cooperation Agreements have been signed with all CASC states except Tajikistan (although the agreement with Turkmenistan has been signed but not yet ratified). Trade with this part of the world on the part of the EU is minor from the EU's perspective (although in some cases quite significant from the point of view of the CASC states) and generally geared toward energy imports. Accordingly, Azerbaijan is the EU's largest trade partner in South Caucasus, and Kazakhstan is the largest in Central Asia (see Chapters Three and Five of this report for more on trade).

Some EU countries have been more involved in bilateral activities than others, however. The United Kingdom is providing security assistance to Georgia, as is Germany, which of the European states has been possibly the most active in providing assistance in the former Soviet states.[24] German-Kazakh cooperation, spurred at least somewhat by the sizable ethnic German population in Kazakhstan (about 40,000 people, or 2.4 percent of the total Kazakhstan population), continues apace. In fact, German military cooperation with Kazakhstan in recent years was more active than that of the United States or Turkey (the latter until recently having had limited success engaging Astana and the former having seen a downturn in relations following Kazakh aircraft sales to North Korea).[25] France, for its part, has played a leading role (alongside the United States and Russia) in international efforts to help resolve the Nagorno-Karabakh conflict and has built a strong relationship with Armenia.[26] More recently, in conjunction with the counterterrorism campaign in Afghanistan, the French have deployed aircraft and personnel to Tajikistan (and, according to some reports Kyrgyzstan) and are developing a plan for

---

[24]On security cooperation by the EC/EU and individual member states in the early 1990s, see Hunter, pp. 155–157. On current EU activities, see the European Union web site, *www.europa.eu.int.* See also Fiona Hill, *The Caucasus and Central Asia*, Washington, D.C.: The Brookings Institution, Brookings Policy Brief No. 80, May 2001.

[25]Author discussions with U.S. government personnel.

[26]Hill.

future military cooperation, to include training and information exchanges, with the Tajiks.[27]

As the EU develops its foreign policy and as energy exploration and exploitation in the Caspian continues, Europe's attitudes toward the region may change. A great deal depends on the extent to which the Caspian becomes a supplier of European energy, and on the routes taken by the pipelines that deliver that energy. If the routes go through Russia, the European states, individually and as part of the EU, are likely to continue policies similar to those now under way: economic assistance and cooperation, private investment, but no significant effort to exert strategic influence over the region. If routes bypass Russia, the Europeans may become more active in the region.

In any case, it is highly unlikely that the next one to two decades will see EU involvement in any CASC conflict independent of a U.S.-led NATO or other international framework. EU states might become involved in the region as part of multinational peacekeeping forces, and there is a fair likelihood that conflict in the region might lead one or more of its states, all of which are NATO Partnership for Peace members, to call for NATO consultations. It is unlikely, but plausible, that those would then lead to NATO action in the region. Finally, the development of the U.S. response to the September 11 terrorist attacks on the United States has the potential to draw its European allies (along with numerous other states) into the counterterrorist effort, some component of which is likely to continue to center around Central Asia.

IRAN

Iran is linked to CASC by ties of proximity, religion (although it should be noted that Iran is predominantly Shi'ite and the post-Soviet Muslim states predominantly Sunni Muslim), and, in the cases

---

[27]"Tajikistan Agrees to Allow French Jets to Use its Air Bases," *RFE/RL Newsline*, Vol. 5, No. 226, Part I, November 30, 2001; "French Troops Arrive in Tajikistan," *RFE/RL Newsline*, Vol. 5, No. 230, Part I, December 6, 2001; "Western Forces to be Based in Kyrgyzstan," *Jamestown Foundation Monitor*, Vol. 7, No. 227, December 11, 2001; Akbar Borisov, "France to Develop Military Cooperation with Tajikistan: Minister," *Agence France-Presse*, January 2, 2002; "French Military Experts Assess Tajik Infrastructure," *RFE/RL Newsline*, Vol. 6, No. 5, Part I, January 9, 2002.

of Tajikistan and Azerbaijan, ethnicity (Tajik ethnicity and language are of the Persian/Farsi family and almost one-quarter of Iran's population is ethnic Azeri). But after some early efforts to build strategic ties and foster the development of its own brand of Islamic fundamentalism, Iran has largely focused on its economic interests in the region since the Soviet collapse. Iran presents the most direct non-Russian route to market for both oil and gas, and it hopes to become a transit state for exports of these resources out of the region. Moreover, along with Russia, Azerbaijan, Kazakhstan, and Turkmenistan, Iran is a Caspian littoral state, with its own claims to the energy wealth of the seabed.

Iran is a state of enormous resources and energy know-how. It is OPEC's second-largest oil producer. Nine percent of the world's oil reserves and 15 percent of its gas reserves are on Iranian territory. But its ability to translate economic resources into power and influence are hampered by a U.S. sanctions regime that imposes penalties on countries that trade with Iran. This prevents Iran's economy from developing at a more rapid pace and becoming integrated into the global economic system. It also ensures that Iran continues to see the United States as a hostile power and its activities as potentially threatening to Iran's interests.

Iran's political system, in which power in both the executive and legislative is split between a popularly elected and a religious leadership, reflects continued divisions in its changing society.[28] With a reformist president in office, the contrast between Iran's conservatives and its reformers has been particularly stark in recent years, with the reformers seeking to open up ties with Western countries while the religious conservatives seek to continue the policies and postures of the revolution. The results of internal conflicts between Iran's political groupings can be expected to have important implications for its domestic and foreign policy choices in coming years.

In the meantime, given continued hostile relations with the United States, one of Iran's primary goals remains the development of political and economic ties with other states. Russia, whose relations with the United States have also been complicated over the last few

---

[28]See Nora Bensahel, *Political Reform in the Middle East,* unpublished manuscript, for a discussion of Iran's political system.

years, presents a good candidate. Iran also seeks to make it more lucrative for a wide range of companies and countries to do business with Iran than to abide by U.S. sanctions. While it is also in Iran's interests to seek to improve ties with the United States so that the sanctions might be lifted, efforts in that direction have thus far fallen short, due both to opposition within Iran and a lack of reciprocal interest from the United States.

Because Russia is a primary partner for Iran, and because it is an important source of weapons and nuclear reactor technology, the relationship with Russia is quite important and often takes priority over other goals in the region. Thus, despite some initial overtures in the early 1990s that appeared geared to supporting Islamic fundamentalism in the CASC region, Iran has generally backed off from such approaches, instead focusing on economic development.[29] In fact, its closest ties in the region are with Christian Armenia, Russia's own closest friend (and client-state) in South Caucasus. In Central Asia, Iran maintains good relations with Turkmenistan. During the Tajikistan civil war, Iran promoted and hosted meetings and discussions between the opposing sides. Despite Iran's reported support of the United Tajik Opposition (UTO) during the war, its relations with Tajikistan have been good in recent years.[30] Iran has also been relatively successful in building relations with Kazakhstan. It has had less luck with Uzbekistan. Russia has been generally supportive of Iran's efforts to build economic and political ties with these states.[31]

Iran agrees with Russia that Western influence over CASC should be limited. It also shares with Russia a perception that stability in the region is an important national security interest for both states. With a large Azerbaijani population in its north, Iran is loath to see conflict in South Caucasus (or Azerbaijani nationalism) spread to its own territory.

---

[29]Further hampering efforts to build ties based on shared religion by both Iran and Turkey is the fact that, as Suny notes, the many predictions of a rise in pan-Islamism in Central Asia were not borne out by historical developments, as regional Muslims, while identifying to some extent with Islam, failed to transfer that into any particular affinity to Muslims outside of their own region. (Suny, "Provisional Stabilities.")

[30]"Central Asia: Fault Lines in the New Security Map."

[31]See Hunter, pp. 129–136, for an analysis of Iran's interests in the region.

Iran sees itself as a natural route for Caspian oil and natural gas, and from a geographic perspective, it has a good point. Iran disagrees with Russia on the proper division of the Caspian Sea (Russia argues that the Caspian seabed alone should be divided, while Iran believes the entire sea should be blocked into five equal sectors), but it also has conflicts with other Caspian states, including Azerbaijan, who have their own views of how Caspian resources should be allocated.[32] Iran and Russia have the most powerful military forces in the CASC region at present, and Iran has threatened the use of force in the Caspian—in fact, in what Azerbaijan considers its territorial waters, leading to harsh words from Azerbaijan and Moscow (see Chapter Five).

Iran's hopes for an oil route through its territory have thus far been stymied as a result of U.S. sanctions, although not a few oil companies (and a number of states) would like to see the sanctions lifted. There has been somewhat more progress with gas, including a gas swap deal with Turkmenistan and Turkey and an agreement to supply natural gas to Armenia (giving Armenia an alternative to its current monopoly supplier: Russia).

Iran is unlikely to do anything that would spur conflict in the Caucasus or Central Asia. Its hopes for an important and lucrative role in Caspian development make peace in the region an important goal for the Iranian government and business interests. While it is possible that Iran's and Russia's goals in the region will diverge over time, it is also unlikely that Iran will try to assert influence over CASC at Russia's expense, given its reliance on Russia as an arms and technology supplier and a balance against the United States. Insofar as Russia has indicated it will not back off from its relationship with Iran,[33] rapprochement between the United States and Russia should not critically change Iran's assessment of this situation, as long as its own relations with the United States remain poor and it remains in need of what friends it can get. If anything, U.S.-Russian cooperation in the counterterrorist effort may even lead Iran to lower its profile in the region further, as it seeks to maintain good relations with Russia.

---

[32]See Chapter Five of this report.

[33]Sergei Blagov, "Moscow Revitalizes Its Old Priorities in Asia," *Johnson's Russia List (Asia Times)*, February 7 (February 6), 2002.

Moreover, Iran's economic interests in maintaining stability in this region appear to outweigh any ideological desire to spread the Islamic revolution or politics built on ethnic ties. This is evidenced by Iran's long-term efforts to develop good relations with the Rakhmanov government in Tajikistan (which has cracked down on Islamic groups and continues to be limited in its power-sharing with the Islamic Rennaissance Party, now incorporated into the government as part of the UTO, to which Iran reportedly provided some level of assistance during Tajikistan's civil war[34]), and its failure to speak out in opposition to Uzbekistan's persecution of Islamic groups and Persian speakers. In fact, Iran continues to actively seek to improve relations with Uzbekistan, despite its policies.[35]

One thing that could change this equation is a significant warming of ties with the United States, such that sanctions are lifted and Iranian routes for Caspian energy are supported by U.S. firms. Although this is tremendously unlikely at any time in the foreseeable future, if it were to take place, Iran would have less need of Russian friendship and could prove less inclined to continue to respect Russia's self-proclaimed sphere of influence in CASC. However, even given closer ties, Iran would be unlikely to welcome too much U.S. and NATO presence so close to its borders.

If conflict in the region develops, Iran is unlikely to get actively involved. The strategic interests are simply not strong enough to create a domestic coalition in favor of such an adventure. Iran will continue to seek to protect its economic interests, including oil and gas fields and pipelines to which it has links, but insofar as it believes that others can and will guarantee these interests, it has minimal incentive to itself send troops into the region—although it may provide support to specific groups, as it did in both the Afghanistan and Tajikistan conflicts. Even if it seems that others cannot control strife in CASC, Iran is likely to sit out any conflict, hoping that its economic

---

[34]"Central Asia: Fault Lines in the New Security Map." See Chapter Two of this report for a discussion of the political situation in Tajikistan.

[35]See Hunter, pp. 132–136. Another example of Iran's pragmatism is its lack of criticism of Russia over the latter's Chechnya campaign. See also country reports in Adrian Karatnycky, Alexander Motyl, and Amanda Schnetzer (eds.), *Nations in Transit, 2001*, New York: Freedom House, 2001, available online at *www.freedomhouse.org/research/nattransit.htm.*

interests are not irretrievably damaged and focusing its efforts on preventing the spread of conflict to its own territory (a particular risk if conflict affects Azerbaijan, or if Islamic fundamentalists or refugees—or both—seek shelter in Iran).

Iran's early attitude toward the emerging anti-Taliban coalition reflected such an approach: Iran wanted to see the Taliban gone but did not want to be directly involved in the operation. That said, because Iran avoids active involvement does not mean that it will not seek to protect its interests in other ways. For example, as the post-Taliban interim government was formed, Iran continued to support its own client groups in Afghanistan (and within the interim government), seeking to ensure their victory in internal Afghan conflict within the Northern Alliance and, according to some, at least, potentially destabilizing the transition. While Iran shared the coalition's interest in destroying the Taliban, it did not share Washington's assessment of how the new government should look, and continued to pursue its own, divergent interests.[36] One aspect of its motivation in doing so, however, may well have been its exclusion from the coalition in any real way and the U.S. government's choice not to seek rapprochement with Iran, which appears to have also weakened domestic proponents of a more Westward-leaning policy.[37] The extent to which this experience is relevant to the pursuit of goals in CASC is uncertain at present, but it is clear that Iran's behavior and involvement will be determined not only by its regional interests, but also by its interaction with the United States, Russia, and other interested parties.

CHINA

China, too, has ethnic links to Central Asia and hopes to benefit from development of its energy resources—as well as from growing trade with the subregion in other commodities. China's northwestern province of Xinjiang is populated predominantly by Uighurs, a Turkic Central Asian ethnic group whose members also live in

---

[36]John J. Lumpkin, "CIA Chief: Al-Qaida Remains Threat," *Associated Press*, March 19, 2002, downloaded from *www.washingtonpost.com* on March 20, 2002.

[37]See John Ward Anderson, "Reform Faction in Iran Is Hurt by 'Evil' Label," *Washington Post*, February 15, 2002, p. A26.

Kazakhstan and Kyrgyzstan, just as ethnic Kazakhs and Kyrgyz live in China. A large multiethnic state in which groups tend to be segregated, China fears that separatist and Islamic fundamentalist political movements will move east from Central Asia into Xinjiang, creating unrest, and/or that Central Asian states will provide a sanctuary for Uighur revolutionaries or help supply them with arms. The extent to which this is already taking place is unclear. The Uighur separatist movement in Xinjiang exists, and there are apparent links with Al Qaeda and reports of Uighur Chinese citizens fighting in Chechnya. However, the movement is also comparatively small and the area heavily militarized by China, keeping the situation apparently under control. The world's second-largest energy consumer, with a rapidly expanding industrial sector, China is increasingly concerned about its long-term ability to acquire oil and natural gas to fuel its economic growth.

China's economic, industrial, and military modernization and development of recent years have worried some countries. Strong states see an increasingly powerful China as a potential competitor, while declining states simultaneously fear its rise and look to it as a potential ally against stronger states.[38] Its growing economy presents a huge and lucrative market. For its own part, China is concerned about the threats to its national security that come from within, embodied in the dangers of dissent and fragmentation of this large state.

Economic growth is a fundamental priority of Chinese foreign and domestic policy. Stemming separatism at home is central to domestic policy. In Central Asia, China has focused its attention on developing economic ties with its neighbors, including discussing the potential for eventual energy purchases by China and pipeline routes to it (although it seems likely that these would be prohibitively long and circuitous). Good relations and cooperation with these states to prevent the rise of Uighur separatism would also have the added benefit of enabling China to decrease its military presence in its own

---

[38]Even though China, too, is a potential threat, states can be expected to align with it against shared greater threats. See Gilpin, *War and Change in World Politics*, Walt, *The Origins of Alliances*, Waltz, *Theory of International Politics*.

western territories.[39] China also has a developing relationship with Russia, from which it buys arms and with which it shares viewpoints on a number of key foreign policy issues, such as opposition to U.S. development of a national missile defense. Both China and Russia have hoped that cooperation between them could somewhat balance U.S. power and what their leaders sometimes describe as "hegemony" or "unipolarity." As with Iran, then, ties with Russia are generally more important to China than interests in developing any sort of influence over Central Asia (China has shown no particular interest in South Caucasus). Even China's involvement in the region is through a Russian-oriented forum, the Shanghai Cooperation Organization (SCO), which aims to cooperate in stabilizing borders and combating terrorism. (In fact, in June 2001 the SCO decided that its planned counterterror center would operate under the auspices of the CIS and in January 2002 decided that its focus would be Chechnya, Xinjiang, and the IMU.[40]) China's primary interest has been in keeping the region quiet and friendly. Conflict makes trade difficult and expensive, and is therefore counterproductive to China's interests.

China has had somewhat strained relations in the past with Kyrgyzstan, having initially refused to recognize borders (of particular concern given past Chinese claims to Kyrgyz territory), and both Kyrgyzstan and Kazakhstan worry somewhat about China's large and powerful presence on their borders and the substantial Kazakh and Kyrgyz populations in China. For its part, China fears that uprisings and Islamic fundamentalist movements could emerge from Central Asia to threaten its control over Xinjiang (a key factor in its ready support for the U.S.-led counterterror efforts in fall 2001), while Kazakhstan and Kyrgyzstan are concerned that separatist movements by Uighurs in Xinjiang could create problems for their own governments.

That said, Chinese-Kyrgyz border negotiations have made headway, and relations between China and both countries have been cordial to date, even involving the possibility of cooperation on rail and trade

---

[39]"Central Asia: Fault Lines in the New Security Map."

[40]"Central Asian Terror Crack-Down to Focus on Three Groups," *Johnson's Russia List (AP)*, January 8, 2002.

routes, as well as pipelines, through Kazakhstan. China is a major trade partner for Kyrgyzstan, and Kyrgyzstan has acceded to Chinese requests to suppress Uighur opposition among the Uighur diaspora on its territory. Moreover, China has provided Kyrgyzstan with about $600,000 in assistance, to include tents and army gear, and in June 2001 the Kyrgyz and Chinese defense ministries agreed that Kyrgyz soldiers would be trained at a training center in Guangzhou, China.[41]

China is also the only state other than Russia to provide lethal aid to a Central Asian state before September 11. In China's case, this took the form of sniper rifles (as well as flak jackets and other material) given (not sold, as all Russian equipment is) to Uzbekistan in 2000.[42] Some military contacts have also begun with Tajikistan, although at a much more general level.[43]

Thus, while there is some possibility that ethnic conflict in western China will create problems for its neighbors in Kazakhstan and Kyrgyzstan or vice versa, in either case creating some potential for Chinese intervention in Central Asia, it is generally highly improbable that China could be a source of Central Asian conflict. Like Iran, China will generally be satisfied to stay on the sidelines and let Russia (or the United States) handle any difficulties in this region. There remains, however, the possibility that China may feel obliged to act if Russia (or the United States) for some reason fails to stem burgeoning conflict in the region. This possibility holds especially true for Kyrgyzstan. That said, China would no doubt prefer to be consulted prior to any significant actions near its borders and may respond if it feels its interests are being slighted. For instance, the Chinese chief of the general staff did say, in the context of the counterterrorist operation on Afghanistan, that any U.S. military deployment to Kazakhstan would threaten China's security.[44] This can be seen less

---

[41]"China to Train Kyrgyz Servicemen," *BBC Monitoring Service, Vecherniy Bishkek* web site, June 14, 2001; "Central Asia: Fault Lines in the New Security Map"; *Recent Violence in Central Asia: Causes and Consequences,* Central Asia/Brussels: International Crisis Group, 2000; "Central Asia: Fault Lines in the New Security Map."

[42]"Central Asia: Fault Lines in the New Security Map."

[43]"Tajik Defence Minister Hails 'Fruitful' Tajik-Chinese Military Cooperation," *BBC Monitoring Service,* text of report by the Tajik news agency *Asia-Plus,* March 29, 2001.

[44]Edward Helmore, "US in Replay of 'Great Game,'" *Johnson's Russia List (The Observer),* January 21 (January 20), 2002.

as a statement that the U.S. presence itself is threatening, and more as a notification that China remains an interested party.

AFGHANISTAN

Afghanistan has been important to CASC far more as an exporter of unrest than as a state whose leadership might have strategic interests in influencing the situation in the region. A weak state, in its third decade of continuing warfare and facing severe drought, Afghanistan even before September 11 was far from what can be called a functioning state. While the Taliban was generally successful in taking control of most of the country militarily, its rule also brought global isolation (and eventually retribution) on Afghanistan. Afghanistan under the Taliban was a state that trampled on the basic human rights of its citizens, especially the rights of women; that had developed into a center of the global narcotics trade (although Northern Alliance forces were no less guilty of involvement in this trade than the Taliban); and that harbored suspected terrorists, most notably Osama bin Laden, and hosted training camps for terrorists and insurgents, preparing them to fight in conflicts in Chechnya, Central Asia, and elsewhere.[45]

Russia, Iran, Pakistan, Uzbekistan, Kyrgyzstan, and Tajikistan have all in various ways been linked to the conflict in Afghanistan during the course of the 1990s. The Northern Alliance against the Taliban was a conglomeration of primarily ethnic Tajik and Uzbek forces that joined together against the Pashtun-based Taliban. These forces were supported by Uzbekistan, Iran, and Russia (there are also some reports of Chinese support). Afghani factions have, in turn, been involved in Tajikistan's civil war, and elements of the Tajik opposition and the Chechen uprising, as well as Islamic revolutionary groups like the Islamic Movement of Uzbekistan (IMU) that have targeted Uzbekistan and Kyrgyzstan have sheltered in Afghanistan and received training and support there.[46]

---

[45]See Chapters Two and Four of this report.

[46]They have also received substantial support from groups in Pakistan. See Chapter Two of this report.

Prior to the events of September 11, it appeared that the Taliban hoped to attain international recognition as the rightful government of Afghanistan; it also seemed likely that if it could hold on to power and stabilize the country, it might even eventually get that acceptance. Positive indicators included an apparent crackdown on the drug trade,[47] and several states had taken steps that, while they fell far short of recognition, did appear to be moving slowly in that direction. Turkmenistan was the first of the Central Asian states to take a pragmatic line, declare itself neutral in the Afghanistan conflict, and develop some official ties with the Taliban (while also maintaining links to the Northern Alliance), including a trade agreement, all while stopping short of official recognition. Turkmenistan also hosted informal talks between Northern Alliance and Taliban factions in 2000.[48] At the end of September 2000, Uzbekistan's President Islam Karimov stated publicly that he did not see the Taliban as a significant threat to his country and urged a coalition government composed of Northern Alliance and Taliban forces. In October of that year, the Uzbek ambassador to Pakistan met with representatives of the Taliban in Islamabad and reportedly reached an agreement for Uzbekistan and Afghanistan not to interfere in each other's affairs. In that same time frame, the Kyrgyz government also spoke of the need to have some sort of contact with Afghanistan's ruling regime, and perhaps even to consider recognition.[49]

Russian officials, too, made some statements in the fall of 2000 to the effect that the Taliban's role as the most important force in Afghanistan should be recognized. Russia continued its support to the Northern Alliance in this time frame, but it also opened up some new contacts with Pakistan, which it used to pressure Islamabad on its continued support to the Taliban and on the question of terrorist training camps in Afghanistan. The Russians reportedly passed intelligence on these camps to Pakistani officials in the hope and expectation of some sort of action against them.[50] Those in Russia and Central Asia who favored improved relations with the Taliban

---

[47]See Chapter Four of this report.

[48]"Central Asia: Fault Lines in the New Security Map."

[49]"Recent Violence in Central Asia: Causes and Consequences."

[50]Ibid.

did so in part out of hope that such ties might translate into an end to the sheltering of revolutionaries on its territory and might limit attacks by insurgencies from Afghanistan, ties with the regime appearing the lesser of available evils.

The U.S. response to the September 11 attacks has created a fundamentally new situation, of course, and one that continues to evolve at the time of this writing. From the perspective of the Central Asian states, the worst-case scenario may be that the United States and its allies will succeed in driving the Taliban from power but then abandon Afghanistan and its neighbors. The former will then deteriorate into anarchy, with the United States taking less interest if it becomes a shelter for terrorists or other groups as long as they do not or cannot target the United States or Europe. This bodes ill, however, for the Central Asian states, Russia, South Caucasus, and China, as the insurgencies that threaten their security might well fit such a category. Moreover, a reinvigorated long-term conflict, with or without substantial foreign involvement, could lead to an influx of refugees into neighboring states, straining their already uncertain economic positions, and polarize political and social groups in the region, potentially creating a threat to government control. This is particularly the case in Tajikistan, where links to Afghanistani factions are strong and central control weak, but it is also true for Uzbekistan, Kyrgyzstan, Turkmenistan, and, to a lesser extent, Kazakhstan. Georgia, where it is believed some number of Chechen militants are hiding among the refugees, may also be at risk. Certainly the U.S. effort to assist Georgia in policing the Pankisi Gorge is predicated on the belief that it is possible that not only are militants there receiving Al Qaeda backing, but also that Al Qaeda militants from Afghanistan or elsewhere might seek shelter in areas of the country such as Pankisi, which are lacking in central control.

It is also worth noting that if narcotics production in Afghanistan continues despite (or because of) the international presence, the trade in these illegal substances will continue to move through Central Asia and Russia, further weakening governments and increasing the likelihood of crisis. If, however, war limits the capacity to produce narcotics in Afghanistan, parts of this industry may move into Tajikistan or Kyrgyzstan.[51] Almost regardless of the specifics of how events unfold, continued chaos in Afghanistan is likely to at least some extent, as no international peacekeeping effort or interim government will be able to consolidate effective control quickly. This will have repercussions for the capability of Central Asian governments to maintain control in their countries—and for the interests of other states.

THE UNITED STATES

There is no question that U.S. interests in the CASC region have been affected by its evolving response to the terrorist attacks of September 11. Prior to considering how U.S. relations with these states are likely to evolve in coming months and years, however, it is worthwhile to examine U.S. policy and interests in the region prior to the events of fall 2001, so as to provide a better context for any analysis of what is and what is not likely to change.

In the decade that followed the end of the Cold War, the United States sought to identify potential threats in what was from its perspective an extremely low-threat environment. It pursued goals and interests that might be termed "nice-to-haves" (as opposed to "need-to-haves"), which might or might not advance security goals but did advance ideological and humanitarian ones: democratization, peacekeeping, etc.[52] It also pursued its economic interests and sought ways to mitigate nonimmediate, but still worrisome, transnational threats that threatened U.S. interests and prosperity, if not in any immediate sense its existence. These included dangers that

---

[51]For more on this, see Chapter Four of this report. See also "Central Asia: Drugs and Conflict," Osh/Brussels: International Crisis Group, 2001.

[52]While proponents of democratization argue that it advances strategic goals as well, because democracies are, according to some data, less likely to fight wars (or, depending on the analysis, fight wars with one another), the literature is, in fact, far from conclusive on this matter. Moreover, according to some analysts, regardless of whether democracies are more or less war-prone, democratizing states are more likely to face conflict. Many of the key arguments in this debate can be found in Michael E. Brown, Sean M. Lynn-Jones, and Steven E. Miller (eds.), *Debating the Democratic Peace*, Cambridge, MA: The MIT Press, 1996. In addition to the papers in that volume, see Carol R. Ember, Melvin Ember, and Bruce Russett, "Peace Between Participatory Polities," *World Politics*, July 1992; and Michael W. Doyle, "Liberalism and World Politics," *American Political Science Review*, December 1986.

were a long way from development, such as a rogue state missile threat, and those that proved notoriously difficult to overcome, such as transnational terrorism and organized crime. Success in resolving these issues has been extremely limited (and some might argue that the efforts were limited as well).

The difficulties inherent in predicting whence threats will emerge can lead to a wide range of goals and involvements throughout the world which can, in turn, develop into involvement in conflicts and issues that, in retrospect, may or may not be found to warrant a significant commitment of forces and efforts on grounds of national security alone. U.S. activities in CASC in the 1990s can be seen in this light. U.S. policy in the region during that period focused on denuclearization assistance to Kazakhstan, low-level military to military contacts (both bilateral and through NATO's Partnership for Peace program), and various forms of democratization and economic assistance throughout the region. The U.S. government's perceived interests in the region focused on energy resource development, although strategic concerns about Russian resurgence and moral and ethical arguments about the continued independence of the post-Soviet states also played a role.

Although, as discussed in Chapter Five of this report, the United States itself is unlikely to become a customer for Caspian oil or gas, the production of the former will affect world oil prices (to what extent depends on how much oil turns out to be in the region), in which the United States certainly has an interest. And even if there is not as much oil and gas in the region as high-end estimates indicate, the resources have significance beyond mere quantity. Central Asian oil and natural gas provide the potential for diversification for many U.S. allies in Asia and Europe, now highly dependent on Russian and Middle Eastern sources of energy.[53]

While a variety of U.S. government officials have voiced support for a network of multiple pipelines leading from the region, the better to minimize dependence on Russian (or Iranian) transport routes for both producers and customers, U.S. policy actions have focused

---

[53]The extent to which this matters given a global oil market is debatable, but the argument for diversification is made frequently enough to create a political reason to diversify, whether or not an economic one exists.

almost exclusively on the development of routes through Turkey. The United States hoped to limit Russian influence in CASC, although its need to maintain good relations with Russia made it difficult to simultaneously pursue both goals. As noted, pipelines that avoid Russia would decrease Russian power over its Caspian neighbors. However, the United States has been wary of unequivocally placing itself in opposition to Russia in the region. Thus, while its cooperation with Caspian states increased, the United States steered clear of any promises of security assurances or guarantees. It also sought to promote Turkish influence in the region, of which support for pipelines through that country was but one component, and the United States worked with Turkey to coordinate military assistance and cooperation in South Caucasus and, increasingly (although still to a small scale, as discussed above), in Central Asia.

More specifically, the sort of assistance the United States provided to Central Asian states prior to September 11 included joint training of U.S. mountain combat units and Uzbek armed forces, as well as some nonlethal military equipment provided to Uzbekistan, for a total of some $10 million promised to that country by 2000 (as well as additional assistance through the Central Asian Security Initiative Program).[54] Kyrgyzstan also received some $4–$6 million in assistance from the United States, primarily in the form of nonlethal equipment such as radios, night-vision equipment, and so forth. An interesting footnote is that upon receipt, the Kyrgyz found that some of the electronic equipment received from the United States was incompatible with their existing equipment.[55]

Energy and Russia were not the only issues of concern from a U.S. perspective. Although the region is geographically distant, events there have implications for U.S. interests. State failure, armed conflict, and major political and economic unrest in the CASC region would add fuel to the fire of criminalization and drug trafficking, as well as potentially leading to sectarian civil wars of the sort that emerged in Afghanistan after the Soviet withdrawal. If this part of the world were to become a terrorist and criminal haven as Afghanistan did, the immediate security threats aside, it would

---

[54]"Central Asia: Fault Lines in the New Security Map."
[55]Ibid

become not just challenging, but impossible to exploit the region's energy resources. Moreover, while distance may isolate the United States from the drug trade to some extent, it does not do so for partners and allies in Europe and Asia. Post-Soviet organized crime has already made its mark in the United States despite the miles, and has the potential to wreak further havoc. Finally, as has been made all the more clear by the September 11 attacks, the terrorist threat is little constrained by distance, as a terrorist group can work from bases in one part of the world to carry out acts of terror far away.

The extent to which the terrorist attacks on the United States will mark a watershed event in U.S. strategic thinking, shifting it from that of a secure state to that of a state facing a clear and defined threat, remains uncertain. The dangers posed to the United States by radical groups with a willingness to use terrorist tactics is categorically different from the threat posed by another state. These groups do not threaten U.S. sovereignty nor its survival as a state.[56] However, terrorism threatens the U.S. way of life, its prosperity, and potentially its freedoms. At the time of this writing, the U.S. response suggests that these threats are seen as significant and vital. The United States is seeking allies against this asymmetric threat, it is responding militarily, and it is seeking to eliminate sources of the threat in a variety of ways.

Because Afghanistan has emerged as a sponsor and a shelter for terrorist groups, particularly Bin Laden's Al Qaeda, which orchestrated the attacks, Central Asia becomes particularly important for the U.S.-led effort. The United States has acquired permission from most states in the subregion to overfly their territories for humanitarian missions, and permission from some to overfly under any circumstances. It has forces, materiel, and facilities in place or available in Uzbekistan, Kyrgyzstan, and Tajikistan, and Kazakhstan has agreed to also provide such support if needed. Although the United States says it does not desire or plan any permanent military presence and has not granted any security guarantees to these states, it has signed an agreement with Uzbekistan promising to "regard with grave concern any external threat" to Uzbekistan. Significant financial assis-

---

[56]Although the acquisition of weapons of mass destruction by such groups could put them into the same range of destructive capacity as some states.

tance was also promised.[57] The United States is also, as noted above, providing equipment and training to Georgia to support its efforts to eradicate what are believed to be Al Qaeda–linked fighters in its Pankisi Gorge area.[58]

The United States has also received unprecedented cooperation from the Russian Federation in this effort. Its overtures to the Central Asian states have been balanced by close and consistent cooperation and discussions with Russian government officials. The United States and Russia have exchanged intelligence in support of the counterterrorism fight and have pledged further cooperation in the long term. While many in Russia have continued to express concern at U.S. involvement in its "back yard," President Putin has been consistent in reiterating that Russia does not oppose the U.S. actions. But the extent to which this cooperation is sustainable and can serve as a basis for further cooperation between the two states will depend on the extent to which they continue to perceive their interests as shared.

There are several possibilities for how this can play out for the states of CASC. An activist U.S. role in CASC will make it difficult to sustain cooperation with Russia. A higher priority on the U.S.-Russian relationship, however, will require the United States to tone down rhetoric and efforts to limit Russian influence in these countries, instead working with the Russians to advance shared goals in the region, which can be a problem insofar as CASC states see a quid pro quo of U.S. security support in exchange for their cooperation. At the same time, the U.S. force presence on and near the soil of these countries means that whatever the United States and Russia may agree between themselves, U.S. influence over the CASC states will grow, as will U.S. involvement in their affairs.

Prior to September 11, ongoing U.S. security cooperation and economic involvement in CASC meant that the prospect of regional conflict was a likely irritant for ongoing U.S. efforts in the area, and

---

[57]Dana Milbank, "Uzbekistan Thanked for Role in War," *Washington Post*, March 13, 2002, p. A23; "U.S., Uzbekistan Sign Military Cooperation Agreement," *RFE/RL Newsline*, Vol. 6, No. 14, Part I, January 23, 2002.

[58]Vernon Loeb and Peter Slevin, "U.S. Begins Anti-Terror Assistance in Georgia," *Washington Post*, February 27, 2002, p. A1.

posed the threat that U.S. assets or forces could become the targets of attack by combatants. This situation is now further exacerbated by the active U.S. involvement in a conflict near the region. U.S. forces have committed themselves to assist local leaders in CASC with their efforts to control and eradicate "terrorist" groups on their territories. This, combined with the physical presence of U.S. forces, greatly increases the risk that the United States will be drawn into local conflict.

It is possible, of course, that the U.S. presence in the region will have the effect of dampening cleavages and making conflict less likely. But the possibility that it will exacerbate some aspects of it, and draw the attention of certain groups to U.S. forces as a plausible target in their campaigns against their governments, must also be considered. Moreover, there is the question of how and under what circumstances the United States will withdraw from the region and its fights. If the United States remains active in the region, it will find itself involved in a range of stabilizing efforts as it seeks simultaneously to fight terrorists, drugs, and crime and to create and/or maintain peace so as to enable its own forces to operate securely—and to fulfill its promises to local governments. If before September 11 there existed the possibility that the interests of allies, such as Turkey, would lead to greater U.S. involvement in the region, or that local conflict would lead to PfP consultations and perhaps even eventual NATO involvement, now the United States has its own imperatives to remain involved. If it withdraws, it runs the risk that the region will degenerate into anarchy and conflict and itself become a breeding ground for the terrorism and violence that drew the United States into the region in the first place.

INDIA AND PAKISTAN

A number of other states have interests in or implications for the CASC region. India and Israel have also provided military equipment to Central Asian states, for example, and India describes that region as its "extended strategic neighborhood" where it must fight against long-time adversaries Pakistan and China for influence over the region.[59] It has built trade ties, including air transport agreements with Central Asian states, and has signed bilateral agreements with Uzbekistan.[60] As of this year, plans appear to be developing for India to assist in the training of the Tajikistan air force and to help modernize the Ayni air force base, which the French rejected for use due to its poor condition.[61] India has also had close relations with Russia, which is its largest arms supplier, and, along with Russia, Iran, and others, it helped supply Northern Alliance forces during the Afghanistan war, largely by way of Tajikistan.[62]

Pakistan sought a role in gas exports from Central Asia and took part in the Tajikistan peace talks. A number of trade and transport agreements have been signed with Central Asian states as well. That said, Pakistan's relationships with many states in the region, but particularly Uzbekistan, were poisoned by its support of the Taliban in Afghanistan and the purported links of Pakistani groups and parties to the IMU.[63] It seems unlikely that Pakistan will now emerge as a major player in Central Asia, but it will have an interest in developments in the region, if only due to simple proximity, its developing ties with the United States, and its continuing competition with India.

GREAT POWER COMPETITION AND GREAT POWER CONFLICT

A wide range of states have varying degrees of interest and involvement in CASC, interests that are variously affected by the events of September 11 and their aftermath. While in principle this could be

---

[59]Ahmed Rashid, "IMU Gradually Developing into Pan-Central Asian Movement," *Eurasia Insight*, April 3, 2001, *Eurasianet.org*, downloaded March 19, 2002; Juli A. MacDonald, "The Reemergence of India as a Central Asian Player," *Central Asia Caucasus Analyst*, 2000.

[60]MacDonald.

[61]"India to Help Train Tajik Air Force," *RFE/RL Newsline*, Vol. 6, No. 23, Part I, February 5, 2002; Sergei Blagov, "Moscow Revitalizes its Old Priorities in Asia," *Johnson's Russia List (Asia Times)*, February 7 (February 6), 2002.

[62]Sergei Blagov, "Moscow Revitalizes its Old Priorities in Asia"; Rashid, "IMU Gradually Developing into Pan-Central Asian Movement."

[63]See Hunter, pp. 135–136; M. Ehsan Ahrari, *Jihadi Groups, Nuclear Pakistan, and the New Great Game*, Carlisle, PA: Strategic Studies Institute, 2001.

seen as having the potential to make the region an arena for conflict between outside interests, as Figure 7.1 illustrates for four of the states discussed in this chapter, the interests of many powers overlap considerably, and disagreements and agreements do not always follow clear lines of alliance, religion, or ideology. Moreover, in the aftermath of September 11, some interests (those in the lighter-lined boxes) may be overshadowed by others (priority interests are enclosed in heavy-lined boxes). Much remains uncertain. To what extent will Russia's fear of terrorism and desire to cooperate with the United States temper its stance on proliferation? How much (and in which direction) will Iran's policy of support for terrorist groups change in the face of U.S. policy and actions?

But the fact remains that for key powers such as Russia, the United States, Iran, and China (not shown in the figure due to its smaller level of involvement to date), areas of agreement appear to be more

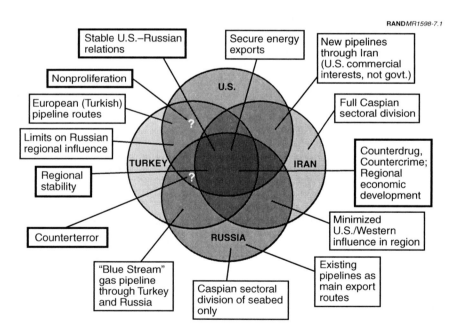

Figure 7.1—Foreign Interests in Central Asia and South Caucasus

important than areas of disagreement, which are in several cases simply the specifics of how to attain shared goals. Thus, while there will no doubt be competition between outside powers in the region, there are strong incentives in place to limit their proclivity to evolve into conflict.

A key component of this is the fact that for most of the outside powers with interests in CASC, their relations with each other are at least potentially more important than their desire for influence in the region. Even before September 11, Iran, China, Turkey, and the United States all had to weigh their desire for influence in CASC against their desire for good relations with Russia. Moreover, in Iran's case, economic interests tended to outweigh any desire to spread potentially destabilizing ideology to the region.

The exception was Russia. Until September 11, Russia was the only outside power that truly saw CASC as vitally important to its national security. While other states saw the potential for increased interest as pipelines were built, this was not likely to lead them to increase their commitment to this part of the world to the level of Russia's.

Today, Russia remains the outside state with the greatest degree of security and economic interest in CASC. But insofar as Central Asia becomes a support base and potential battleground for a U.S.-led coalition fight against terrorism, U.S. interests in the domestic and foreign affairs of these states become far more central to its overall policies. Insofar as these interests align with those of Russia, and both states see the terrorist threat as subsuming any dangers the other poses, it has the potential to boost cooperation between the two. But the United States and Russia maintain conflicting interests on a range of issues, and the strength of their nascent friendship is likely to be tested in a multitude of ways as the counterterror effort continues.

THE LOCAL PERSPECTIVE

An analysis of foreign interests in the CASC region is incomplete without a discussion of how regional states see foreign powers, and their own interests. The CASC states are politically and economically weak. Perhaps even more than Russia, they tend to perceive their security environments as threatening. Some of these threats come from without. The immediate threat of Russian imperialism has in recent years been supplanted by the fear that Afghanistan's mixture of fundamentalist Islam and anarchy will spread, particularly in Central Asia.[64] Moreover, as discussed in detail elsewhere in this report, the political, economic, ethnic, criminal, and other internal sources of conflict in these countries are exacerbated by the danger of refugee flows, support for insurgents, and war stemming from the fighting and the anarchy in Afghanistan. This fear has, of course, been exacerbated by the prospect of reinvigorated fighting and unrest in Afghanistan in the wake of the September 11 attacks.

Because the CASC states expect their political and economic weakness to continue, they have long sought outside assistance to combat the threats they perceive. In the early days of their independence, the most significant threat to survival and security was perceived to be Russia, which made no secret of its desire to reintegrate its periphery in some form. As a result, most of these states hoped that Western assistance would help balance against this Russian threat.

This is what brought many of these states to join and participate actively in NATO's Partnership for Peace. Exceptions to the rule were states that needed more assistance and support than NATO and the United States were offering: Armenia, engaged in a war for the enclave of Nagorno-Karabakh within Azerbaijan, accepted Russian support and assistance, as did Tajikistan, which dissolved into civil war in 1992. Russian peacekeepers were dispatched to resolve the conflict (Kyrgyz and Uzbek forces also took part), and Russia remained actively involved in the peace talks and settlement. Both Armenia and Tajikistan remain close to Russia, and Tajikistan can be described to a large extent as a client state of Russia, given its heavy military presence and close involvement in Tajikistan's government structures. Tajikistan prior to September 11 was hesitant to build ties with the United States and NATO.[65]

To NATO and the United States, PfP was a means to build cooperation with all of the post-Communist world, and something far different from, and far short of, an alliance. To many of the Caspian states,

---

[64]But also in the Caucasus: Georgia's President Eduard Shevardnadze spoke of the "Wahabist" threat to his country in a speech in the United States on October 4, 2001.

[65]"Central Asia: Fault Lines in the New Security Map."

however, it was a step toward closer ties, leading perhaps to eventual alignment. In the meantime, although NATO and the United States offered no security assurances, PfP membership brought military ties, which Caspian states, particularly Georgia and Azerbaijan, hoped would signal to the Russians that they were not without protection. Bolstering that signal, these states resisted Russian efforts to get involved in their affairs. Uzbekistan, too, was seeking a similar route, welcoming U.S. assistance while resisting Russian offers, withdrawing from the CIS collective security treaty and joining the GUUAM (Georgia, Ukraine, Uzbekistan, Azerbaijan, and Moldova) grouping, which, although not a military alliance, was seen as a statement by its members of independence from Russia.[66]

In the middle to late 1990s, the development of domestic threats and the dangers posed by proximity to Afghanistan combined with the lack of clear Western commitment to make many states reassess their viewpoints. Although Georgia and Azerbaijan maintained a pro-Western outlook and continued to make clear their hope for ever-closer ties to NATO (even as their relationships with Turkey continued to deepen), many of the Central Asian states showed signs of warming to Russia, as Armenia and Tajikistan had already done. The Russian government, after all, shared these states' fears of regional conflict and stood willing and ready to offer whatever help was asked of it. This explains why Kyrgyzstan accepted the Russian offer of military assistance. While Kyrgyzstan has avoided a Russian military presence, it has nonetheless maintained good relations with Moscow.[67]

But Kyrgyzstan was particularly weak, having little in the way of natural resources and having as neighbors potential hegemons Uzbekistan and China.[68]   Other states sought other routes. Uzbekistan became less recalcitrant with Russia, but stopped short of accepting any assistance. Turkmenistan maintained its position of

---

[66]Ibid.

[67]Ibid.

[68]Although China is by far the larger state, Uzbekistan, with its past practices of ignoring Kyrgyzstan's borders in its efforts to ensure its own security (see Chapter Two), may actually pose the greater threat, insofar as its actions and statements suggest a more hostile intent (see Walt for a theoretical discussion of the components of threat).

nonalignment even as it increasingly isolated itself from the rest of the world (it never joined the CIS collective security treaty, and although it did recently join PfP, it has not been active). Kazakhstan, with its large ethnic Russian population, continued to tread carefully, balancing ties to Russia with ties to other states (and with the limited resources it could allocate to cooperation with NATO).[69] Kazakhstan also perceives a threat of Islamic/insurgency violence and, after the incursions into Uzbekistan and Kyrgyzstan in August 2000, shifted many of its special forces units to the south of the country.[70]

The Central Asian states also have complicated relationships with one another. Uzbekistan repeatedly accused Tajikistan of allowing the IMU to operate from its territory, while Tajikistan and Kyrgyzstan were unhappy with Uzbek mining of border regions (including some areas that remain undemarcated), which has resulted in dozens of civilian casualties, as well as Uzbek air strikes across their borders, both in response to IMU incursions. Kyrgyzstan, too, has mined borders with Tajikistan and destroyed some mountain passes to prevent incursions. Tajikistan is also concerned about reports of discrimination against ethnic Tajiks in Uzbekistan, which include restrictions on Tajik-language literature and possible deportations from border regions.[71]

Uzbekistan, for its part, supported the Tajikistan government during its civil war (although it later served as the staging ground for at least one opposition incursion) and offered assistance in pursuit of the IMU after the 1999 insurgency attacks (when the assistance was declined, Uzbekistan went ahead with bombing raids into Tajik territory).[72] In 2000, Tajikistan agreed to allow Uzbek helicopters into its airspace, and the two states signed an agreement to cooperate to fight Islamic extremism in September 2000.[73]

---

[69]"Central Asia: Fault Lines in the New Security Map."

[70]"Recent Violence in Central Asia: Causes and Consequences."

[71]"Tajikistan: An Uncertain Peace"; "Central Asia: Fault Lines in the New Security Map."

[72]"Central Asia: Fault Lines in the New Security Map."

[73]"Recent Violence in Central Asia: Causes and Consequences."

Kyrgyz-Uzbek relations have also been tense. In addition to the border mining and air raids, the two states have had disputes over gas and water (see Chapter Five), and Uzbekistan has pressured Kyrgyzstan to crack down on the Hizb ut-Tahrir and other Islamist groups. While Kyrgyzstan has generally complied and carried out arrests of individuals who were then turned over to Uzbekistani authorities, there remain some reports that Uzbekistani security has also taken matters into its own hands and crossed the border to apprehend suspects.[74]

Arguments that Uzbekistan has sought to take advantage of the IMU incursions to strengthen its control over the region culminate in rumors that the Karimov government in fact supported the IMU for this purpose (these appear to be unsubstantiated).[75] There are over 100 border disputes between Uzbekistan and its neighbors, a fact that has not prevented Uzbekistan from claiming that there are none.[76]

Thus, efforts by the Central Asian states to cooperate amongst themselves to enhance their security have generally remained on the level of agreements and meetings, rather than real accomplishment. On the other hand, the appeal of Moscow's offers to Caspian states was tempered by their knowledge that Russia lacked the cash and the know-how to invest advantageously and effectively in its neighbors' economies. Furthermore, to many states in the region, Moscow, long the center of imperial rule, continued to appear as a significant threat to their existence, such that Russian promises of military support rang false, and even dangerous. As Grigor Suny writes, post-Soviet states had some difficulty perceiving Russian involvement in their affairs as a positive factor, given Russia's past imperialism and present ineffectiveness.[77] But in the absence of alternative sources of support against either Russia, foreign-backed insurgent movements, or other dangers and threats, many of the Central Asian states, with

---

[74]*The IMU and the Hizb-Ut-Tahrir: Implications of the Afghanistan Campaign.*

[75]"Central Asia: Fault Lines in the New Security Map."

[76]Ibid. "Uzbekistan Denies It Has Border Disputes with Neighbors," *RFE/RL Newsline*, Vol. 6, No. 24, Part I, February 6, 2002.

[77]Suny, "Provisional Stabilities."

little military power of their own, saw little choice in the long term but to give in to Russia's pressure.

As with everything else in this region, the prospect of energy development and export played (and continues to play) an important role. If in the short term these states seek outside assistance with their security problems, in the long term, the energy producers among them continue to hope that they will be able to transform those resources into economic power and greater independence. States that lack oil and gas reserves hope that they can serve as transit countries and therefore also benefit from energy exploitation in the region.

This requires not only that the energy can get to market, but that there be multiple routes for it to do so. For the oil producers, Azerbaijan and Kazakhstan, this generally means routes through Turkey or Iran, as well as through Russia. For gas-producing states Turkmenistan and Uzbekistan (Kazakhstan and Azerbaijan also produce gas), which are separated from Turkey by the Caspian Sea, the most viable alternative to Russia is Iran (although Afghanistan has also been sporadically considered, it seems an extremely unlikely option today). Turkmenistan is already shipping a small amount of gas to Iran, but the long-term possibilities depend in large part on the United States easing sanctions against those who have dealings with Iran and its businesses (an unlikely prospect given the current situation). In the meantime, an additional problem with the hopes for multiple pipelines is that for multiple export routes to be economically sustainable, it must be feasible to build the routes and there must be sufficient quantities of oil and/or gas to fill all the pipelines. This is more likely to happen for oil, which is easier to transport, than for gas. But in either case it depends on high-end estimates of Caspian energy production proving true. If production proves to be lower, multiple routes may prove impossible for everyone.[78]

Prior to September 11, this meant that for the gas-producing states, and to a lesser extent for the oil producers, there was little choice but to turn to Moscow for economic and security assistance, or perhaps

---

[78]See Chapter Five of this report.

to seek to develop closer ties with Iran and risk antagonizing the United States by doing so. Moreover, the gain in trading export dependence on Russia for export dependence on Iran, a major oil and gas exporter in its own right, is questionable, as Iran could also use this power to control competing Caspian energy exports to their detriment.

Increased U.S. military involvement in Central Asia changes this dynamic. For Uzbekistan, the U.S. forces on its soil provide a means to enlist the United States in its fight against its own insurgents, and the United States has been amenable, at least insofar as targeting IMU bases in Afghanistan has been concerned. Uzbekistan also sees U.S. support as bolstering the Karimov regime and further decreasing security dependence on Moscow. The Karimov regime has been hesitant to reveal to the public the extent of U.S. involvement, however, heavily censoring press reports on the war in Afghanistan. It is also worth noting that Uzbekistan has agreed to access for humanitarian and search and rescue purposes—not combat operations. Moreover, it is unclear the extent to which U.S. pressure on Uzbekistan to democratize will strain the relationship. As noted in Chapter Two, in late January Karimov held a referendum to extend his presidential term from 5 to 7 years, a vote he won overwhelmingly. As Karimov's authoritarian rule continues, and insofar as he uses the war on terrorism as an excuse for further crackdowns on political opposition forces, the United States may find itself in an increasingly awkward situation. Finally, the implications of U.S. presence in Uzbekistan for U.S.-Russian cooperation in the counterterror effort should also be considered. While Russia opposes a long-term U.S. presence, and the United States has said that it does not plan a permanent military presence (although congressional leaders have said that U.S. support is part of a long-term commitment to the region), Uzbekistan has much to gain from keeping the United States in place and engaged for as long as possible.[79]

The dynamic for Tajikistan is somewhat different. The Tajiks were already dependent on Russia for security before September 11, and it

---

[79]Makarenko and Biliouri, "Central Asian States Set to Pay Price of US Strikes"; George Gedda, "U.S. May Remain in Central Asia," *Johnson's Russia List (AP),* February 6, 2002; Olga Dzyubenko, "Franks Sees No Permanent US Bases in Central Asia," *Johnson's Russia List (Reuters),* January 23, 2002.

is unlikely that they have taken or will take any action vis-à-vis the United States without Russian approval. Tajikistan has remained careful in its language and proposals, for instance arguing in December 2001 that peacekeeping in Afghanistan should be carried out by the 6+2 countries (China, Iran, Pakistan, Tajikistan, Turkmenistan, Uzbekistan, the United States, and Russia) except Pakistan under UN auspices.[80] It has permitted coalition forces to use its facilities in support of humanitarian missions (as well as search and rescue and combat "if necessary"), and France received permission to station six Mirage 2000 fighter-bombers in Tajikistan for the duration of the campaign, as well as to use Tajikistan facilities for its forces en route to Afghanistan. Italian and U.S. forces, too, have reportedly flown into Tajikistan, and status of forces agreements were rapidly negotiated. In exchange, Tajikistan is receiving aid packages from a variety of countries, including Japan and France (and India, as noted above), as well as help in refurbishing its airports and facilities, many of which were deemed unusable by coalition forces. Tajik officials have stated that they expect the foreign presence to be long term, as the stabilization of Afghanistan can be expected to take quite some time.[81]

Whether U.S. and coalition presence in the region increases Tajikistan's security over time will depend on how successful U.S. and coalition forces are in controlling the unruly regions that Russian and Tajik troops have had such difficulty with in recent years. If they hope to operate in Tajikistan, they will have little choice but to try, if only in the name of their own force protection needs. As discussed in Chapter Eight, Tajikistan, with its limited central control, high levels of drug and other illegal traffic, and crime, will present unusual challenges.

---

[80]"Tajik Security Official Sees Role for 'Six Plus Two' in Afghan Peacekeeping," *RFE/RL Newsline*, Vol. 5, No. 232, Part I, December 10, 2001.

[81]"Tajik, French Presidents Discuss Afghanistan," *RFE/RL Newsline*, Vol. 6, No. 14, Part I, January 23, 2002; "French Troops Arrive in Tajikistan," *RFE/RL Newsline*, Vol. 5, No. 230, Part I, December 6, 2001; "Western Forces Arriving in Tajikistan," *Jamestown Foundation Monitor*, Vol. 7, No. 225, December 7, 2001; Makarenko and Biliouri, "Central Asian States Set to Pay Price of US Strikes"; Akbar Borisov, "France to Develop Military Cooperation with Tajikistan: Minister," *Agence France-Presse*, January 2, 2002; "French Military Experts Assess Tajik Infrastructure," *RFE/RL Newsline*, Vol. 6, No. 5, Part I, January 9, 2002.

Kyrgyzstan, like Uzbekistan, was fairly eager to welcome a U.S. and coalition presence, and U.S. forces are in place at Manas airfield near the capital, with plans to expand their presence further. A bilateral agreement on the stationing of forces was signed with the United States and ratified by the Kyrgyz parliament in early December 2001. It is valid for one year but can be extended and explicitly allows for U.S. use of Kyrgyz installations in support of humanitarian and military missions. A variety of other coalition states, to include Britain, France, Italy, Canada, Australia, and South Korea, have also asked Kyrgyzstan for basing access. The United States also held a bilateral counterterror exercise with Kyrgyz forces in February. Reportedly, the agreement reached between the United States and Kyrgyzstan called for a payment of $7,000 for each takeoff and landing of a U.S. plane. More recently, reports have surfaced in the Kyrgyz media that the sums actually paid are far lower, and there have been reports of "incidents" (including a hit-and-run accident involving a U.S. officer in March) involving U.S. troops in the surrounding region, as well as of growing resentment of the U.S. presence. The extent to which this resentment reflects the views of the Kyrgyz public is unclear. Moreover, as with Uzbekistan, the United States will face a growing mismatch between its pro-democracy rhetoric and local crackdowns on opposition political forces.[82]

While Kazakhstan has expressed willingness to consider requests to station troops on its soil, no such requests appear to have been forthcoming at present, although U.S. Secretary of State Colin Powell said in December 2001 that Kazakhstan would be making bases and airspace available to the coalition. Kazakh leaders have expressed their willingness to provide humanitarian and economic support to Afghanistan, and the president has suggested that the U.S. presence

---

[82]Boris Volkhonsky, "The US Tries Walking in the Shoes of the USSR," *Johnson's Russia List (Kommersant)*, January 23, 2002; Olga Dzyubenko, "Franks Sees No Permanent US Bases in Central Asia"; "Western Forces to Be Based in Kyrgyzstan," *Jamestown Foundation Monitor*, Vol. VII, No. 227, December 11, 2001; *Johnson's Russia List (Reuters)*, January 23, 2002; George Gedda, "U.S. May Remain in Central Asia," *Johnson's Russia List (AP)*, February 6, 2002; "Kyrgyz Paper Accuses U.S. of Failing to Pay for Use of Airport," *RFE/RL Newsline*, Vol. 6, No. 36, Part I, February 25, 2002; "U.S. Officer in Kyrgyzstan Injures Two Women in Car Crash," *RFE/RL Newsline*, Vol. 6, No. 51, Part I, March 18, 2002.

in Afghanistan should be limited to the time it takes to complete the current operation.[83]

Turkmenistan, for its part, has argued that its neutral status precludes the use of its territory for military forces involved in the war in Afghanistan, although its territory and airspace could be made available for humanitarian missions. In January 2002, Turkmenistan turned down a German request for air base access in support of the coalition effort.[84]

Clearly, the U.S. and coalition forces face somewhat different environments in each of the Central Asian states. In the long term, whether U.S. involvement leads it to build closer ties with the Central Asian states or whether its need to cooperate with Russia will lead it to eschew efforts to exert influence at the Russians' expense, the implications of the ongoing counterterror effort for all of the states of the region will be significant. Influxes of U.S. aid, the physical presence of U.S. and other coalition forces, and the much-increased global attention to this part of the world and its problems may prove a tremendous boon for them. On the other hand, the underlying problems of the region will not go away simply because of a foreign troop presence, and, if anything, the likelihood of foreign (including U.S.) involvement in local problems has increased.

The South Caucasus states face a somewhat different situation. Both Azerbaijan and Georgia have been highly proactive in courting Western support, particularly that of the United States and Turkey. Unlike the Central Asian states, they continued to see Russia as their predominant source of threat. Georgia's domestic secessionists have enjoyed a measure of Russian support, while the refugees and possible militants in Pankisi are there in large part due to the war in Chechnya (although they chose Georgia to flee to not just due to proximity, but also because of the lawlessness and lack of central control in this country). Russian actions in Chechnya, and its de-

---

[83]"Kazakhstan Signals Readiness to Host Antiterrorism Coalition Forces," *RFE/RL Newsline,* Vol. 5, No. 226, Part I, November 30, 2001; "Kazakhstan Again Says it May Join Antiterrorism Coalition . . . ," *RFE/RL Newsline,* Vol. 5, No. 230, Part I, December 6, 2001; "Kazakhstan Offers Use of Facilities to Antiterrorism Coalition," *RFE/RL Newsline,* Vol. 5, No. 232, Part I, December 10, 2001.

[84]"Turkmenistan Rejects German Request for Use of Airfields," *RFE/RL Newsline,* Vol. 6, No. 4, Part I, January 8, 2002.

mands on Georgia and Azerbaijan to assist in that effort, have not made them any less nervous. There can be no question that both of these states initially feared that U.S. rapprochement with Russia would lead to a cooling of relations with their NATO friends, along with increased pressure from Russia to go the way of Armenia and align with their neighbor to the north—or else face Russian political, economic, and potentially military wrath.

In Georgia, the visible U.S. assistance to help fight militants in Pankisi suggests that the United States is choosing a different path. In January and well into February 2002, Georgian officials up to and including the president denied Russian reports of cooperation between the two countries to fight crime and extremist Islam in Pankisi. In fact, a Georgian official said in mid-February that there was no need for joint operations with either Russia or the United States in Pankisi, although his country welcomed "methodological and technical assistance" from either or both. Then, in late February, it became publicly known that the United States was, in fact, providing helicopters and training for Georgian troops to assist in their efforts to eliminate Al Qaeda and other Islamic extremists believed to be in Pankisi. The United States reiterated that it has no intention of sending its own forces into combat in Georgia, and the Russian defense minister Ivanov, on a visit to Washington, reported that he had been fully briefed on U.S.-Georgian cooperation.[85]

Georgia's unwillingness to accept Russia's help and cooperation in Pankisi and its willingness to work with the United States will not do much to improve Russian-Georgian relations, even if Russia's President Putin remains willing to accept U.S. involvement. A congressional vote to loosen restrictions on aid to Azerbaijan and continued efforts to push forward the Baku-Ceyhan pipeline (and apparent Russian warming toward that plan as well) suggest that Azerbaijan, too, will continue to enjoy significant Western support, and that Russia has, for the time being at least, chosen to accept and

---

[85]"Georgia, Russia Agree to Launch Joint Operation in Pankisi Gorge . . ." *RFE/RL Newsline*, Vol. 6, No. 20, Part I, January 31, 2002; "Georgian Officials Exclude Bin Laden's Presence in Pankisi," *RFE/RL Newsline*, Vol. 6, No. 32, Part I, February 19, 2002; Vernon Loeb and Peter Slevin, "U.S. Begins Anti-Terror Assistance in Georgia," *Washington Post*, February 27, 2002, p. A1; Robert Burns, "Russians Tell of Terrorists in Georgia," *Associated Press*, March 13, 2002, from *www.washingtonpost.com*.

perhaps even try to gain from this situation. How long this is sustainable, and what level of commitment the United States is truly willing to give to Georgia given the country's dire need for fundamental restructuring, remain key questions. If the United States does get involved in Georgia to any real extent, moreover, it runs a real risk of being drawn into that country's myriad internal conflicts and will face the challenges of operating in an area of continued instability and limited central control (see Chapter Eight of this report).

The extent to which recent and future events will affect the development of the energy trade is still an open question. Insofar as U.S. support for predominantly Turkish routes was driven by a desire to limit Russian and Iranian influence, U.S. cooperation with Russia (and potentially Iran, although, as discussed above, this appears less likely) may lead it to change its policies somewhat. Turkey will, of course, continue to support pipeline routes through its own territory, and Georgia will remain a vociferous advocate of those options, as it has tremendous amounts to gain from them as a transit state. It is still too early to judge, however, the extent to which U.S. energy policy will change.

CONCLUSIONS

The incentive structure in place for the major outside actors in the CASC region includes shared interests in economic (especially energy) development, political stability, and counterterror, countercrime, and counterproliferation efforts. These combine with the greater importance that most of these states attach to relations with each other over and above relations with the Caspian states, to exert a moderating influence on the propensity for competition between them to evolve into armed conflict. This will continue to be the case for as long as current incentive structures hold. However, these incentives will be challenged as the multinational response to the September 11 terrorist attacks on the United States evolves. Moreover, there exist a number of ways other than war between them in which third parties can develop into potential sources of conflict in the region. Finally, especially considering the importance to Russia, China, Iran, and increasingly the United States that the region remain peaceful, it is likely that if conflict occurs, one or more outside states will be involved in its continuation and/or resolution.

Russia, which is weak relative to the strength enjoyed by its predecessor state, the Soviet Union, remains the outside actor with the most at stake in the region. The risk that in coming years it will seek to reassert its control over the region, perhaps even by force, is somewhat mitigated in the near term by its cooperation with the United States in the fight against terrorism. But because this is a threat born of Russian weakness rather than Russian strength, it does not entirely disappear, and its resurgence will depend in some part on the extent and form of U.S. presence in the next one to two decades. Moreover, if and when conflict occurs in the region, Russia will almost certainly play a role. In fact, the situation may be even worse if it does not. Insofar as states such as Iran and China, which have interests in CASC but also value highly good ties with Russia, believe that Russia will maintain a sphere of influence in the Caspian, they will seek not to tread on Russia's toes. If, however, they have reason to believe that Russia (or some other party, such as the United States) cannot or will not resolve dangers in the region, they may feel obliged to take action themselves. If the United States remains actively involved, these risks are mitigated, particularly if it can cooperate with Russia to maintain control in the region.

The United States will face important strategic choices in CASC in coming years. Prior to September 11, its interests in this part of the world were generally secondary and derivative of the interests of allies and economic actors. Even then, allies like Turkey and global goals such as democratization and the effort to control crime and drugs would have kept the United States involved on some level. Now that the counterterror effort has escalated to armed conflict, the United States has placed forces in the Central Asian region, changing its own incentive structure in several ways. Stability in this inherently unstable region has become far more important. The likelihood that the United States will become involved in regional conflict has become far greater. And whatever choices the United States makes in coming years, as long as it remains involved in the region at all, its local unrest, conflict, and economic and political problems, themselves possibly exacerbated by the evolving situation in Afghanistan, will complicate U.S. military and other efforts in Central Asia, South Caucasus, and beyond.

Chapter Eight

CENTRAL ASIA AND SOUTH CAUCASUS AS AN AREA OF OPERATIONS: CHALLENGES AND CONSTRAINTS
William D. O'Malley

INTRODUCTION

There is no question that the United States can get forces into the South Caucasus or Central Asia, as it has in support of U.S. operations in Afghanistan, known as Operation Enduring Freedom. To date, these operations have been limited to a few airfields in Central Asia from which military and humanitarian support operations have been conducted over Afghanistan. This operational experience has highlighted for U.S. military planners many of the difficulties inherent in deploying forces to and sustaining them in Central Asia, as well as the necessary tradeoffs between speed, cost, combat capability, and effectiveness.

U.S. relations with and security interests in the states of both Central Asia and the South Caucasus have changed dramatically since September 11 and as a result of the U.S. commitment to the international counterterrorist campaign.[1] The U.S. military has been much more proactive in the two subregions, recruiting states into the counterterrorist coalition and expanding its security cooperation and direct military assistance programs. In the long term, this increased military-to-military contact and Western exposure to the region's operational environment will improve the U.S. military's ability both to conduct combat operations in the target countries and to use these areas to project and sustain military forces in nearby countries or regions. The emphasis of this chapter is on the conduct of ground

---

[1]See Chapter Two of this report.

support operations in CASC, but it also addresses briefly the use of the region as a power-projection platform.

To date, this post-September 11 growth in military activity with the regional states has focused first on supporting operations in Afghanistan and then on the broader antiterrorist campaign. In support of Operation Enduring Freedom, the emphasis has been more narrowly focused on gaining essential overflight and base access rights needed to support ongoing combat operations in Afghanistan.

To support a broader range of potential ground support missions in any of these states, military planners will need a more detailed understanding of the capabilities and limitations of the national infrastructure of potential target states than they have so far required. Successful joint military operations demand a precise comprehension of which local operational capabilities are in place and which are not. Often the available local infrastructure will not be able to support the planned deployment of U.S. forces and may in fact hamper the process, forcing alterations in the operation's deployment pattern. U.S. force deployments into Central Asia in support of Operation Enduring Freedom have indeed reinforced this assertion. Deploying forces have identified many problems and shortfalls that they have had to overcome or redress, often requiring the deployment of additional supplies, equipment, and/or personnel, which slows the process and inflates overall lift requirements. This experience is probably not unique, and future deployments will meet similar problems. Moreover, in many of these states U.S. troops are likely to face an uncertain and potentially hostile environment, whatever the type of mission or its requirements.

Regardless of the specifics of the mission, the mechanics of deploying U.S. forces to Central Asia and/or the South Caucasus and sustaining them once there present challenges that must not be underestimated. In the region, forces will find that many of the same factors that make the deployment difficult (and, probably, the same factors that made it necessary) will make their work even harder. Distances to and through the region are vast, the terrain is difficult and often unpredictable, poverty and pollution are prevalent, and political uncertainty is a facet of everyday life.

This analysis discusses some of the geographical and operational challenges presented by CASC as a potential environment for a future U.S. military deployment. It does not postulate the specifics of possible missions; rather, it considers the mechanics of the deployment process, the operational environment, and the capabilities of local forces to work with the United States, work with each other, and to fight their own fights, whether alongside U.S. forces or against them. Although operations in Afghanistan have unique characteristics, there are a number of operational lessons that have implications for any future operations or deployments the two subregions, especially Central Asia. The war in Afghanistan is not over, but a number of the first impressions from that conflict have application and will be discussed briefly in this chapter.

DEPLOYMENT

Whatever the mission, the first step in implementing it will be to deliver forces and equipment into the area of operations. If that area of operations is Central Asia and/or South Caucasus, distances to and through the region make this a particular challenge. Airfields are few and far between, and many of them are in poor operational condition. Only Georgia has access to the open sea, making deployment by ship, especially into Central Asia, even less feasible. Finally, apart from the vast distances to travel, road and rail transit through the region are further hampered by the poor condition of the infrastructure and the difficult terrain across much of the region. While road and rail infrastructure is likely to improve in some parts of CASC as energy development proceeds, it will be largely limited to the energy-producing states (and, to a lesser extent, transit states like Georgia), and even there only to the main traffic arteries, rather than the region as a whole.[2]

Of course, the degree of challenge associated with any airlift mission varies, depending on how much (materiel, equipment, and person-

---

[2] In addition to the traffic arteries, deployment planners must also be concerned about the availability of the right mix of railroad rolling stock necessary to move deploying formations. The rolling stock needed to transport the heavy, outsized equipment associated with a U.S. mechanized formation (battalion or brigade) is in short supply in the region, and this situation is unlikely to improve over the next five years or more.

nel) must be transported into the region; and this will depend on the specifics of the mission. For illustrative purposes, this analysis considers the difficulties inherent in moving a brigade combat team (BCT) into the region. The BCT is today considered the basic building block for Army forces and therefore provides a good starting point for thinking about a deployment.

There are three categories of BCTs (Heavy, Stryker, [Medium],[3] and Light), and Table 8.1 presents the number of troops assigned, the estimated weight of materiel to be moved, and the number of vehicles associated with each type of brigade. The table also outlines the amount of strategic air and sea lift required to transport each of these force packages.

Table 8.1

Key Brigade Combat Team Characteristics and Lift Requirements

	Light	SBCT	Heavy
Passengers, each	2,393	3,494	3,655
Short tons	2,355	12,574	26,865
Square feet	71,896	217,098	315,861
Dismounted infantry, each	945	945	261
Wheels, each	347	930	780
Light tracks, each	0	0	390
Heavy tracks, each	0	0	160
C-17 sorties	53	280	597
LMSRs	1	1	2

---

[3]The Strkyer Brigade Combat Team (SBCT) is the first step in the Army's effort to improve the deployability time of its mechanized combat formations. The SBCT is being built around a new series of combat vehicles that are smaller and lighter than their counterpart in the Army's standard mechanized battalions and brigades. The overall force structure of the SBCT is smaller and its total deployment requirements are much reduced. This medium-weight formation is more deployable than the heavy brigade, but it carries much more firepower and mobility than a light brigade. See John G. Roos, "Tools of Transformation: Army's Sights Focused Far Beyond the Interim Brigade Combat Teams and Future Combat Systems," *Armed Forces Journal International*, October 2001, pp. 56–61, and Daniel Goure, "The Army's Policy Nettle: Transformation: Will It Fix What Ails the Army?" *Armed Forces Journal International*, October 2001, pp. 44–54, for a good description of the Army's long-term transformation program.

The numbers of C-17[4] sorties or LMSRs (Large Medium-Speed Roll-on/Roll-off Ships) indicated are for the brigade combat teams alone and do not factor in additional logistics or other support capabilities that may be demanded by the specific mission and theater's security environment.

As Table 8.1 indicates, the more strategically mobile light brigade combat team requires only one-fifth as much strategic airlift to deploy as the Stryker BCT (SBCT). BCTs of this type are small and light enough to be readily moved exclusively by air into either South Caucasus or Central Asia. Formations of this size and smaller special forces or technical support units can be flown nonstop by C-17 from their CONUS home station[5] or staged through a USAF-managed base nearer the region and transferred to C-130 tactical airlifters for the entry leg of the deployment. For smaller unit deployments, the disadvantage of the smaller cargo space of the C-130[6] is outweighed by the aircraft's ability to effectively operate from almost any type of austere landing strip (see Table 8.2). Moreover, the C-130 places a smaller burden on the supporting host nation airfield. These are both important characteristics when the operational environment is unfamiliar, the airfields are less than optimal, and landing near the operational location is critical.

As Table 8.1 indicates, the light BCT has the same number of dismounted infantry as the SBCT, but less than one-third of the mobility

---

[4]Although the C-17 is used as the standard airlift measure here, all of the combat systems organic to the Army's new medium-weight combat brigade or Interim Brigade Combat Team are C-130 transportable. The smaller cargo body of the C-130 will necessitate more airlift sorties (an estimated 390 versus the 280 for the C-17). This approximately 40 percent increase in the number of aircraft sorties will increase the necessary deployment time and place a greater strain on the host country's infrastructure.

[5]In support of a 1997 PfP-sponsored CENTRAZBAT-97 exercise in Central Asia, about a battalion of 82nd Airborne Division troops flew nearly 8,000 miles nonstop in C-17s from Fort Bragg, North Carolina, to the exercise location in Kazakhstan in about 20 hours and parachuted into the training zone. In addition to the 82nd, elements of the 10th Mountain Division have also participated in this exercise series and gained some operational familiarity with the region and the peacekeeping forces from Kazakhstan, Kyrgyzstan, and Uzbekistan it has worked with, as well as the facilities used.

[6]The C-130 has a cargo capacity of 21 short tons, less than half that of the C-17 (45 short tons). The outsized character of much of the equipment associated with this brigade means that many of the aircraft sorties are cubed out before they are weighted out, thus the less than 50 percent exchange rate of C-130s for C-17s.

assets. Clearly, the light brigade can be deployed more quickly and its deployment will place a much smaller demand on the host country's transportation infrastructure.[7] But it will not have the combat capability, armor protection, or ground mobility inherent in an SBCT and especially not that in a heavy brigade. There is not sufficient organic transportation to simultaneously move all unit personnel, which will constrain the brigade's ground mobility. The HMMWV (high mobility multipurpose wheeled vehicle) is the principal transportation asset organic to the light brigade.[8] The brigade has a number of variously configured models of the HMMWV, as the vehicles are mission configured and carry different weapons and communications packages. What is packaged onboard is constrained by the vehicle's limited space and load-bearing capabilities. The nature of the HMMWV also limits the number and types of C4ISR (command, control, communications, computers, intelligence, surveillance, and reconnaissance) assets that can be self-deployed with the brigade, which could constrain the unit's ability to maintain detailed situational awareness across an expansive operational environment. The light brigade's firepower is limited to lightweight, short-range, towed 105mm howitzers and light mortar indirect artillery systems, and a range of direct-fire, anti-armor systems. The brigade's most effective anti-armor systems will be its direct-fire assets, meaning that enemy armor and artillery assets can with good probability close within range of the unit. The combat effectiveness and operational utility of the light brigade is significantly enhanced when supported by combined lift and attack helicopter units that can add needed mobility and firepower. There are a number of operational environments and mission requirements well suited for such light forces, as the U.S. Army's 10th Mountain Division has demonstrated in the rugged hills and mountains of Afghanistan.[9]

---

[7]Estimates outlined in Table 8.3 suggest that the light brigade can be deployed almost anywhere in the Caspian region in less than four days.

[8]The HMMWV is generally not armored and provides little direct protection from weapons fire or flying debris. The vehicle has good offroad capability, but its truck-like wheel and drive-shaft design is vulnerable to the hazards of both terrain and enemy action.

[9]The missions best suited for this type of light formation include, but are not limited to, the following: seizure and security of airfields and other key facilities, rapid deployment (quickly getting U.S. ground combat forces on the ground), peacekeeping operations, military operations on urbanized terrain (MOUT), counterterrorist opera-

The Army's new medium-weight formation, the SBCT, has greater tactical mobility, armor protection, and firepower than the light BCT.[10] But the tradeoff is a significant increase in the size and weight of the deployment package (see Table 8.1) and in the time needed to deploy the brigade.[11] The SBCT includes about 3,500 troops, 12,600 short tons of cargo (equipment and supplies), and 930 vehicles, and although the SBCT requires less than half of the strategic lift needed to move a standard heavy brigade, it remains a significant lift challenge. The principal combat vehicles assigned to the SBCT will be variants of the Army's new interim armored vehicle (IAV): the wheeled light armored vehicle (LAV III).[12] The size and load-bearing capabilities of the LAV give the unit a more stable and versatile platform than the HMMWV on which to mount a broader suite of weapons, acquisition and systems management tools, C3 (command, control, and communication) assets, and other systems that will enhance situational awareness and the unit's ability to conduct all-weather, day-night operations to greater ranges across the battlefield. The SBCT's overall C4ISR capability is a significant improvement over light brigades. The unit's fire support assets have greater range, higher rates of fire, and a broader range of munitions capability, allowing it to engage enemy forces, including armor, outside of direct-fire range. These mobility, C4ISR, and firepower improvements will allow the SBCT to operate in a broader-range and more robust combat environment. Although the SBCT does not have the operational capability to challenge a heavy mechanized and ar-

---

tions against similarly armed opposition forces, large-scale raids and reconnaissance, operations in rugged terrain (e.g., mountains), timely local security for combat search and rescue (CSAR) operations, and operations requiring shock action (e.g., ambushes).

[10]The SBCT is an evolving unit structure, and the first two teams are expected to be operational in the summer of 2003. See Roos, "Tools of Transformation: Army's Sights Focused Far Beyond Interim Brigade Combat Teams and Future Combat Systems."

[11]See Table 8.3 for a current estimate of the deployment time for an SBCT to key locations in the Caspian region.

[12]The various combat and support variants of the IAV are expected to weigh, on average, 20 tons each, which is significantly less than its counterpart in the heavy BCT. The LAV III is much lighter than the Bradley Infantry Fighting Vehicle, but it sacrifices both armor protection and firepower. It is, however, faster than the Bradley, consumes less fuel, requires fewer man-hours of repair, needs a smaller logistical support base, and is more flexible in complex terrain. Goure, "The Army's Policy Nettle," p. 48.

mored opposition force, it does have much more anti-armor capability than the light brigade and can be expected to operate against lightly armored formations, especially with airborne anti-armor fire support from either Air Force fighters or Army attack helicopters. The SBCT can be effectively used to support most of the same types of missions as the light brigade, but to do so in a security environment that demands greater firepower, personnel protection, situational awareness, and ground mobility. What it clearly cannot do is get there as quickly as the light brigade, but once there, it is better protected and has far better mobility.

The heavy brigade has significantly greater armor protection, firepower, and overall combat capability than either of the other types of brigades, but there are many operational environments where these capabilities are not needed and may, in fact, have only limited utility.[13] As noted in Table 8.1, these enhanced combat capabilities come at a cost in both the size and weight of the unit, as well as how the formation can be deployed, what demands it places on strategic lift, and how long it will take the unit to close in theater.

In the end, the type or mix of formations and capabilities best suited for a given deployment will be determined by a number of factors, including the nature of the mission requirements, the threat environment, local capabilities and limitations, and how soon combat forces need to be on the ground. The discussion that follows focuses on the deployment of pure force packages and is not definitive. It is not anticipated that either the deployment of a pure light or medium brigade will be the best option. Rather, these units are being used to give planners a feel for the range of deployment issues and timeliness possible. In the end, the deployed force package will be tailored to meet specific operational and mission requirements and could easily be a mix of light and medium formations (companies and battalions).

---

[13]For example, heavy formations were a necessity in Desert Storm, but they had only marginal long-term utility in either Bosnia or Kosovo, where the heavy, tracked Bradley IFVs and Abrams tanks were essentially confined to the compounds and provided perimeter security.

DEPLOYMENT BY AIR

As Operation Enduring Freedom so clearly demonstrated, in the absence of standing operations orders, assured access to regional deployment airfields, established air lanes, and the en route infrastructure necessary to support the process, it is difficult to rapidly deploy forces into such a distant theater. Like Central Asia, Afghanistan is landlocked and far removed from stationed U.S. military forces and their traditional deployment support infrastructure. Following the September 11 attacks on the United States, it took U.S. planners nearly three weeks to prepare for Operation Enduring Freedom. This time was used to forge the alliances, prepare the plans necessary to support operations against Taliban and Al Qaeda forces in Afghanistan, and put in place the overflight, basing, and special-access agreements essential for the air bridge linking the operational area to CONUS and the European theater.[14] This latter step was critical because almost all the materiel and equipment moved into the theater has been transported by air. The lack of access or use agreements for airfields with any of the regional states delayed and then constrained airlift operations, as well as combat operations by land-based tactical aircraft.[15] It would take time, but the United States and its allies successfully negotiated access agreements with several of the Central Asian states, which will be discussed in greater detail later.

For the United States to deploy forces effectively by air, it must not only have access to regional airfields, but these airfields must also meet fairly specific infrastructure requirements. As Table 8.2 indi-

---

[14]Ramstein Air Base, Germany, served as the principal strategic hub for all airlift operations in support of Operation Enduring Freedom. Bulgaria, Turkey, Azerbaijan, Georgia, Turkmenistan, and Pakistan were all among those states that granted overflight privileges. Bulgaria also allowed the U.S. Air Force to operate KC-135 tankers from one of its Black Sea bases. See John G. Roos, "Turning Up The Heat," *Armed Forces Journal International,* February 2002, p. 37, and John A. Tirpak, "Enduring Freedom," *Air Force Magazine*, February 2002, p. 36.

[15]During the early weeks of Operation Enduring Freedom, U.S. and allied combat air operations were restricted to the use of long-range bombers and carrier-based aircraft, with U.S. Navy air generating about 90 percent of the combat sorties during these first weeks. Adam J. Herbert, "The Search for Asian Bases," *Air Force Magazine,* January 2002, pp. 51–52. A similar arrangement may be possible to support air operations over the Caucasus from the Black Sea, but most of Central Asia is outside the normal operating range of naval air, underscoring the need for access to regional airbases.

cates, the heavy lifters, especially the C-5 and the tankers, require long, well-reinforced runways and plenty of ramp space to allow for the safe parking and servicing of aircraft and cargo.[16] When fully loaded, the Air Force prefers to operate these larger aircraft from airfields with runways of 8,000 to 10,000 feet.

The preference will be a problem in the area of the Caspian, as it was in Afghanistan.[17] Many local airfields in that region were initially built by the Soviet air force as fighter or fighter-bomber bases, and thus to standard metrics, which included a 7,500-foot runway and an

Table 8.2

Infrastructure Requirements by Aircraft Type

Aircraft Type	Minimum Runway Length for Landings (feet)	Maximum Runway Length for Takeoff at Maximum Weight (feet)	Minimum Runway Length for Takeoff at Minimum Load (feet)	Minimum Runway Width (feet)	Operational Planning Factor (feet)	Ramp Space Required (square feet)	Preferred LCN
C-5	5,000	12,200	7,200	150	$8,000 \times 150$	64,524	48
C-17	3,000	7,500	3,500	90	$4,500 \times 90$	47,500	48
C-130	3,000	6,250	2,600	60	$4,000 \times 80$	15,519	37
C-141	5,000	9,000	5,920	98	$6,000 \times 100$	31,362	50
KC-10/ KC-135	5,400	11,800	8,480	148	$10,000 \times 148$	34,800	77
B-747	6,600	11,000	8,000	142	$8,500 \times 150$	52,500	70

---

[16]The information comes from various sources, including *Jane's All the World's Aircraft 1999–2000*, Jane's Information Group Ltd., 1999, U.S. Air Force Pamphlet 10-1403, *Airlift Planning Factors, 1996*, and U.S. Air Force Pamphlet 76-2, *Military Airlift: Airlift Planning Factors*, May 29, 1987.

[17]During Operation Enduring Freedom, the Air Force has worked around the lack of access to airfields large enough to support its large tankers (KC-10 and KC-135) in several ways. The tankers flew racetrack orbits along the en-route flight paths, refueled the aircraft both inbound and outbound, and staged out of airfields in Turkey and Bulgaria to support the final leg of the flight. This is less than the optimum solution because of the increased daily sortie rate demand it placed on the tanker fleet. Richard J. Newman, "Tankers and Lifters for a Distant War," *Air Force Magazine*, January 2002, pp. 56–60.

LCN (load classification number) ranging from 40 to 45.[18] Only a few commercial airfields and former Soviet strategic military airbases in the area are sufficiently robust to approach the U.S. Air Force's preferences.[19] Moreover, many of the former military installations are not being utilized or, at least, well used and maintained by the local militaries. Also, the facilities are run down and many of their control and safety systems are in disrepair, as U.S. Air Force survey teams confirmed during the ramp up to Operation Enduring Freedom.[20] Because of runway constraints, any deployment to the Caspian by air would probably rely primarily on the C-17 and C-130, which can operate from smaller, more austere airfields than can the C-5, have a much better operational readiness rate than the C-5, and demand less local support.

About 20 airfields in the South Caucasus subregion have runways of at least 7,500 feet. Ten of them are in Georgia, including Babushara, a large commercial airfield not far from the seaport at P'ot'i and two smaller airfields near Bat'umi. The latter are former Soviet fighter bases and have shorter runways but should be able to support C-17 operations. Mureulli air base outside of Tbilisi (see Figure 8.1) is being refurbished to NATO standards with Turkish assistance, and

---

[18]The LCN is a numerical value that represents how much weight a particular runway can hold without causing permanent damage. Each aircraft type has a specified LCN, which identifies how much stress it is expected to exert on the runway. Aircraft type, operational parameters, and gross weight all factor into LCN. Normally, the LCN of an aircraft should not exceed that of the runway, taxiway, or ramp on which it operates. See U.S. Air Force Pamphlet 76-2, *Military Airlift: Airlift Planning Factors*.

[19]The emphasis is on preference, but the Air Force is prepared to and has operated from airfields that fall far short of the preferred standard. The critical concerns are for the length, width, and condition of the runway and its associated ramp space, and for the security of the installation. The Air Force is prepared to overcome or work around most of the other types of shortfalls, bringing in fuel bladders to replace damaged tanks, mobile navigation and control systems, tents or other temporary structures for both operational requirements and life support, etc. Additionally, both the Air Force and the Army can use U.S. contractors to provide specific support utilizing local labor and materials. Air Force operations at both Tazar air base, Hungary, and Tuzla airfield, Bosnia, are good examples of how quickly and effectively these types of upgrades can be made in support of airlift operations. Granted, neither of these airfields had to sustain the operational tempo of airlift operations that would be needed to move and sustain Army units in the Caspian region, since they had access to more efficient rail and road lines of communication (LOCs).

[20]For additional details on the airfields available in these states, see William D. O'Malley, *Evaluating Possible Airfield Deployment Options: Middle East Contingencies*, Santa Monica, CA: RAND, MR-1353-AF, 2001, pp. 123–133.

the Turkish military has negotiated a long-term use agreement for access to this facility.[21] In Azerbaijan, the best deployment support airfield is located outside of Baku, near the Caspian Sea (see Figure 8.1).[22] The Turkish military has indicated that this base and one other in the country can be brought up to NATO standards. Additionally, Turkey has been negotiating base access rights for one of these facilities.[23] In Armenia, there are two airfields with runways greater than 10,000 feet in length and capable of supporting most NATO aircraft.[24]

The airfields in these three states are suboptimal for airlift operations, as they generally suffer from a shortage of adequate parking space, support structure, or equipment needed to handle more than a few large cargo aircraft on the ground simultaneously and would have great difficulty sustaining large-scale airlift operations.

There are 36 airfields with runways longer than 7,500 feet in the five Central Asian states: fifteen in Kazakhstan, two in Kyrgyzstan, six in Tajikistan, three in Turkmenistan, and ten in Uzbekistan. Twelve of these airfields have runways longer than 10,000 feet and seven have runways longer than 9,000 feet. The airfields with the longer runways are concentrated in Kazakhstan and Uzbekistan, with five of the 10,000-foot runways in Kazakhstan and four in Uzbekistan. At a minimum, each of the other countries has an airfield with a 10,000-foot runway servicing its capital. The airfield distribution across each of the countries is shown in Figure 8.2. As in South Caucasus, the larger commercial airfields are in the best shape; many of the smaller airfields have fallen into disrepair. Unless there is a major improvement in the economy such that these less-trafficked airfields become commercially important, it is unlikely that they will improve without direct outside assistance. As noted earlier, in preparation for

---

[21]For more details see Ibid., pp. 128–130.

[22]For more details see Ibid., pp. 125–128.

[23]If the negotiations are successfully completed, it follows the recent Turkish agreement for the right to use an airbase in Georgia and extends Turkish military influence in the region. It also affords Turkey an opportunity to improve the facilities to NATO standards, ensure that they can accept and support a full range of NATO aircraft, and provide another possible NATO access option in the region.

[24]For more details, see O'Malley, pp. 123–125.

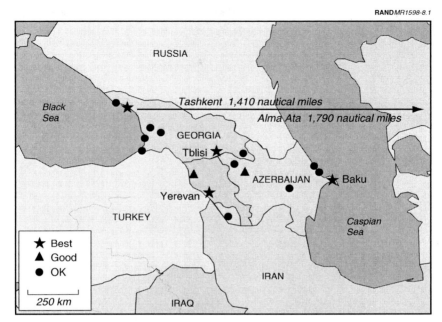

NOTE: This subjective evaluation (best, good, and ok) is based on the author's analysis of the following criteria: length and condition of the principal runway, the number of available square feet of ramp space, the condition of the airfield's command and control structure, support capability, proximity to key LOCs, and available life-support facilities.

Figure 8.1—Airfields in South Caucasus

the war in Afghanistan, USCENTCOM and the U.S. Air Force completed site surveys of many of the airfields in Central Asia, entered into access agreements with three of the countries, and negotiated limited use of airfields in the other two.[25] The airfields in Tajikistan and Turkmenistan appear to be in the worst condition of the subregion. With the possible exception of the larger airfields in Kazakhstan, Kyrgyzstan, and Uzbekistan, few of the Central Asian airfields have adequate space, support structure, or equipment to handle more than a few large cargo aircraft on the ground simultaneously. In their current state, few if any of these airfields could turn around

---

[25]Tamara Makarenko, "Central Asian States Set to Pay the Price of US Strikes," *Jane's Intelligence Review*, November 2001, pp. 34–37.

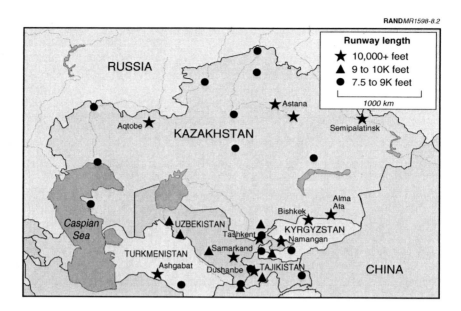

Figure 8.2—Airfields in Central Asia

the approximately 70 to 80 C-17s per day needed to rapidly deploy an SBCT and meet the Army's envisioned deployment timeline.

It is a minimum of 6,220 nautical miles from Fort Stewart, Georgia, into the South Caucasus by air[26] and more than 8,000 nautical miles into Central Asia, far beyond the unrefueled range of the Air Force's strategic airlifters (see Figure 8.3).[27] Therefore, a deployment to Central Asia by air requires a combination of en route staging bases and in-flight refueling. As shown by the U.S. Air Force experience in the initial days of Operation Enduring Freedom, setting up such an

----

[26]As Figure 8.3 shows, the deployment distance could be reduced by approximately 4,500 nautical miles if the unit(s) being moved were stationed or prepositioned in Europe and the transatlantic segment was eliminated. There are, however, no immediate plans to station or preposition an SBCT unit or equipment set in Europe.

[27]The distances portrayed in Figure 8.3 represent the air miles associated with possible legs of an airlift operation, with the aircraft originating near Fort Stewart, landing at the U.S. Air Force's main operating base at Ramstein, Germany, stopping in Georgia, and then staging into Central Asia from there. The distances in nautical miles are for each segment of the route.

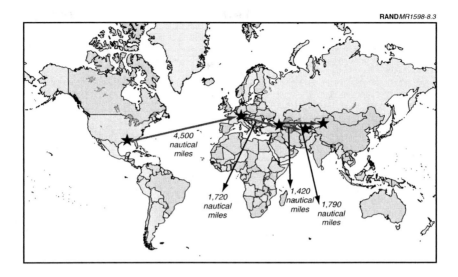

**Figure 8.3—Air Distances Between Staging and Deployment Locations
(distances are in nautical miles and approximations)**

air corridor takes time, the cooperation of many allies, and the dedication of many resources to open and then keep it operating.[28]

As already noted, deploying an SBCT to the region would require approximately 280 C-17 sorties (or 390 C-130 sorties), whereas deploying a light brigade would require only 30 percent of that amount. These sortie numbers, however, are for the brigade alone. It is anticipated that with any combat force deployment, it will be necessary to include a supplementary Army support package, increasing the scale of the deployment and the number of airlift sorties needed.[29] For example, in every major contingency deployment over the last decade, the Army has included aviation assets in its deployment

---

[28]Roos, "Turning Up The Heat."

[29]A composite helicopter battalion with 12 transport helicopters, 2 reconnaissance and command and control helicopters, and 12 attack helicopters would add approximately 450 personnel and 2,000 short tons of cargo to the deployment package. Such an addition would add about 45 sorties and two days to the deployment. Helicopter operations in a number of the regions may be constrained because of high altitudes or rain, snow, ice, fog, or blowing sand and dust.

package. The operational environments in this region strongly suggest the need for the tactical mobility, operational flexibility, and responsive firepower provided by a combined lift and attack helicopter unit. As a frame of reference, it is useful to note that 269 C-17 sorties and more than 20 days were needed for the Army to close all elements of Task Force Hawk into the austere operational environment of Albania in 1999.[30]

In addition to the Army's airlift requirements, the Air Force would likely require another 20 to 25 sorties to deploy its own initial airfield opening package.[31] Once operations begin, daily flights into the region carrying key consumables such as fuel, water, spare parts, and ammunition will also be needed. If the Air Force is also deploying units into the region, the number of airlift sorties supporting their movement and sustainment requirements will increase the total still further, placing greater pressure on the host country's facilities and support capabilities, as well as on the limited number of strategic airlift assets available.[32]

Table 8.3 presents the estimated number of days necessary to close various types of brigade combat teams into the region by air, with the closure time calculated starting with the loading of the first aircraft and ending with the unloading of the last aircraft.[33] In addition to flight time, the estimates include the time needed to move the unit(s) from the installation to the embarkation airfield (APOE), stage and load the unit equipment and cargo onto the aircraft, land and unload

---

[30]Task Force Hawk was a brigade-sized task force with a composite attack helicopter unit, force protection, and a support package.

[31]This Air Force mobility package provides the personnel and equipment needed to open and operate airlift operations from an unprepared airfield and to secure it. The size of the package can be tailored to the specific needs of a given airfield, but it could include 700 to 900 personnel and between 600 and 800 short tons of cargo. The status of the airfield, availability of needed support equipment and service personnel, security, and the status of on-site life-support facilities will be key determiners of what resources are needed and how soon in the deployment process they must be delivered.

[32]Given the most recent experience of Afghanistan, it seems inconceivable that Air Force tactical combat air, reconnaissance, refueling, search and rescue, and special operations assets would not be deployed into theater. These military capabilities are in short supply among the local militaries.

[33]The calculations assume that a minimum of 40 C-17s will be dedicated to the deployment of Army forces to the theater.

Table 8.3

Estimated Days to Close by Air

Days to Close	Light	SBCT	Heavy
Fort Stewart to Georgia	2.5	10.5	22
Fort Stewart to Tashkent	3.1	12.5	26.5
Fort Stewart to Alma Ata	3.2	13	28

the unit at the airfield of debarkation (APOD), recycle the aircraft, and reconstitute the units and move them into their operational sector. For this estimate, the distance of the first leg of the operation was about 4,500 nautical miles from Fort Stewart to Ramstein Air Base, Germany, which is substantially greater than the typical 3,200-nautical mile leg used in standard Air Force planning factors. This was done to simplify the process and provide the reader with a quick estimate of the nature of the deployment time required. Otherwise the analysis used the Center for Army Analysis' deployment methodology and planning assumptions, including the average airspeed for the airlifters, planning load, distances from APOE to APOD airfields where provided (otherwise estimated), the aircraft use rate (hours/day), and the capabilities of the APOE and APOD airfields.[34] Because of the austere nature of the operational environment in both South Caucasus and Central Asia, this estimate employs only the C-17 aircraft.[35] Although the C-130 does not have the range or the lift capacity of the C-17, its ability to operate from almost any type of airfield makes it another good option, if the operational circumstances are right.[36] If the C-130 is used as the principal aircraft, there will be a longer deployment timeline because of the approximately

---

[34]These estimates build on original work presented in a Center for Army Analysis briefing, *Interim Brigade Combat Team Deployment Analysis*, November 9, 2000.

[35]As noted earlier, the C-17's operational characteristics and ability to operate from more austere airfields make it the likely choice for such operations, especially 10 years from now when it will probably be the principal airlift aircraft in the Air Force's fleet. During Operation Enduring Freedom, the C-17 has been the principal airlifter because of the distances involved and the declining operational readiness rate of the aging C-5 fleet. Newman, "Tankers and Lifters for a Distant War," and Bill Sweetman, "Airlift for the 21st Century," *Jane's International Defense Review*, December 2001, pp. 48–52.

[36]The C-17 can readily be used as either a strategic or a tactical deployment support aircraft, because of its range and lift capacity. By contrast, the C-130 is only a theater asset, given the limits on its operational range and lift capacity.

40 percent increase in the number of aircraft sorties required for moving an SBCT.

Note also that these are best-case estimates of the fastest possible closing time for deployment by air. They do not factor in any number of factors that could slow down the process, such as APOD throughput limitations, shortages of airlifters (i.e., higher-priority missions), the nonavailability of needed tankers, overflight restrictions, etc. They also do not factor in the use of a regional ISB,[37] which could change the timeline considerably.

BY SEA

Like airlift, sealift deployment to South Caucasus or Central Asia presents challenges of distance and fairly demanding infrastructure requirements. As noted above, moving an SBCT involves moving at least 12,600 short tons of cargo and 930 vehicles. This means that one SBCT can be deployed in one LMSR and a heavy brigade in two. The steaming distance from Fort Stewart to a Georgian port is approximately 8,300 nautical miles. With current sealift assets traveling at 24 knots, about 14 days would be necessary to complete the sealift portion of the deployment. This number may be reduced over the next decade if new, faster ships, such as the proposed 40-knot ships, enter the sealift fleet. If this happens, total sailing time could be reduced by 35 percent, to about 8.7 days.

This does not, however, mean that even with the faster ships the entire deployment could be complete in nine days. Additional time will be needed to move the unit(s) from the installation to the port, to stage and load equipment and cargo onto the ships, to dock and unload the unit at the port of debarkation, and then to reconstitute the units, move them into their operational sector, and integrate them into the operational task force.

How long this latter phase of the deployment will take depends in part on the condition of the transportation infrastructure and the

---

[37]Intermediate Staging Base(s) are operational bases closer to but outside of the target theater that are used to consolidate, organize, and transship personnel, materiel, and equipment into the appropriate countries. ISBs also frequently serve as the logistical support hub for all forces deployed to and operating in theater.

overall support capabilities of both the receiving port and the host nation. The deploying U.S. forces cannot control these factors, but they will need to plan for them. If support capabilities are deemed lacking at a given seaport of debarkation (SPOD), U.S. planners will have to decide whether it is worthwhile to attempt to improve local facilities. Other possible options are to deploy the necessary support assets to the SPOD to supplement its organic capabilities or to look for a more capable seaport.

In general, the U.S. military's strategic lift assets have not been designed to operate into austere or even mid-level commercial seaports. This is especially true of the U.S. Navy's current generation of strategic sealift ships. These large ships require deep-draft ports with plenty of maneuver room; long, deep, and well-serviced piers; and room in which to offload, store, and stage the deploying unit's equipment and cargo. As shown in Table 8.4, the LMSR has a draft of 35 to 37 feet and is more than 950 feet long. It is estimated that only about 25 to 30 percent of the world's ports are capable of handling ships this size. If the ships are restricted to less than a full load, they can operate in channels and at portsides with a draft of as little as 31 to 35 feet, increasing the number of possible deployment ports. Another option would be to use smaller commercial freighters, but this could significantly complicate the loading and unloading process. Either of these options would increase the number of ships needed to transport U.S. forces and equipment to the theater and extend the deployment timeline.

Finally, note that of all the CASC states, only Georgia has open seaports. To reach Georgia, U.S. ships would have to transit the congested and narrow Bosporus Strait. While a relatively small deploy-

Table 8.4

Strategic Sealift Ship Characteristics

Ship Name	Class	Length	Draft	Deadweight	Knots	Thousands of Square Feet
Pollux	FSS	946	37	27,300	27	173
Gordon	LMSR	956	37	22,150	24	321
Bob Hope	LMSR	949	35	26,600	24	388
Watkin	LMSR	950	35	33,600	24	392

ment is unlikely to strain the waterway to the point of interfering with commercial traffic, it is certain that Turkey's agreement to provide access and willingness to support the mission will be necessary for this transit to occur. A larger deployment and regular deliveries of supplies once the mission is under way may put some strain on the Bosporus. Moreover, Central Asia is entirely landlocked. Unless the crisis is in Georgia and near the coast, cargo shipped through Georgia's ports would still have to be moved by road, rail, water, air, or some combination of these into the crisis zone: this could mean, for example, an additional 600 miles to Baku or 1,400 to 2,400 miles to various locations in Central Asia. There are other ports around the periphery of the region that could support the transhipment of the SBCT and its follow-on sustainment package, but they all include extended transportation requirements from the SPOD to the operational region. A few of these options are reviewed later on in the chapter.

Our analysis suggests that sealift will not on its own be sufficient for most contingencies in the region and that air will probably be the more effective means to move equipment and supplies into and across the region.

INFRASTRUCTURE: TRANSITING THE CENTRAL ASIA AND SOUTH CAUCASUS REGION

Whether forces arrive by air or sea, it is likely that some additional movement will be needed to get them to their final destinations and to distribute additional supplies and support to the force once it is in place. If the force arrives directly in the region by sea, it will do so at one of three commercial ports on Georgia's Black Sea coast: Sokhumi, P'ot'i, and Bat'umi. However, Sokhumi is principally a ferry and light passenger ship port and therefore probably not appropriate. While Bat'umi and P'ot'i are commercial terminals, the channel and pierside draft and size of their various piers are below that preferred by the U.S. military's principal deployment ships, LMSR and FSS (Fast Sealift Ship). U.S. forces could use these ports if the ships carry only a partial load, reducing their draft and improving their ability to maneuver in these harbors. If they go this route, they will probably choose to stage into P'ot'i, currently the more capable port and likely to remain so for the next 10–15 years. Moreover, from

P'ot'i there are direct links to the road and rail network serving the region and the excellent commercial airfield at Babushara (indicated in Figure 8.1 by the star on Georgia's Black Sea coast). Note also that Russian forces stationed in Georgia have facilities in Bat'umi and are using the local airfield and port facilities. While this could present a deployment problem in the near term (depending, of course, on mission), it is anticipated that most of these forces will withdraw within the next decade.

From a Georgian port, deploying forces can move to a crisis zone elsewhere in South Caucasus or in Central Asia by rail, road, water, air, or some combination. Which transportation mode is preferred will depend on the crisis location and the state, dependability, and capacity of the transportation network, which would be called upon to handle high traffic volume and outsized cargo.

RAIL

There are fair rail links between Georgia's Black Sea coast and its two neighboring states, making rail a good choice for transit through the South Caucasus. Rail has traditionally been the preferred and most efficient means for U.S. forces and their allies to transport high volumes of military equipment and cargo from the ports to the crisis zone. The availability of the types and numbers of rolling stock needed to move an SBCT would probably be a problem, however. It is estimated that a minimum of eight trains with 50 flatcars each would be required to transport the 930 vehicles assigned. Multiple trainloads would be needed to move an SBCT, not to mention the other equipment, cargo, and passengers deploying with the SBCT and its support package. It is anticipated that the rail lines linking Georgia's ports to the rest of the South Caucasus will be up to the task in the next 10 to 15 years. But it is unlikely that there will be sufficient heavy-duty rolling stock to support continuous operations. In Central Asia, this option would require the offloading and shipment of the cargo over the Caspian Sea, or using access routes through Russia or Iran. Once in Central Asia, the rail lines across most of the region have deteriorated greatly as a result of years of neglect. Additionally, safety concerns and the uncertain availability of necessary rolling stock would exacerbate the problem.

ROAD

For short hauls, the principal road network, although in need of repair, should be able to support the onward movement of an SBCT.[38] But an onward move of beyond 300 to 400 miles would be much more difficult.[39] Road conditions in Georgia are suboptimal and likely to remain so, and the 600-mile trip to Baku would probably take the better part of two days to complete. Travel by road to Central Asia would be long and arduous, requiring transit of Russia or Iran.

WATER

If road or rail is deemed sufficient to deliver the unit equipment sets and cargo to Baku, the units could then move by water across the Caspian to ports in either Kazakhstan or Turkmenistan. Local Caspian cargo ships could be contracted or the railroad ferry between Baku and Ultra, Turkmenistan, could be used to accomplish this. Once in Central Asia, onward movement could continue by rail or road. Because this option depends on the availability of local shipping that can manage the load, it will probably be much more viable in a decade, as the volume of commercial traffic on the Caspian increases.

---

[38]There are several major structural concerns about moving the heavy, outsized loads associated with the SBCT and heavy divisions on the road network throughout the Caspian region: the state of repair of the roads and whether they can sustain the movement of military convoys and combat movements; the impact of weather on road conditions; and whether the bridges along key LOCs and operational routes can carry the weight of the heavy combat and cargo-laden transportation vehicles.

[39]Outside urban areas throughout these regions, the local communities and rural regions will be able to provide little direct support to military convoys. Force protection and logistics support for the equipment, cargo, and personnel will be an important issue, requiring the establishment of support points along the route. It is estimated that the total number of vehicles needed to move an SBCT alone will be over 1,000; if these are packaged into 20-vehicle convoys, more than 50 convoys would be required. Using a 12-hour travel day, a convoy would be released every 30 minutes over a two-day period, and a minimum of four days would be required to close the SBCT from a Black Sea port to Baku.

AIR: POSSIBLE STAGING LOCATIONS FOR U.S. FORCES OPERATING WITHIN OR OUTSIDE THE REGION

Ongoing global counterterrorist operations and the war in Afghanistan remind us of the difficulties associated with the deployment, staging, conduct of operations, and sustainment of U.S. forces at such distances from their traditional garrisons and support bases. For Afghanistan and Central Asia, the challenge is compounded because they are landlocked and the United States has no operating bases or strong allies guaranteeing access rights nearby. The United States does not have a network of support in South Caucasus, Central Asia, or along much of the strategic air route into these areas. In addition, the in-place airlift support network of transportation hubs and refueling stations linking CONUS to Europe and on to the Middle East is not ideally suited for supporting such an air route. Recent experience in Bosnia and Kosovo suggests that the most efficient and effective way to support operations at such a distance is to establish at least one regional staging base. This proximity to the crisis zone will allow U.S. planners to insert combat resources and supplies more quickly in response to the operational commander's needs.

As noted earlier, Georgia is unique because it is the only country in the CASC region that is not landlocked. Its Black Sea ports and the transportation network that feeds from them could provide an important avenue for both the deployment and sustainment of any U.S. forces deployed in South Caucasus or deeper into Central Asia. In addition to Georgia's role as a transportation transition point for sealift, there are a few airfields in each of three countries in South Caucasus that could serve as transportation/logistics hubs for airlift operations and staging bases for tankers supporting deployments deep into Central or even South Asia.[40]

---

[40]During Operation Enduring Freedom, the Air Force staged about 12 KC-10/135 tankers out of Burgas air base, Bulgaria, to refuel airlifters over the Black Sea. Radu Tudor, "Temporary US Airbase Opens in Bulgaria," *Jane's Defence Weekly*, December 5, 2001, p. 4. If the airfields in Azerbaijan are adequately improved and the fuel supplies are available, these airfields (or for that matter other regional airfields) could similarly be used to support the refueling of airlifters over the Caspian Sea.

Georgia's location on the Black Sea and proximity to the Middle East (only 500 to 600 nautical miles from Baghdad) also means that its airfields provide a good platform from which to conduct operations into the northern Persian Gulf region, such states as Iraq, Iran, or Turkey. Although Georgia's airfields are not a viable replacement for Turkish airbases, they do provide a limited alternative or supplement if access is denied to or operations restricted from airfields in Turkey. For example, several of Georgia's airfields are no further from Iraq than the U.S. Air Force's main regional operating base at Incirlik, Turkey.[41] Although they are not as good an option as the Georgian airfields, there are also capable airfields in Azerbaijan and possibly Armenia that are similarly well located to support any range of possible operations into the northern Persian Gulf region.[42]

In South Caucasus, the assessment is based on speculation. For Central Asia, the assessment is built on the U.S. military's ongoing deployment experience in support of Operation Enduring Freedom.

In Central Asia, Uzbekistan has the best support infrastructure and LOCs and (from a capabilities perspective) can most readily support major airlift operations. Furthermore, although force protection remains a concern in Uzbekistan, it should be less challenging than in most other states of the region. If the contingency is within Central Asia, Uzbekistan could serve as a regional ISB or Forward Operating Location (FOL),[43] relieving some of the burden from the host country and keeping most of the key logistics infrastructure (footprint) out of the conflict zone. Uzbekistan's strategic location and its well-placed and reliable LOCs and transportation hubs suggest that its facilities can support U.S. power projection operations in the Uzbek-Tajik-Afghan border region, across Central Asia, into Afghanistan, or even elsewhere in south Asia. For these reasons, immediately after the

---

[41]For more details, see O'Malley, *Evaluating Possible Airfield Deployment Options: Middle East Contingencies*, pp. 128–131.

[42]Ibid., pp. 123–128.

[43]FOLs are designated regional airfields from which the Air Force expects to be able to operate (access assured). The Air Force supports the development and maintenance of these airfields to certain operational standards. Equipment, munitions, fuel, or other assets may be prepositioned in order to ensure the rapid ramp up of these facilities to support an operational deployment. For details, see Paul S. Killingsworth et al., *Flexbasing: Achieving Global Presence for Expeditionary Aerospace Forces*, Santa Monica, CA: RAND, MR-1113-AF, 2000.

decision was made to attack the Taliban and Afghanistan, U.S. military planners began to pursue access to former Soviet military airfields in Uzbekistan.

Uzbekistan was the first country to offer access rights to U.S. military forces for operations in Afghanistan. Several C-17 capable airfields in Uzbekistan were considered, including three in Uzbekistan's part of the Ferghana Valley and its border region (see Figure 8.2). Although concerns were raised early in the Operation Enduring Freedom planning process about the current status and utility of these airfields, military planners were unwilling to dismiss the option without first conducting an onsite assessment to determine the overall condition of each of these facilities.[44]

The Air Force airfield survey teams' key concerns focused on the operational condition of the runway (length, width, and status), proximity to the crisis zone, and the security of the base. The deterioration of the other elements of the base infrastructure may be an inconvenience and slow down the process of opening the field to full-scale operations, but it is likely that the Air Force can work around, quickly repair, or upgrade most of these types of infrastructure problems.[45] Their report plays a key part in the planner's initial assessment of what additional operational and troop support personnel, equipment, and materiel will be needed to bring the facility up to at least minimal operational standards. This type of survey was done prior to the deployment to airfields in Central Asia; the teams found that many of the "bare bones" installations had little habitable infrastructure, poor sanitation conditions, and no potable

---

[44]According to Mikhail Khodaryonok, a Russian military analyst quoted in Moscow's *Nezavisimaya Gazeta*, "Most aerodromes in Central Asia have a limited operational capacity and the infrastructure they inherited from the Soviet Union is in poor conditions. . . . Even if the aerodromes' technical facilities are still in working order, they would be unlikely to meet US standards. . . . Moreover the aerodromes lack even minimal living conditions for pilots and technical personnel." See "Central Asian Air Bases 'Obsolete, Run-Down': Russian Expert," *Agence France-Presse*, September 29, 2001.

[45]For example, the fuel storage tanks can be supplemented or replaced by fuel bladders, the troop support facilities can be replaced by tent cities, the airfield's command and control systems can be replaced by mobile systems, tents and other temporary structures can stand in for deteriorating housing and other buildings, and so on.

water, to mention but a few of the problems encountered.[46]   In a scene that was repeated at all of the airfields used, the Air Force deployed into the site, as soon as possible, Tanker Airlift Control Elements (TALCE) personnel and equipment to set up or upgrade existing command and control, navigation, maintenance, and logistics support operations.   For each of these installations, the size of the team and amount of equipment deployed was outside the norm—just about everything was needed.[47] Air Force civil engineer units (Red Horse) deployed in early, like the TALCE, and were responsible for all engineer and construction work needed to improve airfield operations and provide life-support facilities for troops on the ground.[48]

Based on the estimated status of the runways and overall facilities, two of the Uzbek bases, Kakaidi and Karchi-Khanabad,[49] were assessed to have the best potential for handling heavy, outsized aircraft and large cargo flows.[50] These airfields can support the deployment of forces, the staging of forces, offensive air or intelligence-gathering operations, or the provision of humanitarian assistance.[51]   These

---

[46]These problems were reported for the airfields surveyed in Uzbekistan.   Richard J. Newman, "Tankers and Lifters for a Distant War," p. 58.

[47]Ibid.

[48]The Air Force has prepackaged, transportable bare base kits that contain everything from tents to latrines to support a thousand troops.   The Red Horse units use these equipment sets, local materials and labor, and heavy equipment flown in to establish both the operational base and those troop encampments needed to support deploying Air Force and Army units.   "CE Sets Up Bare Base Camps," *Air Force Magazine*, February 2002, p. 27.

[49]Khanabad is the largest and best maintained of Uzbekistan's military air bases and was used to support Soviet fighter operations during Moscow's occupation of Afghanistan.   The Uzbek air force's Su-24 Frogfoot ground attack aircraft are currently stationed there.   Kakaidi is the home station for a fighter unit.

[50]These two airfields were used extensively by the Soviets during their invasion and long occupation of Afghanistan to support both combat and logistics operations.

[51]In the future, these facilities could serve as a forward support location for U.S. forces operating in the region.   Forward support locations are regional support facilities outside CONUS, located at sites with high assurance of access. They will be upgraded and stocked to support the rapid deployment of forces into the region, but can be maintained with only a nominal or periodic U.S. presence.   For details on this concept, see Killingsworth et al., *Flexbasing: Achieving Global Presence for Expeditionary Aerospace Forces.*

fields also lay astride a good LOC and any number of goat-trail infiltration routes leading into Afghanistan.[52]

Khanabad was chosen as the staging base for U.S. Special Operations units and elements of the 10th Mountain Division. From Khanabad, these forces were deployed into Afghanistan and resupplied. Uzbekistan authorized the use of Khanabad for all but offensive combat operations, restricting the staging of combat aircraft. Uzbekistan did not place a time limit on the U.S. use of this facility.[53] We anticipate that U.S. forces will remain deployed there during the course of operations in Afghanistan, but do not anticipate that a significant presence will remain. Given the improvements being put into the facility, the United States may try to retain a string on it in the event of a future regional deployment.

Tajikistan, with its 800-mile border, also proved to be extremely important for the movement of personnel, equipment, supplies, and materiel into Afghanistan. Like Uzbekistan, it has a number of ground routes leading into Afghanistan, including direct access to the regions that were controlled by the Northern Alliance. The operational environment in Tajikistan (noted earlier[54]) complicates any deployments and compounds force protection concerns. Internal strife from the 1992–1997 civil war is still present, and Tajikistan still depends on about 8,000 troops from Russia's 201st motorized rifle division and an additional 8,000 or so border guards (also Russian commanded and predominantly Russian in makeup) for its defense/security.[55] The central government does not control all

---

[52]The strategic bridge crossing the Amu Darya River into Afghanistan is located at Termez, Uzbekistan. This bridge, which had been closed since the Taliban occupied the region across the bridge, links Uzbekistan to the key LOC linking the north with Kabul.

[53]Tamara Makarenko, "The Changing Dynamics of Central Asian Terrorism," *Jane's Intelligence Review*, February 2002, p. 39.

[54]See also Chapters Two and Four of this report.

[55]Kazakhstan also has a small number of forces deployed to Tajikistan, and some of Tajikistan's own troops serve under Russian command in the border units. Estimates of Russian/CIS force size vary from a low of about 14,000 to a high of 25,000. *The Military Balance: 2000–2001*, London: The International Institute of Strategic Studies, 2000, pp. 175–176; Anthony Davis, "Interview with Brigadier General John Hvidegaard, Chief Military Observer for the United Nations Mission of Observers in Tajikistan," *Jane's Defence Weekly*, July 21, 1999, *www.janes.com/regional_news/europe/interviews/dw990721_i.shtml;* and the Periscope Database.

elements of the state bureaucracy any more than it controls all of its territory. Moreover, the country remains a principal transit route for drugs, other contraband, and terrorists crossing into Central Asia. There is a strong possibility that personnel collaborating with local warlords, criminal elements, or even terrorist cells have infiltrated government bureaucracies, including the civil defense and emergency preparedness directorates.[56]   The airfield at Dushanbe is probably the most secure location within the country for any air operations, but there are also two southern airbases much closer to the Afghan border, Kulyab and Kurgan-Tyube.   Like the airfields in Uzbekistan, these can support the deployment of forces, the staging of forces, offensive air or intelligence gathering operations, the transiting of assistance and supplies into northern Afghanistan, or a broader humanitarian assistance effort.   In early 2002, U.S. forces deployed to Kulyab air base, from which they conducted a range of logistics support, search and rescue, troop deployment, and air operations.   Allied (French and Italian) air and ground forces also deployed through and operated from this base.   Location is the value added by the airfield at Kulyab, and once the mission is completed in Afghanistan, there appears to be little attracting the United States to extend its stay.

In December 2001, the United States signed a one-year lease/access agreement with Kyrgyzstan for use of Manas International Airport, near the capital of Bishkek.   The U.S. military is building a 37-acre base extension to the airport with an administrative headquarters, housing, warehouses, munitions bunkers, fuel tanks, etc.   In addition, the United States and its allies are making significant improvements to the airfield, and current expectations are that there will eventually be up to 3,000 international troops (ground and air forces) stationed there.[57]   According to Brigadier General Christopher A. Kelly, commander of the 376th Air Expeditionary Wing, "we're establishing a mini-air force base from which we can fly a variety of military missions, mainly airlift, aerial refueling and tactical air."[58]

---

[56]See Chapters Two and Four of this report.

[57]Daan van der Schriek, "US Military Forces Build Up Strength in Kyrgyzstan," *Eurasia Insight*, January 23, 2002.

[58]A telephone interview from Kyrgyzstan reported in Schmitt and Dao, "U.S. Is Building Its Military Bases in Afghan Region," January 9, 2002.

Unlike the agreements made with the other regional allies, the one-year agreement signed with the Kyrgyz government does not limit the type of aircraft or missions that allied air forces can fly from Manas. Given the investment being put into airfield upgrades, the United States may try to retain a presence, though the nature of that presence may vary greatly, including simply a marginal caretaker arrangement that will allow for the base's responsive availability to any future power projection requirement in the region.

Kazakhstan and Turkmenistan both provided critical overflight rights and provided limited access to their airfields. The Kazakh government indicated a greater willingness to support the allied effort in Afghanistan, but it has not been officially called on to provide more. Turkmenistan's professed neutral status will likely constrain its willingness to provide anything more than assistance to the humanitarian support efforts.

Overall, the United States has made its first force deployments into the region, gained exposure to the power projection platforms available in the region, made significant upgrades to several facilities that will facilitate their future use and increase the aircraft throughput, and opened the door to future access, if needed. Increases in U.S. military assistance programs to and operations and training with the region's armed forces will help in this respect. It can not be overemphasized that these countries provided critical staging bases on the perimeter of Afghanistan that allowed the United States to more effectively and efficiently move assets into the combat zone.

INTERMEDIATE SUPPORT BASE POSSIBILITIES

Distances and poor local infrastructure argue for the establishment of an intermediate support base (ISB) for operations in Central Asia or South Caucasus. The distance from Ramstein Air Base to Alma Ata, for instance, is more than 3,500 nautical miles. The unrefueled range of the C-17 is approximately 2,600 nautical miles, so if U.S. forces were to stage from Ramstein, they would require refueling while en route, full-service support at the APOD, or both.[59] An ISB

---

[59]As noted earlier, the Air Force was doing this with KC-10/135 tankers operating out of Burgas air base, Bulgaria.

would also place U.S. forces closer to the problem and make it easier for them to respond to changing in-country needs and to reduce the in-country logistics footprint.

Known facilities with the necessary support infrastructure and capabilities already in place are preferable. Turkey, which is 1,700 nautical miles closer to Central Asia than Ramstein, has obvious advantages. Both Incirlik and Antalya are NATO support bases that frequently support NATO operational requirements, deployments, and exercises. Both have excellent runways of 10,000+ feet and plenty of apron space to support airlift operations. Moreover, Incirlik is USAFE's[60] only MOB (Main Operating Base) in the region. Both installations are close to major Turkish seaports, allowing for seaborne resupply (see Figure 8.4).

Turkey is not the only option, however, and several locations along the Black Sea coast would also provide viable facilities. For example, although southern Russia's transportation infrastructure has suffered from the economic downturn, it remains superior to what

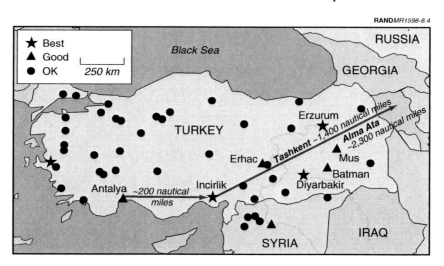

Figure 8.4—Airfields in Turkey

---

[60]U.S. Air Force, Europe, the Air Force's component command within U.S. European Command. This command is headquartered at Ramstein Air Base in Germany.

exists in either the South Caucasus or Central Asia. Assuming Russian cooperation, U.S. forces could easily be accommodated at a number of sea or airports.

Southern Russia has a large constellation of C-17 capable airfields and several with runways longer than 10,000 feet (indicated by stars in Figure 8.5) in locations convenient to CASC. Excellent international commercial ports along the Russian coast could support LMSR-size ships. Although road networks to South Caucasus or Central Asia present some concerns, the rail network into either sub-region is still in fairly good operating order, and no transloading

RANDMR1598-8.5

NOTE: This subjective evaluation (best, good, and ok) is based on the author's analysis of the following criteria: length and condition of the principal runway, the number of available square feet of ramp space, the condition of the airfield's command and control structure, support capability, proximity to key LOCs, and available life-support facilities.

Figure 8.5—Airfields in Southern Russia

would be required along the route because the same rail gauge is in use throughout the former Soviet Union. Moreover, access to needed rail stock may take time, but should be possible. As noted earlier, rail across South Caucasus and Central Asia remains questionable and in major need of repair. Unlike with Turkey, however, U.S. forces would be unfamiliar with Russian facilities, equipment, and terrain, and Russian cooperation would, of course, be required. Acclimatization to Russian infrastructure and geography would add approximately 7–10 days of preparation time to the mission. Finally, in Russia, as elsewhere, security could also pose significant concerns.

As with the use of facilities in southern Russia, the current political environment makes Iran an unlikely option now, but this may change over the next 10 to 15 years.

From an operational perspective, access through Iran has many benefits. Excellent airfields (indicated by stars and triangles in Figure 8.6) include several with 10,000-foot runways, and many are well placed near the southern borders of CASC. They could support U.S. forces as ISBs, tanker support bases, sustainment bases, etc.[61]

Iran also has a number of excellent international commercial seaports that could service LMSR-size ships and link the cargo to a rail network that runs into both South Caucasus and Central Asia. It is anticipated that this network will continue to grow over the next decade as trade links strengthen. Plans to extend and expand both the road and rail links from Iran into CASC to support an expanded trade relationship are under consideration. On the other hand, it is possible that the required type of heavy-duty rolling stock will be unavailable. Moreover, due to differences in rail gauge, transloading would be required at the Iranian border.

OPERATIONAL ENVIRONMENT

The operational environment in CASC—the geography, local infrastructure, the nature and scale of the security threat, local force capabilities, political and economic situations, U.S./Western security

---

[61] For a general description of the capabilities of Iran's airfields and the feasibility of using these assets, see O'Malley, *Evaluating Possible Airfield Deployment Options: Middle East Contingencies*, pp. 102–104.

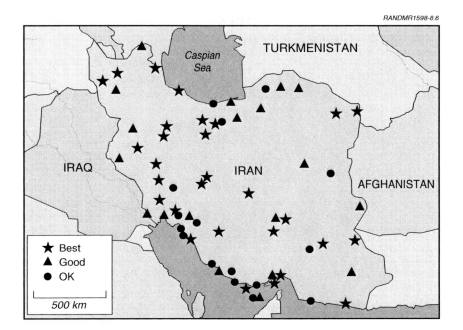

Figure 8.6—Airfields in Iran

relations with each of the regional states, and so forth—will have significant implications for the nature of the operational environment and, in turn, what sort of force package needs to be deployed, how the forces will operate, what support will be necessary, and how much of it needs to be forward deployed. While the operational environment in CASC will continue to evolve, it is still possible to identify the areas where more or less change is likely, and to assess how current trends in, for instance, local military reform and development are likely to progress over the next one to two decades.

That said, the operational environment of CASC is a set of complex, interdependent, and interlocking environments that can be looked at from both the macro and micro level. Depending on the mission, U.S. forces may have to operate in one or more countries, and conditions can change significantly as forces cross borders. Even if actual activities are limited to a single country, as the above discussion illustrated, reaching the area where U.S. forces are needed may well require transit of other countries.

To a large extent, this is a geographical phenomenon. The fact that Georgia is the only country of those under discussion with an outlet to the open sea, the mountainous and inhospitable terrain in much of the region, the lack of potable water, and the widely varying (by time as well as location) climate will all drive where and how forces move, and what supplies they will have to bring with them. The fact that the road and rail infrastructure of the region varies from primitive to acceptable creates other implications and requirements. That said, expectations for energy resource exploitation and energy trade development over the next few years are likely to have beneficial effects on the transportation infrastructure, as well as the economy, making travel easier across at least parts of the region.

But improvements will come first, and possibly only, to main transportation routes, and then only to energy-producing states or transit countries. Roads in Armenia, Tajikistan, and Kyrgyzstan will therefore almost certainly remain poor, as will secondary and tertiary routes throughout the region. These tend to be hardpacked dirt roads, at times covered by gravel. During the rainy season they can be treacherous or completely impassable, especially for heavy or outsized vehicles. Especially in Central Asia, the road infrastructure is marked by great distances between possible entry points, few hard-surfaced roads outside or between major urban centers, and little support infrastructure along even the major routes. The rugged, winding, climbing roads linking Georgia's coastal plain with Armenia and Azerbaijan also have little support infrastructure for those traveling them. Moreover, few of the existing maps of South Caucasus or Central Asia are sufficiently detailed to include much of the secondary road network. Especially in the mountains of Central Asia, only locals know many key transit routes.

Absent complete political stabilization in the region, highly unlikely in the next 10 to 20 years, there will continue to be threats of bandit and paramilitary activity, particularly in but not limited to South Caucasus, where these types of groups take advantage of the isolation of mountain roads to rob and kidnap travelers. Furthermore, many countries suffer from limits to central control—not only along isolated mountain paths, but also in places like Georgia and Tajikistan, outside the capital cities. The lack of effective law and order in much of this region also extends to a certain independence of local bureaucracy, which may necessitate the paying of bribes and customs duties as U.S. forces seek to deploy and ensure that supplies can reach forward-deployed forces effectively.

Rail line improvements will probably also focus on the energy-producing states, and on transit states like Georgia, although limits on the number and types of available rolling stock will probably remain. The Soviet rail network provides a good backbone, and it is likely that in those countries rail will become a dependable means of transport, although even with improvements, capacity will probably remain somewhat limited.

Widespread poverty and high levels of environmental contamination mean that few supplies will be readily available in the region, and that food and water may be unsafe to use even if they are available. Forces will have to bring in supplies, purification equipment, and so forth if they are to be in the region for any significant period. This will increase the logistics tail of the operation, which will, as already noted, probably be further hampered by local corruption as well as by distances and terrain.

Finally, the state of U.S./Western security relations with the regional states is the least stable and among the most diverse of the factors under discussion. This relationship has changed dramatically during the months following the September 11 attacks on the United States, and it will undoubtedly continue to evolve. As noted earlier, the United States is taking a much more proactive role in the region's security environment, seeking to expand its security cooperation and military assistance programs with many of the states, enlisting their support in the war in Afghanistan and the broader counterterrorist campaign, and pursuing access and use rights to facilities needed to support Operation Enduring Freedom. Many of the regional states are looking quite favorably on the U.S. efforts to change the nature and depth of its security relations with them. There are costs and benefits associated with these developments for the United States, each of the regional actors, and for each of the other external international actors, i.e., Russia and China.[62]

While the above generally hold true throughout CASC, there are nuances specific to individual countries that should be considered in more detail. As noted, climate, terrain, infrastructure, and the degree of government control all vary from country to country.

SOUTH CAUCASUS

Armenia

Armenia today has probably the best-maintained transportation infrastructure in the South Caucasus; unfortunately, it is largely limited to the country's major cities. The country's continued political and economic problems have translated into poverty and frequent shortages, including energy supplies. Armenia is not an energy producer in its own right, and poor relations with Caspian energy producer and neighbor Azerbaijan limit Armenia's options for energy supplies. It is therefore unlikely that Armenia could support the fuel, food, and water requirements of deployed U.S. forces. Some proportion of support infrastructure would also have to be brought in.

While Armenia has little internal discord, its dispute with Azerbaijan over Nagorno-Karabakh (with implications for Nakhichevan) remains volatile, with occasional clashes. Armenia has a security assistance treaty with Russia. It receives military equipment, spare parts, supplies, and training from the Russian armed forces, and Russian units are stationed in Armenia. Armenia's security reliance on Russia will probably continue at least as long as the Nagorno-Karabakh dispute does. By contrast, the United States provides modest military assistance to Armenia, but this has kept the door open for U.S. military interaction with Armenia's ministry of defense and maintains direct military-to-military contacts. After September 11, in exchange for Armenia's support of the counterterrorist campaign, the United States has increased its security cooperation

---

[62]See Chapter Two of this report for further discussion of this issue. This chapter will focus on the implications of these developments for U.S. military operations.

Figure 8.7—South Caucasus

efforts.[63] Armenia is also an active participant in NATO's Partnership for Peace program, which opens the military to Western military procedures, training, and operational concepts.

Azerbaijan

The Nagorno-Karabakh conflict affects Azerbaijan in some ways even more than Armenia, since the disputed territory is within Azerbaijan and about 750,000 refugees displaced by the conflict remain in Azerbaijan today. The country is less developed industrially than

---

[63]The United States has reportedly allocated $4.3 million in military assistance for Armenia in 2002, which is far less than reported for Georgia and Azerbaijan for the same period. It does, however, represent a significant expansion in military assistance over previous years. "U.S. Military Team Arrives in Armenia," *Eurasiaweek*, March 1, 2002, electronic version, *thisweek@eurasianet.org*.

either Armenia or Georgia and also differs from them in its majority Muslim population. High structural unemployment and low standards of living are more typical of the post-Soviet space as a whole. Pollution of the air, water, and soil are significant problems, particularly on the Apsheron Peninsula (Baku and Sumqayit) and near the Caspian Sea.

The economic and structural situation may begin to change as Azerbaijan's oil and gas resources are developed. However, it is far more likely that instead of widespread economic growth, energy development will simply widen the gap between the rich and the poor, with poor living conditions remaining the norm in much of the country. The transportation infrastructure, however, is likely to benefit significantly from oil and gas development and trade.

The country's growing energy exploration, extraction, production, storage, refineries, and distribution pipelines also represent lucrative targets for terrorist activity. The extended pipelines linking Azerbaijan's energy production centers to its markets are critical and highly vulnerable targets. Armed bands from the north Caucasus (e.g., Chechnya) have sought sanctuary in Azerbaijan, aggravating relations with Russia and creating security problems for the Azeris. This is a factor of continued conflict in the northern Caucasus and will likely remain a problem for Azerbaijan for the foreseeable future. Borders with all of Azerbaijan's neighbors are generally porous and difficult to patrol, a factor that may have an impact for possible U.S. force deployments.

Azerbaijan has avoided Russian efforts to build closer defense ties and has turned instead to Turkey for significant military assistance. In the shadow of the U.S. counterterrorist campaign in Afghanistan, Georgia, Azerbaijan, and Turkey have finalized a tripartite agreement on regional security that solidifies Turkey's growing military relations with the two states.[64] Turkey's military assistance programs with

---

[64]According to a Turkish diplomat, "The agreement between Turkey, Azerbaijan and Georgia on cooperation in the military field envisages a number of measures relating to the carrying out of [a] joint struggle against smuggling, terrorism, as well as the protection of the main export pipeline, . . . [The] new concept envisages, among other things, an upgrading of the Turkish-Azerbaijani military cooperation to a 'qualitatively new level.'" Igor Torbakov, "A New Security Arrangement Takes Shape in the South

both Azerbaijan and Georgia continue to grow, with an increased Turkish military presence in both states.[65] Azerbaijan is also active in NATO's Partnership for Peace and in the GUUAM grouping with Georgia, Ukraine, Uzbekistan, and Moldova.[66] Although relations with the United States have been friendly overall, the military component has been constrained by U.S. laws that limit the types of military assistance that can be provided.[67] U.S. officials have linked the removal of this constraint to Azerbaijan's support for the counterterrorist campaign. In March 2002, the United States lifted the arms sales restrictions on Azerbaijan.

Georgia

Heavily mountainous Georgia presents particularly inhospitable terrain. It has one of the worst transportation networks in the region, due in part to the activities of bandits and other criminal groups who prey on travelers using the badly maintained roads. Moreover, fuel shortages are a persistent problem, and economic conditions are dismal throughout the country. A general lack of central control outside of the capital makes travel in Georgia particularly challenging and dangerous. Largely local authorities administer both the South Ossetian and Abkhazian regions. While conflict with the regions has ended, there is always a possibility that it will resume.

While Georgia is not and will not itself be a major oil or natural gas producer, it is an important transit route for Azerbaijan's energy resources. As these are developed, Georgia's main (road and rail) traffic arteries are likely to enjoy significant refurbishment. The extent to which this also improves conditions elsewhere in the country

---

Caucasus," *Eurasia Insight,* electronic version, *www.eurasianet.org/departments/insight/articles/eav012402.shtml,* January 24, 2002.

[65]There are large numbers of Turkish military trainers working with the local military, while officers and troops from local militaries are being trained at military academies in Turkey.

[66]GUUAM was formally founded in 1997 as a political, economic, and strategic alliance designed to strengthen the independence and sovereignty of these former Soviet Union republics. Uzbekistan joined the group at the GUUAM summit, which was held during the NATO/EAPC summit in Washington, D.C. on April 23–25, 1999.

[67]Section 907 of the Freedom Support Act bars direct U.S. government aid, especially military, to Azerbaijan until such time as the Nagorno-Karabakh conflict is resolved (or the laws changed).

depends on the government's ability to re-establish control beyond the capital.

Borders with Russia remain porous, and Georgia hosts a large number of refugees from the Chechen conflict. Russian spokesmen have accused Georgia of harboring Chechen rebels, particularly in the refugee camps and settlements in the Pankisi Gorge region. However, Georgian government complicity in any Chechen rebel presence in the Pankisi Gorge is not a given. The situation exacerbates relations with Russia, which has overflown and reportedly dropped munitions on Georgian soil in its efforts to attack fleeing Chechen rebels and control the border. Georgia has rejected Moscow's proposals for joint military actions in the Pankisi region. There are good reasons to believe that the Russian government supported uprisings in Georgian separatist regions of Abkhazia and South Ossetia.[68] Russian troops remain present at two bases in Georgia, having pulled out of two others. There is a general commitment to the eventual withdrawal of Russian combat troops, but it is proceeding slowly.

In an effort to improve regional cooperation and security, Georgia is a member of the GUUAM grouping. Georgia has developed close ties through NATO's Partnership for Peace program, most notably with Turkey and the United States. It receives defense assistance of various sorts from both countries.[69] As noted earlier, Georgia, Azerbaijan, and Turkey have finalized a tripartite agreement on regional security and military cooperation that will solidify Turkey's growing military assistance efforts with the two states.[70] As with Azerbaijan, the Turkish military presence in Georgia is increasing,

---

[68]Ariel Cohen, "Paving the Silk Road: US Interests in Central Asia and the Caucasus," *Harvard International Review*, Winter/Spring 2000, electronic version.

[69]The United States has over the years supported a full range of training for the officers and staffs of the Georgian ministry of defense, including counterterrorist training, and has provided military equipment to assist the restructuring of the Georgian armed forces and improve their combat capability. The most notable equipment transfer was 10 Huey helicopters late in 2001.

[70]According to a Turkish diplomat, "The agreement between Turkey, Azerbaijan and Georgia on cooperation in the military field envisages a number of measures relating to the carrying out of joint struggle against smuggling, terrorism, as well as the protection of the main export pipeline . . ." Igor Torbakov, "A New Security Arrangement Takes Shape in the South Caucasus," *Eurasia Insight*, January 24, 2002.

with military advisors and trainers working with the armed forces, both in-country and at military schools and academies in Turkey. In 2001, Turkey also completed a lease agreement for use of a Georgian air base and maintains a permanent military presence there.

After September 11, the U.S. Defense Department proposed to increase its security cooperation and direct military assistance support to Georgia, as part of the counterterrorism campaign. The effort was further fueled by growing concerns over the Georgian security forces' inability to control the border with Russia's Chechen Republic and the destabilizing affects of ongoing terrorist/criminal activity in the Pankisi Gorge region of the country. The $64 million program reportedly includes the deployment of approximately 200 military advisors in spring 2002 to train about 1,000 Georgian troops (four 300-man battalions) and "equip these units with light weapons, vehicles, and communications."

CENTRAL ASIA

Kazakhstan

Vast in size yet lightly populated, Kazakhstan has fairly diverse terrain, with temperature extremes in the desert, the high steppe, and the mountains. Kazakhstan's porous borders present the possibility of IMU-type (Islamic Movement of Uzbekistan) insurgencies and potential spillover of terrorist activity from China's western provinces, although such problems have not manifested themselves as yet. A more immediate concern is Kazakhstan's growing role in smuggling, the drug trade, and other criminal activity. High levels of environmental contamination and soil and water toxicity make Kazakhstan yet another place to which most consumables would need to be brought.

Kazakhstan's energy exploration, production, storage, and distribution industries are rapidly expanding. This can both spur infrastructure development and present new targets in the event of conflict. Protecting Kazakhstan's energy industry could be challenging given the many lengthy pipelines and the sparsely situated oil and gas fields that are frequently located in relatively underpopulated areas.

Figure 8.8—Central Asia

Kazakhstan has maintained close ties, including military ties, with Russia, although it is also a participant in NATO's Partnership for Peace and has implemented bilateral and multilateral activities with U.S. and other NATO forces. But it continues to cautiously balance its relationships with both Russia and the West/United States. It has also received significant military and related assistance from the United States, in large part through the Cooperative Threat Reduction (CTR) program of assistance to eliminate weapons of mass destruction and related infrastructure. After September 11, the United States enlisted Kazakhstan's support in the war in Afghanistan, but its response has been tempered, endorsing the counterterrorist campaign and U.S. actions in Afghanistan and providing overflight rights. Kazakhstan also reportedly agreed to limited U.S. use of facilities, but no major presence.[71]

---

[71]To date, no Kazakh facilities have been used repeatedly. This may be a function of proximity to the target area and the availability of adequate alternative bases.

Turkey is also an active provider of military assistance and equipment, including patrol boats, and in August 2001 it opened a military representation office in Astana to coordinate bilateral military cooperation. Locally, Kazakhstan took part in the CIS peacekeeping operation in Tajikistan, established a joint peacekeeping battalion with Kyrgyz and Uzbek forces, and developed a regional joint counterterrorist "Central Asian Collective Rapid Deployment Force" along with the militaries of Russia, Tajikistan, and Kyrgyzstan.[72] To date, this latter organization remains only a notional headquarters and a vehicle for some joint training.

Kyrgyzstan

More than 50 percent of Kyrgyzstan is at altitudes of 9,800 feet or higher, and 75 percent of that land is permanently frozen. Although adequate roads exist in the valleys, roads into the foothills and mountains are predominantly narrow and in poor repair. Extremes in weather create operational concerns, and most local roads are dirt trails that are easily affected by rain, snow, and ice. There is no reliable overland connection between the country's north and south. It is highly unlikely that this situation will change in the foreseeable future.

Worries that the growing Uighur separatist movement in China may spill over into Kyrgyzstan are overshadowed by other more immediate security threats. Drugs and other contraband reach Kyrgyzstan from Tajikistan, which also serves as a haven for criminal and terrorist groups that threaten Bishkek's rule, including the Islamic Movement of Uzbekistan, which has staged incursions into Kyrgyz territory. IMU activity is particularly a problem near the Uzbek-Kyrgyz border and in northern Krygyzstan and the Ferghana Valley. The valley is divided with convoluted and porous borders between Kyrgyzstan, Tajikistan, and Uzbekistan, all of which contest some aspects of the current border arrangements (see Figure 8.8).

Kyrgyzstan's poverty and lack of natural resources make it highly unlikely that its present problems will be resolved in the next 10 to 15

---

[72]Frederick Starr, *Central Asia's Security Needs and Emerging Structures for Addressing Them*, URL *www.sais-jhu.edu/caci/Publications/Security%20needs.htm*, undated.

years. It is, in fact, possible that economic and political deterioration will eventually lead to government collapse, perhaps following a succession crisis.[73]

As Kyrgyzstan has become more uncertain of its security, it has looked to Russia and regional security structures to help address its security concerns. It participates in the CIS collective defense agreement and took part in its peacekeeping mission in Tajikistan. Regionally, Kyrgyzstan is a member of the Central Asian peacekeeping battalion (along with Kazakhstan and Uzbekistan) and helped establish the joint counterterrorist "Central Asian Collective Rapid Deployment Force," along with the militaries of Russia, Tajikistan, and Kazakhstan. This latter organization is headquartered in Bishkek and looks to coordinate and improve both the national and collective capabilities of the member states to confront terrorism. As noted earlier, this organization is not yet a viable joint security command. Keeping its options open, Kyrgyzstan was an early member of NATO's Partnership for Peace program and has security ties with the United States, which provides assistance and training;[74] Turkey, which has begun doing the same; and China, which recently provided some equipment and agreed to plans for joint training efforts. Kyrgyzstan's security relationship with the United States and the West has changed greatly after September 11. It signed a one-year access (lease) agreement for Manas International Airport—just outside of the capital—in December 2001.[75] The lease agreement reportedly does not restrict the nature of the operations staged from the base (humanitarian, combat support, or combat), and access has been extended to a number of allied air forces (including the British, Canadian, French, Danish, German, Spanish, and South Korean).

---

[73]See Chapters Two and Four of this report.

[74]Since 1999, CENTCOM's Special Operations Command has been the lead provider of U.S. training to the Kyrgyz, Kazakh, Uzbek, and Tajik militaries. The training focused on counterinsurgency operations, with Special Forces (SF) A-Teams spending about a month each quarter in each country working with their elite SF counterparts. This training established strong military-to-military contacts and relations that helped encourage other security cooperation and assistance programs. Glenn W. Goodman, Jr., "Central Asian Partners: Low-Key Spadework By Green Berets Reaps Valuable Benefits for War in Afghanistan," *Armed Forces Journal International*, January 2002, p. 60.

[75]Although the lease is only for a year, it is reportedly automatically renewed unless either country opts out.

The population of military personnel from the United States and its allies is expected to grow to about 2,000 by summer 2002, with temporary facilities under construction. The United States is carving out a 37-acre military support base as an adjunct part of Manas International Airport. This former Soviet bomber base has the longest runway in the region and can support the deployment of all types of U.S. and NATO aircraft, including the U.S. Air Force's heavy, wide-body aircraft—C-5 and C-17 airlifters, and KC-135 tankers—as well as an array of tactical combat aircraft. This facility is a strategic logistics, refueling, and operational hub for air forces supporting operations over Afghanistan. The facility is already being used to move troops and cargo to bases in the Afghan cities of Kandahar, Bagram, and Mazar-i-Sharif; stage tactical fighter operations over Afghanistan; support refueling tanker operations over Central Asia and Afghanistan; and launch unmanned aerial vehicle (UAV) reconnaissance missions. Manas is clearly the best operational base that U.S. forces have direct access to in the region.[76] The nature and scale of the ongoing upgrade program suggests that the United States hopes to retain long-term access to this facility.

Payment for use of the airfield reportedly includes an economic compensation package totaling an estimated $40 million a year, upgrading of the airfield to meet NATO standards, and increased military assistance through training and joint exercises.[77] Kyrgyzstan is apparently hoping that the U.S. military presence will provide a number of benefits, including stimulation to a stagnant economy, assistance that will help the country rebuild its small military and improve its combat capability, and improvements in the security/stability situation both within the country and on its immediate borders. Whether or not U.S. forces are stationed perma-

---

[76]Like so many Soviet-built airfields, Manas does not have much hard-surface ramp space on which to park heavy aircraft. Reportedly there is currently only room along the taxiway for four C-5 type aircraft, which discourages the permanent stationing or even overnight stay of large numbers of such aircraft.

[77]Bruce Pannier, "Tajikistan, Kyrgyzstan Balancing Relations with West, Russia," *Eurasia Insight*, December 8, 2001. In part, the lease agreement's terms reportedly include the payment of $7,000 every time a plane lands or takes off from the airport, and $1,000 and $500 for every truck and car entering the airport. In addition, the United States promised Kyrgyzstan $3.5 million to be used toward the repair of its combat equipment and the provision of spare parts. Makarenko, "The Changing Dynamics of Central Asian Terrorism," p. 37.

nently at Manas, the upgrading of the base by the U.S. Air Force is an investment in the future in terms of base availability for future contingencies.

Tajikistan

Over 93 percent of Tajikistan is mountainous, and half is above 9,500 feet. The terrain and problems it creates are similar to those discussed for Kyrgyzstan, but even more rugged. Economic development is minimal and poverty and crime are widespread.[78] There is little chance of local purchase of needed consumables, and the availability of potable water also is a problem. Any deploying formations must plan to deploy all consumables. The successful management of a logistics support hub in-country will be crucial.

Although a cease-fire remains in place, the central government currently controls little of Tajikistan outside of the capital. Paramilitary groups and regional warlords control much of the country. The population is concentrated in the Ferghana Valley in the north, and the Kofarnihon and Vakhsh Valleys in the southwest. The country has evolved into the principal transshipment route for Afghanistan's illegal drug production, and Uzbekistan and Kyrgyzstan believe that IMU insurgents have been attacking their countries from bases within Tajikistan. While the situation may improve over the next 10 to 15 years, it is equally probable that it will instead deteriorate further or at best improve only moderately.

Russian military and border guard troops have been stationed in Tajikistan since the collapse of the Soviet Union. Russian security forces play a critical role in maintaining what order there is. They patrol Tajikistan's borders, especially its 1,200-kilometer border with Afghanistan. Many of the better roads entering Afghanistan from Central Asia cross through this border region. The high, rugged terrain, few villages, poor roads and trails, and harsh climate make operations along this border difficult. Many of the mountain trails and passes are not on maps, ensuring the advantage to those with local knowledge of the terrain. In December 2001, Tajikistan, like its neighbor Kyrgyzstan, offered the United States the use of former

---

[78]See Chapters Two and Five of this report for more details.

Soviet air bases to support its counterterrorism campaign. The United States identified one of these as suitable for the staging of fighter-bombers, search and rescue aircraft, helicopters, and a transportation/logistics hub for supplies, equipment, and personnel moving into Afghanistan. Although genuinely concerned about the outcome of the war in Afghanistan and its implications for refugee flow and stability on its southern border, the government in Dushanbe also saw potential economic, military, and security benefits that could accrue. In exchange, the United States is increasing its military assistance and security cooperation programs, as well as its economic assistance efforts.[79]

Turkmenistan

Most of Turkmenistan is desert, with high temperatures and low rainfall. In this, it more closely resembles parts of the Middle East, such as Saudi Arabia and Kuwait, than the rest of Central Asia. A mountainous border with Afghanistan was for many years patrolled with the assistance of Russian border troops, but the Russian security presence was withdrawn more than a year ago. This 450-mile border has been porous to illegal traffic over the years, with smuggling and drug traffic from Afghanistan posing significant problems. The porous nature of the border presents many security concerns; among them is potential refugee traffic fleeing fighting or poverty in Afghanistan.

Energy exploration, production, storage, and distribution industries continue to develop for Turkmenistani gas, but most of the population receives little benefit. Although a handful of hard-surfaced roads link the few population centers, much of the country is not tied to the transportation network in any real way, and there is little support infrastructure. As elsewhere in the region, toxic agricultural chemicals and pesticides have contaminated the soil and groundwater; and there are many contaminants in the Caspian Sea. All

---

[79]On January 9, 2002, U.S. State Department spokesman Richard Boucher stated that restrictions imposed in 1993 on the transfer of military equipment to Tajikistan have been lifted due to that country's close cooperation with the international counterterrorist coalition.

deployed forces would have to have good cross-country mobility and be self-sufficient.

Turkmenistan has declared itself a nonaligned state, even though it participates in NATO's Partnership for Peace and generally maintains good relations with Iran. Security cooperation with the United States has been minimal, but the country did authorize overflight of its territory in support of operations in Afghanistan and the limited use of an airfield in its southern border region to support humanitarian relief flights into Afghanistan.

Uzbekistan

Uzbekistan's terrain includes areas of desert, river valleys, and mountains. The country's advantages include the best transportation infrastructure in Central Asia. Moreover, the government has established long-term programs for the refurbishment of existing and the construction of additional road and rail. The principal international airport in Tashkent has been upgraded (with foreign assistance), as have several major regional airfields. More improvements are planned. Pollution remains a significant problem, and visitors must be aware of contaminated areas, avoid use of the local water, and take care when purchasing local foodstuffs.

Disputes with Kyrgyzstan and Tajikistan over the Ferghana Valley, domestic political and economic tension, drug trafficking from Afghanistan, crime, and the growth of the insurgent Islamic Movement of Uzbekistan all create security concerns for Uzbekistan. One aspect of its response has been increasing authoritarianism.[80] Uzbekistan's short 90-mile border with Afghanistan is a security concern and has been a principal route for contraband moving north; it is a likely route for refugees as well.[81]

Uzbekistan has been consistent in refusing Russian offers of military assistance, although it has periodically shown signs of being willing to improve relations with Moscow. It is a member of the GUUAM

---

[80]See Chapter Two of this report.

[81]During the Soviet occupation of Afghanistan, roads and highways from Uzbekistan and Tajikistan were the principal military deployment and resupply routes.

grouping but tends to view it as a means of attaining economic, rather than security, goals. It is an active participant in NATO's PfP program and receives security assistance from the United States and, recently, Turkey. Uzbekistan was the first Central Asian republic to offer assistance to the United States in support of operations in Afghanistan. It authorized U.S. access to the Khanabad air base, which is about 120 miles north of the border with Afghanistan, for all but offensive combat operation. As early as September 22, 2001, U.S. military transport aircraft began arriving at Khanabad, and the population of U.S. airmen and soldiers, as well as allied troops, swelled to several thousand. Because of the constraint on the conduct of combat operations from the base, Khanabad has been used essentially as an ISB and logistics hub to support the movement and sustainment of ground forces into Afghanistan,[82] search and rescue operations, and the launch and recovery of UAV reconnaissance vehicles.

On March 12, 2002, U.S. Secretary of State Colin L. Powell and Uzbekistan Foreign Minister Adulaziz Kamilov signed a broad-based bilateral agreement that outlines a framework for future cooperation. The agreement provides for economic, political, legal, and humanitarian cooperation, as well as an enhanced security arrangement.[83] In exchange for Uzbekistan's commitment to the war against terrorism, the United States will "regard with grave concern any external threat to Uzbekistan" and denounce the IMU as an international terrorist group.[84] This latest agreement ties the United States to the security of the Uzbek state, underwrites future U.S. security cooperation and military assistance programs, and suggests long-term security ties between the two states and a U.S. commitment to Uzbekistan's national security.

---

[82]U.S. Special Forces and 10th Mountain Division units were among the ground force formations that staged through this facility.

[83]The United States also promises to triple the foreign aid for Uzbekistan to $160 million and guaranteed another $55 million in credit from the U.S. Export-Import Bank. The Uzbek government has committed itself to the "democratic transformation of its society."

[84]"United States-Uzbekistan Declaration on the Strategic Partnership and Cooperation Framework," U.S. State Department Fact Sheet, March 12, 2002.

OPERATIONAL ENVIRONMENT: IMPLICATIONS

Poverty and shortages of everything from food to services to energy will make it difficult for countries in CASC to provide any significant logistics or maintenance support for a U.S. force deploying to the region. Exceptions are Uzbekistan, where if anticipated improvements proceed over the next decade, the country should be able to efficiently support a high-speed aerial deployment of U.S. forces into the region and serve as a regional logistics hub for operations elsewhere, and Kazakhstan, which may also be able to provide a certain level of host-nation support. Elsewhere, logistical support will have to be brought into country in advance of the force and then be capable of moving with it.

Consumables—food, water, fuel, etc.—will also have to be brought in and distributed given shortages, contamination, and poor water quality throughout the region. Although the development of energy resources may well improve the economic situation in oil-producing states like Azerbaijan and Kazakhstan over the next one to two decades, gas producers Turkmenistan and Uzbekistan will see less growth, transit state Georgia will lag behind, and Armenia, Kyrgyzstan, and Tajikistan are unlikely to benefit particularly from energy development.

Energy trade will also spur important infrastructure improvements in the oil-producing states, pipeline transit states, and to a lesser extent the gas-producing states. While this should make travel and transport easier, it should be noted that pipelines and related infrastructure might also prove an inviting target for terrorists or enemy forces in a conflict.[85] Planners should also be aware of the dangers posed by criminal groups and possibly terrorists in much of this region, particularly in (but not limited to) countries where central control is limited (e.g., Georgia and Tajikistan today).

Caucasian and Central Asian terrain favors small-unit operations. Local military and paramilitary formations (state and nonstate) have little high-speed mobility and very little long-range engagement capability. In part, this is a result of the terrain and poor state of the transportation network and would therefore similarly affect outside

---

[85]See Chapter Five of this report.

forces. In Central Asia, extreme distances and wide variations in terrain and climate will impose additional challenges. Throughout all these states, there are few major hard-surfaced roads outside the towns and cities. While energy development may improve the main traffic arteries, most roadways will remain primitive. If combat is centered in the hills and mountains on dirt roads and paths or offroad (as much of it was in Afghanistan), this will present problems, requiring the use of troops that are well trained and equipped for this type of environment. The U.S. 10th Mountain Division units in Afghanistan were effectively used in this capacity, e.g., Operation Anaconda near Gardez in March 2002. Obviously, if activities are in or around the major regional cities, MOUT-type combat will impose an entirely different set of requirements.

Because hostile forces will most likely be based on small units, they will be able to take advantage of the terrain to confound efforts to identify their locations in near-real time. Tactical reconnaissance and intelligence will be needed to detect and target adversary formations.[86] Maps will be essential, but planners must recognize that much of the terrain in CASC has never been adequately mapped, giving a clear operational advantage to the local units. Rapid-reaction forces and firepower that can be quickly moved to crisis areas will be important, as will air mobility, particularly to cover the distances of Central Asia.[87] Lightly armored, highly mobile ground formations, supported by good airborne reconnaissance and fire support, will have the advantage in most of this region. In areas where terrain is especially mountainous, such as Kyrgyzstan and Tajikistan, there may be a need for special equipment and personnel

---

[86]U.S. forces effectively used unmanned aerial vehicles (UAVs) for this tactical reconnaissance and targeting role in Afghanistan.

[87]U.S. ground force operations in Afghanistan faced similar operational challenges. They effectively used helicopters to provide the high-speed mobility, and responsive and precise airborne fire support (bombers, fighters, and attack helicopters) to provide the long-range engagement capability as well as close air support for both local and alliance ground forces. The combination of precision-guided munitions and good target designation/identification from the ground proved to be a deadly combination that made it possible to effectively use high-flying bombers for close support missions.

prepared for high-altitude operations.[88] At the other extreme are the stretches of hot, dry desert in Turkmenistan.

LOCAL MILITARY CAPABILITIES: CAPACITY AND INTEROPERABILITY DIRECTIONS OF MILITARY REFORM IN CENTRAL ASIA AND SOUTH CAUCASUS

The military forces that the CASC states inherited from the Soviet Union were structured, equipped, and trained to fight the Soviet Union's wars. Such forces were inappropriate for the new states' actual security needs. However, resource constraints and changing priorities over the last decade have precluded significant attention to military reform, not only in CASC, but throughout the post-Soviet space. This has led to oversized, undertrained, and often unpaid military forces fielding equipment that is rapidly aging and falling into disrepair, in part due to the absence of spare parts. In the CASC region, where the equipment deployed in Soviet times was older and less capable than that maintained in Europe and elsewhere, this process has been accelerated.

CASC state militaries also inherited Soviet military doctrine, tactics, procedures, and training regimens. Most senior military officers in these states came up through the Soviet Union's ranks, and this is the education and philosophy in which they were prepared and which, in many cases, they continue to hold and propagate. Of course, these are no more appropriate to post–Cold War needs than the force structures these states inherited. Soviet-style thinking as well as the conservatism of these older senior officers has often hampered what efforts toward reform have been attempted.

To a certain extent, Uzbekistan has been the exception. With a military leadership somewhat more open to change and dedicated to casting off its Soviet legacy, along with resources devoted to the

---

[88]Toward this end, U.S. Special Operations Forces have been engaged in training their Uzbek and Kyrgyz counterparts for counterterrorist operations in the mountains since 1999. These small elite formations are rated as highly capable. In similar environs in Afghanistan, U.S. planners made effective use of small Special Forces teams to support local formations and conduct small-scale special missions reconnaissance, and targeting for air. For larger operations, elements of the 10th Mountain Division or the 101st Airmobile Division were employed.

effort, they have recently been able to adopt a new national security strategy and national military strategy and establish relevant mission requirements. They have also downsized and restationed forces and taken steps toward professionalizing their military. But even in Uzbekistan, these changes are concentrated in a few elite, higher-readiness formations rather than uniformly applied to the entire force.[89]

The transition process is proceeding even more slowly elsewhere. It is only within the last year or two that some Caspian states have begun to adopt national security strategies that more realistically reflect their security environments. Most states have made selective progress, seeking to change the focus and improve the quality of military training, to downsize the legacy forces and restructure them to better meet real operational requirements, and to improve operational readiness in at least some components. As a result, a few elite formations in a few states are combat-capable, but they are the exception, with most forces in extremely poor condition.

Participation in the Partnership for Peace has provided exposure to NATO tactics, techniques, and procedures, although this exposure, too, is still limited in most countries to only a few units and personnel. Turkey has been particularly involved in assisting Azerbaijan and Georgia, signing a formal tripartite agreement on military assistance and security cooperation with the two. It has also recently expanded its military assistance programs with both Uzbekistan and Kyrgyzstan. Cooperation with Kazakhstan has been fitful but has recently enjoyed a resurgence with the August 2001 opening of a Turkish military mission in Astana to coordinate bilateral military ties, which will include assistance with military reform, equipment transfers, and the continuation of ongoing programs through which Kazakh military personnel are trained in Turkey. Russia continues to provide training for many Central Asian militaries, as well as to provide training and assistance to Armenia. Kyrgyzstan has received some assistance from China.

The United States is active in PfP activities and provides bilateral assistance as well, with particular beneficiaries being Georgia,

---

[89]This assessment is based on in-country interviews with members of the Uzbekistan ministry of defense staff and NATO defense attachés in Tashkent.

Azerbaijan, Uzbekistan, and Kyrgyzstan. Relations with Kazakhstan have somewhat cooled in recent years. U.S. military relations with the states of Central Asia may evolve significantly in the next few years, as the United States responds to the September 11 terrorist attacks and as a global coalition determines its approach to the terrorist threat. It is too early to predict the long-term implications of this evolution, as much will depend on the actions of the Central Asian states, the United States, Russia, and others.

Over time, more states in the region will seek to restructure their legacy forces into smaller, more mobile formations that can conduct a broader range of missions. Plans also call for professionalized militaries and some limited equipment acquisition. But if the military transformation processes in CASC are to be truly effective and successful, such that small to mid-size modern military establishments can become the norm, these countries must reach a level of economic development that has to date eluded them. Even given economic growth, the political will required for an extended, phased military transformation program is likely to be difficult to sustain. Finally, it is unlikely that effective military reform will be possible without significant outside assistance to provide the necessary guidance, training, and probably equipment and technology to fuel this process. The post–September 11 U.S. effort to enhance its security cooperation programs with and direct military assistance to many of these countries may help stimulate this effort, but the effect will probably be mixed across the region. To date, U.S. political and military activity seems to be focused in order on the states of Uzbekistan, Kyrgyzstan, and Kazakhstan in Central Asia, and Georgia and to a lesser degree Azerbaijan in South Caucasus. These efforts appear to be directed toward establishing assured access to the region and thereby stabilize the operational planning process and speed up any future deployments.

Given all these difficult requirements, there can be no expectation that most of these states will successfully reform their militaries in the next ten to twenty years. While some progress can be expected by the wealthier states, real improvements in readiness and combat capability will most likely be limited to elite "rapid-reaction force" formations, while poorer states (such as Tajikistan) will probably deteriorate further. Professionalization will continue to present challenges throughout the region for as long as the resources necessary to make the military an appealing career are not available to the armed forces. Even in the wealthiest states, the acquisition of the C4ISR elements critical to high-speed, highly integrated, U.S.-type conventional operations are outside the realm of the possible in the next decade, and quite probably beyond.

That said, PfP membership, exercise participation, and collective and individual training with and by NATO member states is exposing Central Asian and Caspian militaries to Western tactics, techniques, and procedures (TTP), as well as Western training methods. The more progressive states have already begun to change their Soviet-based system to reflect NATO TTP. They are moving away from the highly structured, centrally planned, set-piece operations that were the norm under the Soviet system to small-scale, independent maneuver operations that are more common in the West and more appropriate to their security needs.

Within the next decade, Uzbekistan, Kazakhstan, and Armenia are most likely to develop this sort of capability with higher-readiness, rapid-reaction formations. If Azerbaijan devotes the economic resources and political will to the program of development it has outlined, it too could get close to this standard within the next decade. The current defense ministry leaderships of both Georgia and Kyrgyzstan are dedicated to making a similar transition, but it is unlikely that their economies will be strong enough to support the resource requirements. These two states are both hoping that U.S. post–September 11 commitments will help them take a major step forward in the development of a reasonable military capability.[90] Tajikistan and Turkmenistan lag far behind their neighbors and are expected to continue to do so for the foreseeable future.

---

[90]For example, the United States is providing Kyrgyzstan military assistance and economic rewards as an incentive to lease its airfield and allow the United States to build a semipermanent presence. The intent appears to be to upgrade Manas International Airport in Kyrgyzstan and Khanabad air base in Uzbekistan to nearly full-service U.S. Air Force operating bases that can be activated in the event of a future deployment. It is likely that the United States will retain a presence there as long as the current crisis exists, but it is also likely that this presence will be reduced to a mere caretaker status in the future, living up to General Franks's assurances that the United States was seeking no permanent bases in the region.

Overall, it is reasonable to conclude that despite these improvements, military forces in the region will remain, for the most part, low-tech and based on light formations. Training and readiness will remain problems in all but a few states, and even there, in all but a few elite units. For the foreseeable future, all the Caspian states will have low combat potential if faced with a well-trained, advanced, and technologically sophisticated military force. But the low proficiency of the Caspian militaries in conventional engagements does not necessarily hold across the full spectrum of operations. Depending on the circumstances, an asymmetric strategy of irregular warfare against a technologically superior and better-trained adversary could enable even a low-proficiency force to inflict substantial casualties on the stronger opponent. This could be particularly effective if the stronger force was on unfamiliar territory, while the conventionally less capable force was on home soil.

The most probable threat to security across the CASC region remains organized crime and isolated terrorism. Like the regional militaries, the paramilitary and terrorist organizations involved in these types of activities are low tech and prefer to operate in small, mobile bands (units) that are difficult to track and attack. Hit-and-run guerrilla-type operations by generally lightly armed units will be more common, and these do not require the higher-tech response discussed above. Moreover, the light formations will be most effective if they are complemented by the tactical intelligence needed to find and fix opposition troops and the mobility and firepower needed to quickly attack such fleeting targets.[91]

IMPLICATIONS FOR U.S. FORCES: INTEROPERABILITY AND REQUIREMENTS

If U.S. forces deploy to the CASC region, they cannot expect local militaries to fulfill the role that a NATO coalition partner might be able to do. Neither will the local militaries be able to conduct similar combined arms operations anytime soon. To operate within the capabilities of these militaries, U.S. forces can plan for and fight a

---

[91]Although Afghanistan is a much different operational environment than most of the Caucasus and Central Asia, the guerrillas' use of the hilly and mountainous terrain and primitive road and trail networks to mask their movement are not.

multispeed campaign, with responsibilities and missions assigned to local forces commensurate with their capabilities, or settle on different, i.e., more modest, campaign objectives. A more appropriate model appears to be Operation Desert Storm, in which non-NATO and non-Western military units were integrated into a multinational combat force. If U.S. forces are to fight alongside CASC militaries, similar nontraditional approaches will be called for to overcome operational concerns and interoperability problems, and to ensure that all allied commanders have equal access to the airborne fire support and reconnaisance that U.S. forces bring to the battle. Of course, approaches will have to be tailored to the specific challenges posed by this region and its militaries. Communications, command and control, TTP, mobility, maneuver, firepower, logistics support, medical assistance, and national civil and military infrastructure are all factors for which differences between U.S. and local procedures, systems, and capabilities have the potential to create real problems. Language barriers also cannot be ignored. Moreover, if conscript armies are retained in the region, training and experience shortfalls will present additional difficulties and operational concerns. In many cases, U.S. forces must be concerned that local units may not be able to complete mission requirements and protect coalition units on their flanks.

The above notwithstanding, if local forces successfully create the small, light capable formations that many of them are trying to build, it may be possible to overcome some of the interoperability problems and to work around others. While the litany of challenges certainly precludes combined arms maneuver with local states, it should be possible to attain interoperability at the small-unit level if local forces attain sufficient capability to be reliable partners. If this happens, the Gulf War model becomes applicable, although the United States will probably seek a strong command and control role, with U.S. military liaison personnel integrated into the operational staff of the local formations. This model was revisited during Operation Enduring Freedom, as the United States detailed Special Forces teams to commanders of regional formations as liaisons and operational assistants and to provide an interface with U.S. Air Force and intelligence assets. One of the successes of U.S. operations in Afghanistan was how effectively they supported the local ground operations with U.S. strategic and tactical airpower. Such an approach might prove useful to a mission in Central Asia or South Caucasus as well.[92]

The other main workaround will simply be to bring along whatever is lacking in the region. U.S. forces train for and expect to operate in an information-rich operational environment, with the information management capability to observe and influence activity on the total battlefield. This applies to U.S. expectations of a long-range secure communications package; a tactical intelligence-collection, analysis, and dissemination capability; battlefield surveillance and target acquisition; and a tailored logistics support package. The militaries in the CASC states are far below this level and cannot be expected to have in their operational inventory many of the capabilities standard in or available to U.S. formations. Thus, if these or other capabilities—such as composite transportation and attack helicopter units, additional medical personnel, dedicated transportation assets to support logistics tail, etc.—are deemed necessary to U.S. operational or mission requirements, they will have to be deployed into the region, which will increase the strategic lift requirement, extend the deployment timeline, and increase the U.S. force presence (footprint) in-country. Hiring a U.S. contractor to provide and manage specific support functions utilizing local labor and materials can reduce some of this additional footprint.[93] The services have used this method during most of their recent contingencies in the areas of troop support, transportation, supply operations, and construction, reducing the deployment requirement for logistics support troops, equipment, and materiel.[94]

Finally, there is the issue of local militaries' abilities to work with each other. If the operation is multilateral in nature, local capacity to combine forces can lessen the burden on the United States. On the

---

[92]Bryan Bender, Kim Burger, and Andrew Koch, "Afghanistan: First Lessons," *Jane's Defense Weekly*, December 19, 2001, pp. 18–21.

[93]The role of Brown and Root in providing a broad range of support in several recent contingencies is a good example of how this tool can be used and what types of services and functions contractors can effectively perform.

[94]In the absence of standing local contracts, it will take time to get this type of support in place and operating efficiently. The early-deploying units must be prepared to provide most, if not all, of their own logistics support. It will be important to identify early on what services can and cannot be provided through local contract, so that deployment and sustainment plans can be adjusted accordingly.

other hand, if these militaries are more compatible with the United States. than with each other, it will fall on U.S. forces to facilitate their interactions, increasing the burden.

Current trends are mixed. While the forces of the region inherited compatible equipment (although they are now drifting apart in capability, structures, and procedures), and language barriers can be overcome (if sometimes by speaking Russian), successful interoperability requires significant preparation, experience, and practice. To date, this has been limited, partly because of a history of distrust among many of the states of CASC. Georgia and Azerbaijan have been making some progress, such as through the effort to establish a GUUAM peacekeeping battalion, operations under Turkish command in KFOR, and the most recent tripartite security cooperation agreement that ties them to common Turkish military assistance and training. PfP and NATO have also provided a common forum for military-to-military contacts between representatives of Central Asia's militaries, as well as common training, exercises, and planning activities, such as those found in the Central Asia peacekeeping battalion. In addition, growing regional security concerns are forcing a level of cooperation, including intelligence sharing and coordinated operations against terrorist and criminal groups such as the IMU. Similar security concerns have spawned a number of regional security cooperation organizations and joint military formations, such as the counterterrorist Central Asian Rapid-Reaction Force, that may foster a better environment for combined operations in the future, if it indeed becomes a viable operational command.

CONCLUSIONS

Central Asia and South Caucasus present a myriad of challenges for deploying and sustaining U.S. troops, among them the distances, the lack of established facilities with which U.S. forces are familiar, and a political environment marked by uncertainty, crime and corruption, and, in many areas, weak central control.

Distances alone will introduce friction and vulnerabilities, as well as add challenges to the operations planning and execution process. Any U.S. deployment will be asset-intensive and time-consuming, and will place extreme demands on host country resources.

Currently, the only way to responsively get U.S. military assets into Central Asia and much of South Caucasus is by air. The extreme distances from traditional home bases for Army and Air Force units to possible deployment locations in the region are only the first problem. The real challenge will be to get access to airfields in the region that can effectively support the deployment and then to complete the upgrades/improvements necessary to accommodate the types of aircraft, troop population, and operational tempo anticipated. When one is looking to operate in a little-known environment and use facilities that are unfamiliar, the negotiation for access and the planning and execution stages of the deployment process may well take some time. The ramp up to U.S. operations in Afghanistan underscore these problems and their effects on the deployment timeline and how quickly units can be operationally readied. The United States was able to deploy forces into staging bases in Central Asia—Kyrgyzstan, Uzbekistan, and Tajikistan—but not quickly.

As U.S. planners recently found, in Central Asia austere reception facilities and limited host nation support must be expected in all but one or two countries. Moreover, a high percentage of the first several weeks' sorties into these facilities carried the airfield support personnel, equipment, and materiel to bring the facility up to acceptable standards and establish an adequate life-support condition for deployed troops. There is a high probability that all of this support activity slowed down the deployed unit's ability to establish full operational readiness.

After establishing presence in these countries, the United States negotiated its initial access/lease agreements that allowed it to upgrade these facilities. Although the United States is unlikely to maintain a long-term presence in any of these countries, a major step has been taken toward improving the Air Force's ability to responsively transport troops and equipment into them. These airfields are no longer an unknown quantity, the logistics and transportation networks linking them to CONUS and Europe have been tested, and the airfields have been improved. The United States is continuing ongoing efforts to gain "assured access" to deployment bases in the region.[95]

A lack of alternative deployment options will add predictability and possible vulnerability. U.S. forces are most vulnerable while in transit and during staging into the host country. Opposition forces may take the opportunity to attempt to discourage, disrupt, or prevent deployment and sustainment operations.

Much depends on the initial decision on how forces will be transported to and through the theater. The most direct approach may not provide the most efficient follow-on force projection and sustainment. Sustainment will be another potential vulnerability and place additional intensive demands on U.S. strategic lift resources. For one thing, the extended distances involved and the limited possibility of local purchase will create strain. An ISB outside the deployment zone could be considered one way to provide a necessary management, transportation, and logistics hub while reducing the in-country footprint and demand on host nation support, although these cannot be eliminated entirely.

Due to the relatively low projected capabilities of the local militaries and their limited capacity to offer host nation support, the deploying brigade's organic support assets will probably be inadequate for mission requirements. An additional support package will be necessary to ensure the availability of the logistics, transportation, C4ISR, secure communications, force projection (including tactical helicopter and fixed-wing lift), and force protection assets that are demanded by the security environment and mission requirements.

Deployment planners must also be concerned with the stability of the country that will be receiving their forces and the types of social problems that may arise. Table 8.5 outlines the relative character of the domestic measures across these eight states, summarizing the

---

[95]The United States has signed lease/access agreements for airfields in both Kyrgyzstan and Uzbekistan. Turkey has negotiated similar agreements with both Azerbaijan and Georgia and is upgrading these airfields to NATO standards. Although future access may not be guaranteed by these agreements, the process of renegotiation or reinstatement should be much simpler, which should improve the timelines and throughput significantly. It is likely that Turkey would support U.S. or alliance access to its leased facilities in Azerbaijan and Georgia.

Table 8.5

Relative Measures of Domestic Stability

	Armenia	Azer-baijan	Georgia	Kazakh-stan	Kyrgyz-stan	Tajikistan	Turkmen-istan	Uzbek-istan
Poverty	W	W	W	L	W	W	W	L
Urban	L	L	L	I	L	W	W	I
Rural	W	W	W	W	W	W	W	L
Crime	L	W	W	L	L	W	L	I
Terrorist activity	N	L	L	I	L	W	I	I
Pollution	I	L	L	L	L	L	L	L

W = widespread; L = localized; I = isolated; N = not a concern.

NOTE: Although these measures are subjective, they represent key areas of environmental concern that must be factored into the planning for and execution of any operations in these countries. The list does not represent a definitive checklist of what should be considered, but rather is meant to provide a quick snapshot of some of the expected planning concerns. Assessment of these factors is also subject to change and should be re-evaluated frequently.

concerns briefly discussed earlier for each country. These measures are subject to dramatic change, especially the first three factors, if the economies improve substantially. The last factor is included to highlight that all forces deploying into this region must be concerned with pollution. All these problems and concerns have broader implications for the security of any deploying troops, their sustainment, and ultimately the conduct of operations. The nature and level of criminal and/or terrorist activity may well affect the stability of local, regional, and national governments and magnify security problems.

The local operational environment also has implications for the types of units and equipment needed. Terrain and operational environments vary from country to country, but there are some common challenging features such as the inadequate road and rail networks, likely shortages of needed supplies, and limited support infrastructure. Table 8.6 provides a relative comparison of the nature of the existing transportation infrastructure and the availability of food, water, and fuel in the needed quantities and qualities to support deploying forces. A detailed appraisal of each of these factors will contribute to the planner's assessment of what needs to be deployed, when in the process (airfield and troop support versus combat assets) this must happen, and what the anticipated throughput of the

Table 8.6

Transportation Infrastructure and Support Capabilities Vary Dramatically Across South Caucasus and Central Asia

	Armenia	Azer- baijan	Georgia	Kazakh- stan	Kyrgyz- stan	Tajikistan	Turkmen- istan	Uzbek- istan
Transportation								
Road—rural	G	F	B	F	F	B	B	G
Rail	B	F	F	F	P	P	P	G
Air	F	F	F	F	F	B	B	G
Available support								
Food	F	B	B	F	B	P	P	F
Water	F	B	B	F	F	P	P	F
Fuel	B	F	P	F	P	P	P	F

E = excellent; G = good; F = fair; B = bad; P = poor.

facility will be. It also has broader implications for the reception, onward movement, and sustainment phases of any ground component deployments.

While the operational environment may improve over the next 10 to 15 years, it is unlikely that improvements will be sufficient to significantly mitigate concerns. Moreover, the sheer distances that operations in Central Asia would involve magnify the problem and create requirements for light and highly mobile ground forces and tactical air.

Military reform in CASC states will have an impact on local capabilities. All the militaries in this part of the world are in transition, but not all are equally far along. The forces these states inherited from the Soviet Union remain incompatible with their security environments. The legacy equipment, infrastructure, human capital, and operational concepts are all dated. Repair and conversion are proving difficult and painful.

While CASC states have for the most part recognized the need to adapt their armed forces to their real security environments, only a few states have yet committed needed resources to the process. Uzbekistan began early, is furthest along, and has the most professional and capable military in the region. Kazakhstan is just now

Table 8.7

Snapshot of the Relative Capabilities of the Militaries of Each Country

	Armenia	Azer-baijan	Georgia	Kazakh-stan	Kyrgyz-stan	Tajikistan	Turkmen-istan	Uzbek-istan
Military								
Readiness	F	P	P	F	B	P	P	G
Equipment	F	B	B	F	B	P	P	G
Capability	F	B	B	F	B	P	P	G
Compatibility w/NATO	B	B	B	F	F	P	P	G
Contact w/Western militaries								
PfP	B	F+	F+	F	F+	P	P	G
Bilateral tng	F	F+	F+	F	F	P	P	F+
Military ast	F	F	F+	F	F	B	P	F

E = excellent; G = good; F = fair; B = bad; P = poor.

seriously beginning a reform and restructuring process, but it is at least five years behind Uzbekistan and is unlikely to catch up in the next decade. See Table 8.7.

Development of modern, capable, and professional militaries from post-Soviet legacy forces will require major commitments of time and resources. The nascent military reform processes in these countries can be sustained only if economies improve and the commitment is firm. It seems likely that Uzbekistan will continue on its positive path. A few other states, namely Kazakhstan and potentially Azerbaijan, Kyrgyzstan, and Georgia (less likely, but there is a renewed U.S. effort to provide direct military assistance, training, and equipment) will also probably move forward over the next decade, but real improvements will be limited to a few elite, combat-ready formations in each country's rapid-reaction force. Low-tech, poorly trained units will likely remain the norm for the armed forces of all the CASC states, with the possible exceptions of those few states that benefit from improving economies and energy wealth.

Even with improvements, it seems likely that a decade into the future, these militaries will still be hampered. Limits on their mobility and on their capacity to conduct reconnaissance and tactical intelligence, as well as secure long-range or tactical communications, will all constrain capabilities. With the possible exception of Uzbekistan, any joint operations with the United States would be restricted to the small-unit level (most likely company but possibly battalion). Given the current security environment in most of these states, the most likely conflict will be low-level, small-unit operations against an unsophisticated military and paramilitary force. U.S. forces should expect that in a cooperative mission in this region, they will have to provide almost everything both (or all) forces will need. They will also have to prepare for difficulties with interoperability. Carefully designed planning and management arrangements and circumscribed roles and responsibilities for the local militaries can ease the difficulties but will not be able to eliminate them entirely.

Chapter Nine

SOURCES OF CONFLICT AND PATHS TO U.S. INVOLVEMENT
Olga Oliker and Thomas S. Szayna

The preceding chapters have outlined numerous causes of and potential pathways to conflict in the Central Asia and South Caucasus region. Most of these causes are deeply entrenched and are likely to remain in place for the foreseeable future. Moreover, none of them operates in a vacuum: economic and political grievances, for example, reinforce each other and, combined in environments of political weakness, create far more risk of conflict than either would alone.

This chapter seeks to identify the key sources of conflict for each of the states and subregions in question, as well as to note which states within and outside the region are most likely to get involved. This analysis does not present scenarios for conflict evolution, but rather seeks to identify some of the ways that conflict can evolve in and around each of the states of the region. It then assesses the U.S. interest in this evolution and possible U.S. involvement/responses.

At the end of each country analysis, a table illustrates some of the key indicators of conflict drawn from this report and how they apply to the country in question. These are not so much causes of conflict per se as likely precursors—and thus useful indicators to watch for. Derived from the analyses in the preceding eight chapters of this report, these indicators are also in some cases syntheses of those analyses. For instance, the politicization of ethnicity (see Chapter Six) is not in itself a cause for conflict, but combined with group-level grievances and a perception of threat and insecurity at the group level, which may translate into more radical agendas, such politicization becomes a useful indicator that the potential for conflict is increasing. An example of such a grievance may be an ethnic redress policy, carried out by the state, that privileges the eponymous ethnic group over groups that previously enjoyed advantages (for instance, Russophones). Mobilization by Russophone groups that seeks to combat this discriminatory policy may be an additional indicator of conflict ahead. Similarly, the privatization of force increases the capacity for individuals or groups to take extralegal violent action, which, as already discussed, is fairly likely to be met with violence by the state.

Insofar as transitions, whether to democracy or toward greater authoritarianism, are statistically linked with an increased risk of conflict (see Chapter Two), both processes need to be watched carefully. Moreover, whatever the political structures in place, the rise of political groups, legal or otherwise, that have clear ethnic, religious, linguistic, or clan affiliation and radicalized agendas, especially ones that identify other groups or the state as the source of the politicized group's problems, should be watched. The emergence of such groups has been a precursor to conflict in other parts of the world. Extralegal political activity of this sort is a sign that disenfranchised groups have found legal channels insufficient to address grievances, and are now seeking to change the system (see Chapter Two). Finally, the increased public awareness of corruption and rent-seeking behavior within a state is an important indicator that the state's legitimacy is waning, and a possible precursor to government collapse (see Chapters Two and Four).

There are also a number of factors relating to how states in and near the region interact that are likely precursors to conflict. Again, none of these will necessarily lead to violence, but they may make it more likely. For instance, a Russian military presence (as well as Russian economic behavior) can be a stabilizing factor, or it can be a sign that conflict is more likely. Which it is depends on the specifics of the situation, regional attitudes, and the responses of others, as well as what other indicators of conflict are present. If Russian presence or action is perceived as hostile by one or more states, the risk of conflict increases.

The increased militarization of the Caspian Sea is also dangerous and an indicator of increased risk even if Caspian claims are resolved, as the presence of armed forces placed close to each other increases the risk of misunderstandings and military responses to other disagreements. Today, all of the Caspian littoral states have some level of military force on or near the Caspian, but Russia and Iran have the most significant and capable forces there. If current trends continue, however, within 10–15 years, Azerbaijani, Turkmenistani, and Kazakh force strength on and near this body of water will increase.

The development of alliances with neighboring or far-off states (including the United States) can also catalyze conflict in the region. Given the dynamism of the current situation, it would be downright foolhardy to attempt to predict the future of interstate alliances over the next 10–15 years in the region. However, it is possible to predict how states might respond to a range of scenarios by assessing their overall strategic interests (see Chapter Seven). For instance, given a combination of Russian pressure on the South Caucasus states and increasingly close relations between those states and Turkey, it is possible that, under certain circumstances, the Russian response to Georgian or Azerbaijani alignment with Turkey could be violent. Increasing perceptions of an Uzbek alignment with the United States, should that develop out of ongoing cooperation in the counterterrorist effort, may well make other states in the region nervous about Uzbek intentions, crystallizing an anti-Uzbek alliance in the region, perhaps even including Russia. Finally, a U.S.-Russian alliance (whether spurred by counterterrorism cooperation or by some other strategic development) may give Russia a sense that it has more freedom to pressure regional states to abide by its wishes, including by military means.

It is worth noting up front that a number of domestic factors historically linked to conflict and instability, especially when combined with other problems (see Chapters Two and Three), are present in all the states of this region. These include:

- A widening income and standard-of-living gap between the rich and the poor, combined with perceptions of relative deprivation.

- Increased macroeconomic disturbances such as high inflation, shortages and queues, wage arrears, and labor strife.

- Demographic downtrends such as low birth rates, high/young death rates, health, drug use, etc.

Not only are all of these factors present in the states of the region today, current trends suggest that they will persist over the course of the next 10–15 years and may in fact worsen in some countries. As with the other domestic indicators, the true risk of conflict depends in large part on a state's capacity to respond to problems and crises in ways that do not aggravate risks. In this sense, the weak state capacity and political institutions of this region do not bode well for their ability to do so.

Finally, one of the most likely precursors to conflict in this region is a succession crisis in one or more states. Successions can be catalysts for unrest and civil strife, particularly in authoritarian and transitional regimes. In Azerbaijan and Georgia, these are something to watch for in the immediate future. President Aliev of Azerbaijan is nearly 80 years old, ailing, and making efforts to designate his son as his successor. President Shevardnadze of Georgia is well into his 70s, is facing increasing discontent among the populace, and has said he will not run for re-election in 2005. In both countries, these two leaders have been instrumental in maintaining the state in the absence of lasting institutions. Their departure from power could easily lead to scenarios involving internal, and potentially external, strife.

In many of the Central Asian states, there may be time for the risk of a succession crisis to be averted through democratization, as the leaders of Uzbekistan, Turkmenistan, Kazakhstan, and Kyrgyzstan are in their 50s and early 60s. However, these authoritarian regimes are at risk of the sudden death, through illness, accident, or perhaps assassination, of their leaders. Moreover, as already noted, the democratization process itself is far from risk-free. Finally, it is worth highlighting once more that the Armenian polity is comparatively stable, and a succession crisis there is less likely (if not entirely impossible given the presence of extremist political parties and occasional political violence).

The evolution of the U.S. military presence and involvement in the region will also affect how conflict may or may not evolve. If U.S. military forces remain in place in CASC, the likelihood that they will become involved in regional conflict is increased. At the same time, for some states at least, the U.S. presence may mitigate the likelihood of conflict emerging, playing a stabilizing role by helping to support the government and strengthen its control and possibly legitimacy. In other cases, however, the U.S. presence may make certain forms of conflict more likely. For example, local militant groups in one or more states may target U.S. forces, or regional states who see the U.S. presence as bolstering their own power may crack down on local opposition forces or take action against neighbors, spurring reprisals.

A country-by-country summary of indicators that may herald impending conflict is presented below. Data from individual chapters have informed the summaries.

CENTRAL ASIA

Kazakhstan

Kazakhstan's continued stability and growth depend in large part on the potential for large energy exports. Oil exploration and sales have fueled its economy to date, ensuring that it remains in relatively good condition, particularly when compared to its neighbors. Kazakhstan's high estimated reserves and the fact that it is likely to have the greatest diversification of export routes suggest that it can count on this situation continuing to improve—although it should be noted that should something go wrong, there is little for this fuel-export-dependent state to fall back on. As noted in Chapter Three, Kazakhstan is the only regional state to have attained a per capita GDP of over $1,000 ($1,250 as of 1999). The government has set up an oil fund to direct proceeds from energy development into other economic sectors, a pragmatic move that can help make its economic growth more sustainable. That said, 30 percent of Kazakhstan's population remains below the poverty line, and wealth is concentrated in the hands of a relatively small minority.

Kazakhstan is, like much of Central Asia, an increasingly autocratic state politically, with limited press freedom and power concentrated around President Nazarbayev and his inner circle. Corruption is routine, although not as bad as in some other countries of the region. Organized crime has had an important role in the local economy for years, and criminal groups are believed to be much involved in the oil sector. The drug trade has had an effect as well, with increasing numbers of users and at least one identifiable major trafficking route through the country.

Thus, the potential for discontent on the basis of political and economic grievances exists, although it may be somewhat mitigated by expected economic growth driven by energy exports. The potential for ethnic grievances is probably highest among the Russophone population in the country, which has lost much of its former privilege under Kazakhstan's policies of ethnic redress. Certainly, there are some rumblings of secessionism in Kazakhstan's heavily Russian-populated north, and there has been some development of ethnically based parties, an indicator of the politicization of ethnicity. However, the policies promoting the Kazakh language have been relatively mild to date, and there is little likelihood of conflict arising from the grievances engendered by them unless the Kazakh government undertakes a radical shift in approach. The government is also somewhat worried about the possibility of spillover ethnic tension among Uighurs in Kazakhstan as a result of Uighur separatism in neighboring China. From the religious perspective, Kazakhstan does not have a substantial militant Islamic movement, although groups like the Hizb ut-Tahrir have been distributing leaflets and seeking to attract membership here as elsewhere. Regardless of the true extent of the Islamist threat, the government has expressed concern about it, and Kazakhstan also perceives a threat of Islamic/insurgency violence. After the incursions into Uzbekistan and Kyrgyzstan in August 2000, Kazakhstan shifted many of its special forces units to the south of the country.

All that said, Kazakhstan, of all the states of the Central Asian region, can probably be expected to be relatively free of internal strife in the short term, at least until such time as Nazarbayev leaves power. At that point, the succession crisis that is such a danger for autocratic regimes such as Kazakhstan has become in recent years may well bring to the surface the range of economic, political, ethnic, and religious grievances that autocracy and comparative economic health had kept submerged. Another possible immediate source of internal conflict might be a sharp economic crisis, which could lead to public discontent with the government. Over the longer term, factors such as the development of ethnic relations in the country, the growth of organized crime and extralegal political, religious, or other movements, corruption, etc. should be watched carefully as possible indicators that internal strife is becoming more likely.

In terms of Kazakhstan's relations with neighbors and outside powers, there is also little immediate cause for concern. It has high levels of trade with its fellow Central Asian states, as well as with Russia. Kazakhstan took part in peacekeeping in Tajikistan, and established a peacekeeping battalion with Kyrgyzstan and Uzbekistan. While there is some continuing competition with Uzbekistan, the other large and relatively powerful state in Central Asia, relations are not hostile. While relations with China have not always been easy, they are at present fairly good, with the two countries discussing a range of possible trade ties, to include energy sales to China. Kazakhstan and China are also both founding members of the Shanghai Five/Shanghai Cooperation Organization. Kazakhstan enjoys relatively good relations with Iran, with which it has arranged oil swaps. It also has close ties with Germany and has received some assistance from Turkey (although bilateral relations have been on and off). Relations with the United States had cooled somewhat in recent years, but the United States has also provided a great deal of support to Kazakhstan, particularly through the Cooperative Threat Reduction program to eliminate the nuclear weapons infrastructure left in Kazakhstan by the collapse of the USSR. Ties with these Western states have also not precluded Kazakhstan's maintenance of close ties with Russia (from which it also imports energy and other goods). Along with Kyrgyzstan and Tajikistan, Kazakhstan takes part in a customs union with Russia and Belarus, the Eurasian Economic Community.

The potential for resource-based conflict involving Kazakhstan must also be assessed as fairly low. Like the other energy-rich states, Kazakhstan is dependent on energy-poor Tajikistan and Kyrgyzstan for water for irrigation. This dispute, described in more detail in Chapter Five, has been a significant one, but it seems unlikely to lead to actual strife. Insofar as Caspian seabed division is concerned, Kazakhstan has supported the Russian proposal of dividing the seabed and subsoil into national sectors while holding the waters in common. If the Caspian becomes increasingly militarized and an arena for hostile competition, Kazakhstan is likely to be involved. Although weaker than Russia or Iran, it does have more military capacity than many of its neighbors, and this advantage is expected to increase in coming years.

Table 9.1

Indicators of Conflict: Kazakhstan

Indicator	Currently in Evidence	Likely in 10–15 Years	Possible in 10–15 Years
Domestic			
Popular movements form outside of legal channels, develop secretive, militaristic, radical agendas			✓
Privatization of force			✓
Increasing political "democratization"		✓	
Increasing authoritarianism	✓	✓	
Ethnic, clan, linguistic or religious political parties with radical agendas gain influence			✓
Widespread reports of corruption; frequent government-related scandals and crackdowns on same		✓	
Regionalization/secessionism			✓
Succession crisis			✓
Regional			
Unresolved Caspian claims	✓		✓
Russian efforts to exert influence by cutting off energy export routes		✓	
Foreign (Russia, Iran, other) support of insurgents/secessionists			✓
Militarization of Caspian Sea		✓	
Negative impact from revolution in Xinjiang, China			✓

Thus, prospects for conflict in Kazakhstan must be seen as focusing primarily on the danger of a succession crisis (which is unlikely in the immediate future), with a somewhat smaller likelihood of conflict emerging for other reasons. From the U.S. perspective, this means that involvement would probably be limited to some sort of international peacekeeping effort, if one develops. The one factor that could alter this situation would be a substantial U.S. presence in Kazakhstan in conjunction with the war on terrorism. To date, Kazakhstan has expressed willingness to host forces, but it has not been asked to provide any support beyond overflight access. That said, Kazakhstan's facilities, which include fairly good infrastructure and long runways, may make it appealing for future aspects of this or future operations. Moreover, its efforts at defense reform suggest that Kazakhstan will in the next 10–15 years have at least a small number of effective rapid-reaction forces (although the balance of its military will remain low-tech and with limited training and equipment). Thus, Kazakhstan could emerge as a partner for some regional missions, which might in some ways lead the United States to become more closely tied to this state and more likely to be drawn into a crisis.

Kyrgyzstan

Kyrgyzstan has a per-capita income of only about $300/year, marking it as one of the poorest states in the region. Moreover, the situation is not improving: Kyrgyzstan's ranking on the UN human development index has dropped since 1995. In part, this is because the growing burden of international debt (as a percent of GDP, among the highest in the region, along with Tajikistan) has precluded spending on domestic programs, deepening poverty.

The country's principal export is energy, in the form of electric power stemming from its (and Tajikistan's) control of the headwaters of the major river systems of Central Asia. It also exports gold. Despite its production of electricity, Kyrgyzstan is overall a major energy importer, with 85 percent of oil coming from abroad, although half of the fuel consumed in the country is illegally smuggled in. Much of the economy is dependent on local trade, with sales to Kazakhstan and Tajikistan and purchases from Kazakhstan and Uzbekistan. Kyrgyzstan belongs, along with Tajikistan, Kazakhstan, Russia, and Belarus, to the Eurasian Economic Community customs union. Kyrgyzstan's sizable debt to Moscow has recently been offset by the transfer of shares in 27 Kyrgyz industrial enterprises. Kyrgyzstan has had little success drawing Western investment into its economy, but increased Russian ownership of assets in Kyrgyzstan has the potential to distort some aspects of its economic interests.

Crime and corruption are major problems, with the illegal economy at nearly the same size as the official economy. Extortion and organized crime include a variety of activities such as car theft, trafficking in human beings and wildlife, drugs, money laundering, and various financial crimes. On a more local level, livestock theft is a common problem. As Kyrgyzstan is a major thoroughfare on the route that illegal narcotics have been taking from Afghanistan to Russia and on to Western Europe, there is increasing concern that rising drug use in the country will contribute to the spread of HIV, straining the under-funded and low-capacity health system. Here, as in Tajikistan, opium was used as a barter currency in the middle 1990s.

Given this starting point, even under the best of economic circumstances, the best that Kyrgyzstan can hope for over the next 10 to 15 years is a very slow level of growth. Its balance of payments and debt problems will almost certainly persist over the next decade and beyond, as will the attendant problems, although it is possible that regional security stabilization could boost trade, helping to ease the situation somewhat. This, however, is a best-case scenario. Under less favorable circumstances, economic crisis becomes probable.

Once seen as Central Asia's model of democracy, Kyrgyzstan has also exhibited increasing authoritarianism under President Akaev in recent years. Nervous about the rise of Islamicism in the country, combined with the effect of Islamic Movement of Uzbekistan (IMU) incursions in 1999 and 2000, Akaev's government has been cracking down on Islamist movements and groups, but it has also imprisoned members of the opposition. Partly in response to concerns voiced by China, it has also become increasingly repressive in relation to its Uighur minority.

While the threat from the IMU, which sheltered in Afghanistan and received training and support there, has been diminished, other Islamist groups continue to gain support. The Hizb ut-Tahrir, for example, has been growing in popularity in Kyrgyzstan, starting from a primarily ethnic Uzbek, rural support base, but more recently spreading to other areas and ethnic groups. Hizb ut-Tahrir members, leaders, and pamphlet distributors are subject to arrest in Kyrgyzstan. Islamic political parties are banned in Kyrgyzstan as they are in all states of the region except Tajikistan.

The combination of a weak economy, widespread poverty, and increasing autocracy is a dangerous one. In this context, the potential for ethnic conflict also cannot be overlooked, especially as it overlaps with the religious dimension. Uighurs and Uzbeks in Kyrgyzstan are generally perceived as more prone to Islamic fundamentalism, and thus subject to more government attention. Assuming continued stabilization in Afghanistan, there seems little likelihood of a resurgent IMU launching the sorts of incursions that it did in previous years. However, the possibility of lower-level terrorist attacks by this group or other radical Islamist groups should be considered. Finally, while Akaev is relatively young, the increasingly authoritarian nature of his rule suggests the possibility for a succession crisis when he leaves power, and a variety of groups battling for control of the state. Thus, the risk of internal conflict in Kyrgyzstan, while not presenting an immediate threat, must be judged as real, and the situation in the country worth watching.

Although Kyrgyzstan also sought to build ties with Western states—particularly the United States and Turkey—in part as a means of diversifying its security away from dependence on Russia, after the IMU incursions and faced with a deteriorating situation in Afghanistan in the late 1990s, it became more accepting of Russian assistance—and influence. Russia has provided some military assistance, and Kyrgyzstan is a member of the joint counterterrorist "Central Asian Collective Rapid Deployment Force" that also includes Russia, Tajikistan, and Kazakhstan. Assistance from Turkey and the United States prior to September 11 was in the form of nonlethal supplies and counterinsurgency training.

Kyrgyzstan is also an original member of the Shanghai Cooperation Organization. As noted, it hosts a substantial Uighur minority, while a number of ethnic Kyrgyz live in China. Chinese-Kyrgyz relations have been strained in the past due to China's failure to recognize borders, combined with its historical claims to Kyrgyz territory. More recently, however, relations have been positive. The Kyrgyz and the Chinese share a fear of Islamic fundamentalist political movements, and China has provided Kyrgyzstan with some $600,000 worth of assistance, including tents, army gear, and at least the intention of training Kyrgyz soldiers in China.

Because of the interlocking borders and ethnic groups of the Ferghana Valley, where Kyrgyzstan, Tajikistan, and Uzbekistan meet, ethnic unrest and conflict in any one of these states would be unlikely not to affect the others. The vast majority of Kyrgyzstan's Uzbek population lives in Ferghana, and borders in the region are uncertain and often contested. Following the IMU incursions,

Uzbekistan mined its borders and staged some military strikes into its neighbors' territories. Kyrgyzstan, too, has sought to mine and otherwise tighten up its border with Tajikistan. While to some extent the three states have sought to cooperate against what they agree is a common threat, they are also deeply suspicious of each other, often to a degree that precludes effective cooperation.

Given their tight connections, there is no question that, for example, a reignited civil war in Tajikistan would threaten Kyrgyzstan's capacity to maintain control. Renewed fighting there or in Afghanistan could create refugee flows that would strain resources. The drug trade that affects these states is also a potential source of continuing instability, as it is unlikely that the peace settlement in Afghanistan (much less its failure) will fully stem the traffic in one of the country's few cash crops.

Kyrgyzstan, like Uzbekistan, was eager to welcome a U.S. and coalition presence to its soil after September 11. At the time of this writing, U.S. forces are in place at Manas airfield near the capital, with plans to expand the presence further (and to make substantial improvements to the infrastructure in place). A bilateral agreement on the stationing of forces was signed with the United States and ratified by the Kyrgyz parliament in early December 2001. It is valid for one year but can be extended, and it explicitly allows for U.S. use of Kyrgyz installations in support of humanitarian and military missions (unlike agreements with other regional states, which are limited to humanitarian operations). A variety of other coalition states, including Britain, France, Italy, Canada, Australia, and South Korea, have also asked Kyrgyzstan for basing access.

While the United States has said that it does not plan to maintain a permanent presence in Kyrgyzstan, the facilities it is building there suggest a desire for at least the capacity to return. Brigadier General Christopher A. Kelly, commander of the 376th Air Expeditionary Wing, said of the facility that "we're establishing a mini-air force base from which we can fly a variety of military missions, mainly airlift, aerial refueling and tactical air."[1] The United States has also boosted its program of military-to-military contacts with Kyrgyzstan,

---

[1]Telephone interview reported in Eric Smith and James Dao, "U.S. Is Building Up Its Military Bases in Afghan Region," *The New York Times,* January 9, 2002.

Table 9.2

Indicators of Conflict: Kyrgyzstan

Indicator	Currently in Evidence	Likely in 10–15 Years	Possible in 10–15 Years
Domestic			
Popular movements form outside of legal channels, develop secretive, militaristic, radical agendas		✓	
Privatization of force		✓	
Increasing political "democratization"		✓	
Increasing authoritarianism	✓	✓	
Ethnic, clan, linguistic or religious political parties with radical agendas gain influence		✓	
Widespread reports of corruption and crackdowns thereon; frequent government-related scandals		✓	
Succession crisis			✓
Regional			
Energy cutoffs by oil/gas suppliers	✓	✓	
Hostile/semi-hostile Russian military presence			✓
Foreign (Russia, Iran, other) support of insurgents/secessionists		✓	
Extended U.S. military presence		✓	
Formal alignment with the United States			✓
Spillover from neighboring Central Asian states		✓	
Negative impact from revolution in Xinjiang, China			✓

holding a bilateral counterterror exercise with Kyrgyz forces in February. The U.S. presence brings a variety of benefits to Kyrgyzstan. Directly, the United States is paying for the use of Kyrgyz facilities. Less directly, Kyrgyzstan is benefiting from a program of increased military and economic assistance.

Kyrgyzstan is not a particularly appealing environment for a long-term presence, given high altitudes and poor infrastructure. While the coalition involved in the Afghanistan conflict was able to move forces into the country, the effort was complicated and lengthy. That said, the infrastructure that the United States is now helping to put in place will change this. From Bishkek's perspective, a long-term U.S. and allied military presence is very much a positive factor. It can help stimulate Kyrgyzstan's weak economy, help the country's military build, train, and equip a capable force, and provide a measure of security against possible future incursions like those by the IMU of 1999–2000. Moreover, a U.S. presence sends a signal to Russia, China, and Uzbekistan that Kyrgyzstan has a very strong ally and protector.

That said, a U.S. presence is a two-edged sword for both parties. The U.S. presence may provide a measure of stability, but those forces are also a possible target for militants; and if anti-U.S. Islamist feeling continues to grow in the country, attacks on U.S. bases, facilities, and personnel become more likely. This could be exacerbated if the U.S. presence garners public hostility, as there are some signs it may be doing. Insofar as it raises hackles in Russia, China, and Iran, it can also have negative political repercussions for the strategic interests of both the United States and Kyrgyzstan. Moreover, none of the factors that make violence and conflict in Kyrgyzstan possible will immediately disappear simply due to the presence of U.S. forces. Kyrgyzstan hopes, and the United States fears, that this will make the United States more likely to get involved in helping to settle Kyrgyzstan's problems. Even if the U.S. presence is not permanent, but the bases are maintained to provide access to U.S. forces if necessary for future contingencies, a closer U.S.-Kyrgyz relationship, while far from a commitment to Kyrgyzstan's security, does make it more likely that the United States will feel pressured to get involved in stabilizing conflict on Kyrgyz territory should it occur. The potential for spillover of conflict into Tajikistan (if spillover from Tajikistan is not in fact the cause) creates further incentives for the United States and others to become involved.

Tajikistan

Tajikistan is among the poorest states in the world and is the poorest in this region, with poverty over 50 percent (the average monthly wage is $10), a per-capita annual income of $290, and rampant unemployment (over 80 percent in some regions). Tajikistan has dropped on the UN Human Development Index since 1995 and is the lowest-ranked state in the region. Entire sections of the country subsist largely on the assistance provided by humanitarian organizations. Tajikistan's exports include electric power and aluminum, the latter in turn heavily dependent on the country's imports of alumina. Like Kyrgyzstan, it is a heavy importer of oil and gas, and carries a large debt burden and faces a difficult balance of payments/debt situation. In addition to large public-sector external debts, Tajikistan has substantial bilateral debt, half of it within the CIS. Russia is a particularly large creditor.

To some extent, Tajikistan's continuing problems can be attributed to the aftereffects of its civil war of 1992–1997, in which government loyalists fought a coalition of Islamic, democratic, regional, and ethnic opposition factions. It was a conflict overlaid by regional and clan feuds and ethnic rivalries and further exacerbated by struggles among warlords, criminal groups, and drug traffickers. As the war continued, drug and arms trafficking became the major economic activity, enabling warlords to consolidate power in key areas, power they largely kept after peace was negotiated.

The end of the war brought with it some genuine political liberalization, but central control remains limited; tribal, criminal, and other leaders remain in charge (if not control) of large swaths of land. Organized crime maintains high levels of influence over government bodies (local and national). Corruption is pervasive and reaches all sectors of the government, as well as members of the Russian armed forces that continue to be deployed in Tajikistan. While the power-sharing regime that incorporates opposition members into President Rakhmonov's government represents a step forward, tension between groups and regions remains a volatile factor, and many regional leaders, despite ostensible incorporation into the government, are not trusted by the Rakhmonov regime. Local groups, in turn, assert that the government does not distribute funds and resources to former opposition strongholds. On the one hand, this level of state weakness suggests that Tajikistan is one of few states in the region not at risk of a succession crisis. On the other hand, this is less comforting when it is recognized that this is largely because there is little power to succeed to, and that the country remains in a very real political crisis as it is. Moreover, the Rakhmonov regime, despite its limited control, is exhibiting some dangerous signs of authoritarianism, namely the crackdowns on opposition members who are not incorporated in government structures, and the results of the 1999 presidential election, which Rakhmonov reportedly won with 97 percent of the vote and a 98 percent turnout.

The drug trade remains one of the few sources of income for local residents (opium was used as a currency in the middle 1990s), and insurgent groups such as the IMU have repeatedly taken advantage of good relations with local leaders (IMU leaders fought alongside the opposition in the civil war) in parts of the country outside of central government control to establish and maintain bases. The arms trade and other illegal trafficking also continue, and the unofficial/shadow economy is estimated to be at least as large as the official economy.

Thus, the prospects for a continued peace in Tajikistan do not inspire confidence, as almost all of the identifiable risk factors are in place in this country. Economic and/or political crisis of some sort seems almost inevitable in coming years, with the only question being the extent to which it further destabilizes the country as a whole (and with it the interconnected region). The tribal/ethnic/religious/ regional components of divides within the country stem from continued distrust and a real absence of national consolidation and identity. Moreover, although Tajikistan is alone in Central Asia in accepting a measure of Islamic participation in government (in the form of the former opposition Islamic Renaissance Party, or IRP), the central government continues to arrest members of other groups, such as the Hizb ut-Tahrir. Moreover, Islamicism appears to be spreading in Tajikistan, with the IRP expanding its membership in regions once considered predominantly secular, even as it appears to be losing ground to groups such as the Hizb ut-Tahrir in more traditionally religious areas. As in Kyrgyzstan, the Hizb ut-Tahrir has spread its base of support beyond the ethnic Uzbek population to include more Tajiks and others.

With the large (if debatably effective) Russian military presence in Tajikistan, it is little wonder that relations between the two countries remain close. To a large extent, Tajikistan can accurately be described as a client state of Russia, given the troops and Russia's influence over government structures. A founding member of the Shanghai Cooperation Organization, Tajikistan has also had some small-scale bilateral military contacts with China. Iran, which reportedly supported the opposition during Tajikistan's civil war, was also active in seeking a settlement, hosting and promoting meetings and discussions between the combatants. Since 1997, relations between Iran and Tajikistan have been fairly good.

Tajikistan was a route for supplies being sent by Russia, and to some extent Iran, to the Northern Alliance as it fought the Taliban for control of Afghanistan in the late 1990s and early 2000s. Moreover, the Northern Alliance itself was largely composed of ethnic Tajik and Uzbek forces, united against the Pashtun-based Taliban. Afghani factions were also involved in Tajikistan's civil war, and elements of the Tajik opposition, as well as the IMU, received support and training from the Taliban.

As already noted, there remains tension as well as common interests among Kyrgyzstan, Uzbekistan, and Tajikistan. While Uzbekistan supported the Tajik government during its civil war, it also served as the staging ground for at least one opposition incursion. After the IMU incursions into Uzbekistan and Kyrgyzstan in 1999, Uzbekistan offered Tajikistan assistance in going after IMU rebels in its territory. When that offer was not accepted, Uzbekistan nevertheless went ahead with bombing raids into Tajikistan. In 2000, however, Tajikistan agreed to the presence of Uzbek helicopters in its airspace. But it remains concerned about Uzbek and Kyrgyz border mining and continuing border disputes with Uzbekistan. It has also expressed worries about reports of discrimination against ethnic Tajiks in Uzbekistan, which includes restrictions on Tajik-language literature and possible deportations from border regions.

Prior to September 11, Tajikistan was hesitant to build ties with the United States and NATO. This can be seen as a reflection in large part of its security dependence on Russia. Even after September 11, Tajikistan initially took great care in its language and proposals. It has, however, permitted U.S. and other coalition forces to use its facilities in support of humanitarian missions (as well as search and rescue and combat "if necessary"). France received permission to station six Mirage-2000 fighter-bombers in Tajikistan for the duration of the campaign and to use Tajikistan facilities for its forces en route to Afghanistan. Italian and U.S. forces, too, have reportedly flown into Tajikistan, and status of forces agreements are in place. In exchange, Tajikistan is receiving aid packages from a variety of countries, including Japan, France, and India, as well as help with refurbishing its airports and facilities, many of which were deemed unusable by coalition forces. Tajikistan and France are developing a plan for future military cooperation, to include training, and there are reports of Indian assistance in both base modernization and air force training.   Tajikistan has also recently joined NATO's Partnership for Peace, the last of the post-Soviet states to do so.

Tajik officials have stated that they expect the foreign presence to be long term, since the stabilization of Afghanistan is likely to take quite some time. Certainly, as with Kyrgyzstan, the stationing of foreign forces and assets in Tajikistan (other than the Russian forces, which remain as well), has implications for the country's security. Tajikistan, however, presents even more challenges than Kyryzstan, for in addition to poverty and difficult terrain (even worse than that in Kyrgyzstan), the lack of central government control over much of the country creates challenges for operations and movements. Moreover, the internal situation in Tajikistan is more immediately volatile than that in Kyrgyzstan, and, as already noted, the likelihood of further conflict is high. The criminalization of much of the country means that if conflict erupts, the same factors that came into play during the civil war will return—including struggles for control of drug routes (and if narcotics production begins to move out of Afghanistan, for that as well), ethno-tribal-regional conflict, etc.— with a very real potential for Tajikistan, or at least some parts of it, to begin to look something like Afghanistan did circa 2000. If this happens, the international community will face clear incentives to seek to prevent the development of Tajikistan as a center of the drug trade and potentially a safe haven for terrorism. If this happens while foreign forces are already in place in Tajikistan, and building relations with what state structures exist, there is little doubt that the conflict would quickly be internationalized and that some or all of these foreign forces, including Russia's, could find themselves operating in an environment of increasing hostility. Moreover, as already noted with respect to Kyrgyzstan, it is unlikely that conflict in Tajikistan would be limited to that state alone; there is a clear risk of spread to Uzbekistan and Kyrgyzstan.

Table 9.3

Indicators of Conflict: Tajikistan

Indicator	Currently in Evidence	Likely in 10–15 Years	Possible in 10–15 Years
Domestic			
Popular movements form outside of legal channels, develop secretive, militaristic, radical agendas	✓	✓	
Privatization of force	✓	✓	
Increasing political "democratization"	✓	✓	
Increasing authoritarianism	✓	✓	
Ethnic, clan, linguistic or religious political parties with radical agendas gain influence	✓	✓	
Widespread reports of corruption and crackdowns thereon; frequent government-related scandals	✓	✓	
Regionalization/secessionism	✓	✓	
Regional			
Energy cutoffs by oil/gas suppliers	✓	✓	
Foreign (Russia, Iran, other) support of insurgents/secessionists	✓	✓	
Extended U.S./European military presence			✓
Conflict spillover from neighboring Central Asian states		✓	
Negative impact from revolution in Xinjiang, China			✓

Turkmenistan

If most of the CASC states exhibit some signs of personalized authoritarianism, or "sultanism," Turkmenistan is furthest along on this particular path. Saparmurat Niyazov's rule is based on Soviet structures, loyal security forces, and increasingly a cult of personality, the closest parallel to which might be found today in North Korea. Political parties are banned, and the media are entirely controlled by the government. Public meetings are forbidden. Niyazov has named himself president for life, but he has also promised to step down in 2010, although there are rumors that rather than holding an election, Niyazov will proclaim himself king so as to ensure succession by his son.

Politically isolated by choice, Turkmenistan is not the poorest state in the region. Although its UN Human Development Index ranking has dropped since 1995, with a per-capita annual income of $670, it is in better shape than many. However, gas, water, energy, and salt rations are provided to citizens, and the price of bread is regulated. The water that Turkmenistan depends on for irrigation is controlled by Kyrgyzstan and Tajikistan. Like the region's other fuel exporters, Turkmenistan has heavy export concentration, with most of its exports derived from its gas sales. But Turkmenistan is alone in the region in continuing to sell over half of its gas to other CIS states, a factor attributable in large part to sales to Ukraine. It actually imports less from Russia, proportionately to its other imports, than from other states in the region. It also has substantial trade with Iran, with which it has arranged gas swaps.

Autocracy and poverty have fed crime and corruption here as they have elsewhere in the region. The shadow economy in Turkmenistan is estimated to be 60 percent the size of the official GDP. Although not a narcotics producer of any volume, Turkmenistan has become a route for drug traffickers and those who smuggle precursor chemicals to Turkey, Russia, and Europe. Here, too, the country's role as a transit state for the drug trade is increasing domestic illegal drug use, with the U.S. State Department's INCSR estimating unofficially that over 10 percent of the population may use illegal drugs.[2]

Niyazov's autocratic rule has to some extent limited the development of radical Islam in his country, although accurate and reliable information on this and similar domestic issues in Turkmenistan is difficult to come by. People of Turkmen ethnicity make up nearly 80 percent of the country's population. The largest minority group is the Uzbeks (just under 10 percent), followed by Russians (about 5 percent). The population is expected to continue to grow in coming years. If Niyazov's control falters, either in a transition of power or for some other reason, ethnic, religious, political, and economic

---

[2] *International Narcotics Control Strategy Report,* U.S. Department of State, Bureau for International Narcotics and Law Enforcement Affairs, March 2001. See *http://usinfo.state.gov/topical/global/drugs.*

conflict all become possible as grievances whose expression the state has suppressed seek outlets in the absence of institutions capable of channeling them.

Over the next decade, Turkmenistan's share of Caspian natural gas export potential is expected to rise as Uzbekistan's declines due to domestic consumption. But this is also dependent on Turkmenistan's capacity to secure markets, particularly in Turkey and the Far East. The most viable alternative/supplement to routes through Russia is Iran, and it is likely that swaps with Iran will increase. But supplies from Iran and Azerbaijan may well be sufficient to saturate the Turkish market, leaving the Far Eastern option. The possibility of a route through Afghanistan to Pakistan and perhaps on to India has been discussed and may become possible if and when a political settlement of the Afghanistan conflict stabilizes that country. Other options for transporting and monetizing Turkmenistani gas hold promise, such as liquefying it for overwater transport or using other means of physical or chemical transformation for easier transport.

As a Caspian littoral state, Turkmenistan contests some areas of the Caspian with Azerbaijan. Although it was ambivalent about its stance on the division of the sea and seabed until recently, it now advocates the position that each littoral state have a national coastal zone of control that extends 10–20 miles into the Caspian. It also argues that no development of subsoil gas and oil deposits in disputed areas should take place until agreement is reached.

Turkmenistan has been consistent in insisting on its nonalignment, to the point of isolationism. Although it remains vulnerable to Russian economic pressure stemming from its dependence on Russian gas pipeline routes, it has not tried to balance that pressure by building political relationships with a variety of other states, as have many of its neighbors. While it has sought alternative pipelines and routes (for instance through Iran or Afghanistan, as noted above), it has avoided formalizing relationships within or outside the CIS. For instance, Turkmenistan never joined the CIS collective security treaty, it has signed but not ratified an EU Partnership and Cooperation Agreement, and although it did join Partnership for Peace, it has not been active in that organization.

Turkmenistan has been somewhat more amenable, however, to relations with Iran, driven in part by its desire for an alternative gas export mechanism. It also took a pragmatic line to Taliban-controlled Afghanistan, negotiating a trade agreement and hosting informal talks between Northern Alliance and Taliban factions in 2000, although stopping short of official recognition of the regime. This can be at least partially explained by a belief that through good relations with the Taliban, Turkmenistan could avoid being targeted by insurgents trained in Afghanistan and could preclude Taliban support to whatever Islamist opposition might emerge on its own soil.

Since the collapse of the Taliban, Turkmenistan has discussed a range of possible cooperative projects with representatives of the interim government. In addition to gas pipelines, these include highway investments and electricity infrastructure. But the continued uncertainty of the political, economic, and military situation in Afghanistan makes any near-term implementation of such plans unlikely.

When it comes to the coalition as a whole, however, Turkmenistan has argued that its neutral status precludes the use of its territory for military forces involved in the war in Afghanistan, although it is willing to allow overflight for humanitarian missions. In January 2002, Turkmenistan acted on this policy and turned down a German request for airbase access in support of the coalition effort. That said, it should be noted that other states in the region, too, have excluded the use of their territory or airspace to support combat operations, and that Turkmenistan did allow the limited use of an airfield near the border with Afghanistan for humanitarian support.

Turkmenistan may see internal unrest, as noted above, in the event of a succession crisis or other economic or political crisis (and the latter could bring on the former). Turkmenistan is likely to get involved in conflict over the Caspian, as a littoral state. It will continue to be a battlefield of the war on narcotics, although not the most significant one of the region. It is not, however, a likely locale for major international conflict of any sort.

Other than multinational peacekeeping in the event of internal conflict, U.S. involvement in Turkmenistan is likely to be limited for as

Table 9.4

Indicators of Conflict: Turkmenistan

Indicator	Currently in Evidence	Likely in 10–15 Years	Possible in 10–15 Years
Domestic			
Popular movements form outside of legal channels, develop secretive, militaristic, radical agendas			✓
Privatization of force			✓
Increasing political "democratization"		✓	
Increasing authoritarianism	✓	✓	
Ethnic, clan, linguistic or religious political parties with radical agendas gain influence			✓
Widespread reports of corruption; frequent government-related scandals and crackdowns on same			✓
Succession crisis			✓
Regional			
Unresolved Caspian claims	✓		✓
Russian efforts to exert influence by cutting off energy export routes	✓	✓	
Foreign (Russia, Iran, other) support of insurgents/secessionists			✓
Militarization of Caspian Sea		✓	

long as the country maintains its current isolationist foreign policy. If policy shifts, for whatever reason, the United States might seek to build stronger relations with this gas-producing state, particularly if planned gas pipeline routes connect Turkmenistan to Asia, increasing its strategic significance. If this happens, the likelihood of the United States taking a more active role in Turkmenistan's problems, and potentially conflicts in or near that state, would increase. That said, Turkmenistan, along with Tajikistan, has some of the worst infrastructure of Central Asia, with much of the country not tied in to transport infrastructure. Its military is weak and likely to remain so for the foreseeable future. Even with major political reforms and economic growth, it would take years for Turkmenistan to reform its military to a point of real competence. Contamination of soil and water is a problem, as it is in neighboring states. The terrain is mostly desert. Thus, as long as alternatives exist, Turkmenistan is not an appealing operational environment. That said, plausible scenarios can be envisioned in which alternatives are not sufficient to rule out the need to plan for the possibility of operations in Turkmenistan.

Uzbekistan

Uzbekistan is in second place after Turkmenistan as the most authoritarian/sultanistic regime of the Central Asian region. President Karimov has banned all opposition parties, restricts and censors the press, and maintains strict control over religious bodies. All opposition has been forced underground, and media censorship has extended to coverage of the ongoing war in Afghanistan: Karimov has limited the extent to which the U.S. and coalition presence in his country is discussed by its media. In January 2002, Karimov extended his presidential term from five years to seven by means of a referendum that made barely a pretense of democracy: 91 percent of voters were recorded as supporting the extension of Karimov's term.

From the economic perspective, Uzbekistan is in comparatively good shape when considered alongside its neighbors. Of the CASC states, only Uzbekistan has regained the GDP level of 1991. Annual income per capita is $720. It is the only state in the region that is not heavily dependent on imports and has the most balanced trade structure of the eight regional states. That said, figures may well be unreliable. Uzbekistan appears to have a substantial debt burden as a percent of its GDP. The government has fought efforts to liberalize foreign exchange and trade regimes, making longer-term prospects questionable. It is the only state in the region that does not have a World Bank/IMF poverty reduction program in place. Foreign investment has gone down recently, in part due to government regulation and corruption.

Despite its large reserves, Uzbekistan is not a major exporter of natural gas. Its share of gas production is likely to decrease further in coming years, as domestic consumption rises. By 2005, its gas exports should be negligible, and Uzbekistan will become a net importer of crude oil to fill its energy needs. This may limit its capacity in the future to use gas exports to pressure neighbors that currently depend on it for that resource, namely Kyrgyzstan and Tajikistan, on which Uzbekistan in turn relies for its water.

As is typical in the region, Uzbekistan has burgeoning and substantial problems with crime and corruption. There are close links between major criminal organizations and at least some political leaders. Foreign criminal groups, for instance from Korea, have also been active in Uzbekistan, particularly in the Ferghana Valley. That said, crime is a factor more of corruption than of economic development. Compared to other states in the region, Uzbekistan's shadow economy is low compared to its official economy. This is attributable, in part, to government control of economic activity and slow economic reform. Uzbekistan's role as a transit state for narcotics has also led to a burgeoning health crisis within the country. The United States government has estimated some 200,000 drug abusers in Uzbekistan (out of a population of about 24–25 million).

The combination of autocracy, corruption, and limited economic development, here as in neighboring states, creates real risks of internal conflict. If Karimov's grasp on power should fail, for whatever reason, a struggle for succession may emerge involving economic and political interests, as well as criminal groups, in a variety of short- and long-term alliances. A situation in some ways similar to the civil war in Tajikistan in the 1990s becomes plausible.

This is of particular concern because in Uzbekistan, too, political and economic divides overlay ethnic and religious allegiances. Ethnic Uzbeks make up just over three-quarters of the population of Uzbekistan, and the government has to some extent pursued policies of "ethnic redress," privileging Uzbeks over other ethnicities. However, the more likely source of internal ethnic conflict may be Karakalpakstan, a special administrative region in western Uzbekistan with substantial autonomy. Because Karakalpaks in Karakalpakstan enjoy a measure of self-rule and an elite structure independent of that of Uzbekistan as a whole, this area carries the potential for secessionism (as has happened with similar regions elsewhere in the former Soviet Union). This is unlikely in the near term, but it might become more probable if and when the regime in Uzbekistan weakens.

Insofar as religion is concerned, there can be no question that Islam Karimov's regime views political Islam as hostile. To some extent, the feeling is mutual. Groups such as the IMU and the Hizb ut-Tahrir take as their primary goal the removal of Karimov from power. The danger that such movements will become a true grassroots opposition that can challenge the regime is increased by the general crackdowns on all Muslims in Uzbekistan. It does appear that the appeal of such groups in Uzbekistan is growing, spreading beyond its traditional rural, Ferghana Valley base.

As already noted, the question of ethnic and religious rifts in any of the countries of Central Asia cannot be viewed in a vacuum. Aside from the shared concern about Islamic militants—and the somewhat differing views on how to respond to those concerns—Uzbekistan and its neighbors are caught in a tangle of shared and conflicting interests. Uzbekistan's Karimov and Kazakhstan's Nazarbayev both see themselves and their countries as regional leaders, and therefore each sees the other as a rival. Uzbekistan claims territory in all of its neighboring states, while the large Uzbek diaspora provides a potential pretext for Uzbek meddling in the affairs of others—something those neighbors fear will turn into an excuse for imperialistic behavior on the part of Uzbekistan. Similarly, some neighbors fear that Uzbekistan's efforts to police and pacify the Ferghana region, and its pressure on neighbors to track down militants and extremists, are part of a larger effort to extend influence, rather than just guarantee security. Events over the last two to three years do suggest that, if nothing else, Uzbekistan's evolving security policy appears to include the right to intervene in neighboring states if it perceives its own interests to be threatened.

If the IMU is likely to have had its capacity substantially degraded by the operations against the Taliban in Afghanistan, it and similar organizations may well retain or regain the capacity for at least small-scale harassment and terrorist acts, in Uzbekistan and elsewhere. Uzbekistan's own desire and perceived security need for regional leadership can also spark conflict, given its extraterritorial enclaves within Kyrgyzstan, the intermixing of Uzbek, Kyrgyz, and Tajik populations in all three countries, and resource tensions. Conflict could begin with Uzbek assistance for co-ethnics abroad, or an effort to track down and prevent attacks from militants who have fled to or are based in neighboring states. Insofar as the U.S. military presence in Uzbekistan bolsters the regime and its perception of its regional influence, such scenarios may be even more likely today than they were prior to the September 11 attacks.

Beyond the region, Uzbekistan has sought to preserve as much independence as possible, refusing to accept Russian military assistance and instead seeking to build ties with the United States and Turkey, efforts that were, until recently, limited in large part by Uzbekistan's continued autocratic policies and human rights abuses. Uzbekistan withdrew from the CIS collective security treaty and joined GUUAM, the Georgia, Ukraine, Uzbekistan, Azerbaijan, and Moldova grouping whose existence was intended and seen, at least in part, as a statement of independence from Russia. After the IMU incursions of 1999–2000, Uzbekistan appeared to warm somewhat to Moscow and its offers of assistance, but it stopped short of accepting any substantial military aid.

Prior to September 11, U.S. assistance to Uzbekistan was limited. It included some joint training of U.S. mountain combat units and Uzbek armed forces, as well as provision of some nonlethal military equipment. Turkey and Uzbekistan had begun to build a relationship, in which Turkey provided some material assistance and Turkish troops helped train Uzbek special forces units. Iran, which cooperated with Uzbekistan to some extent in the efforts by both countries and Russia to support Northern Alliance forces in Afghanistan, had little luck building more solid relations with the Uzbeks. Uzbekistan also joined the Shanghai Cooperation Organization in June 2000 and accepted assistance from China. Because this assistance included sniper rifles, it made China the only state other than Russia to provide lethal assistance to a Central Asian state prior to September 11. Uzbekistan has also signed bilateral agreements with India. Relations with Pakistan were strained due to Pakistan's reported links to the IMU.

The IMU certainly received support from Al Qaeda and the Taliban, and it established bases in Taliban-held areas of Afghanistan in the late 1990s and early 2000s, providing impetus for Uzbekistan's continuing support to the Northern Alliance (which was, as noted, predominantly Uzbek and Tajik in makeup). However, in middle to late 2000, it appeared that Uzbekistan might be seeking a different approach, perhaps hoping that rapprochement with the Taliban could result in an end to its support of the IMU and increased security along Uzbekistan's southern border. In fall 2000, Karimov stated that he did not see the Taliban as a significant threat and urged a coalition government composed of Northern Alliance and Taliban forces. A few weeks later, the Uzbek ambassador to Pakistan met with representatives of the Taliban in Islamabad and reportedly reached an agreement for Uzbekistan and Afghanistan not to interfere in each other's affairs.

With the commencement of the U.S.-led coalition operation in Afghanistan, the situation changed drastically. Uzbekistan has a tremendous interest in peace in Afghanistan, and a reignited and/or protracted conflict posed the risk of an influx of refugees into Uzbekistan, straining resources, introducing possible insurgents, and threatening the survival of the regime. This, combined with Uzbekistan's wish to establish independence from Moscow and its longstanding desire for a closer relationship with the United States makes it not surprising that Uzbekistan was the first country to offer access rights to U.S. military forces for operations in Afghanistan. For Uzbekistan, this was an unprecedented opportunity to enlist the United States as a partner, to bolster the government and the stature of the country, as well as to assist in alleviating some of its security concerns. To date, the United States has repaid Uzbekistan's generosity by targeting IMU bases in Afghanistan, providing economic assistance, refurbishing infrastructure that U.S. forces are using in country, and signing a bilateral agreement promising to "regard with grave concern any external threat" to Uzbekistan. This is, of course, far short of any sort of security guarantee or alliance. That said, the very presence of U.S. forces in Uzbekistan suggests a tripwire, if not a political commitment, to Uzbekistan for at least as long as they remain in place.

While the United States has stated that support and assistance are contingent on democratization and improvement in the human rights sphere, Karimov's January referendum does not say much for the prospects of this being a successful mechanism for changing the nature of the regime. It is also worth noting that Uzbekistan has agreed to access for humanitarian or search and rescue purposes—not combat operations. Over time, Karimov's authoritarian rule and efforts to use the war on terrorism as an excuse for further crackdowns on political opposition forces will place the United States in an increasingly awkward situation. Moreover, the United States may face a tension between its growing cooperation with Russia (and its relations with other states) and its presence in Uzbekistan and other Central Asian states. To date, the United States has been insistent that it does not plan a permanent presence in the region, but in Uzbekistan, as in Kyrgyzstan and Tajikistan, it may well find it difficult to leave entirely, particularly as Uzbekistan has much to gain from keeping the United States in place and engaged for as long as possible.

Despite the pitfalls, there may be strategic reasons for maintaining at least the option of presence in/access to Uzbekistan. It has the best support infrastructure of the region, and it has 10 of the region's 36 airfields with runways over 7,500 feet (including 4 of the 12 longer than 10,000 feet). This makes it the most capable base for major airlift operations in the region. It also has some of the most capable military forces in the region (although this is a fairly low bar, and Uzbekistan's forces remain largely in poor condition), and possibly the best potential to develop a small number of truly competent elite units in coming years.

That said, U.S. forces found that even these "best" facilities required that they deploy with more personnel and equipment than is standard—they needed to bring far more in the way of support infrastructure than is generally the case. Uzbekistan's terrain is not as challenging as, say, Tajikistan, but its desert, river valleys, and mountains are not particularly hospitable, either. Pollution and contamination are real problems, as is the food supply.

An extended U.S. presence in Uzbekistan runs a real risk of involving the United States in Uzbekistan's internal cleavages, as well as its tensions with neighboring states. The withdrawal of forces in the near term, combined with the maintenance of close military ties and provision of economic assistance, mitigates that danger but does not remove it completely. U.S. forces, facilities, and personnel may also emerge as an appealing target for anti-Karimov forces insofar as they are seen as bolstering his regime. It is therefore plausible to argue that insofar as conflict in or involving Uzbekistan is likely over the course of the next 10–15 years, U.S. involvement in some form in that conflict has recently become far more probable.

Table 9.5

Indicators of Conflict: Uzbekistan

Indicator	Currently in Evidence	Likely in 10–15 Years	Possible in 10–15 Years
Domestic			
Popular movements form outside of legal channels, develop secretive, militaristic, radical agendas		✓	
Privatization of force		✓	
Increasing political "democratization"		✓	
Increasing authoritarianism	✓	✓	
Ethnic, clan, linguistic or religious political parties with radical agendas gain influence		✓	
Widespread reports of corruption; frequent government-related scandals and crackdowns on same		✓	
Succession crisis		✓	
Secessionism		✓	
Regional			
Extended U.S. military presence		✓	
Formal alignment with the United States			✓
Russian efforts to exert influence by cutting off energy export routes			✓
Foreign (Russia, Iran, other) support of insurgents/secessionists	✓	✓	
Conflict spillover from neighboring Central Asian states		✓	
Negative impact of revolution in Xinjiang, China			✓

Trans–Central Asian Conflict

As the above discussion indicates, ethnic and religious conflict in Central Asia, if it emerges, is unlikely to be limited to a single state. Just as IMU incursions affected Uzbekistan, Kyrgyzstan, and Tajikistan, any similar movement will not limit itself to any one of these regimes, linked as they are by ethnicity, religion, and intercutting borders. The IMU itself, now significantly degraded in its capacity, will continue (insofar as it survives) to see Islam Karimov's government in Uzbekistan as its primary target, but it is likely to continue to carry out operations in Kyrgyzstan and may also seek to shelter once more in Tajikistan, where it can easily find sanctuary in the Pamir mountains. In fact, as long as Tajikistan remains a country with large swaths of land outside of central government control, it will remain an appealing base of operations for the IMU and similar groups with targets throughout the region. Whether or not the Hizb ut-Tahrir itself continues to adhere to its nonviolent philosophy for attaining some of the same goals as those held by the IMU, it is also likely that some of its members may become radicalized over time (particularly as they are likely to develop contacts with more radical individuals and groups as a result of the prison sentences that local regimes impose on Hizb members). The increasing alienation of the population in Central Asia, where the majority of residents are faced with political and economic disenfranchisement, benefits radical groups who not only provide a mechanism for political expression, but are often able to pay their members and soldiers with monies received from foreign sources and illegal enterprises (such as narcotics smuggling). Because it appears that such groups are growing beyond their traditional poor and rural support bases, they are likely to remain a real concern to regional states and, if the United States remains either physically present or otherwise involved in the region, to U.S. forces and personnel as well.

Prior experience indicates that regional states may have difficulty cooperating against these or other common threats, and that their own conflicts over influence, resources, and terrorism also present a danger of conflict. Uzbekistan and Tajikistan have accused each other of harboring violent oppositionists, and not without evidence. All the states of the region have land claims and border disputes with their neighbors; Uzbekistan has some sort of territorial dispute with every other Central Asian state. Large ethnic diasporas of the eponymous ethnic groups of each of these states on the territories of their Central Asian neighbors (as well as in China and Afghanistan) combined with policies of ethnic redress in most of these states create a danger of international conflict as states seek to support their co-ethnics on the other side of national borders.

Moreover, the other Central Asian states are concerned that Uzbekistan will use cooperation to counter common threats or to support/defend its co-ethnics as an excuse for imperialistic behavior. It has justified the mining of borders with Kyrgyzstan and Tajikistan, including in contested areas, by arguing that it is done to prevent IMU-style insurgencies, although the only result so far has been civilian casualties. The Uzbek air force has also launched unsanctioned attacks into the territories of these countries. At the same time, as noted above, Kyrgyzstan too has mined its borders with Tajikistan. Also, as already discussed, Uzbekistan has pressured these states to crack down on Hizb ut-Tahrir and similar groups. Kyrgyzstan has generally complied and has extradited some individuals, but the situation continues to create tension. Disputes over gas and water have also marred relations between Uzbekistan and Kyrgyzstan and Tajikistan.

SOUTH CAUCASUS

Armenia

Armenia is something of an outlier in the region. It has maintained a relatively stable domestic political situation despite economic stagnation, debilitating emigration, and the murders of a prime minister and a speaker of parliament. It has been able to do so in large part because the cease-fire in its conflict with Azerbaijan over the Nagorno-Karabakh conflict, although oft-challenged, remains in place.

That said, Armenia faces severe economic decline, attributable in part to the costs of holding on to the enclave of Nagorno-Karabakh, within Azerbaijan, and the resultant blockade by Azerbaijan and Turkey. Income inequality is high, and the annual per-capita income is low at $490. It is estimated that about 80 percent of the population lives at or below the poverty level of less than $25/month. Though the official unemployment rate is 17 percent, unofficial estimates put it as high as 50 percent. The extralegal economy is estimated at 78 percent of the size of the official economy. Corruption is a problem here, as it is throughout the region.

Armenia is a large importer of oil and gas and heavily dependent on Russia for its imports. Its continuing conflict with Azerbaijan makes it unlikely to have a role in Caspian energy development as a transit state, although transit through Armenia would be shorter and possibly less dangerous than planned transit through Georgia. Armenia does have plans to diversify its gas imports by means of natural gas from Iran, lessening its dependence on Russia.

In the meantime, its debt for gas deliveries from Russia have mounted, and Armenia agreed to a debt-equity swap that granted Russian gas suppliers controlling interest in Amrosgazprom, the Armenian gas distribution monopoly. Negotiations for stakes in other Armenian enterprises are ongoing. That said, Armenia's debt sustainability problem does not appear to be unmanageable.

Unlike other countries in the region, economic or other discontent can be expressed in protests and demonstrations. While there has been violence in the parliament and continues to be tremendous disagreement within the government and among the polity, Armenia is more prone to contentious elections than to succession crises. The population is largely ethnically homogenous and predominantly of the Armenian Orthodox faith. Thus, the risk of internal conflict in Armenia is relatively low, although the risks that conflict with Azerbaijan will be renewed remain significant, and there is a substantial domestic constituency for a more belligerent attitude (see discussion below).

Armenia maintains very close ties with Russia, relying on it for security assistance. Russia provided support during the war with Azerbaijan and continues to do so, in the form of military equipment, spare parts, supplies, and training. Russian units and equipment are also stationed in Armenia. The two countries have signed a security assistance treaty. Armenia also has some military ties with the United States, but these have been limited in part by constraints placed on the United States by the Freedom Support Act, which prevented real military assistance to either combatant in the Nagorno-Karabakh war. With these restrictions eased in the wake of September 11, it is expected that ties between the United States and Armenia will grow. Armenia is also an active participant in NATO's PfP program.

Armenia's relationship with Turkey remains tense over Turkey's insistence that its government was not at fault in the mass deaths of Armenians in Turkey in 1915, a tension exacerbated by Turkey's support for Azerbaijan. Armenia does have a strong relationship with

Table 9.6

Indicators of Conflict: Armenia

Indicator	Currently in Evidence	Likely in 10–15 Years	Possible in 10–15 Years
Domestic			
Popular movements form outside of legal channels, develop secretive, militaristic, radical agendas			✓
Privatization of force			✓
Increasing political "democratization"	✓		
Increasing authoritarianism			✓
Widespread reports of corruption; frequent government-related scandals and crackdowns on same		✓	
Regional			
Russian efforts to exert influence by cutting off energy export routes			✓
Conflict with neighboring states		✓	

France, which has been involved, along with the United States and Russia, in mediating the Nagorno-Karabakh conflict. It also has good ties with Iran.

Armenia is unlikely to become a major staging area for U.S. operations, and it is an unlikely place for U.S. troops to be deployed in the foreseeable future. That said, it does have some capable airfields, two with runways over 10,000 feet, which would be capable of supporting most NATO aircraft. These could potentially be useful for operations not just locally, but into the northern Persian Gulf region. It has one of the more capable militaries in the region and is one of the more likely to develop a capable rapid-reaction force in coming years. On the other hand, while roads in and between the major cities are better maintained than those elsewhere in the region, secondary and tertiary roads and related infrastructure are poor.

Azerbaijan

Like Kazakhstan, Azerbaijan's hopes for prosperity rest on its oil reserves. Petroleum accounts for 83 percent of its exports, demonstrating a high degree of export concentration. Sixty percent of this oil goes to the EU. Azerbaijan also has the highest level of imports from Russia in the region (21 percent). A portion of this is natural gas. Although Azerbaijan is a gas producer in its own right, it does import a small amount from Russia—enough that when Russia cut off gas supplies in October 2000, Azeris organized street protests. Depending on the success of exploration, Azerbaijan can be expected to be a significant oil producer into 2010–2015. Kazakhstan, however, is increasingly seen as the more important oil state of the Caspian, with Azerbaijan increasingly viewed as a prospective gas producer over coming decades. In the meantime, it is reasonable to assume that Azerbaijan will glean profits from both oil and gas exports.

In an effort to offset some of the problems that export concentration in the fuels sector can engender, the IMF made a recent installment of loans to Azerbaijan contingent on the creation of an "oil fund" that would redirect energy development proceeds to other sectors of the economy. With the fund now in place, the IMF and the Azerbaijani government disagree on whether it should be managed by the executive or the legislative branch of Azerbaijan's government.

Despite the prospects that its oil wealth would suggest, the people of Azerbaijan remain poor. Per-capita income is $460 per year, and Azerbaijan scores lower on the UN Human Development Index than neighbors Armenia and Georgia. The shadow economy is large, estimated at 90 percent of the size of the official economy. Corruption is a tremendous problem—Azerbaijan is consistently ranked near the bottom of global rankings of states on this measure.

Azerbaijan must be seen as somewhere between an autocracy/ sultanistic regime and a democracy, although increasingly leaning toward the former. Aliev, as president, has been increasingly authoritarian, and his rule ever more personalistic. As he ages, the dangers of a succession crisis begin to loom large, and he has sought to take steps to name his son his successor. Azerbaijan does have an opposition, composed of a variety of diverse movements and groups. Opposition leaders (and members) of a certain stripe (for instance, Islamists) or those who are seen as a real threat by the Aliev regime find themselves harassed and subject to arrest on trumped-up charges. Some have left Azerbaijan and gone into exile. The press, too, is increasingly subject to censorship, and there is reason to think that elections and voting are rigged.

The Islamist movement in Azerbaijan appears to be fairly small and to have limited appeal, although continuing crackdowns on it by the Aliev regime could in time further radicalize its members. Moreover, continued economic deprivation combined with increasing limits on political freedom may in coming years make the Islamist movement more appealing to some segments of the population. Azerbaijan is fairly homogenous ethnically (over 90 percent Azeri). Past incidents of ethnic violence have been directed against the Armenian minority. That said, there are some subnational identities in Azerbaijan with the potential to become more important if political entrepreneurs are able to take advantage of them to mobilize groups. This is possible if the regime begins to weaken and the many economic and political grievances in Azerbaijan rise to the surface. Finally, conflict in Russia, in the northern Caucasus, could spill over into Azerbaijan. Of particular interest are Lezgin nationalists in Dagestan and the broader possibility of strife in that region.

In the more immediate term, however, Azerbaijan is at more risk from reignited conflict with Armenia over Nagorno-Karabakh. The 1994 cease-fire left 20 percent of Azerbaijan under Armenia's control and hundreds of thousands of Azeris internally displaced from that territory (estimates suggest that between 700,000 and one million people are affected). If war returns, Azerbaijan's political and economic growth and development will suffer. If a peace settlement is reached and all or part of the displaced people return to their homes, the resulting strain on the economy of Azerbaijan could foment a crisis. As in Armenia, there is strong domestic support among the opposition for actions that could well reignite conflict.

As a Caspian littoral state, Azerbaijan has claims on oil and gas fields therein. Azerbaijan is a supporter of Russia's proposed solution to Caspian claims: that the seabed and subsoil be divided along international boundary lines while the waters are held in common. Azerbaijan and Turkmenistan have competing claims over several oil fields, including ones that Azerbaijan is already developing. In July 2001, Iranian gunboats threatened a British Petroleum research vessel in what Azerbaijan considers its territorial waters in the Caspian.

Azerbaijan has a strong relationship with its neighboring state Georgia, with which, along with Ukraine and Moldova, it is a founding member of the GUUAM grouping (now also including Uzbekistan, as noted above). At present it remains largely dependent on Russia for export routes for its natural gas and oil, although a "Western route" for oil to Europe through Georgia now supplements the "Northern route" through Russia. Azerbaijan, Georgia, Turkey, and the United States have supported the construction of the Baku-Tbisli-Ceyhan (BTC) pipeline, which would begin in Azerbaijan, transit Georgia, and terminate at the Mediterranean port of Ceyhan in Turkey (oil could then transit the Mediterranean by tanker). There are also plans for a parallel gas export route (although gas cannot be transported over water as easily, as noted in the discussion of Turkmenistan above).

Azerbaijan's relations with Russia have been tense. Aliev's government has been adamant and consistent in its refusal to allow Russian troops to be stationed in Azerbaijan and more recently has largely rebuffed Russian efforts to re-establish close ties. One of the reasons for Azerbaijan's interest in developing multiple pipeline routes for oil and gas is to minimize its dependence on Russia, and thus limit Russia's leverage. The expectation that these routes will be built has already helped Azerbaijan chart a more independent foreign policy. Azerbaijan also hopes that by building close ties with Turkey, the United States, and NATO as a whole, it can guarantee its independence from Russia for the long term.

Azerbaijan has built a close cooperative relationship with Turkey. Turkey sponsors its (and Georgia's) participation in NATO-led peacekeeping in the former Yugoslavia (as part of NATO's KFOR stabilization force in Kosovo) and provides military assistance, including training and refurbishment of bases. Turkey is also Azerbaijan's largest single trade partner. Most recently, Turkey, Azerbaijan, and Georgia have signed a tripartite security cooperation agreement that commits Turkey to provide more military assistance and training. While this is still far short of formal alignment, it does cement the relationship even further than before and, combined with the Turkish presence in Azerbaijan, sends a clear signal to other states, including Russia.

Table 9.7

Indicators of Conflict: Azerbaijan

Indicator	Currently in Evidence	Likely in 10–15 Years	Possible in 10–15 Years
Domestic			
Popular movements form outside of legal channels, develop secretive, militaristic, radical agendas			✓
Privatization of force			✓
Increasing political "democratization"		✓	
Increasing authoritarianism	✓	✓	
Ethnic, clan, linguistic or religious political parties with radical agendas gain influence			✓
Widespread reports of corruption; frequent government-related scandals and crackdowns on same		✓	
Succession crisis		✓	
Regional			
Unresolved Caspian claims	✓		✓
Militarization of Caspian Sea		✓	
Formal alignment with Turkey		✓	
Russian efforts to exert influence by cutting off energy export routes	✓	✓	
Foreign (Russia, Iran, other) support of insurgents/secessionists			✓
Conflict with neighboring states		✓	

Azerbaijan's relationship with the United States was limited by arms sales and assistance restrictions imposed on the warring parties in the Nagorno-Karabakh conflict by the Freedom Support Act. In March 2002, however, these restrictions were lifted, and the United States has, since September 11, shown signs that the relationship with Azerbaijan will be developing more in the future, particularly in areas related to the coalition against terrorism. Azerbaijan has the potential to build some capable military formations in coming years, particularly with assistance from states such as Turkey and the United States, although this would require that it devote considerable effort and resources.

As things stand, crisis or conflict in or relating to Azerbaijan
sonably likely to draw in Turkey and involve Russia, which is understandably ambivalent about U.S. and Turkish ties to its close southern neighbor, in some capacity. As the U.S. relationship with
Azerbaijan develops, the likelihood that the United States will be
involved also increases. Moreover, as a possible basing area for military operations outside its territory, Azerbaijan offers some advantages, including proximity to the Persian Gulf region. Access rights to
an Azerbaijani airfield are reportedly being sought by Turkey, which
argues that there are two airfields in Azerbaijan that could be
brought up to NATO standards. On the other hand, Azerbaijan is relatively underdeveloped industrially compared to Armenia or
Georgia. High unemployment and poverty typical of the post-Soviet
region are a problem in Azerbaijan as well, as is pollution and poor
water, air, and soil quality. Road conditions are poor in ways typical
of the region.

Georgia

Georgia's economy has been ravaged by years of domestic unrest,
which has included civil war and secessionist movements in several
regions. Georgia's GDP in 2000 was half the level of 1991, and the
shadow economy is estimated to be 85 percent the size of the official
economy. In fact, it is difficult to overestimate the extent to which
crime and criminal groups are involved in Georgia's economy and
political system. Georgia is very dependent on Russia for natural gas
and has a high debt burden, with half of its debt bilateral. Sixty percent of the population lives at or below the poverty level. Georgia's
debt has, in fact, fed its poverty problem, as debt service has precluded higher spending domestically. Insofar as the balance of payments and debt situation is unlikely to change significantly for
Georgia, even under the best of circumstances it will continue to
experience severe economic difficulties. In this environment, external shocks or crises could prove particularly volatile.

In the meantime, the domestic political situation continues to be in
turmoil, with de facto separatism in Abkhazia and South Ossetia, an
influx of refugees (reportedly including a number of militants) from
Chechnya in the Pankisi Gorge, and general lawlessness and lack of
control in many regions. While Georgia under President Eduard

Shevardnadze has made a public commitment to political and economic liberalization, corruption is rampant, even compared to other states in the region, and Shevardnadze's rule has come under increasing criticism from within his country. At the same time, the president's ability to command respect abroad has helped him maintain foreign support, which in turn has helped him stay in power at home. As Shevardnadze ages, and the Georgian public gets increasingly unwilling to tolerate the corruption and economic collapse that has continued under his rule, the likelihood increases that there will be a change in power. Given the political and economic situation in Georgia, and the history of conflict, it is extremely optimistic to expect that a peaceful political transition would be easy to achieve. While it is possible that Shevardnadze's eventual departure from power will help Georgia begin to develop as a democracy, it is also possible that it will spark a succession crisis that destroys the few institutions and government structures that exist in this country.

Other possible flashpoints for conflict in Georgia include spillover from the war in Chechnya, which could culminate in Russian intervention and perhaps even takeover of parts of northern Georgia. Various other Russian North Caucasus conflicts (the Ingush-Ossetian conflict, tensions between the Karachai-Balkars and the Circassians) could also spill over into Georgia if they flare up. Russian support for separatists within Georgia has precedent (Russians are widely believed to have aided the Abkhaz movement) and may recur, given the many ethnic and subethnic groups and identities in Georgia. The one thing that seems unlikely to be a factor in Georgia is political Islam. Ajaria, a region inhabited by Muslim ethnic Georgians, tends to be a secular place, where the people identify far more as Georgians than as Muslims.

Georgia has sought to develop a Western political orientation even as Russian troops remained in place on its soil. Russia maintains ground and air force bases within Georgia, in part with an ostensible peacekeeping mission, although its forces have been accused of assisting separatists in Abkhazia and South Ossetia (and not without evidence). Although Russia has withdrawn forces from two of its four bases in Georgia, it was guilty of foot-dragging in doing so, and negotiations on the two remaining bases remain difficult. It has also overflown and reportedly attacked Georgian territory in pursuit of Chechen rebels.

Georgia's effort to demonstrate and cement its independence from Russia has taken two primary forms. One was a role in the Caspian energy trade, for which Georgia promises to be a key transit state for oil and gas en route from the Caspian to Europe. The other was a concerted effort to build ties with Western states. The two are, of course, related, as the United States and Turkey have supported efforts to build the pipelines through Georgia even as they have developed military and other ties. Georgia has been particularly successful in building ties with Turkey, which sponsors its (and Azerbaijan's) participation in NATO-led peacekeeping in the former Yugoslavia (as part of NATO's KFOR stabilization force in Kosovo), provides military assistance, and has become Georgia's single largest trade partner. Georgia, Azerbaijan, and Turkey have signed a tripartite agreement on regional security (noted above in relation to Azerbaijan). Turkish military advisors are in place in Georgia, and Turkey leases a Georgian airbase, where it now has a military presence. As with Azerbaijan, Turkey's increasing political and military involvement in Georgia, while short of actual alliance, does send clear, and unwelcome, messages to Moscow.

Assistance from the United States to Georgia had been more low-key throughout the middle to late 1990s, with the United States pleased to let Turkey take the leading role in building ties with Georgia, Azerbaijan, and several Central Asian states. Since September 11, however, U.S. ties with Georgia have grown to encompass assistance to the Georgians in efforts to eradicate Chechen rebels and other groups or individuals believed to be linked to Al Qaeda, who Georgia has said may be sheltering in the Pankisi Gorge among Chechen refugees. It is worth noting that Georgia has for years refused to accept Russian arguments that such rebels were in Pankisi, in part because Russia was offering its military support (and thus stepped up military presence). U.S. assistance is in the form of training and equipment provided to Georgia, and it has been careful to maintain consultations with Russia with regard to this endeavor.

In addition to the fight against Al Qaeda and related groups, Georgia offers some strategic advantages for other potential operations. As the only state in CASC with access to the open sea, it is a possible entry point for operations throughout the Caspian region. It is also sufficiently close to the Middle East that its airfields could be used for operations in the northern Persian Gulf, Iraq, Iran, or Turkey. Half of the twenty airfields in the South Caucasus with runways over 7,500 feet are in Georgia. Georgia has fair rail links to Armenia and Azerbaijan, although the road network is in poor condition and the lack of government control over large areas of the country may make land transit dangerous.

At the time of this writing, the United States has been insistent that its presence in Georgia will be minimal and will not include combat operations. In the meantime, Russian, Turkish, and U.S. forces are now operating on Georgian territory. Georgia's hope is almost certainly that U.S. and Turkish involvement will help speed the final withdrawal of Russian forces and cement Georgia's independence from Russian influence and leverage. However, the very reasons that U.S. troops are now in place—the possible presence of Al Qaeda–backed militants and the Georgian military's own insufficient capacity to patrol its borders—effectively combine with the many other faultlines and possible causes of conflict in Georgia to create a very volatile situation. Conflict in Georgia at some level has been almost constant since independence, and escalation of one or more of the existing fights seems relatively likely. With both Turkey and the United States now more deeply involved in Georgian security, their involvement in such developing conflicts becomes increasingly probable. Insofar as their efforts appear to be supportive of the existing (and increasingly unpopular) government, moreover, U.S. forces stand the risk of becoming a target of opposition groups, creating additional dangers. Finally, as the consolidation of central control over Georgia and establishment of a functioning state on its territory will be a long-term and difficult endeavor, one must ask to what extent the United States will be willing and able to commit personnel and resources to it—as well as taking on the difficult task of managing relations with Russia, given its strategic interests in what it sees as its southern "underbelly." Without help and support to consolidate central control and build a functioning state, however, Georgia runs the risk of disintegrating into a state of anarchy and war, where terrorists, criminals, and others may find safe havens. Certainly the United States, Russia, Turkey, and, indeed, all interested parties share an interest in preventing such an outcome. Their capacity to achieve it, and moreover to do so cooperatively without doing irreparable damage to other strategic interests, remains in question.

Table 9.8

Indicators of Conflict: Georgia

Indicator	Currently in Evidence	Likely in 10–15 years	Possible in 10–15 years
Domestic			
Popular movements form outside of legal channels, develop secretive, militaristic, radical agendas	✓	✓	
Privatization of force	✓	✓	
Increasing political "democratization"	✓	✓	
Increasing authoritarianism			✓
Ethnic, clan, linguistic or religious political parties with radical agendas gain influence	✓	✓	
Widespread reports of corruption; frequent government-related scandals and crackdowns on same	✓	✓	
Succession crisis		✓	
Secessionism	✓	✓	
Regional			
Extended U.S. military presence			✓
Formal alignment with Turkey		✓	
Formal alignment with the United States			✓
Russian efforts to exert influence by cutting off energy export routes	✓	✓	
Foreign (Russia, Iran, other) support of insurgents/secessionists	✓	✓	
Conflict spillover from neighboring states	✓	✓	

Trans-Caucasus Conflict

The Nagorno-Karabakh conflict is the most likely cause of renewed interstate fighting in the South Caucasus. Nagorno-Karabakh, a region inside the territorial borders of Azerbaijan that is populated primarily by Armenians, sparked an outright war between the two neighbors that ended with a cease-fire in 1994—and with Armenian control of Nagorno-Karabakh (which in principle is independent) as well as a swath of Azerbaijani land connecting Armenia to it (as noted above, this has led to a large number of internally displaced refugees in Azerbaijan). Peace talks have continued since that time. It is generally agreed that any settlement would require the return to Azerbaijan of the land outside of Nagorno-Karabakh occupied by Armenia, as well as some sort of land bridge to Nakhichevan, an Azeri-populated territory that is administratively part of Azerbaijan but located on Armenian territory, on the border with Iran. Recently, with both sides increasingly recognizing the war's economic and political costs, a settlement has begun to appear more possible. However, the success of peace talks remains far from assured, and opposition movements in both Azerbaijan and Armenia that take a more belligerent view than the current leadership will grow stronger if they fail—making a resumption of conflict more likely. Certainly, public opinion in both states is a long way from pacifist, and Armenian politicians speak in favor of outright annexation, while Azerbaijan is far from resigned to the loss of Nagorno-Karabakh, much less any other territory. As both sides raise their military spending and Armenia plans for a larger army, it appears that these states may be considering renewed conflict as a real possibility (or seeking to deter each other in an arms race, which in turn may also increase the risk of conflict).

In addition to the Nagorno-Karabakh crisis, the presence of many ethnic and subethnic groups and identities in Georgia has repercussions for neighboring states. One possible scenario over the next 10–15 years, for example, might include Armenian efforts to support co-ethnics in Armenian-inhabited parts of Georgia that are contiguous to Armenia. If Georgia remains weak, it is even possible to speculate that Armenia might seek to annex some portion of this territory.

Trans-Caspian Conflict

A critical issue that affects all the states of the Caspian region is, of course, the legal status of the Caspian Sea itself and the division of its fossil fuel–rich seabed. Until the question of which countries control which portions of the seabed are resolved, the Caspian's energy resources cannot be fully exploited. While the legal questions hinge on whether the Caspian should be seen as a sea (in which case it is covered by the Law of the Sea Convention, and the sea and undersea resources should be divided into national sectors) or a lake (in which case the resources should be developed jointly), the negotiations that have been ongoing since the collapse of the Soviet Union have reflected somewhat more complex concerns.

Russia has advocated a solution that calls for the division of the seabed and subsoil of the Caspian into national sectors along international boundary lines, with the waters held in common. Kazakhstan and Azerbaijan also support this approach. Iran argues that the Caspian seabed and waters should be divided so that each of the five littoral states controls 20 percent (Iran would receive less than 20 percent if the Caspian is divided by the mechanism Russia, Kazakhstan, and Azerbaijan favor). Turkmenistan, which insists that no one should begin development on subsoil gas and oil deposits in disputed territories until these issues are resolved, has advocated a condominium principle (which would apply if the Caspian were deemed a lake), with each state having a national coastal zone of 10–20 miles into the sea, but does not disagree with the principle of dividing the sea as an alternative option. Despite many meetings and discussions, the five states have remained unable to reach agreement as of the time of this writing.

The extent to which this problem can lead to actual conflict appears limited, but not entirely negligible. In July 2001, as noted above, Iranian gunboats threatened force against a British Petroleum research vessel in what Azerbaijan sees as its territorial waters. This earned Iran stark rebukes from not only Azerbaijan, but also its partner on many issues, Russia. Soon after, however, Turkmenistan declared that Azerbaijan was illegally claiming fields in the Caspian, as no demarcation was as yet agreed. Meanwhile, although Russia and Iran currently maintain the largest and most capable military forces in or near the Caspian, the other littoral states are building up their capabilities. As long as the Caspian issue remains unresolved, each of them has a strong incentive to deploy increasing numbers of forces to the Caspian itself, both to deter attacks or conflict, and to ensure that they can respond if it occurs. Of course, insofar as other states see this militarization as threatening, such a situation can lead to further militarization, thus raising the overall risk of conflict.

PATHS TO CONFLICT AND U.S. INVOLVEMENT

All of the analyses suggest that there are numerous causes of and potential pathways to conflict in CASC. Most of the causes are deeply entrenched and are likely to remain in place for the next 10–15 years and probably much longer. The general conclusion emerging from the research is that, in view of the faultlines and risk factors in place, it would be surprising if some form of armed strife did not break out in the region during the next decade and a half. But that in no way means that U.S. military involvement is likely in any such strife. The most likely forms of armed conflict in the region are incidents of internal strife, whether they take the form of Islamist-supported insurgencies, unrest that may accompany a breakdown of state control in one area and the assumption of state-like functions by non-state bodies, or violence that follows mobilization along ethnic lines because of local grievances, or a mixture of any or all of the above. However, such incidents of armed conflict are also the most likely to be localized, and most are apt to be contained by the regime in question. The connection between such a form of strife and the threat to U.S. interests that would lead to the decision to deploy U.S. forces in the region is not obvious or automatic, and such conflict is unlikely to trigger quick U.S. deployment to deal with the strife.

CONFLICT LIKELIHOOD, CONFLICT SEVERITY, AND POTENTIAL FOR ARMY DEPLOYMENT

We differentiate the pathways to potential deployment of Army forces with a mission that is internal to the region (rather than external, such as deploying to Uzbekistan in support of operations in Afghanistan) by *subregion* and *severity of conflict*. We use "subregion," of course, to distinguish Central Asia and the South Caucasus as distinct areas. We use "severity of conflict" to describe the scope (extent of contested space) and intensity (extent of casualties) of hostilities. In the context of the Caspian region, we see severity as a continuum, ranging from intrastate, localized, and usually temporary mob violence, to intrastate organized armed action against a regime (and usually associated with an alternative political program), to an interstate armed conflict, all the way to an interstate war that involves several states and their armed forces. Admittedly, the categories sketched above overlap and some insurgencies may be more severe in terms of casualties than some interstate wars. But on the average, as signposts on the continuum, and especially as these types of armed strife might play out in CASC, we believe that the continuum roughly approximates the range of low conflict severity associated with various forms of civil unrest, to insurgency, to an interstate war, all the way to high conflict severity associated with a regional war. Figure 9.1 provides a notional representation of the relationship between conflict likelihood and conflict severity in a perspective of the next 10–15 years. The likelihood of U.S. involvement varies along both axes. We stress that the figure is notional and subject to modification if basic conditions were to change. The rationale for the representation is discussed below.

The likelihood of different types of conflict varies between the two subregions. Intrastate, unorganized, and localized unrest of some form is more likely in Central Asia than in the South Caucasus because of the presence of more entrenched authoritarian regimes, lower socioeconomic levels, greater vulnerability to the appeal of

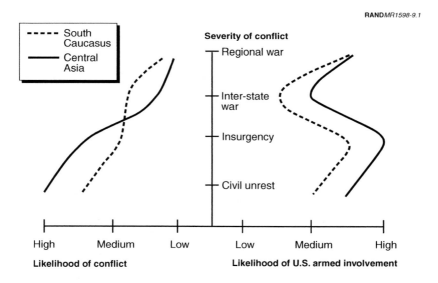

RANDMR1598-9.1

Figure 9.1—Notional Representation of Conflict Severity, Conflict Likelihood, and the Potential for Army Deployment in Central Asia and South Caucasus

Islamists, and greater ethnic heterogeneity. The high conflict likelihood in Central Asia at the low levels of conflict severity stems from the general thrust of all the analyses in this report, which have pointed to the existence of a multitude of grievances and to the expectation of some form of armed unrest in one or more of the Central Asian states, even if the unrest is not organized by an alternative political group seeking power. Most of the same reasons are present in South Caucasus, though not all and not always at as high a level of severity. The relative difference between the two subregions notwithstanding, there is high likelihood of conflict in an absolute sense.

The same reasons for differentiating between South Caucasus and Central Asia apply to the assessment of the likelihood of the two subregions to drift toward more organized forms of politically motivated conflict, with insurgencies and guerrilla wars being more likely in Central Asia than in South Caucasus. Although conflict types more akin to an insurgency are less likely in both regions than the sporadic and probably localized forms of strife that may accompany civil unrest, Central Asia retains a fairly high vulnerability to insurgency in an absolute sense.

We reverse our assessment of conflict likelihood in the two subregions at the higher levels of conflict severity, with South Caucasus more vulnerable to interstate war than Central Asia. The currently dormant Azerbaijani-Armenian conflict is the primary cause for this assessment, though it is not the only plausible conflict pairing in the subregion. Whether stemming from potential Georgian alignment with Turkey or from Georgia's internal implosion, an Armenian-Georgian conflict is also plausible in a long-term perspective. There is also the potential for one of the South Caucasus states to become involved in a border war with a state external to the region, with plausible scenarios centering on Russia, Iran, and Turkey. But interstate war in Central Asia is limited mainly to Uzbekistan resorting to force in pursuit of its perceived ethnic, resource, or economic goals in the region. The already high preponderance of power wielded by Uzbekistan in the region and the likelihood that this will continue lowers the likelihood of any use of force, since it isn't needed to achieve the regime's regional goals. In terms of conflict potential for a war with a state external to the region, the likelihood is also relatively low, in that geography limits interaction with Iran,

Afghanistan, and China, and there are fewer existing (and potential) interstate disputes in place. Russia is an exception in that it has important interests in and many potential areas for dispute with Kazakhstan, but here the Russian preponderance of power is so overwhelming that it is difficult to imagine that Russia would have to resort to the use of force to secure its interests. As long as Russian policy continues to be cautious regarding support for Russophones in Kazakhstan and as long as the Kazakhstani regime continues to be careful in its treatment of that population, the potential for Russophones in Kazakhstan to provoke a conflict remains low. In any event, because internal causes of conflict in South Caucasus in almost all cases have a direct link to disputes with external state actors, the potential for interstate war does not differ greatly from the potential for organized intrastate conflict in that subregion. On the other hand, the link between internal causes of conflict and external state actors in Central Asia is more tenuous, leading to a lower assessment of likelihood for interstate war in Central Asia.

In an absolute sense, we assess the likelihood of a regional war as fairly low in both subregions, though, for the same reasons mentioned in the discussion of the likelihood of an interstate war, there is greater likelihood of a regional war in South Caucasus. The link between internal causes of conflict and external state actors is more intertwined in South Caucasus. In Central Asia, an Uzbekistani turn to the use of force stands as the most important factor that could lead to a regional war. However, as outlined earlier, Uzbekistani predominance of power also makes the turn to the use of force in support of regime goals less necessary.

The pathways to deployment and armed involvement of Army forces to CASC as part of U.S. military involvement are a function of U.S. interests and an assessment of risks and benefits, and thus they vary by subregion and conflict severity. The September 11 attacks and the consequent U.S. presence on the ground in Central Asia has elevated the likelihood of involvement of U.S. troops in armed strife in Central Asia. An S-shaped curve portrays the likelihood of U.S. deployment and armed involvement in strife in both subregions, though the likelihood is higher in Central Asia. Any insurgency in Central Asia is likely to have Islamist elements and, as such, carries a strong likelihood of provoking a U.S. armed response. Because of the lesser role of Islam in South Caucasus, and the potential for other ideological motivations for an insurgency, a U.S. response in that subregion may not be as automatic. The same rationale is behind the lower U.S. likelihood for deployment and armed involvement in both sub-regions if mob violence/civil strife were to break out. The caveat that accompanies the above assessment is that the existence of many unknowns and the fact that the security environment (especially in Central Asia) is highly fluid make the assessment highly subject to change. The context for U.S. involvement will be crucial, and much depends on the behavior of external actors (Russia, China, Iran, Afghanistan).

Nevertheless, the likelihood of Army deployment to Central Asia with a mission that is internal to the region has increased greatly in the post–September 11 security environment, at least for the near term. For one, the United States has committed itself to provide assistance to Uzbekistan in case of spillover of combat operations from Afghanistan. Similarly, certain types of armed strife and unrest in Uzbekistan (or, to a lesser extent, in Tajikistan), if led or organized by sympathizers of Al Qaeda or the Taliban, may lead to the involve-ment of Army troops in an advisory role to the Uzbekistani (or Tajik) military. Finally, the developing close relationship between Uzbekistan and the United States introduces the potential for reverse influence and manipulation of the patron by the client, which could draw the United States into combat operations in defense of Uzbekistan and its regime.

We assume that U.S. involvement in a conflict in CASC at the higher levels of conflict severity would have to stem from geopolitical (realist) concerns, primarily the counterterrorist campaign, but also defense of or assistance to an ally or acting to secure energy supplies. Uncertainty about the likely length of U.S. presence in Afghanistan and Central Asia complicates any assessment. That said, interstate conflict in Central Asia is most likely to involve Uzbekistani regional ambitions, and in such a case the United States would be most likely to try to limit the strife and keep out of the fighting. In South Caucasus, interstate conflict is most likely to feature renewed Azerbaijani-Armenian fighting. The United States has stayed out of the conflict previously and will probably try to do so in the future. U.S. actions may be limited to preventing or moderating such a conflict to stop its escalation to a regional war.

At the highest levels of conflict severity, larger geopolitical concerns are likely to be present in any decision to deploy, and such a deployment may be a part of a larger U.S. policy aimed at Russia, China, Iran, or Afghanistan. Since regional war in South Caucasus is likely to involve either a NATO ally (Turkey) and/or Russia and/or Iran, U.S. likelihood of involvement in such a war is greater than in a purely interstate war in South Caucasus. Because of the ramifications of a regional war in the Caspian region on the counterterrorist campaign, U.S. involvement in both subregions is assessed as equal in likelihood and fairly high in an absolute sense.

At lower levels of conflict severity, geopolitical concerns are supplemented by a humanitarian rationale for U.S. involvement, making potential Army deployment both more likely (because of additional reasons for involvement) and easier (in the sense of being potentially less costly because of a lower likelihood of casualties). A multitude of humanitarian scenarios can be constructed for each subregion. Of course, any U.S. military involvement in a contingency in South Caucasus or Central Asia is likely to be a coalition operation, and the views and roles of U.S. allies as well as potential adversaries would have to be taken into account in any assessment of the risks involved.

A critical determinant of the potential for U.S. involvement in CASC in the future will be the evolution of the counterterrorist campaign. Success against the Islamist and terrorist elements in Afghanistan and its environs and subsequent pacification of Afghanistan will probably bring about a lessening of U.S. interest and presence in Central Asia and a gradual return of pre–September 11 geopolitical considerations to govern U.S. military involvement in the region. A lower level of success will probably mean an increased U.S. presence in the Caspian region. The pace of the development of energy resources in the region is another important consideration and has a primary link with the growth of U.S. interests in the area. When it comes to energy resource exploitation, oil is more important than gas, and assuming no major new discoveries of oil in the region, the importance of Azerbaijan and Kazakhstan is likely to rise in importance to the United States from the perspective of the next 10–15 years. Kazakhstan's dependence on a Russian pipeline network means that its importance to the United States is not likely to grow as much as Azerbaijan's.

The important caveat for the conclusions above is to note that high likelihood of conflict does not mean that conflict is inevitable. There are important dampeners of conflict, especially at the higher levels of conflict severity, that can counteract the many conflict accelerators in place. For example, the presence of authoritarian regimes has the effect of channeling dissent into more conflictual modes, but it also raises the price for dissent and thus deters some of it. In addition, parallel state structures and shadow economies soften the impact of the corrupt and sometimes inept policies of the regimes upon the citizens of the state. There are also safety valves in place, such as the potential for migration to Russia (either permanently for Russophones or as labor migrants for most of the others).

BIBLIOGRAPHY

Books, Monographs, Pamphlets, Reports

Ahrari, M. Ehsan, *Jihadi Groups, Nuclear Pakistan, and the New Great Game*, Carlisle, PA: Strategic Studies Institute, 2001.

Anderson, Robert, et al., *California's Vulnerability to Terrorism*, Santa Monica, CA: RAND, MR-1430-OES, 2002.

Armenia Economic Trends, October–December 2000, EU Tacis Georgian–European Policy and Legal Advice Centre; *http://www.economic-trends.org*.

Azerbaijan Economic Trends, January–March 2001, EU Tacis Georgian–European Policy and Legal Advice Centre; *http://www.economic-trends.org*.

Barnes, Joe, *US National Interests in the Caspian Basin, Getting Beyond the Hype*, Austin, TX: James A. Baker III Institute Working Paper, 1998.

Beblawi, Hazem, and Giacomo Luciani, *The Rentier State*, London: Croon Helm, 1987.

Benningsen, Alexandre, and S. Enders Wimbush, *Mystics and Commissars, Sufism in the Soviet Union*, Berkeley: University of California Press, 1985.

Bensahel, Nora, *Political Reform in the Middle East*, unpublished manuscript.

Blainey, Geoffrey, *The Causes of War*, New York: The Free Press, 1988.

Bodio, Tadeusz (ed.), *Uzbekistan: History, Society, Policy*, Warsaw: Elipsa, 2001.

Brezinski, Zbigniew, *The Grand Chessboard*, New York: Basic Books, 1997.

Brinton, Crane, *Anatomy of Revolution*, New York: Vintage Books, 1957.

Brown, Michael E. (ed.), *The International Dimensions of Internal Conflict*, Cambridge, MA: MIT Press, 1996.

————, Sean M. Lynn-Jones, and Steven E. Miller (eds.), *Debating the Democratic Peace*, Cambridge, MA: MIT Press, 1996.

Brubaker, Rogers, *Nationalism Reframed: Nationhood and the National Question Reframed in the New Europe*, Oxford: Cambridge University Press, 1996.

Carter, Ashton B., and William J. Perry, *Preventive Defense: A New Security Strategy for America*, Washington, D.C.: Brookings Institution Press, 1999.

Central Asia/Brussels: International Crisis Group, 2000, *Recent Violence in Central Asia: Causes and Consequences.*

Chelabi, H.E., and Juan Linz (eds.), *Sultanistic Regimes*, Baltimore: Johns Hopkins University Press, 1998.

Chowning Davies, James, (ed.), *When Men Revolt*, New Brunswick, NJ: Transaction Publishers, 1997.

Collier, Paul and Anke Hoeffler, *Greed and Grievance in Civil War*, October 21, 2001; *http://www.worldbank.org/research/conflict/ papers/greedandgrievance.htm.*

Dawisha, Karen (ed.), *The International Dimension of Post-Communist Transitions in Russia and the New States of Eurasia*, Armonk, NY: M.E. Sharpe, 1997.

—— and Bruce Parrot (eds.), *Conflict, Cleavage and Change in Central Asia and the Caucasus*, Cambridge: Cambridge University Press, 1997.

—— and —— (eds.), *The End of Empire? The Transformation of the USSR in Comparative Perspective*, Armonk, NY: M.E. Sharpe, 1997.

Ebel, Robert, and Rajan Menon (eds.), *Energy and Conflict in Central Asia and the Caucasus*, Lanham: Rowman & Littlefield, 2000,

Energy Information Agency, *Country Analysis Brief: Turkey*, August 2000; *http://www.eia.doe.gov/emeu/cabs/turkey. html.*

Fairbanks, Charles, C. Richard Nelson, S. Fredrick Starr, and Kenneth Weisbrode, *Strategic Assessment of Central Eurasia*, Washington, D.C.: The Atlantic Council of the United States and the Central Asia–Caucasus Institute of Johns Hopkins University, Paul H. Nitze School of Advanced International Studies, 2001.

Ferdinand, P. (ed.), *The New Central Asia and its Neighbors,* London: RIIA/Pinter, 1994.

Fleming, Jeff, and Barbara Ostdiek, *The Impact of Energy Derivatives on the Crude Oil Market*, Austin, TX: James A. Baker III Institute Working Paper, 1998.

Georgian Economic Trends, EU Tacis Georgian–European Policy and Legal Advice Centre; Quarters 3–4, 2000; *http://www.economic-trends.org.*

Gilpin, Robert, *War and Change in World Politics*, Cambridge: Cambridge University Press, 1981.

Gorst, Isabel, and Nina Poussenkova, *Petroleum Ambassadors of Russia: State Versus Corporate Policy in the Caspian Region*, Austin, TX: James A. Baker III Institute Working Paper, 1998.

Gurr, Ted, *Why Men Rebel,* Princeton, NJ: Center of International Studies, Princeton University Press, 1970.

Hannesson, Rognvaldur, *Petroleum Economics: Issues and Strategies of Oil and Natural Gas Production*, Westport, CT: Quorum Books, 1998.

Heslin, Sheila, *Key Constraints to Caspian Pipeline Development: Status, Significance and Outlook*, Austin, TX: James A. Baker III Institute Working Paper, 1998.

Hill, Fiona, and Regine Spector, *The Caspian Basin and Asian Energy Markets*, Washington, D.C.: The Brookings Institution, Conference Report No. 8, September 2001.

————, *The Caucasus and Central Asia*, Washington, D.C.: The Brookings Institution, Brookings Policy Brief No. 80, May 2001.

Hunter, Shireen T., *Central Asia Since Independence*, Westport, CT: Praeger, 1996.

Huntington, Samuel P., *Political Order in Changing Societies*, New Haven, CT: Yale University Press, 1968.

International Crisis Group, *Central Asia: Crisis Conditions in Three States*, August 7, 2000; *http://www.intl-crisis-group.org/projects/showreport.cfm?reportid=291.*

International Energy Agency, *Black Sea Energy Survey*, Paris, 2000.

International Monetary Fund, *Direction of Trade Statistics Yearbook* (geographic), Washington, D.C., 2000.

————, *Kyrgyz Republic: Selected Issues and Statistical Appendix*, Staff Country Report 00/131, Washington, D.C., October 2000.

————, *Turkmenistan: Recent Economic Developments*, Staff Country Report 99/140, Washington, D.C., December 1999.

————, *Republic of Tajikistan: Statistical Appendix*, Country Report 01/69, Washington, D.C., May 2001.

————, *Republic of Uzbekistan: Recent Economic Developments*, Staff Country Report 00/36, Washington, D.C., March 2000.

———— and World Bank, *Armenia, Georgia, Kyrgyz Republic, Moldova, and Tajikistan: External and Fiscal Sustainability—Background Paper*, Washington, D.C., February 6, 2001.

International Narcotics Control Strategy Report 2000, Washington, D.C.: Department of State, March 2001; *http://www.state.gov/g/inl/rls/nrcrpt/2000/index.cfm?docid=891.*

International Narcotics Control Strategy Report 2001, Washington, D.C.: Department of State, March 2002.

Interstate Statistical Committee of the CIS, *Main Macroeconomic Indicators on CIS Countries;* see *www.cisstat.com/mac1_an.htm.*

Jane's All the World's Aircraft 1999–2000, Jane's Information Group Ltd., 1999.

Joseph, Ira B., *Caspian Gas Exports: Stranded Reserves in a Unique Predicament,* Austin, TX: James A. Baker III Institute Working Paper, 1998.

Karl, Terry Lynn, *The Paradox of Plenty,* Berkeley, CA: University of California Press, 1997.

Kazakhstan Economic Trends, January–March 2001, EU Tacis Georgian–European Policy and Legal Advice Centre; *http://www.economic-trends.org.*

Kazakhstan Economic Trends, April–June 2000, EU Tacis Georgian–European Policy and Legal Advice Centre; *http://www.economic-trends.org.*

Kemp, Geoffrey, and Robert E. Harkavy, *Strategic Geography and the Changing Middle East,* Washington, D.C.: Carnegie Endowment for International Peace, 1997.

Killingsworth, Paul S., et al., *Flexbasing: Achieving Global Presence for Expeditionary Aerospace Forces,* Santa Monica, CA: RAND, MR-1113-AF, 2000.

Kortunov, Andrei, *Russia and Central Asia: Evolution of Mutual Perceptions, Policies, Interdepence,* Austin, TX: James A. Baker III Institute Working Paper, 1998.

Kugler, Richard L., *Changes Ahead: Future Directions for the U.S. Overseas Military Presence,* Santa Monica, CA: RAND, MR-956-AF, 1998.

Lapidus, Ira M., *A History of Islamic Societies*, Cambridge: Cambridge University Press, 1988.

Menon, Rajan, Yuri Federov, and Ghia Nodia (eds.), *Russia, the Caucasus and Central Asia: The 21st Century Security Environment*, Armonk, NY: M.E. Sharpe, 1999.

The Military Balance: 2000–2001, London: The International Institute of Strategic Studies, 2000.

Moore, Barrington, *Social Origins of Dictatorship and Democracy*, Boston: Beacon Press, 1966.

National Petroleum Council, *Securing Oil and Natural Gas Infrastructures in the New Economy*, Washington, D.C.: June 2001.

Nunn, Sam, Barnett Rubin, and Nancy Lubin, *Calming the Fergana Valley*, Report of the Fergana Valley Working Group for Preventative Action, New York: Century Foundation Press, 1999.

Nye, Joseph S., Jr., *Bound to Lead: The Changing Nature of American Power*, New York: Basic Books, 1990.

Olcott, Martha Brill, *Central Asia's New States*, Washington, D.C.: United States Institute of Peace Press, 1996.

O'Malley, William D., *Evaluating Possible Airfield Deployment Options: Middle East Contingencies*, Santa Monica, CA: RAND, MR-1353-AF, 2001.

Organski, A.F.K., *World Politics*, 2d ed., New York: Knopf, 1968.

Osh/Brussels: International Crisis Group, *Central Asia: Drugs and Conflict*, 2001.

Osh/Brussels: International Crisis Group, *Central Asia: Fault Lines in the New Security Map*, 2001.

Osh/Brussels: International Crisis Group, *Tajikistan: An Uncertain Peace*, 2001.

Osh/Brussels: International Crisis Group, *The IMU and the Hizb-Ut-Tahrir: Implications of the Afghanistan Campaign*, 2002; see *http://www.crisisweb.org/projects/showreport.cfm?reportid=538.*

Pirseyedi, Bobi, *The Small Arms Problems in Central Asia: Features and Implications*, Geneva: UNIDIR, 2000.

Pomfret, Richard, *The Economies of Central Asia*, Princeton, NJ: Princeton University Press, 1995.

Reno, William, *Warlord Politics and African States*, Boulder: Lynne Rienner, 1999.

Report of the President's Commission on Critical Infrastructure Protection, *Critical Foundations: Protecting America's Infrastructures*, Washington, D.C., October 1997.

Republic of Armenia, *Interim Poverty Reduction Strategy Paper*, March 2001.

Rueschmeyer, D., E.H. Stephens, et al., *Capitalist Development and Democracy*, Chicago: University of Chicago Press, 1992.

Rywkin, Michael, *Moscow's Muslim Challenge, Soviet Central Asia*, Armonk, NY: M.E. Sharpe, 1982.

Sachs, Jeffrey D., and Andrew M. Warner, *Natural Resource Abundance and Economic Growth*, Cambridge, MA: Harvard Institute for International Development, Development Discussion Paper No. 517a, October 1995.

Sickes, Robin, and Patrik T. Hultberg, *Convergent Economies: Implications for World Energy Use*, Austin, TX: James A. Baker III Institute Working Paper, 1998.

Snyder, Jack L., *From Voting to Violence: Democratization and Nationalist Conflict*, New York: W.W. Norton, 2000.

Social, Cultural, and Religious Factors That Affect the Supply of Oil from Central Asia and the Caucasus, Austin, TX: James A. Baker III Institute Working Paper, 1998.

Sokolsky, Richard, and Tanya Charlick-Paley, *NATO and Caspian Security, A Mission Too Far?* Santa Monica, CA: RAND, MR-1074-AF, 1999.

Soligo, Ronald, and Amy Jaffe, *The Economics of Pipeline Routes: The Conundrum of Oil Exports from the Caspian Basin*, Austin, TX: James A. Baker III Institute Working Paper, 1998.

Starr, S. Frederick, *Central Asia's Security Needs and Emerging Structures for Addressing Them*, undated; *http://www.sais-jhu.edu/caci/Publications/Security%20needs.htm.*

Suny, Ronald Grigor, *The Revenge of the Past: Nationalism, Revolution, and the Collapse of the Soviet Union*, Stanford, CA: Stanford University Press, 1993.

Szayna, Thomas (ed.), *Identifying Potential Ethnic Conflict: Application of a Process Model*, Santa Monica, CA: RAND, MR-1188-A, 2000.

Talwani, Manik, Andrei Belopolski, and Dianne L. Berry, *Geology and Petroleum Potential of Central Asia*, Austin, TX: James A. Baker III Institute Working Paper, 1998.

U.S. Air Force Pamphlet 10-1403, *Airlift Planning Factors*, 1996.

U.S. Air Force Pamphlet 76-2, *Military Airlift: Airlift Planning Factors*, May 29, 1987.

Uzbekistan Economic Trends, January–March 2001, EU Tacis Georgian–European Policy and Legal Advice Centre; *http://www.economic-trends.org.*

von der Mehden, Fred R., *Islam and Energy Security in Central Asia*, Austin, TX: James A. Baker III Institute Working Paper, 1998.

Walt, Stephen, *The Origins of Alliances*, Ithaca and London: Cornell University Press, 1987.

———, *Revolution and War*, Ithaca and London: Cornell University Press, 1996.

Waltz, Kenneth, *Theory of International Politics*, New York: McGraw-Hill, 1979.

Weisbrode, Kenneth, *Central Eurasia: Prize or Quicksand?* Adelphi Paper Number 338, London: International Institute for Strategic Studies, 2001.

Xu, Xiaojie, *Oil and Gas Linkages Between Central Asia and China*, Austin, TX: James A. Baker III Institute Working Paper, 1998.

Papers, Articles, Reviews, Briefings, and Speeches

Abazov, Rafis, "Economic Migration in Post-Soviet Central Asia: the Case of Kyrgyzstan," *Post-Communist Economies*, Vol. 11, No. 2 (1999), pp. 237–252.

Akbarzadeh, Shahram, "National Identity and Political Legitimacy in Turkmenistan," *Nationalities Papers*, Vol. 27, No. 2 (1999), pp. 271–290.

Akbarzadeh, Shahram, "Political Islam in Kyrgyzstan and Turkmenistan," *Central Asian Survey*, Vol. 20, No. 4 (2001), pp. 451–465.

Akiner, S., "Post-Soviet Central Asia: Past Is Prologue," in P. Ferdinand (ed.), *The New Central Asia and Its Neighbors*, London: RIIA/Pinter, 1994.

Aleksandrov, Ivan, "Is the Islamic Threat to Uzbekistan Real?" *Nezavisimaya Gazeta—Religii*, October 10, 2001.

Anderson, John, "Elections and Political Development in Central Asia," *Journal of Communist Studies and Transition Politics*, Vol. 13, No. 4 (1997).

Auvinen, Juha, "Political Conflict in Less Developed Countries 1981–1989," *Journal of Peace Research*, Vol. 34, No. 2 (1997), pp. 177–188.

Barrington, Lowell, "Russian Speakers in Ukraine and Kazakhstan: 'Nationality,' 'Population,' or Neither?" *Post-Soviet Affairs*, Vol. 17, No. 2 (2001), pp. 129–158.

Becker, Abraham S., "Russia and Caspian Oil: Moscow Loses Control," *Post-Soviet Affairs*, Vol. 16, No. 2 (2000), pp. 91–132.

———, "Russia and Economic Integration in the CIS," *Survival*, Vol. 38, No. 4, Winter 1996–97, pp. 117–136.

Bender, Bryan, Kim Burger, and Andrew Koch, "Afghanistan: First Lessons," *Jane's Defence Weekly*, December 19, 2001, pp. 18–21.

Bichel, Rebecca M., "Deconstructing Constitutionalism: The Case of Central Asia and Uzbekistan," *Interactive Central Asia Resource Project (ICARP) paper*, 1997; *http://www.icarp.org/publications/pub-deconstruct.html.*

Blanche, Ed, "West Turns Attention to Afghan Drugs Trade," *Jane's Intelligence Review*, January 1, 2002.

Blank, Stephen, "Armenia at the Crossroads of War and Peace," Bi-Weekly Briefing, *The Analyst*, May 23, 2001.

————, "Every Shark East of Suez: Great Power Interests, Policies and Tactics in the Transcaspian Energy Wars," *Central Asia Survey*, Vol. 18, No. 2 (1999), pp. 149–184.

Bobrovnikov, Vladimir, "Muslim Nationalism in the Post-Soviet Caucasus: The Dagestani Case," *Caucasian Regional Studies*, Vol. 4, No. 1 (1999); *http://poli.vub.ac.be/publi/crs/eng/0401-01.htm.*

Brazhko, Vasilina, "Afghanistan Remains Main Supplier of Illegal Drugs to Central Asia and the CIS," *The Times of Central Asia*, July 19, 2001.

Campos, Nauro, and Jeffrey Nugent, "Who's Afraid of Political Instability?" *William Davidson Institute Working Paper*, No. 326, July 2000.

Collier, Paul, "Rebellion as a Quasi-Criminal Activity," unpublished draft, January 17, 2000.

————, and Anke Hoeffler, "Justice-Seeking and Loot-Seeking in Civil War," unpublished draft, February 17, 1999.

Cornell, Svante E., "Conflicts in the North Caucasus," *Central Asian Survey*, Vol. 17, No. 3 (1998), pp. 409–441.

————, "Religion as a Factor in Caucasian Conflicts," *Civil Wars*, Vol. 1, No. 3 (1998).

————, "Democratization Falters in Azerbaijan," *Journal of Democracy*, Vol. 12, No. 2 (2001), pp. 118–131.

David, Steven R., "Saving America from the Coming Civil Wars," *Foreign Affairs*, Vol. 78, No. 1 (Winter 1999), pp. 103–116.

Davis, Anthony, "Interview with Brigadier General John Hvidegaard, Chief Military Observer for the United Nations mission of observers in Tajikistan," *Jane's Defence Weekly*, July 21, 1999; *http://www.janes.com/regional_news/europe/interviews/dw990721_i.shtml.*

————, "How the Afghan War Was Won," *Jane's Intelligence Review*, February 2002, pp. 6–13.

Davis, Graham A., "Learning to Love the Dutch Disease: Evidence from the Mineral Economies," *World Development*, Vol. 23, No. 10 (1995).

Davis, James C., "The Revolutionary State of Mind: Toward a Theory of Revolution," in James Chowning Davies (ed.), *When Men Revolt*, New Brunswick, NJ: Transaction Publishers, 1997, pp. 133–148.

Davlatov, Vladimir, and Turat Akimov, "Dushanbe Alarmed Over IMU Activity," Osh/Brussels: International Crisis Group, 2001.

———— and ————,"Central Asia: Drugs and Conflict," Osh/Brussels: International Crisis Group, 2001.

Deutsch, Karl, "Social Mobilization and Political Development," *American Political Science Review*, Vol. 55 (September 1961), pp. 493–514.

Doyle, Michael W., "Liberalism and World Politics," *American Political Science Review*, December 1986.

Edmunds, Timothy, "Power and Powerlessness in Kazakstani Society: Ethnic Problems in Perspective," *Central Asian Survey*, Vol. 17, No. 3 (1998), pp. 463–470.

Eitzen, Hilda, "Refiguring Ethnicity Through Kazak Genealogies," *Nationalities Papers*, Vol. 26, No. 3 (1998), pp. 433–451.

Ember, Carol R., Melvin Ember, and Bruce Russett, "Peace Between Participatory Polities," *World Politics*, July 1992.

Esenova, Saulesh, "'Tribalism' and Identity in Contemporary Circumstances: The Case of Kazakhstan," *Central Asian Survey*, Vol. 17, No. 3 (1998), pp. 443–462.

Evangelista, Matthew, "Historical Legacies and the Politics of Intervention in the Former Soviet Union," in Michael E. Brown (ed.), *The International Dimension of Internal Conflict,* Cambridge, MA: MIT Press, 1996.

Fierman, William, "Language and Identity in Kazakhstan: Formulations in Policy Documents 1987–1997," *Communist and Post-Communist Studies*, Vol. 31, No. 2 (1998), pp. 171–186.

Fox, Jonathan, "The Ethnic-Religious Nexus: The Impact of Religion on Ethnic Conflict," *Civil Wars*, Vol. 3, No. 3 (2000).

———, "Is Islam More Conflict Prone Than Other Religions? A Cross-Sectional Study of Ethnoreligious Conflict," *Nationalism and Ethnic Politics*, Vol. 6, No. 2 (2000).

Gammer, Moshe, "Post-Soviet Central Asia and Post-Colonial Francophone Africa: Some Associations," *Middle Eastern Studies*, Vol. 36, No. 2 (April 2000), pp. 124–149.

Gleason, Gregory, "Counterinsurgency in Central Asia: Civil Society is the First Casualty," January 8, 2001; *http://www.eurasianet.org/ departments/recaps/articles/eav092200.shtml.*

———, "Tajikistan Minister's Murder Points to Drug-Route Conflict," *The Times of Central Asia; http://www.times.kg/ times.cgi?D= article&aid=1017175.*

Goldwyn, Daniel R., Martha Brill Olcott, Julia Nanay, and Thomas R. Stauffer, "Symposium: The Caspian Region and the New Great Powers," *Middle East Policy*, Vol. 7, No. 4 (October 2000), pp. 1–21.

Goodman, Glenn W., Jr., "Central Asian Partners: Low-Key Spadework by Green Berets Reaps Valuable Benefits for War in Afghanistan," *Armed Forces Journal International*, January 2002, pp. 60–61.

Goure, Daniel, "The Army's Policy Nettle: Transformation: Will It Fix What Ails the Army?" *Armed Forces Journal International*, October 2001, pp. 44–54.

Grebenshchikov, Igor, "Central Asian Leaders Think Alike," *http://www.iwpr.net/index.pl?archive/rca/rca_200103_45_4_eng.txt.*

Griffiths, Hugh, "A Political Economy of Ethnic Conflict Ethnonationalism and Organised Crime," *Civil Wars*, Vol. 2, No. 2 (1999).

Gurr, Ted, "Peoples Against States—Ethnopolitical Conflict and the Changing World System 1994," Presidential Address, *International Studies Quarterly*, Vol. 29, No. 1 (March 1999).

Hancilova, Blanka, "Prospects and Perils of an Armenian-Azerbaijani Settlement," Bi-Weekly Briefing, *The Analyst*, Wednesday, May 23, 2001.

Hanks, Reuel R., "A Separate Space? Karakalpak Nationalism and Devolution in Post-Soviet Uzbekistan," *Europe-Asia Studies*, Vol. 52, No. 5 (2000), pp. 939–953.

Hawley, General (ret.) Richard E., and John R. Backschies, "Closing the Global Strike Gap," *Armed Forces Journal International*, September 2001, pp. 38–46.

Helman, Gerald, and Steven R. Ratner, "Saving Failed States," *Foreign Policy*, No. 89 (Winter 1992–93), pp. 3–20.

Herbert, Adam J., "The Search for Asian Bases," *Air Force Magazine*, January 2002, pp. 50–54.

"In Brief—Kazakhstan Receives Turkish Aid," *Jane's Defence Weekly*, August 22, 2001.

"Interim Brigade Combat Team Deployment Analysis," Center for Army Analysis Briefing, November 9, 2000.

Karl, Terry Lynn, "The Perils of the Petro-State: Reflections on the Paradox of Plenty," *Journal of International Affairs*, Vol. 53, No. 1 (Fall 1999).

Karpat, Kemal H., "The Role of Turkey and Iran in Incorporating the Former Soviet Republics into the World System," in Karen Dawisha (ed.), *The International Dimension of Post-Communist Transitions in Russia and the New States of Eurasia*, Armonk, NY: M.E. Sharpe, 1997, pp. 168–196.

"Kazakhstan—Turkey: Military Cooperation," *The Times of Central Asia*, July 30, 2001.

Klaassen, Ger, et al., "The Future of Gas Infrastructures in Eurasia," *Energy Policy*, Vol. 29 (2001), pp. 399–413.

Klare, Michael T., "The New Geography of Conflict," *Foreign Affairs*, Vol. 80, No. 3, pp. 49–61.

Klitgaard, Robert, "International Cooperation Against Corruption," *Finance and Development*, Vol. 35, No. 1 (March 1998), pp. 3–7.

Lee, Ebon, "Central Asia's Balancing Act: Between Terrorism and Interventionism," *Harvard International Review*, July 2001.

Liberman, Peter, "The Spoils of Conquest," *International Security*, Vol. 18, No. 2 (Fall 1993).

Lieven, Anatol, review of H.E. Chelabi and Juan J. Linz (eds.), *Sultanistic Regimes*, Baltimore: Johns Hopkins University Press 1998, November 8, 2000; *http://www.eurasianet.org*.

Lubin, Nancy, "An Old Story with a New Twist," in Rajan Menon, Yuri Federov, and Ghia Nodia (eds.), *Russia, the Caucasus and Central Asia: The 21st Century Security Environment*, Armonk, NY: M.E. Sharpe, 1999.

MacDonald, Juli A., "The Reemergence of India as a Central Asian Player," *Central Asia Caucasus Analyst*, May 24, 2000.

Makarenko, Tamara, "Crime and Terrorism in Central Asia," *Jane's Intelligence Review*, Vol. 12, No. 7 (July 1, 2000).

———, "Patterns of Crime in the Caspian Basin," *Jane's Intelligence Review*, April 1, 2001.

———, "Seeking Security in Central Asia," *Jane's Intelligence Review*, Vol. 13, No. 1 (January 2001), pp. 23–25.

———, "The Changing Dynamics of Central Asian Terrorism," *Jane's Intelligence Review*, February 2002, pp. 36–39.

——— and Daphne Biliouri, "Central Asian States Set to Pay Price of U.S. Strikes," *Jane's Intelligence Review*, November 2001, pp. 34–37.

Mann, Poonam, "Fighting Terrorism: India and Central Asia," *Strategic Analysis*, Vol. 24, No. 11 (February 2001).

Mansfield, Edward D., and Jack Snyder, "Democratization and the Danger of War," *International Security*, Vol. 20, No. 1 (Summer 1995), pp. 5–38.

Masanov, Nurbulat E., "The Clan Factor in Contemporary Political Life in Kazakhstan," Mark Eckert (trans.), *Johnson's Russia List*, February 20, 1998.

Matveeva, Anna, "Democratization, Legitimacy and Political Change in Central Asia," *International Affairs*, Vol. 75, No. 1 (1999), pp. 23–44.

McCutcheon, Hilary, and Richard Osbon, "Discoveries Alter Caspian Regional Energy Potential," *Oil & Gas Journal*, December 17, 2001.

Menon, Rajan, "The Security Environment in the South Caucasus and Central Asia," in Rajan Menon, Yuri Federov, and Ghia Nodia (eds.), *Russia, the Caucasus and Central Asia: The 21st Century Security Environment*, Armonk, NY: M.E. Sharpe, 1999.

———, and Hendrik Spruyt, "The Limits of Neorealism: Understanding Security in Central Asia," *Review of International Studies*, Vol. 25 (1999), pp. 87–105.

Newman, Richard J., "Tankers and Lifters for a Distant War," *Air Force Magazine*, January 2002, pp. 56–60.

Oliker, Olga, "Ukraine and the Caspian, an Opportunity for the United States," Santa Monica, CA: RAND, IP-198, 2000.

Pain, Emil, "Contagious Ethnic Conflicts and Border Disputes Along Russia's Southern Flank," in Rajan Menon, Yuri Federov, and Ghia Nodia (eds.), *Russia, the Caucasus and Central Asia: The 21st Century Security Environment*, Armonk, NY: M.E. Sharpe, 1999, pp. 177–202.

Pandey, Gyanendra, "Can a Muslim Be an Indian?" *Comparative Studies of Society and History*, 1999, pp. 608–629.

Paul, C. Edward, "Moving Forward with State Autonomy and Capacity: Examples from Two Studies of the Pentagon During WWII,"

Journal of Political and Military Sociology, Vol. 28, No. 1 (2000), pp. 21–42.

Poppe, Edwin, and Louk Hagendoorn, "Types of Identification Among Russians in the 'Near Abroad,'" *Europe-Asia Studies*, Vol. 53, No. 1 (2001), pp. 57–71.

Posen, Barry, "The Security Dilemma and Ethnic Conflict," *Survival*, Vol. 35, No. 1 (1993), pp. 27–47.

Postel, Sandra L., and Aaron T. Wold, "Dehydrating Conflict," *Foreign Policy*, September/October 2001, pp. 61–67.

Raczka, Witt, "Xinjiang and Its Central Asian Borderlands," *Central Asian Survey*, Vol. 17, No. 3 (1998), pp. 373–407.

Rashid, Ahmed, "China Forced to Expand Role in Central Asia," *Central Asia–Caucasus Analyst*, July 19, 2000.

———, "The New Struggle in Central Asia: A Primer for the Baffled," *World Policy Journal*, Vol. 17, No. 4 (Winter 2000/2001), pp. 33–45.

———, "Pamirs Offer IMU Secure Base," *Eurasia Insight*, August 12, 2001.

———, "Central Asia: Trouble Ahead," *Far Eastern Economic Review*, May 9, 2002.

———, "IMU Gradually Developing into Pan-Central Asian Movement," *Eurasia Insight*, April 3, 2001; *www.eurasianet.org*, downloaded March 19, 2002.

Redo, S., "Uzbekistan and the United Nations in the Fight Against Transnational Organized Crime," in Tadeusz Bodio (ed.), *Uzbekistan: History, Society, Policy*, Warsaw: Elipsa, 2001.

Roberts, Sean R., "The Uighurs of the Kazakhstan Borderlands: Migration and the Nation," *Nationalities Papers*, Vol. 26, No. 3 (1998), pp. 511–530.

Roos, John G., "Tools of Transformation: Army's Sights Focused Far Beyond Interim Brigade Combat Teams and Future Combat Systems," *Armed Forces Journal International*, October 2001, pp. 56–61.

———, "Turning Up the Heat," *Armed Forces Journal International,* February 2002, pp. 36–42.

Ross, Michael L., "The Political Economy of the Resource Curse," *World Politics,* Vol. 51 (January 1999), pp. 297–332.

———, "Does Resource Wealth Lead to Authoritarian Rule? Explaining the 'Midas Touch,'" World Bank Research Group workshop on "The Economics of Political Violence," Princeton University, March 18–19, 2000.

Rowland, Richard H., "Urban Population Trends in Kazakhstan During the 1990s," *Post-Soviet Geography and Economics,* Vol. 40, No. 7 (1999), pp. 519–552.

Ruseckas, Laurent, "Turkey and Eurasia: Opportunities and Risks in the Caspian Pipeline Derby," *Journal of International Affairs,* No. 1 (Fall 2000), pp. 217–236.

Rywkin, Michael, "Kazakstan and the Rest of Central Asia: Fifteen Shades of Difference," *Nationalities Papers,* Vol. 26, No. 3 (1998), pp. 573–579.

Sachs, Jeffrey D., and Andrew M. Warner, "Natural Resource Abundance and Economic Growth," Development Discussion Paper No. 517a, Harvard Institute for International Development, October 1995.

Safizadeh, Fereydoun, "On Dilemmas of Identity in the Post-Soviet Republic of Azerbaijan," *Caucasian Regional Studies,* Vol. 3, No. 1 (1998); *http://poli.vub.ac.be/publi/crs/eng/0301-04.htm.*

Salukvadze, Khatuna, "The Struggle for the Remains of Geopolitical Weight: Russia Dodges from Disengaging Militarily from Georgia," *The Analyst,* Vol. 21, Issue 23 (July 19, 2001); *www.cacianlayst.org.*

Schatz, Edward A.D., "Framing Strategies and Non-Conflict in Multi-Ethnic Kazakhstan," *Nationalism and Ethnic Politics,* Vol. 6, No. 2 (2000).

————, "The Politics of Multiple Identities: Lineage and Ethnicity in Kazakhstan," *Europe-Asia Studies*, Vol. 52, No. 3 (2000), pp. 489–506.

Selimov, Seymour, "Peace over Nagorno-Karabakh Remains Elusive as Populaces Drift Further Apart," *Transitions Online*, August 24, 2001.

Shenoy, Bhamy, and William James, "Caspian Energy Exports: Turkmenistan Fumbling Opportunities Afforded by Trans-Caspian Pipeline," *Oil & Gas Journal*, May 28, 2001.

Shevardnadze, Eduard, "Georgia, the United States, and the New Security Paradigm in Eurasia," speech given at the Willard Hotel in Washington, D.C., October 4, 2001.

Smith, Robert, "Politics, Production Levels to Determine Caspian Area Energy Export Options," *Oil & Gas Journal*, May 28, 2001.

Snyder, Jack L., and Edward D. Mansfield, "Democratization and the Danger of War," *International Security*, Vol. 20, No. 1 (Summer 1995), pp. 5–38.

Snyder, Jack L., and Karen Ballentine, "Nationalism and the Marketplace of Ideas," *International Security*, Vol. 21, No. 2 (Fall 1996), pp. 5–40.

"Special Issue: Confronting the Political-Criminal Nexus," *The Times of Central Asia, Trends in Organized* Crime, Vol. 4, No. 3 (Spring 1999).

Specter, Michael, "Letter from Tbilisi: Rainy Days in Georgia," *New Yorker*, December 18, 2000.

Starr, S. Frederick, "Making Eurasia Stable," *Foreign Affairs*, January/February 1996, pp. 80–92.

Suny, Ronald Grigor, "Provisional Stabilities," *International Security*, Vol. 24, No. 3 (Winter 1999), pp. 139–178.

————, "Southern Tears: Dangerous Opportunities in the Caucasus and Central Asia," in Rajan Menon, Yuri Federov, and Ghia Nodia (eds.), *Russia, the Caucasus and Central Asia: The 21st Century Security Environment*, Armonk, NY: M.E. Sharpe, 1999.

Svante, E. Cornell, "Conflicts in the North Caucasus," *Central Asian Survey*, Vol. 17, No. 3 (1998), pp. 409–441.

Sweetman, Bill, "Airlift for the 21st Century," *Jane's International Defense Review*, December 2001, pp. 48–52.

Szayna, Thomas S., and Ashley J. Tellis, "Introduction," in Thomas S. Szayna (ed.), *Identifying Potential Ethnic Conflict: Application of a Process Model*, Santa Monica, CA: RAND, MR-1188-A, 2000.

Szporluk, Roman, "The Fall of the Tsarist Empire and the USSR: The Russian Question and Imperial Overextension," in Karen Dawisha and Bruce Parrott (eds.), *The End of Empire? The Transformation of the USSR in Comparative Perspective*, Armonk, NY: M.E. Sharpe, 1997, pp. 65–95.

Tirpak, John A., "Enduring Freedom," *Air Force Magazine*, February 2002, pp. 32–39.

Tsepakalo, Valery, "The Remaking of Eurasia," *Foreign Affairs*, Vol. 77, No. 2, pp. 107–126.

"U.S. to Train Central Asian Border Police," *World*, August 22, 2001.

"Uzbekistan, Kazakhstan: Repression Spreads In Central Asia," *The Times of Central Asia*, February, 16, 2000.

Ware, Robert Bruce, and Enver Kisriev, "The Islamic Factor in Dagestan," *Central Asian Survey*, Vol. 19, No. 2 (2000), pp. 235–252.

Young, David, "Mideast Political Changes Seen Creating Oil Opportunities," *Oil & Gas Journal*, October 1, 2001.

Zelkina, Anna, "Islam and Security in the New States of Central Asia: How Genuine Is the Islamic Threat?" *Religion, State and Society*, Vol. 27, No. 3–4 (1999), pp. 355–372.

Zhuangzhi, Dr. Sun, "China and Central Asia in the New International Climate," *The Times of Central Asia*, January 25, 2001.

Newspapers, Press Digests, and Wire Services

Agence France-Presse

Alexander's Gas & Oil Connections

Associated Press

BBC Monitoring Service

BBC News Sunday

Christian Science Monitor

Defense Link News

The Economist

Foreign Broadcast

FSU Oil and Gas Monitor

Information Service

Jamestown Foundation Monitor

Jane's Defence Weekly

Lenta.ru

Moscow Times

The New York Times

Nezavisimaya Gazeta

Nezavisimoye Voyennoye Obozreniye

Reuters

RFE/RL Newsline

Rossiysbaya Gazeta

Russia's Week

Segodnya

Tbilisi Rezonansi

United Press International (UPI)

Washington Post

Web Sites

Eurasianet.org

The European Union web site: *www.europa.eu.int*

http://www.freedomhouse.org/ratings/

Hizb ut-Tahir: *www.hizb-ut-tahrir.org;* also see *www.khilafah.com*

The India DME Project web site:
   http://www.dmeforpower.net/pg_theproject.html

Karatnycky, Adrian, Alexander Motyl, and Amanda Schnetzer (eds.),
   Nations in Transit, 2001, New York: Freedom House, 2001:
   http://www.freedomhouse.org/research/nattransit.htm

Kyrgyzstan National Statistics Committee:
   http://nsc.bishkek.su/Eng/Database/Index.html

National Statistical Committee of the Kyrgyz Republic, Direction of
   Trade Statistics:
   http://nsc.bishkek.su/Eng/Annual/Xc.htmlandMc.html

Periscope Database: *http://www.periscope.ucg.com/*

Transparency International: *http://www.transparency.org*

www.undp.org/hdro/anatools.htm

http://www.undp.org/hdro/highlights/past.htm.
   For the text of the Convention, see
   http://www.odccp.org/palermo/convmain.html

The World Bank: *http://www.worldbank.org*

Interviews

In conducting the research for this report, the authors spoke with a
   range of U.S. military and government personnel and other specialists.